Psychology and Instruction

A Practical Approach to Educational Psychology

Psychology and Instruction

A Practical Approach to Educational Psychology

Benjamin B. Lahey University of Georgia

Martha S. Johnson University of Detroit

Scott, Foresman and Company • Glenview, Illinois
Dallas Tex. • Oakland, N.J. • Palo Alto, Cal. • Tucker, Ga. • London, England

The credit lines for copyrighted materials
in this book are placed in the acknowledgments
section, which begins on page 375 and runs
through page 378. These pages are considered
an extension of the copyright page.

Library of Congress Cataloging in Publication Data
Lahey, Benjamin B
   Psychology and instruction.

   Bibliography: p. 366
   Includes index.
   1.   Learning, Psychology of.   2.   Intelligence
levels.   I.   Johnson, Martha S., joint author.
II.   Title. [DNLM: 1.   Psychology, Educational.
LB1051   L183p]
LB1051   L16   370.15'2   77-12255
ISBN 673-15040-2

12345678910-RRC-858483828180797877

PREFACE

Many decisions must be made in writing a textbook. Our first decision was based on a belief that students of education want and need to be taught more than just abstract theories of learning and instruction. They need to be given information that is directly useful in the *practice* of teaching. We have provided a textbook for the basic course in educational psychology that gives the greatest possible emphasis to the application of information to the classroom, without ignoring the basic principles that underlie the discipline. We have employed practical examples throughout the text; provided three chapters illustrating how the basic concepts discussed in other parts of the book can be applied to preschool, elementary, secondary, and exceptional students; and included a special chapter on classroom discipline. For this reason, we have subtitled the text, "A Practical Approach to Educational Psychology."

A second major decision concerns the orientation of the text. Rather than blindly adhering to a particular point of view, we have been empirical, practical, and skeptical in the selection of material to include. In other words, we have attempted to write a book about ideas that are *important* to teachers and about teaching methods that *work*. In following these guidelines, we have produced a text that has a dominant "behavioral" orientation, but one that is very different from any previous behavioral treatment of education. Because we set out to include all concepts that have been empirically shown to be useful in the classroom, we have written a full treatment of educational psychology including not only the topic of learning, but also development, motivation, social factors, cognition, and measurement.

The result is a broad, practical, and eclectic text whose dominant theme is the role played by teachers in actively structuring the learning environment of students. We have emphasized the works of Glaser, Gagné, Bloom, Ausubel, Skinner, and Bijou, but we have also drawn on the theories of Bruner, Piaget, and others.

The final decision that must be made is whether the project is worth the effort. Although an enormous amount of work went into this book, writing it was mostly an enjoyable experience. We will be most pleased if students get as much out of reading it as we did from writing it. We would like to offer special thanks to Richard Tucker for the key role he has played in the development of this book. We sincerely appreciate the contributions of the many other individuals who devoted their time and talents to the text, especially David Halfen, Jim Romig, Joanne Tinsley, Andrew Rojecki, Elaine Kurisu, Jackie Johnson, Muriel Price, and the friendly, patient ladies who operate the switchboard at Scott, Foresman. This book is dedicated to our spouses, Susan and Eric, with very special thanks for their contributions, support, and patience, to Megan, Edward, and Erin, and to Professor Jay Ostwalt, to whom this text was promised ten years ago.

CONTENTS

Psychology and Instruction

A Practical Approach to Educational Psychology

Introduction

The functions of teachers are twofold: First, they should help students learn in ways that are meaningful and efficient. This will allow children to reach their highest level of achievement and to have the greatest number of options in chosing an adult life-style. This will also provide society with the educated people necessary to strive to create a thriving civilization that will support happy, meaningful lives.

Second, teachers should see to it that children enjoy themselves while they are in school. We spend a sizable portion of our lives in classrooms. Not only should the educational system prepare children to be happier and more successful adults, it should also ensure that they are happy while they are in school. Fortunately, the goals of meaningful achievement and happiness are compatible. Children need not be tense and competitive in order to succeed. Our best educational practices can develop effective learners who are also having a good time.

Society builds schools and entrusts teachers with the responsibility of pursuing these goals. No other human-services profession has such prolonged and convenient access to children. Teachers are our first line of defense in solving the problems of childhood and preventing the problems of adulthood. We are far from having solutions to every problem of growing up, and we may be even farther from implementing the solutions that we do have. But we now possess much information that when properly applied will take us closer than ever before to the goal of happy, achieving children.

THEORIES OF EDUCATION

Two broad, opposing points of view dominate educational theory and practice today. One point of view holds that children have an innate interest in learning that, when given the proper amount of freedom, will stimulate children to learn and to grow at their maximal rate. As long as children are allowed to learn only when they are interested in learning and are only given opportunities to learn but are never forced, learning will be efficient as well as joyous. The teacher's primary duties are to be available when the child wants to ask questions and to provide materials from which the child can learn new principles. For example, a teacher might provide sticks of varying lengths from which the child could learn about serial order and would then be available for discussing this concept with the child, *if the child initiated such learning*.

A key assumption of this philosophy is that only the children know when they are ready to learn, and that any attempt on the teacher's part to teach a fact or a principle before the children are ready only inhibits the learning process. This approach assumes that the child's readiness for each new principle is tied to a maturational process that cannot be speeded up through teaching or through enriched experience.

The opposing view also sees children as having an innate potential for learning, but holds that learning will occur only when the appropriate experiences are provided for them. Efficient and enjoyable learning takes place when the children's experiences are carefully arranged and programmed for them.

Thus, the teacher's job is to arrange and to sequence the program of learning experiences for the child. For example, the teacher must insure that each child masters such skills as counting objects and making "greater than" and "less than" comparisons between two groups of objects before teaching addition. Learning will be a worthwhile experience when children are taught each set of principles in an effective way that reduces errors and when they are allowed to master one set of principles before proceeding to the next.

This division of educational theory into two camps is only a rough one; there are many theorists who take their own positions between these two views. Educational theories can be viewed on a continuum with the two approaches that we described lying at extreme ends. We will call these extreme positions *free* and *programmed* education, respectively. Although they characterize most current disputes over educational theory, these views have been with us in one form or another since Plato began having intellectual disputes with his student, Aristotle. This dialogue takes many different forms and assumes many different labels throughout history, from the early Greeks, through the empiricist-nativist debates of the Renaissance, to current times. Fortunately, however, the greatest number of educators fall towards the middle of this continuum rather than at the extremes.

This book, too, will be written from the middle ground of thought. On the one hand, we believe that children should be regimented as little as possible, but we also believe that the teacher should play a *major role* in guiding and arranging learning experiences. Children need not follow rigid schedules in order to learn, but a certain amount of organization and arrangement of learning is necessary.

Stated differently, the issue is how often should the teacher guide the student? Both of the opposing theoretical viewpoints recognize the importance of guidance, but differ on the amount necessary. You can avoid both extreme viewpoints by adopting a flexible, pragmatic approach, as the following classroom experiment illustrates.

The experiment took place in the Laboratory Preschool of the University of North Carolina at Charlotte, which serves children from middle- and upper-income families (Haskett & Lenfestey, 1974). The teachers were concerned that the children were not interested enough in the children's books that were distributed about the classroom. As Figure 1–1 shows, none of the children spent any significant amount of time looking at the books during the first part of the study (labeled "baseline" on Figure 1–1).

The teachers asked how they could encourage their students to read the books without adding undue regimentation to their activities. First, novel books were added to the collection in an attempt to attract the students' attention. The second part of Figure 1–1 shows that the addition of ten to fifteen new books each day did lead five of the children to spend more time with the books, but the teachers felt that this was still inadequate. They decided, therefore, to set an example for the children.

For the next five days, two to four of the teachers picked up a book at the beginning of each session, found a place to sit down, and began reading aloud. The children responded by looking frequently at the books (as the "models" part of Figure 1–1 shows). To check to see if their modeling was responsible for the changes in their students' behavior, the teachers stopped reading, but continued adding novel books for five days, and then began modeling reading again for three more days. As Figure 1–1 shows, the amount of attention the children paid to the books fell when the teachers stopped setting an example, but rose when the teachers resumed modeling the desired activity again.

This study illustrates the orientation of this text. Education requires guidance, but it need not result in a loss of the joy of learning. Teachers can effectively guide learning without creating a dull and regimented atmosphere.

BASIC PRINCIPLES OF TEACHING

Through years of experience, teachers gradually formed opinions about the effectiveness of methods of instruction. More recently, educators have used the methods of science to compare methods more objectively and have developed a "science of instruction." This chapter summarizes what we feel are some of the most useful principles of education in order to give a general overview of the orientation of this text. Support for these principles will be cited in the more specific discussion that follows.

Create a Favorable Classroom Climate

As a prospective teacher, you will need to give considerable thought to the kind of place your classroom will be. Will you have

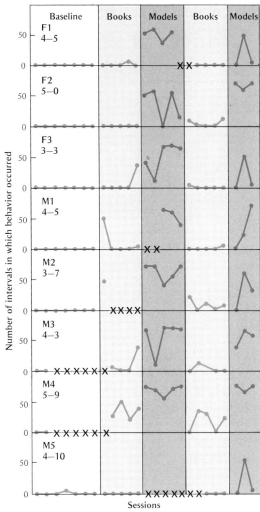

Figure 1–1. *The number of intervals in which each student attended to a book. Each student is identified by age in years and months and by sex (M-male, F-female). Absences are indicated by Xs. The students were observed under typical classroom conditions during the "Baseline" phase; novel books were placed in the classroom during the "Books" phase; and the teachers modeled reading the books during the "Models" phase. (From Haskett & Lenfestey, 1974)*

DOES GOOD TEACHING MAKE A DIFFERENCE?

"Studies published in the mid-1950s (Bloom, 1956; Bloom & Statler, 1957) compared the achievement of students in the 48 states at the end of 12 years of school. . . . Put in terms of grade equivalents in the highest state, the average student in the lowest state had completed only an eighth-grade education in 12 years.

"Recently, the International Study of Educational Achievement completed studies of achievement in mathematics, science, literature, reading, English as a second language, French as a second language, and civic competence. Altogether, about 28 nations have been involved in these comparative survey studies (Comber & Keeves, 1973; Husén, 1967; Purves, 1973; Thorndike, 1973). When one considers only the so-called 'developed' nations, the difference between the mean scores of the highest and the lowest nations on a particular subject field also approximates one standard deviation on the total distribution of scores at the end of about 12 years of school. When a few 'developing' nations are included in the distributions, the mean score for the students in the developing nations is about two standard deviations below the highest mean of the developed nations. Again, put crudely in terms of time and learning, an average student in a developing nation has obtained about 6 years of learning in 12 years and an average student in a low-scoring developed nation has obtained 8 years of learning in 12 years, in contrast to what the average student in the highest scoring of the developed nations has learned in 12 years. . . .

"While time and learning are not so easily equated, it is evident in these national and international studies that the accidents of birthplace and geography determine that a student in one set of communities and schools may spend 1½–2 years to learn what a student in another set of communities and schools will learn in 1 year. Or, to put it into time and human resources spent, it may cost twice as much for a particular level of learning in one place as it does in another place." (Bloom, 1974, p. 682)

Clearly, it is not geography that matters as much as the quality of education.

a classroom that fosters achievement and enjoyment? Will you arrange the desks so that they encourage studying rather than kicking? In short, will your classroom be a nice place to be? With some planning, you can use the atmosphere of the classroom to facilitate your educational programs, rather than to fight against them. For example, there could be one area in elementary classrooms where children can quietly work sitting in their seats and another area where they can engage in group discussions and behave in more informal ways. This physical arrangement encourages quiet when it is appropriate and encourages talking when that is appropriate. Many different areas of

this sort might be provided in an open classroom, but the teacher in an overcrowded self-contained room could accomplish the same goals by arranging different seating areas or by putting mats on the floor for different types of activities.

You can also make your classroom more pleasant and effective by using audio-visual aids, creative learning games, interesting reading materials, and bright decorations. These activities and decorations make a classroom an enjoyable place to spend the better part of the day. Playing rock records may give middle-school students a better understanding of poetry, and it will certainly make the classroom a more exciting place to

COMPUTERS AS TEACHERS?

In cities from Palo Alto, California, to Mc-Comb, Mississippi, to New York City, children are learning from teachers who are computers. They receive their lessons on small television screens and "talk" to their "teachers" by way of typewriters. Extensive research suggests that children enjoy this type of teaching and learn a great deal from it.

A study conducted in rural Mississippi by Patrick Suppes, one of the principal developers of computer-assisted instruction at Stanford University, showed that a group of children who were given daily 15-minute computer lessons in mathematics gained from 1.10 to 2.03 years of academic achievement, compared to gains of 0.26 to 1.26 years of achievement for students who did not receive computer tutoring (Suppes, 1966).

These results suggest that computers can function as very effective teachers indeed. But it seems very unlikely that computers will ever take jobs away from people-type teachers. It is not feasible to develop computer tutoring in the foreseeable future for anything except very clear-cut, repetitive instructional tasks. Computers, therefore, may someday free you from some of the drudgery of teaching, giving you more time and energy for more creative and human kinds of teaching.

be. Many such strategies for improving the atmosphere for learning are possible and can help ensure good teaching.

The most significant factor for creating a favorable classroom environment, however, is your own behavior as the teacher. A considerable amount of research supports this assertion. Several studies show that student achievement is highest when teachers show enthusiasm, present information in a clear and organized manner, preview and review the topics in their lessons, teach relevant material, show concern that the students will learn what they need, make flexible use of teaching materials and methods, and give informative personal feedback rather than harsh criticism (Firestone & Brody, 1975; Rosenshine & Furst, 1973).

Evidence also suggests that effective teachers display warmth, give their students an expectation of success (Rappaport & Rappaport, 1975), and know their pupils as individuals (Johnson, 1970). Coercive and dominating teachers tend to produce rebellion, distraction, and a lack of spontaneity in their students; psychologically unstable teachers tend to produce students with adjustment problems (Johnson, 1970). And as we shall see later, the most effective teachers are the ones that make learning meaningful, involve their students in decisions about goals and standards in a democratic way, and make wise use of rewards.

Understand the Characteristics of the Age-Group You Teach

We all know that behavior changes with age, but we often fail to grasp the implications of this fact. Children's behavior varies considerably within age levels, but not as much as across age levels. For example, the actions of a group of six-year-olds will be different from a group of twelve-year-olds. While most male six-year-olds claim to "hate" girls, few twelve-year-olds make the same claim. We must keep this in mind in deciding what to expect from a group of children. (Chapters 2 and 3 will focus on this issue.)

✓Define Educational Goals - Pinpoint

Simply stated, if you want to be an effective teacher, you must know what you want to teach. Teachers, of course, "know" what they must teach, but do they really? The first-grade teacher knows that the students must learn to read, and the social science teacher knows that students must understand cultural differences. Teachers, however, cannot always list all of the skills they want their children to learn and give *specific, meaningful* definitions for them. Definitions such as "understanding what they read" are too vague to be useful.

In order to maximize useful learning, you must clearly define the desired educational skills in terms of *what the student does*. This is the only way you can know what your students should be working on and how to accurately evaluate their progress. For example, reading for comprehension might be defined as including answering questions about material that the student has just read orally, following written directions, or summarizing a passage in the student's own words. The same rule applies for all subjects, from arithmetic to history. Defining instructional objectives in behavioral terms is an essential element of good teaching.

The computer as teacher

There are three main reasons for taking the time to define specific objectives for instruction:

(1.) It is much easier for teachers to know when to correct and reward their students if each step toward the objective has been clearly defined. For example, an arithmetic teacher cannot wait until a child has acquired an "understanding of numbers" to give praise for a job well done. Students must be patted on the back each time they perform one of the elements of "number concepts" (counts, seriates objects, etc.) and must be corrected each time an error is made if learning is to be maximally efficient. The more clear and specific the definition, the easier it is for the teacher to know whether the student has done the right or the wrong thing.

(2.) Learning is more efficient when tasks are taught in a sequence in which each skill builds on the previously learned ones and when *mastery* is achieved on each skill before proceeding to the next. For example, multiplication cannot be effectively taught until the student masters addition. This seems obvious, but it is often difficult to decide when a child should progress to the next higher step unless each element of the task has been carefully defined. This is one of the most frequently made mistakes in the classroom. When children are allowed to progress before they are ready, each step becomes more difficult than the last because the children face tasks for which they are increasingly unprepared.

(3.) It is only when instructional objectives have been adequately defined that the teacher can accurately assess the performance of a student or the effectiveness of a method of instruction. Objectives must be so clearly defined that the instructor can simply count how many objectives have been attained per unit of time. This allows the teacher to meaningfully compare a student with others and to compare teaching methods.

This final suggestion for better teaching is a simple one. You should be able to define what you want your students to learn in terms that are clear enough that allow you to recognize when learning takes place. This will allow you to monitor progress, to ensure mastery at each level, and to determine which teaching methods are the most effective.

The importance of instructional objectives will become clearer later in the book. Because they are so important, they should be defined in consultation with administrators, with curriculum specialists, with school psychologists, with other teachers, and, whenever possible, with parents and students.

Make Learning Meaningful

We all know from our own experience that learning is easier and is more enjoyable if it means something to us. In like manner, we need to teach in ways that will make learning meaningful to our students. Meaningful learning has two important components. First, learning is meaningful if it is in some way related to the life of the student. Students who want to be automobile mechanics will learn geometry better if it is related to their interest in mechanics, for example. It is simply a matter of explaining how the new knowledge relates to topics that are already meaningful to the students.

Second, the term *meaningful* also means *understanding* what you are learning. It is easier to learn the steps in dissecting a laboratory specimen, for example, when the reason for those steps is explained. Learning will always be more enjoyable and effective if it is meaningful rather than if it is rote.

Individualize Instruction   *children learn at their own rates*

History is made in the search for knowledge when a new generalization can be stated that holds for diverse things in varied circumstances, such as Newton's law of gravity. Psychology has such a shrewd generalization: *All children are different.* Children do,

HOW MUCH MUST A STUDENT LEARN TO BE "EDUCATED"

" 'Reeling and Writhing, of course, to begin with,' the Mock Turtle replied; 'and then the different branches of Arithmetic — Ambition, Distraction, Uglification and Derision.'
— Alice's Adventures in Wonderland

"To many worried parents, the new math — new methods of teaching that swept public schools in the '60s made as much sense as Lewis Carroll's Turtle. When they complained that children were no longer learning basic reading, writing and arithmetic, however, no one listened. Until, that is, test scores began plunging, and legislators and officials discovered that the supposed mess in public education could be a dangerous political issue.

"The result: in the past year, 'minimal competency testing' has become the hottest new catch phrase in public education. Described by educators as a 'man on the street' effort to halt the devaluation of a high school diploma, minimal competency requires students to pass proficiency exams, in addition to course work, in order to graduate. So far, six states — California, Florida, Maryland, New Jersey, Virginia and Washington — have enacted minimal competency laws. Florida has also outlawed traditional 'social passing,' by which illiterate students eventually graduated after merely attending school enough years. In ten more states, boards of education have decreed minimal competency on their own authority, and boards of over a dozen states are on the verge of doing so. Colleges, too, have caught the fever, and are increasingly requiring students to pass a writing exam before graduating. . . .

"Once a state has ratified minimal competency testing, however, the rhetoric ends and the problems begin. Foremost among them: What constitutes 'functional literacy'? Should only reading and math be tested? Or should the exams include such 'survival skills' as how to balance a checkbook or read a road map? Should standard statewide exams, which might be biased against, say, inner-city children, be used? Or should individual tests be developed by local school districts? . . .

"Nor do the problems stop there. When should students be tested? Many states, realizing that students must have time for remedial work if they fail a competency exam, are studying programs that would test students from early elementary grades upward. Extended remedial programs, however, would clearly cost additional tax dollars which may not be available. Warns Paul Hubbard, executive secretary of the Alabama Education Association: 'Without a commitment of funds, the real danger is that we'll give a test that will put the stamp of failure on thousands of Alabama young people, and no alternative course will be available.'

"Yet another fear is that minimal competency might turn into maximum competency as well. Says Titus Singletary, associate state school superintendent in Georgia: 'We must be wary of tailoring our programs to meet one need and concentrating so much on it that we don't teach anything else.' And, of course, there is the ultimate question: What to do with the student who fails?" (*Time*, Feb. 28, 1977, p. 74)

of course, share many characteristics, but a key feature from an educational point of view is their individual differences. Of particular importance are the wide variations in the rate and in the style with which children learn.

If children are to master each educational step, and if there are large differences in the time it takes children to reach these objectives, then it is obvious that children need to progress through the academic program at their own rates and in their own ways. Most schools long ago gave up the notion that all children of the same age are ready to be taught the same things and divided their children into "slow" and "fast" groups. But schools need to permit *all* children to progress at their own unique rates in order to

maximize achievement and to minimize frustration and failure. No child need be placed in a situation in which he or she does not "pass" a grade. Some children will just progress less rapidly than others.

Furthermore, treating children as individuals means that you can reward students for doing a good job *at their own level*, rather than comparing them to the rest of the class. If you praise only those who are at the top of the class, your class will have too few winners and far too many losers. Remember that being a loser during one's school days can contribute to a lifelong pattern of failure. Individualization is only one of the steps necessary to create optimal learning conditions, but it is an essential one.

Base Instruction on Entering Behavior

A major corollary of the last two suggestions is that you should know what each student can and cannot do before you start to teach. If you are going to develop learning experiences that will get a student to an educational goal, you must know in a clear and precise way where you need to begin. Some students who walk into your math class to learn calculus will be ready to learn the first concepts in the course, while others will be unprepared until you have given them remedial work on the foundations upon which calculus is built. In both cases, you must know what the students know, what their motives are, how they behave in the classroom, and how good their study skills are before you can begin. That is, you need to know what their **entering behaviors*** are.

*Boldface terms in the text and lightface terms in the boxed features are defined in the glossary at the end of the book.

It is equally important that you understand the concept of entering behavior before you attempt to individualize instruction. One of the major ways in which students differ is the set of entering behaviors that they present to you.

A simple framework for instruction adopted from Glaser (1962) can be stated in these terms:

(1.) Develop clear and precise instructional objectives.

(2.) Measure entering behaviors to determine how far each student has already progressed toward the objective, the way that she or he studies, her or his motives, and so on.

(3.) Develop instructional procedures that base current learning on each student's entering behavior.

(4.) Measure each student's progress toward the educational goals.

(5.) If one or more students have not reached the goals, provide additional instruction, modify the instructional procedures, or perhaps modify the instructional goals or·your methods of assessing entering behavior.

This model gives the teacher an active role in structuring the learning environment. It should be made clear, however, that structure does not equal regimentation. The teacher should assess and should teach in ways that are not obtrusive or coercive and that do not detract from the joy of learning. This is a tough task, but this text will provide you with some specific ideas for accomplishing this.

Allow Mastery Learning   *individualize instruction in order to master a concept*

We must be aware of an important implication of the fact that children learn at differ-

ent rates. If, for example, you teach a unit on finding the area of right triangles and then give a test, you will find that some of the students will be able to solve all of the problems, while others will not. What does this mean? What do you do next? Teachers sometimes deal with this problem by deciding that some children are "smart" in geometry and some are not. The students who learn triangles the first time they are presented are thought to be smart, while the ones who do not are seen as incapable. Although teachers usually do not spend much time thinking about this issue, they often implicitly assume that there is no use in wasting time on students who are not good in math anyway. This is a convenient way for teachers to look at the problem of differences in learning rates as it lets them off the hook. They can simply blame slow learning on the students' lack of ability. This does nothing to help slow-learning students, but it does remove the responsibility from the teacher.

Perhaps the most unfortunate aspect of this way of thinking is that it tends to confirm itself through a self-fulfilling prophecy. When teachers move on to the next topic (such as finding the area of irregular polygons, which requires a prior knowledge of how to find the area of triangles), sure enough, those students who were "not capable" of learning triangles will do even less well with polygons. This, of course, will tend to confirm the teacher's impression that the slower-learning students are truly incapable.

The concept of individualized instruction, on the other hand, is based on the premise that, assuming adequate teaching is available, nearly all students can master all academic tasks if they *have the right background* and if they are *given enough time* (Bloom, 1974). If the students who had floundered on polygons had been given enough time to *master* triangles, then they would have had the prerequisite skills to learn how to find the area of polygons (if they were given enough time to do that!). When children move from one task to another before they master the lower-level task, failure is likely. When instruction is individualized so that the child is allowed to learn each skill or concept to mastery before proceeding to the next, a slow child may learn fewer things in twelve years of formal education than a fast child, but at least the slow child will have experienced success in *mastering* what was learned. The concept of mastery has important implications for all areas of education, but is most important when learning directly builds on previous learning. For example, it is essential that students master multiplication before tackling division, but less important for them to master a poetry unit before moving on to short stories. Like individualization, mastery learning is a goal to aim for, but not one that can always be reached in large classrooms.

Provide for Active Learning

In many instances an American classroom can be described as a place where the teacher talks and the students listen (or at least are supposed to). Occasionally the students will write and the teacher will read what they wrote, but these occasions take up only a small part of the total classroom time. If, however, you are going to follow the recommendations given above, you must create conditions in which the children will be encouraged to do a considerable amount of talking and writing. This is essential if you are to accurately monitor progress and to give frequent feedback and rewards.

To a great extent, the more time that students spend on work that you can observe and respond to, the more rapid and painless learning will be. This can be very difficult for you to arrange, as it is much easier to lecture than to arrange meaningful independent work for the students. We will make many suggestions for making it easier in later sections of the book.

Reduce Student Failure   *encouragement*

The student who is frequently unsuccessful in academic work is an unhappy child who may soon give up, cause trouble, and drop out. The successful student, on the other hand, can have a good time and work to capacity. We do learn from our mistakes, but too much failure can be defeating. It is possible to engineer the situation so that failure is infrequent for most children by designing small steps for poor learners and large steps for good learners, and, again, by allowing each child to progress at his or her own rate.

Seek Help from Others   *resources*

Many teachers realize that the best college of education and the best in-service training program cannot teach them everything that they need to know, that even the most judicious teachers can fall into bad habits, and that even the most fundamental concepts can be misunderstood or misapplied. This is why the best teachers will take the time and the trouble, placing pride and prestige on the line, to seek feedback on their teaching skills. They will seek feedback from experts, administrators, other teachers, parents, and students. Perhaps more importantly, they will take the time to monitor the progress of their own students to seek out and to correct weak spots in their teaching repertoires.

ONE SCHOOL'S APPROACH TO HUMANISTIC EDUCATION

"The fifth-graders at Denver's Thomas A. Edison elementary school sit in a circle with their principal, Forest Fransen. Placing an empty soda bottle on the floor, Fransen and the kids spin it to choose the order of children who will 'tell about themselves.' After a few embarrassed giggles, a boy named Paul says: 'I like to go fishing a lot. There's six in my family and two are babies. That's all.' Don reveals that 'I've got a sister in junior high; I had another sister but she had cancer.' The children are fidgetless and fascinated. Finally the bottle points to Fransen, who tells of his pride in a father who came from Sweden to homestead in a sod house.

"So goes the first class in 'emotional skills,' a new course that has spread to several dozen public and private schools in cities from New York to San Francisco. Increasing numbers of states are mandating some form of classroom instruction in mental health. The goal: helping children forestall the emotional scars that lead to drug abuse, delinquency and adult happiness. . . .

"For one fifth-grade lesson, the teacher induces jealousy by repeatedly choosing the same bright, attractive youngster to do blackboard work. When the class balks at this favoritism, the teacher admits her ploy, then tries to coax the students into conceding that they feel jealous. 'It is important,' says the teacher' guide, 'that no one feel he is strange or wicked if he is jealous from time to time. By admitting jealousy and talking about it, children are less likely to act out their aggressive feelings.'

"At four schools in Colorado Springs, where the courses have been taught for the past two years, about half the parents say their children have become more willing to discuss their problems. 'Before,' said one mother, 'my daughter just threw a fit.' Teachers report fewer discipline cases; social workers say they get more 'self-referrals—kids with problems they sense they can't handle alone.' Among the few criticisms, one parent said 'these attitudes and insights are training I would rather my child received at home.'

"Despite this seeming success, no one is yet sure how much of the kids' improvement is due to normal growing up or merely the extra attention they get in the course. Noting that the Colorado teachers have been trained in special seminars, critics also fear that untrained or insecure teachers could easily confuse the kids they are trying to help. . . .

"Emotional-skills courses are obviously well-intentioned efforts to forestall critical social problems. As the courses spread, though, mistakes seem inevitable. Thus sharp questions are likely to be raised about whether those efforts are pointed in the right direction." (*Time,* Feb. 22, 1971, p. 74)

Some psychologists and parents applaud this effort to improve the emotional development of children. Others oppose it as ill-conceived, as dangerous, and as a violation of the rights of parents to raise children as they see fit. How do you feel? The decision to include emotional education in your curriculum will be up to you and your colleagues.

Protesting the content of social-science textbooks in Kanawha County (West Virginia)

HUMANISTIC EDUCATION

Recently an old controversy arose again about the need for broadening the goals of education. Schools often focus exclusively on teaching academic skills and forget that children and youths also need to learn to be "people." The advocates of this point of view suggest that education must be *humanistic* as well as intellectual. This recurring controversy raises two important points: Humanists are concerned with both what is taught in the classroom and how it is taught.

Children acquire their attitudes and values through learning from other people. Both the home and the school play significant roles in this process. The question is should schools intentionally teach values and attitudes?

People who say that they should suggest that schools should, for example, teach individuals to understand their own emotions and those of others, to relate easily with peers, and to tolerate and even enjoy the cultural differences among people. Although this seems a worthy venture, it is quite controversial.

It is one thing to favor humanistic education when the values that are being taught are your own, but what if your children were being taught values that conflicted with your own? Recently some Fundamentalist Christian groups burned books they judged offensive to their beliefs and advocated a return to Bible readings in school, actions bitterly opposed by atheists and by non-Christians.

DRUG EDUCATION OR DRUG PUSHING?

One of the more favorable trends in humanistic education is toward teaching information and skills that are relevant to "real life." In addition to traditional academic subjects, many schools offer courses in consumer education, vocational training, and health and physical fitness. These courses seem to be important ways to directly improve our students' lives, but we must be careful to evaluate what these programs actually accomplish. A health education program in Michigan provides a case in point.

A study was conducted in a suburban junior high school of the effects of a drug education program (Stuart, 1974). A total of 935 seventh- and ninth-grade students of both sexes were randomly assigned either to a group that received drug education or to one that did not. At the end of the program, all the students filled out an anonymous questionnaire about drugs. Relative to the group that did not participate, the students in the drug education program were more knowledgeable about drugs and were less worried about them. This seems desirable, but the results also showed that the students in the drug education program *increased their use* of alcohol and drugs (marijuana and LSD), and even *sold* drugs more often than the students who were not in the program.

These results do not mean that all drug education programs will necessarily encourage drug use and sales, but they do tell us to be careful of what we teach and to *evaluate* the effects of our efforts.

Some groups of ecologists protested the showing of movies to children of Eskimos killing seals; while, on the other hand, some industrialists objected to teachers, having their pupils write letters protesting pollution. This sort of disagreement probably will go on as long as we are a pluralistic society.

Such conflicts support arguments against humanistic education, but there is another side to the controversy. Children learn values from their teachers whether their teachers intentionally teach them or not. This is because people *live* their attitudes and their values, and children learn from the way we live. It may make sense, therefore, to be systematic about what we teach them. This, however, is a very complicated matter. For example, we believe that teachers should teach their students to find nonviolent solutions to conflicts. This seems justified, even though some communities and families believe that children need to be physically aggressive to survive in a tough world, because a student's use of violence necessarily violates the rights of others. We also urge that steps be taken to reduce racial, sexual, and other forms of prejudice in the classroom, but believe that personal issues such as religious beliefs should be decided upon in the home. Similarly, we strongly favor sex education in the schools, but only if minor students have parental permission. We shy away from these issues not because they are sensitive, but because they are *personal.* They are personal in the sense that religious attitudes and sexual standards do not ordinarily affect the rights and values of others. Teachers may feel free to challenge personal beliefs in free and open discussion, but not to unilaterally usurp the rights of parents by changing the personal beliefs of their students. In general, you should be very hesitant to transmit your own values to your students without community guidance and consent. We say this for the best of humanistic reasons: respect for the values of others.

But, humanistic educators are concerned with more than just the content of education; they are vitally concerned with the *way* students are taught. They ask teachers to respect the individual characteristics and autonomy of students in the same way they would respect other adults. This is a controversial position as it conflicts with the traditional conception of children as clay to be shaped to conform with adult society. The authors take issue with it, however, primarily because it is excessively vague. We believe in giving children as much autonomy as they are able to handle, but some interpret it to mean that we should allow children to do whatever they please. As we have already made clear in our discussion of the free and programmed educational philosophies, we believe that adult guidance is an indispensable part of education.

Humanistic education, then, involves many important but difficult issues. The authors have taken a stand in this book that is strongly supportive of most aspects of humanistic education, but not all. We believe the process of education must respect the inherent worth of each student, and that teachers sometimes have the right and obligation to teach values to their students. But, while we vigorously support most of the goals of humanistic education, we disagree with some humanists about the best methods to use.

First, we believe that you show the most meaningful kind of respect for the rights of students when you provide enough guidance to ensure that they will grow and learn appropriately. Permissively allowing children to do whatever they wish out of "respect" for their self-determination does not promote effective development.

Second, many humanistic educators downplay the importance of academic instruction in their advocacy of more humanistic learning experiences. We believe the development of academic skills is an *essential* part of the development of the whole person. Educational achievement is an important part of adult competence.

Third, we disagree with some of the specific learning experiences advocated by some humanists. For example, we do not support the use of "encounter groups" designed to "get children in touch with their own feelings." It is our opinion that these experiences are often confusing to children and may cause more harm than good.

The authors, therefore, have adopted a position on humanistic education that is somewhat middle-of-the-road. You may want to give considerable thought to the development of your own opinions on this very important issue, and you may want to consult other professionals. We hope the remainder of this book will assist you. The principles and methods most relevant to humanistic education are not placed in a separate section, but are spread throughout the text.

REVIEW 1-1

Answer the following questions before going on to the next section in this chapter. Compare your answer to each question with the answer given at the end of the chapter. Make sure you achieve *mastery* on these questions before going on. Repeat the self-testing process until you can correctly answer each question without hesitation. You will enhance your understanding of each section if you thoroughly master each preceding section. Do not "read now," with a promise to "learn later."

1. Define the concepts of "free" and "programmed" education. What approach do most educators follow?

2. What are two functions of a teacher?

3. List the nine basic principles of teaching discussed in this chapter.

4. What does the term *favorable classroom environment* mean? Give examples of some things that would help to create such an environment.

5. What does it mean to say that a teacher should allow students to "act their age"?

6. How should educational goals be defined? Give an example.

7. What are the three main reasons for defining educational goals?

8. What is the main reason for allowing children to progress at their own rate in individualized instruction?

9. What does mastery learning mean?

10. What is meant by the term *entering behavior*? Give two examples and describe how you would measure it.

11. Put the five steps of designing an educational program adopted from Glaser's model of instruction into your own words.

12. Why should the teacher bring about active learning?

13. Why should the teacher reduce the frequency of failure for the student?

14. What benefit would a teacher receive from a habit of frequent consultations with parents, with children, and with other professionals throughout his or her career?

If you do not understand the answer to any of these questions, reread the appropriate section of the book. If you still have a question, ask your instructor. Never study for a test until after you fully understand all of the material.

SUMMARY

Teachers play a vital role in the development of society's children. Good teachers help to ensure happy and successful growth. They create classrooms that are fun to be in and that encourage learning. They allow their students to "act their age" by knowing what to expect from each age-group and by realizing that enjoying childhood is as important as enjoying any other part of life. They maximize learning without encouraging an overemphasis on success by clearly defining educational goals, by allowing students to progress at their own pace, by avoiding failure, by mastering each task before progressing to the next, and by stimulating active learning. They also seek the assistance of others in sharpening and maintaining their teaching skills. They may define successful education in a way that includes learning values in addition to mastering academic skills (humanistic education), but they do so in a way that balances their own values with those of the community.

ANSWERS TO REVIEW QUESTIONS

1. Proponents of "free" education feel that children have an innate desire to learn that guides their education from within, if adults do not stifle self-directed learning with too much regimentation. Advocates of "programmed" education feel that children learn only when the proper experiences are arranged for them by teachers. They view learning as coming from the outside rather than from the inside. Most educators today hold a view that is some combination of these extreme viewpoints.

2. Two functions of teachers are to create conditions in which children can learn at their maximal rate, and to see to it that children enjoy themselves while they are learning.

3. The nine basic principles of learning discussed in this chapter are create a favorable classroom climate, understand the characteristics of the age-group you teach, define educational goals, individualize instruction, base instruction on entering behavior, allow mastery learning, provide for active learning, reduce student failure, and seek help from others.

4. The term favorable classroom environment includes everything from proper seating arrangements and the use of teaching aids to the behavior of the teacher. Research suggests that teacher characteristics such as enthusiasm, warmth, and clarity lead to improved achievement.

5. Teachers need to understand the behavior that is characteristic of the age-group they teach. It is normal for children to be "childish" or "immature," and teachers should guard against expecting their students to learn or to behave in ways that are too advanced for their age.

6. Educational goals should be defined in terms of what the student *does*, rather than what the student *knows*. It is very difficult to know when students understand the concept of a fair and speedy trial, but it is relatively easy to determine when they have stated a definition and given examples of this concept.

7. The three main reasons for defining goals are to facilitate knowing when to give corrective feedback or rewards, to make it easier to design instruction in appropriate sequences, and to aid in assessing student progress toward those goals.

8. Allowing children to progress at their own rates allows them to completely learn one concept or skill before attempting to learn another one that is based on the first, thus reducing the amount of failure.

9. Mastery learning, as in the previous question, means allowing the child to completely learn a skill or concept even if that child requires considerable time to learn it.

10. Entering behavior refers to what the child can do *before* instruction on a new skill or concept begins. For example, counting is a necessary entering behavior for instruction in arithmetic.

11. Glaser suggests that we know and define what we want the student to learn in behavioral terms; that we find out what the child can do before we begin instruction (paying particular attention to those skills and concepts that the new learning will be based upon); that we build the new learning on what the student can presently do; that we measure the student's progress; and that we revise the instructional methods if they have not been completely successful.

12. Students must generate a great deal of behavior if the teacher is to be able to continually monitor progress and to provide corrective feedback or rewards.

13. Students who frequently fail may stop working, cause trouble, and drop out.

14. A teacher's training is never complete, nor is a teacher ever immune from developing poor teaching habits. Consulting with other professionals will help improve skills and maintain competence.

1

HUMAN DEVELOPMENT

From preschool to high school, children grow up. The chapters in this section are presented to give you a better understanding of changes in behavior associated with age and to discuss the teacher's role in guiding development. In Chapter 2 we will discuss differing viewpoints on the nature of development. Some theorists believe psychological development is biologically predetermined with the individual's learning experiences having little power to shape development. Other theorists see learning as having a much more important role than heredity, while the authors of this text take a moderate stand. Like most current thinkers, we believe that both heredity and experience interact to determine development. In Chapter 3 we will look at some of the typical patterns of behavior that are associated with each age-group from preschool to high school. This chapter is included in the belief that a key to understanding the behavior of any child is a knowledge of how behavior typically changes with age.

Chapter 2

Concepts and Theories of Development

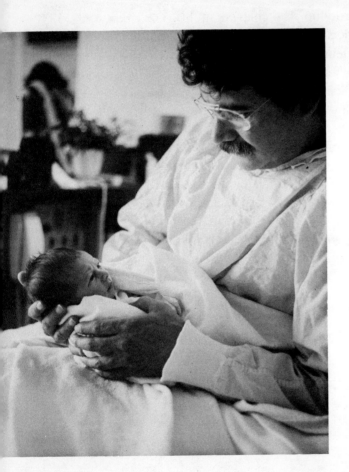

One of the basic principles of teaching mentioned in Chapter 1 was "understand the characteristics of the age-group you teach." It is clear that children of different ages behave differently and that teachers have different expectations for their students' behavior, depending upon the student's age. Indeed, our whole educational system is based on the notion that children differ with respect to age and that this makes different teaching strategies necessary. This emphasis on the student's age can be seen in our teacher training programs, in our certification standards, and in the divisions we make in our school programs—early childhood, primary, intermediate, middle school, and high school.

Psychologists, in their attempt to understand human behavior, also show great interest in the relationship between age and behavior. In this chapter we will draw heavily from the field of **developmental psychology,** the field within psychology that is most clearly concerned with how people change and grow through time. We will examine the concept of human development and various theories that attempt to account for development. In doing so, we hope to lay the foundation for a discussion in the following chapter of the normal sequences of development from infancy through adolescence and the implications these sequences have for classroom instruction.

"UNFOLDING" AND "MOLDING": ANCHOR POINTS IN UNDERSTANDING DEVELOPMENT

As the human grows from infancy to adulthood, vast changes take place in his or her characteristics and abilities. Newborn babies are relatively helpless and dependent organisms whose behaviors are closely tied to biological needs. As time passes, infants change in many ways. They grow physically, as they gain in weight and height and as their muscles and bones develop. They grow intellectually, as they begin to explore their environment and acquire language and thought. They grow socially and emotionally, as they interact first with their parents and siblings and later with their peers and other members of society. Many of these changes in physical, in intellectual, and in social-emotional characteristics are *developmental* in nature; that is, they are systematically related to the age of the individual. We know this because psychologists put considerable effort into the careful observation of children at various age levels.

As we pinpoint, for example, the ways in which most five-year-olds are alike, as well as the ways in which the typical five-year-old differs from the typical three-year-old or seven-year-old, we begin to see a pattern of development. We see that the behavior of a child is, to a large extent, a function of his or her age. There are, however, many important differences in the behavior of children of the same age. Different children grow up at different rates and in different ways. Variability in development is normal unless it is extreme and is the rule rather than the exception. But there is more than enough similarity in the development of children to make a study of age-related changes in behavior important to our understanding of our students.

Few would dispute that age is an important variable in explaining similarities and differences among children. But there is much disagreement as to *why* age is so important. In other words, why do children develop as they grow older? Perhaps it will be helpful to anchor our discussion of the "why" of development by referring to the unfolding/molding dichotomy summarized in Table 2–1.

Unfolding Theories

This dichotomy represents the two most extreme viewpoints on development. On one end is the "unfolding" view that sees the child first and foremost as a biological organism. **Maturation** is defined as the orderly growth processes that are genetically determined and that occur independent of exercise and training. This is seen as the underlying principle that guides development. According to the unfolding viewpoint, the behavior of most one-year-olds is similar because most one-year-olds are at the same level of biological maturation. They are, for example, ready to walk because the muscles and the centers in the brain that control motor movement have matured sufficiently so that coordinated and voluntary walking is possible. One-year-olds are unable to run or to skip or to speak in complete sentences, because these behaviors require more complex neurological development that comes at a later age.

Changes in behavior occur as the result of the automatic unfolding of biological processes within the child. These changes occur sequentially as the nervous system matures and are similar from one person to another. The environment has only a minor influence on development, according to this view.

Proponents of the unfolding viewpoint have been particularly interested in describ-

---

TABLE 2–1

Issues Defining the "Unfolding"-"Molding" Dichotomy

Unfolding Viewpoint	Molding Viewpoint
Age depicts the underlying process of biological maturation, as determined by the genes.	*Age* depicts the backdrop against which specific experiences accumulate as a result of the children's interaction with their environment.
Norms and *stages* are the benchmarks of the natural process of unfolding.	*Norms* and *stages* are useful only as descriptions of what has occurred in a given environment.
Learning is a function of maturation—what children can learn depends on their biological readiness.	*Learning* is a function of the acquisition of prerequisite skills—what children can learn depends on what they have learned previously.
Teachers and *parents* play the role of a "gardener," planting the seeds and cultivating, but waiting for the final product to emerge from "within" the child.	*Teachers* and *parents* play the role of a "potter," starting with a ball of clay and actively shaping the final product by structuring learning experiences.

ing typical behaviors of children at various age levels. They call these typical patterns of development **developmental norms** and often use them as guidelines or "rulers" to measure and to understand the underlying process of biological maturation. Any deviations from these norms are believed to result from the natural genetic distribution that characterizes most biological processes — some individuals simply mature (in the biological sense) faster than others. This experience plays a minor role in influencing development.

Developmental stages also play an important role in the unfolding theories of development. Stages refer to sequential time periods that are characterized by qualitative differences in the person's behavior. The term "qualitative difference" means a change in *kind*. A basket that contains three oranges differs from one that contains one orange quantitatively, that is, in number. But, a basket that contains apples differs from one that contains oranges qualitatively, that is, in kind. In the same way, unfolding theories of development focus on qualitative changes in behavior.

A child who learns to speak more words in longer sentences over a period of six months has only changed quantitatively. His or her verbal behavior is not radically different; rather, it is just more extensive. A child who in the course of six months changes from a child who *cannot* communicate verbally to one who *can* talk, however, has changed qualitatively. This child is a different "kind" of a person with a different kind of capacity. In the terms of the unfolding theories, the child has entered a new "stage."

According to the unfolding viewpoint, children go through many stages in their physical, intellectual, moral, and social-emotional development. Their behavior differs from one stage to another. Similarly, children are unable to learn new skills and concepts, according to this view, until they have reached the proper stage for such learning. Under the control of biological mechanisms, the stages are passed through in a fixed sequence. A later stage of development cannot be reached until the child has passed through all earlier stages in the sequence. Experience plays a limited role in determining the rate at which the stages will be completed, in the same way that sun, water, and nutrients play a role in influencing the growth of a tree. A child growing in a poor environment can be stunted like a tree growing in a poor soil, but experience cannot influence the nature or sequence of the stages any more than soil can determine what kind of tree will grow from a seed. Acorns always produce oaks, regardless of the soil they are planted in.

Molding Theories

On the other end of the continuum are the molding theories. They see age as important in development only in that with increasing age children increase their range of experiences. Changes in behavior do not emerge autonomously from within children, but result from events in the environment that act upon them in lawful and predictable ways.

Thus **learning,** which is defined as any relatively permanent change in behavior that is due to experience, is the principle that guides development. Like the unfolding theories, the molding theories also see ''readiness'' to learn playing an important role in influencing what will be learned from experience. Children at different points in their development will be more or less able to learn certain things, but this readiness is not seen as coming from a biologically determined process of maturation. Readiness to learn does not just happen; it must be acquired. The acquisition of readiness is simply a matter of preparing for more complex behaviors through the learning of prerequisite skills.

Followers of the molding viewpoint agree that norms and stages may be helpful guideposts in understanding child behavior. But they criticize the notion that certain behaviors invariably appear at given ages and that all children develop in the same sequence. Instead they emphasize the similarities in the environments of most children that cause certain behaviors to usually appear at certain ages and in sequence.

Let us take, for example, the norm that states that the average child begins to use her first words around age one. Most one-year-olds live in roughly similar environments which might account for the similar changes in behavior. The child has heard her parents speak for a year now and might be making some sounds of her own. The parents have probably shown their delight in the child's vocalizations by smiling, by cuddling, and by praising the child when she coos and babbles. They have paid particularly close attention to any sounds the baby makes that approximate the English language and may be actively shaping speech. Furthermore, they have begun to teach the child, intentionally or not, to label events, objects, and people in her environment. The mother may point to herself, for example, and say "mama." The baby might imitate, and the proud parents might provide reinforcement.

Thus it may be "normal" for a one-year-old to begin to use single words, but it is normal only because the typical child has been exposed to certain experiences. Simply being alive for a year is insufficient *cause* for the child to speak. If a psychologist who is oriented toward the molding viewpoint encounters a child who deviates from the norm (for example, a child of eighteen months who is not yet labeling objects), he or she will first look for differences in the child's environment that might account for the child's idiosyncratic behavior.

A COMPARISON OF THEORIES

The most salient difference between the unfolding and molding viewpoints for teachers concerns the role that adults play in the child's development. The gardener-potter analogy referred to in Table 2–1 highlights the differences between these approaches. A gardener is most interested in providing a favorable environment in which the young plant can flourish. He does what he can to ensure that the plant receives the nutrients

necessary for growth, and he attempts to protect it from harmful influences such as weeds, predators, and harsh weather. Aside from these minimal precautions, he does little else, allowing the innate genetic mechanisms within the plant to govern its development. Extending the analogy to the classroom, we see a teacher who provides a favorable environment in which the children can develop according to their own innate potential. The teacher sets a minimum number of rules designed to protect the health and safety of the students and to maintain some order in the classroom. The teacher also makes available a variety of stimulating materials and activities. Beyond these simple preparations, however, the teacher intervenes as little as possible and allows the children to follow their own interests and abilities, serving primarily as a resource person to help guide their development.

The potter, on the other hand, starts with a ball of clay and some ideas of what she would like the clay to become. She then actively shapes the clay so that it begins to take on the characteristics desired in the final form. Extending this analogy to the classroom, we see a teacher who structures the students' social and academic experiences so that they learn the skills society values. The teacher not only sets rules and provides a pleasant classroom atmosphere, but also defines objectives for each student, depending upon the student's current abilities. By providing carefully sequenced instructional experiences, the teacher plays an active role in shaping the development of each child.

Above and opposite page: motor coordination in an eight-month-old child

You may recognize by now that the unfolding/molding viewpoints of child development correspond closely to the free/programmed viewpoints of education introduced in Chapter 1. We will return to some of the implications that developmental psychology has for education in Chapter 3, when we look at the concepts of developmental norms, and particularly the readiness issue, more carefully. We now turn, however, to an examination of several specific theories of development and of their relationship to the unfolding/molding dichotomy.

EARLY THEORIES OF DEVELOPMENT

The unfolding/molding dichotomy is useful only to the extent that we consider these two positions to be at the extremes of a continuum. They are only two of many approaches to understanding development; and they are currently out of fashion. In fact, the dichotomy is more characteristic of the early history of developmental psychology than it is of present approaches. Present approaches tend to emphasize the interaction between biological maturation and environmental experiences. Early theories, however, did not.

One of the earliest contributors to developmental psychology and one of the strongest proponents of the unfolding viewpoint was Arnold Gesell. In the early 1900s Gesell began a series of research projects at the Yale Child Development Center that involved the observation of large numbers of children. Although he first studied infants, Gesell gradually included children at all age levels from birth through adolescence. Gesell's research was *normative* in nature; that is, he wanted to develop norms that described the typical characteristics of child behavior at various ages.

Gesell used two different methods in collecting this normative data. In some cases he used the **longitudinal method,** observing the same child or group of children at different times in order to chart growth. In other cases he used the **cross-sectional method,** observing at one time the behavior of different groups of children at various age levels (comparing, for example, the height of four-year-olds versus that of five-, six-, and seven-year-olds). Gesell used both methods to gather huge amounts of data on characteristics such as motor abilities, personal hygiene, emotional expressions, fears and dreams, interpersonal relationships, play and pastimes, school adjustment, and ethical beliefs. Gesell culminated these ambitious projects in a series of three books published in the 1940s and 1950s dealing with infancy, childhood, and adolescence (Gesell & Ilg, 1943; Gesell & Ilg, 1946; Gesell & Ilg, 1956). In each of these books, Gesell and his colleagues provide detailed descriptions of "the two-year-old," "the three-year-old," and so on—descriptions to which parents still turn in order to know what to expect of their children, to determine if their course of development is normal.

Gesell believed strongly that development is a function of biological maturation (Gesell, 1954). He was fascinated by the similarities he observed in the behavior of children of the same age and proposed that these similarities were due to the unfolding or the "ripening" of the nervous system. This, in turn, was under the control of the genes, the basic units of heredity. Gesell placed little emphasis on learning, as the following quote illustrates: "Environmental factors support, inflect, and modify; but they do not generate the progression of development. . . . The maturational matrix is the primary determinant of child behavior" (Gesell, 1954, p. 358).

An early experiment by Gesell and Thompson (1929) provided support for the unfolding position. In this experiment they used the "co-twin control method" to investigate the relative effects of maturation and learning. This method involves studying a pair of identical twins under conditions in which one child is given training and practice in a certain behavior while the other is not. In their experiment they studied stair-

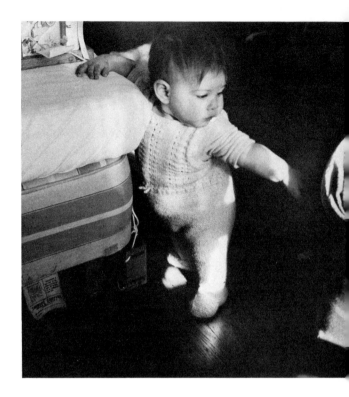

climbing. The experimenters began training one child (twin A) to climb a staircase at the age of forty-six weeks. By the end of the six-week training period, twin A was climbing the stairs with considerable proficiency. It certainly looked as if she was *learning* how to climb. At this point twin B, who had no previous experience with staircases or climbing, was brought into the experiment. When first placed on the staircase, twin B climbed without assistance and at a respectable rate, even though she had received no training. Gesell and Thompson concluded that the crucial events during the six-week period that paved the way for stair-climbing were

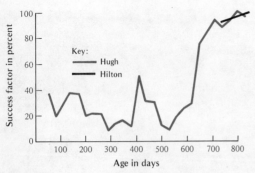

Figure 2–1. *Achievement curves showing the effect of early toilet training. (From McGraw, 1940)*

related *not* to training or to practice, but to the children's maturing physical and neurological processes.

Another early proponent of the unfolding viewpoint was Myrtle McGraw (1940), who also published a study using the co-twin control method. In her experiment McGraw observed toileting. McGraw toilet trained one member of a pair of twins from a very early age. As soon as the trained twin had achieved bladder control, she introduced the other twin to similar training. Figure 2–1 shows the results. Because the second twin rapidly and easily became toilet trained (although, unlike his brother, he had not been given an extended period of training), McGraw concluded that maturation was the key. Toilet training before the child is biologically ready will be useless. Once the child is ready, however, training can proceed with little difficulty.

Additional support for the unfolding position came from early studies by Wayne Dennis. In one study, Dennis (1941) examined the development of twin girls who were raised in his home until the age of fourteen months. Dennis wanted to see if their behavior would develop normally under conditions of restricted stimulation and social isolation. The infants received no toys and lay in their cribs with minimal contact from other humans (their physical needs were adequately met). Dennis then compared the ages at which these children reached certain motor milestones such as grasping, reaching, sitting, standing, and walking to standard norms. Dennis concluded overall that the motor behavior of the restricted infants developed at a similar rate and in the same sequence as that of infants given a normal amount of environmental stimulation.

In a second study, Dennis (1940) found a larger sample of subjects to examine. One group consisted of Hopi Indian infants whose parents still followed the tradition of binding the infants to a cradleboard for the first few months of life. The comparison group consisted of Hopi infants whose parents had given up this practice. Again, Dennis found little difference in motor development between the restricted and the unrestricted children. These early studies suggested that early motor behavior develops regardless of experience.

The experimental work of Gesell, McGraw, Dennis, and other pioneers in the field of developmental psychology focused almost solely on the development of motor and physical characteristics in childhood. Yet Gesell and his co-workers believed intellectual and social-emotional characteristics developed in the same way, from *within* the child.

One early psychologist who took the opposite point of view was John B. Watson. Watson believed that in order for psychology to progress as a science it was necessary to focus on the relationship between observable behavior and environmental events that affect that behavior. Watson chose first to study the behavior of infants, as infants could be easily observed in the laboratory under controlled environmental conditions. In 1920 Watson and Raynor conducted what was to become a classic experiment in psychology. They conditioned an eleven-month-old boy, known today as "Little Albert," to be afraid of white rats by pairing the presence of a rat with a sudden loud noise. Convinced that fear in children was a learned response, Watson went on to formulate a theory of development that placed total emphasis on learning as the process that shapes the child. Watson's (1925) extreme environmentalist position is best illustrated in his famous statement:

Give me a dozen healthy infants, well-formed, and my own specified world to bring them up in and I'll guarantee to take any one at random and train him to become any type of specialist I might select—doctor, lawyer, artist, merchant chief and, yes, even beggar-man and thief, regardless of his talents, penchants, tendencies, abilities, vocations, and race of his ancestors (p. 82).

Watson believed so strongly in the power of the environment to shape behavior that he later wrote a book on child-rearing, in which he called child-rearing "the most important of all social obligations" and urged parents to take an objective and firm, yet kindly stance toward their children. He urged parents to put considerable thought into the training of their children and warned them against the unfolding viewpoint (Watson, 1928):

. . . Educators have been insisting for the last twenty years upon a method of training which allows the child to develop from within. This is really a doctrine of mystery. It teaches that there are hidden springs of activity, hidden possibilities of unfolding within the child which must be waited for until they appear and then be fostered and

tended. I think this doctrine has done serious harm. It has made us lose our opportunity to implant and then encourage a real eagerness for vocations at an early age (p. 40).

Although this was a small part of Watson's contribution to psychology, it was these extreme views on child development that caught the attention of Watson's critics. Many rejected altogether Watson's work, fearing his vision of a society in which the environment could be engineered to modify human behavior and disagreeing with his attempt to be totally objective about human nature. Others, as we shall see later in this chapter, accepted at least part of Watson's theory and expanded upon it, seeing in it the hope for a better development of human potential.

REVIEW 2-1

1. What is *developmental psychology*?

2. Define the "molding" and "unfolding" approaches to child development by relating them to the gardener and the potter analogies.

3. What roles do the molding and unfolding approaches play in current theories of developmental psychology?

4. What does the term *maturation* mean? What role does it play in the molding or unfolding approach?

5. What are developmental norms? What restriction should be placed on our use of them?

6. Define the term *learning* as it is used in the text. What role does it play in the molding or unfolding approach?

7. Compare and contrast the longitudinal and cross-sectional methods of studying developmental changes in behavior.

8. Place Arnold Gesell, Myrtle McGraw, Wayne Dennis, and John B. Watson on the molding/unfolding continuum.

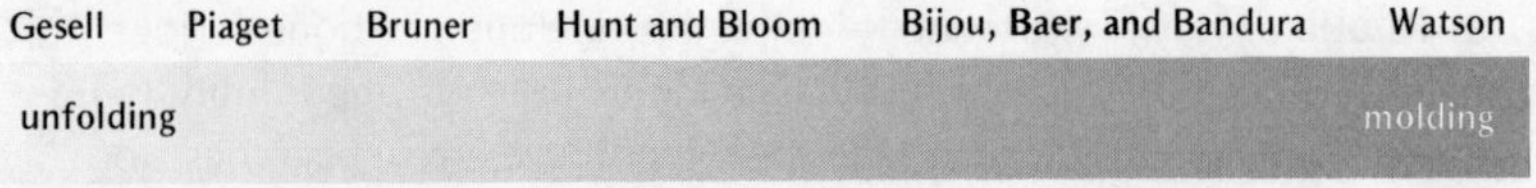

Gesell	Piaget	Bruner	Hunt and Bloom	Bijou, Baer, and Bandura	Watson
unfolding					molding

Figure 2–2. *The unfolding/molding continuum.*

CURRENT THEORIES OF DEVELOPMENT

Although the extreme positions of Gesell and Watson serve a useful purpose by anchoring the ends of our unfolding/molding continuum, they are primarily of historical interest. Recent theorists have moved away from these extremes and have emphasized the *interaction* between the child's biological makeup and his or her environmental experiences. Still, current theories do not all fall at the midpoint of the continuum. Some are clearly more unfolding in nature, emphasizing that development occurs in stages and that successful completion of each stage is dependent on maturational readiness. Others stress the learning experiences that mold the child, resulting in the acquisition of behaviors necessary to master new, more complex behaviors. Thus, we will organize our discussion of current developmental theories by placing the theorists at appropriate points along the unfolding/molding continuum, as shown in Figure 2–2.

There are many more theories of human development than we can possibly discuss in one chapter. In choosing the particular theories covered in this section, we have used three major criteria: (1) The viewpoints expressed represent the range of ideas falling along the complete continuum; (2) considerable scientific support exists for each of the theories; and (3) in explaining development, the theorists chosen make pertinent statements to the classroom teacher. In the discussion that follows, we hope to give you a feel for the importance of theory in educational psychology, as well as the background necessary to translate theoretical considerations into classroom practice.

Jean Piaget: A Stage Theory

Jean Piaget, who was born in Switzerland in 1896, began his career as a zoologist, rather than as a psychologist. From an early interest in biology and in the classification of animal species, Piaget turned next to epistemology, the branch of philosophy concerned with the nature and the origin of knowledge. Combining his interests in biology and in philosophy with his fascination with the development of his own children, Piaget next began a comprehensive analysis of the ways in which children come to think about their world. It is clear that Piaget's work (e.g., Piaget, 1929, 1952) has had a monumental effect on how we think about children.

From the outset, Piaget was convinced that the thought processes of children differ from the thought processes of adults in two major ways. First, children's thought is *quantitatively* different—children have fewer facts and less knowledge to work with. Second, children's thought is *qualitatively* different—the ways in which children acquire and use knowledge differ from adults. It is this latter aspect of the child's thinking that captivated Piaget and to which he devoted over fifty years of study.

Piaget's theory of cognitive development is first and foremost a stage theory, in that he believes children go through a series of sequential stages in the development of their thinking abilities. The characteristics of children's thought—the ways they think, the kinds of things they think about, and the kinds of errors they make in solving problems—change as they pass from stage to stage.

Moreover, Piaget believes that all children, regardless of culture or learning experiences, go through these stages in the same sequence and that a child cannot achieve a higher stage of thinking without having first gone through the lower stages. Piaget assigns ages to each stage, implying maturational unfolding of the child's thinking abilities. Let us now examine Piaget's four stages and some of the concepts he uses to characterize thought at each stage.

Sensorimotor stage (birth–2 years). Piaget names this stage after his belief that infants are primarily occupied with processing sensory input and with coordinating motor behavior in response to sensory stimuli. Newborn infants have no language; they are unaware of their relationship to their environment. What they do have is a set of reflexes—behaviors like sucking, crying, and kicking—which occur automatically in response to specific internal or external stimulation. For example, if you place your finger in the palm of a newborn baby's hand, she will grasp tightly in response to that specific stimulation. She will not, however, intentionally reach out and grasp a rattle laying in her crib. Intentional behaviors come later in this stage, as infants begin to explore their environment and receive feedback that they can have an effect on objects and people around them.

The one-year-old, for example, may delight in repeatedly banging a toy against his playpen in order to hear the sound. He is beginning to make sense of his environment. His knowledge of the environment, however, is based on his motor behavior, his physical contact with it. His crawling, his reaching, and his manipulation of objects is the way he knows his world. It is only toward the end of the sensorimotor period, when the child makes rapid strides in the use of language, that the beginnings of **internalized thought** appear. As evidence of this internalization, Piaget cites the two-year-old child's mastery of the concept of **object permanence:** She can think about and systematically search for objects that are out of her sight. She also displays what Piaget calls **deferred imitation,** observing, for example, how her father drives a car and repeating these behaviors in sequence later in her play.

Preoperational stage (2–7 years).   During the second stage of cognitive development we find an elaboration of the basic thinking abilities formed in infancy—the child's language becomes functional. At first the child's language and thought is **egocentric,** having idiosyncratic labels for objects and events and seeing things from his own point of view only. Early in this stage the child often errs in his understanding of cause and effect. He may, for example, think that spiders make the basement warm. Indeed, there *are* spiders in the basement and the basement *is* warm. Here the child reasons that one event causes a second event, when the two are not related. Piaget calls this type of thought **transductive reasoning.**

The tendency of the preschool child to treat two objects as the same, even though they are alike in only one respect, is another case of transductive reasoning. For example, many young children who initially call all four-footed animals "dogs" are using **pre-concepts** in their reasoning. They have yet to reach the level of cognitive development necessary to understand the general category of "animals" and to differentiate among the concepts of dog, cow, cat, and so on.

Experiment designed to test child's understanding of conservation: *Does the tall glass contain more water than the short glass?*

During the last half of the preoperational stage, children begin to grasp logical concepts. They become less egocentric in their thinking, make fewer errors in the attribution of cause and effect, and are able to grasp simple concepts such as size, shape, color, and number. Nevertheless, their conceptual thinking is still unsophisticated. In particular, they have difficulty manipulating more than one concept at a time. For example, if given a bag of marbles of different sizes and colors, they could probably pick out all of the blue marbles or all of the big marbles. But if asked to pick out all of the big, blue marbles, they might have trouble. In addition, there are difficult concepts, such as time and space, that preoperational children have yet to master.

Concrete operational stage (7–11 years). About the time children enter elementary school, critical changes take place in their thought processes. The most important change is their newly acquired ability to use mental operations in making sense of their environment. Piaget uses the term **operation** to refer to the ability to manipulate concepts internally in complex ways. Children at this stage now understand that concepts can be arranged hierarchically. For example, they understand that the category food can be broken down into subcategories, like fruits, vegetables, and so on. Moreover, fruits can be classified further into apples, peaches, grapes, and the like. They know that an object can belong to more than one class at a time; a marble can be big, blue, round, and hard. They are able to perform the logical operations necessary for solving math problems. For example, they can combine concepts $(7 + 2 = 9)$ and once having done that, can reverse the operation $(9 - 2 = 7)$. They can order objects according to some physical dimension such as weight, a process called **seriation.** And, they have mastered the concept of **conservation:** They can see that an object maintains its essential identity, even when its appearance is changed in some way. One task often used to illustrate conservation involves presenting the child with a short, wide container filled with water. The water is then poured into a tall, narrow container. A child who is able to conserve will recognize that even though the water level is higher in the tall, narrow container, it still contains the same amount of water as the short, wide container. According to Piaget, conserving children are able to focus on more than one aspect of the situation at a time, as their thought is **decentered.** They can consider both the height and width of the containers and reason that the increased width of one container makes up for the increased height of the other, leaving an equal amount of water. A preoperational child, on the other hand, might focus or center on only one dimension and decide, for example, that the second container has more water "because it's taller." Being able to see that things can be different and yet the same through conservation is essential to understanding upper and lower case letters, addition, and many other school concepts.

In summary, the thought processes of the concrete operational child are becoming more logical and flexible. Nevertheless, the child's thinking is still very closely tied to objects and events that are present or that he or she has previously experienced in a direct manner.

Formal operational stage (11–15 years).   As children approach adolescence, their thought takes on an abstract quality absent in previous stages. Adolescents are able to consider objects and events they have never experienced directly. For example, they can— and often do—speculate about philosophical, social, and political issues. In solving problems, they can formulate hypotheses and set out to test them in a systematic manner. They can also understand abstract scientific principles and can apply these principles in novel ways. As children pass through adolescence their thought processes come to resemble those of adults.

The role of learning in Piaget's theory.   We have oversimplified Piaget's theory in suggesting that all children pass through the stages of development at the same speed. Some children develop much faster than others, and some very slow children may not ever pass through all of the stages. For this reason, the ages assigned to each stage should only be considered as the average and not the specific ages at which all children reach each stage.

We have also oversimplified Piaget's theory by making it appear that the change from one stage to another is more sudden than it actually is. Children usually do not acquire all the characteristics of a new stage at once; rather, they acquire them one by one over a period of time. For example, the child who is passing into the concrete operational stage may be able to seriate objects a year before understanding conservation. Moreover, a child may be able to conserve volume (understand that a given amount of substance has the same volume regardless of its shape), well before the ability to conserve number (understand that the number of objects remains the same regardless of how they are arranged) and vice versa.

Piaget attributes this variability in development partly to variations in biological maturation and partly to variations in learning. For all of his emphasis on the biological determination of development, Piaget does see a role for learning. He has, in fact, developed a two-part theory of learning; but it is a theory that suggests there is a close relationship between learning and development (Piaget, 1952, 1970). Piaget's views on learning are as follows.

When children learn new information, they learn it in ways that are consistent with their existing level of intellectual development. For example, the young child may incorporate bluejays, finches, butterflies, and bats into his or her concept of birds, without noticing their distinctive characteristics. Piaget calls this changing of new information to fit the existing intellectual structure **assimilation.** At a later point, however, the child may have experiences that will lead him or her to alter the concept of birds so that birds and flying insects become different categories (he or she may be stung by a bee and see a bird eat a moth). He terms the changing of existing intellectual structure by new information **accommodation.**

Piaget sees these two aspects of learning as playing an important role in development, but he never strays far from the concept of maturation. It is important to note that Piaget believes that children cannot accommodate new learning experiences until they have reached the appropriate maturational stage. This assumption places learning under the control of development, rather than vice versa.

Evaluation of Piaget's Theory

We have placed Piaget to the right of Gesell near the unfolding end of our continuum for several reasons. First, Piaget clearly emphasizes that genetically determined changes in the maturity of the child's nervous system provide the main impetus for cognitive growth. Children will not move from one stage of development into the next until they are biologically capable of doing so. Thus, Piaget's conception of development is similar to Gesell's.

On the other hand, Piaget places slightly more emphasis on learning, recognizing that biological readiness by itself does not guarantee that a child will begin to acquire more sophisticated ways of thinking. Crucial to Piaget's theory is the idea that cognitive growth is an active process, with the child acting upon and adapting to the environment. If the opportunities for learning are severely restricted, if there are few opportunities for the child to interact with objects or with other people, the child's cognitive abilities will not develop normally.

MATCHING LEARNING AND DEVELOPMENTAL LEVEL

The majority of contemporary psychologists fall between the "molding" and "unfolding" ends of the continuum and believe that both learning and the process of development play important roles in intellectual growth. Harvard Psychologist Jean Carew and her associates (Carew, Chan, & Halfar, 1976) have published observations of young children in natural situations that they feel illustrate this interaction of learning and development. The following excerpts describe two parents informally "teaching" their young children. In the first example, the parent seems to successfully match his child's "developmental level," but the information given by the second parent seems unusable to the young child.

EXCERPT 1: Good Match with Developmental Level

"Father is reading to John, age thirty-three months, Ezra Keats' story 'Goggles.' They turn to a picture showing the dog Willy running away with the goggles through a hole in a fence. In the picture the dog's face is half hidden behind the fence. John looks and tells Father: 'Doggie face broken.' Father explains, 'No, it's not broken. It's hiding behind the fence.' John looks puzzled. He asks, 'Hiding?' Father demonstrates. 'See my hand. Now, see it hide when I move it behind the book?' John watches intently. Father continues, 'Now, see it come out again. It's not broken. It was hiding.' John imitates Father's action several times, passing his hand behind the book and watching it reappear." (pp. 59–60)

EXCERPT 2: Poor Match with Developmental Level

"Amy and her mother are putting together a puzzle. (On the cover of the box is a picture of the completed puzzle: Raggedy Ann, Teddy Bear, and Doggie having a tea party.) Amy tries to fit one of the pieces but is having no success. The piece she holds is a picture of a cookie. Mother tells her, 'See, the cookie is going into Teddy's mouth, not his foot. Look at the picture. That piece doesn't go there.' Mother points to the detail in the picture on the box. Amy looks briefly but immediately resumes her attempt to place the piece incorrectly. Amy announces, 'It doesn't fit. It's too fat.' She takes another piece and tries to place it in the puzzle without referring to the picture, apparently relying on shape correspondence and memory. Mother asks her, 'You don't think the picture helps?' Amy replies, 'No, it's the way it comes out after.' " (p. 61)

Although Piaget acknowledges the harmful effect of a restricted environment, it does not necessarily follow from his theory that providing children with very stimulating learning experiences will speed up their cognitive growth. In fact, Piaget has expressed considerable disdain for the issue of accelerating cognitive development in children (Piaget, 1970), calling it the "peculiarly American" interest in making children learn more quickly. He points to the biological factors that place limits on what a child is capable of understanding at a given age. This implies that while it may be possible to teach children certain concepts or mental operations before they are maturationally ready, any gains exhibited by these children will be only superficial; they will be unable to use these concepts or operations meaningfully in a variety of situations. True understanding will come only when children are ready and will be maximized by providing children with a reasonably stimulating environment and by allowing them considerable freedom in exploring that environment on their own.

Whether or not cognitive development can—or should—be accelerated is a controversial issue. In Chapter 3 we will discuss some of the research on acceleration and look more closely at what Piaget's theory has to say about classroom instruction. For the time being, it should be sufficient to note that even those who strongly disagree with Piaget on the importance of learning in development or his stance on acceleration have considerable appreciation for his many insights into the thought processes of children.

MARIA MONTESSORI AND THE MONTESSORI SCHOOLS

The name of Maria Montessori is a familiar one to Americans who are interested in children and education. Her name and her approach to early childhood education can be found in nearly every city in the U.S.

Maria Montessori was born in rural Italy in 1870. She was the first woman ever to be awarded a Medical Doctor's degree in Italy, later specializing in child psychiatry. Throughout her career, her major interest was in the education of young children. During the early 1900s, she wrote a guide to her approach, published in English as *The Montessori Method*. It outlined a philosophy of education that was very similar to that of Jean Piaget. Although they were writing on the same topic in adjacent countries (Piaget was in Switzerland), they never directly collaborated. Still, they arrived at remarkably similar points of view.

Both saw children as natural learners whose curiosity would lead them to learn on their own, but only if adults did not stifle it through rigid discipline and drill. It was the teacher's responsibility to provide materials and other opportunities for learning, but not to directly teach new concepts and facts to their children. The Montessori curriculum, therefore, consists of a variety of learning materials for children to explore, with strict instructions to teachers to let their pupils learn at their own pace. Teachers are a resource that children can call on, but only when they want to seek information from the teacher. The Montessori approach was briefly popular in the United States in the 1920s, but fell out of popularity until the 1950s when a major resurgence of interest occurred that has lasted until today.

Jerome Bruner

Jerome Bruner is an American psychologist who took an early interest in the work of Piaget and his colleagues in Switzerland. But, although Bruner formulated a stage theory of cognitive development that closely parallels Piaget's, enough differences exist between the two theories to warrant a separate discussion of each. It may be helpful to keep in mind that Piaget and Bruner approached the topic from somewhat different perspectives. You may recall that Piaget began his studies as a biologist and philosopher interested in classifying thought processes, primarily for theoretical purposes. Although Piaget's theory has many practical implications, these have been pointed out primarily by American followers of Piaget. They have not, for the most part, been suggested by Piaget. In contrast, Bruner was motivated by a strong commitment, not only to the discovery of how children acquire and use information, but also to the application of this knowledge so as to improve education. This commitment can be seen in his books dealing with educational reform (Bruner, 1960, 1971).

Bruner's view of development. Bruner's theory received considerable attention after he published an article proposing that the key to understanding how children think can be found in a process called **representation** (Bruner, 1964). Representation refers to the cognitive behaviors that occur when people process and remember information, that is, when they take in information from their environment and code and store it in such a way that they can retrieve it for use at some future time. Representation, then, is a process we use to make sense of our environ-

ment. Without the ability to code, store, and retrieve past experience, the complexity of events in our lives would overwhelm us.

According to Bruner, children at different stages use different techniques to represent their environment. Like Piaget, he sees children as passing through stages that are more or less related to age. In infancy and in very early childhood, **enactive representation** predominates. In enactive representation children represent past experience through their motor acts; they "know" a stimulus in their environment only by the actions associated with that stimulus. We can observe the behavior of a two-year-old as she pedals her tricycle and infer that she has learned something from past experience about tricycles. She cannot, however, describe to us how tricycles operate; nor can she tell us how tricycles differ from bicycles. Indeed, if she sees a tricycle next door she might tell us the meaning of the tricycle by going through the motions of riding one. The actions stand for or "represent" the object.

During the preschool and early elementary school years, perceptual images begin to play a more important role in the child's thought. At this stage of development, children use **iconic representation.** They are able to form visual images of stimuli encountered in their environment, to retain these images, and to recall them in the absence of the real object or event. There is a certain autonomy in their thinking—objects exist independent of their actions toward them. The perceptual images formed by preschoolers, however, are based primarily on physical appearance and are inflexible. A picture of a tricycle in school stands for the tricycle at home because they look alike. If the physical appearance of the picture is altered (e.g., if it is cut up into several pieces and presented as a jigsaw puzzle), the correspondence may be missed. The difficulties preschoolers have in completing puzzles, in finishing incomplete drawings, and in recognizing partially hidden or "embedded" figures suggest the dominance of iconic representation at this stage.

During the later elementary school years, children begin to use **symbolic representation.** Their thought becomes more flexible and abstract and is not tied strictly to concrete images. Bruner attributes this flexibility to the child's increasingly complex use of language. Words, as symbols, may stand for real objects and events, but a word does not in any way resemble the real object in the sense that a picture does. Further, words may represent ideas and relationships for which there are no concrete referents. Thus language has characteristics of remoteness and arbitrariness which allow the child to go beyond immediate experience and to translate experience in novel ways.

Reference to two experiments by Bruner and his colleagues will help illustrate the differences among the different types of representation. In one experiment, sixty children, ages six to nineteen, described likenesses and differences among various items (Olver & Hornsby, 1966). For example, they were asked "How are a banana and a peach alike?" After a third item such as a potato was added, the children were asked to tell how all three were alike and how the potato differed from the first two. Additional items were added until the children were comparing and contrasting nine items. The most important finding for our purposes was that the younger children relied on physical appearance for grouping the items (e.g., "A

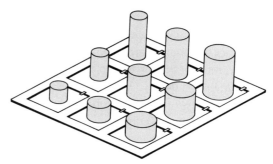

Figure 2-3. *Bruner and Kenney's (1966) glass matrix.*

radio and telephone are both sort of square on the bottom"). These children displayed iconic representation. In contrast, the older children used symbolic representation. They went beyond the immediate visual dimension of the objects and grouped them instead according to the more abstract dimension of utility (e.g., "They're all food" or "You use them to communicate").

In a second study (Bruner & Kenney, 1966), fifty children, ages three through seven, were presented with a three-by-three matrix of glasses, similar to the one shown in Figure 2-3. The glasses differed in height and diameter and were arranged according to these dimensions. At first the children were asked how the glasses were alike and different. One, two, and then three glasses at a time were removed from the matrix, and the children were then asked to replace them in the correct position. Then the actual experiment began.

All the glasses were removed and scrambled, and each child was instructed to reconstruct the original arrangement. Significantly, most of the three- and four-year-olds were unable to do so. They were still at the level of enactive representation and seemed unable to retain and copy a visual image of the glasses, preferring instead to manipulate the glasses randomly. The five-, six-, and seven-year-olds, however, had little difficulty with reconstructing the arrangement.

To further differentiate among these older children, another, more difficult task was presented. This time the glasses were removed, and the glass that was formerly in the lower *left* corner of the matrix was placed in the lower *right* corner. The children were then asked to make a similar arrangement of glasses, leaving the one glass in the new position. This task required them to use some underlying rule in **transposing** the matrix. The children could not rely solely on a visual image, since they had not seen the correct transposed arrangement. Bruner found that all of the five-year-olds failed on the transposition task, while 80 percent of the seven-year-olds succeeded. He interpreted these results to mean that the five-year-olds could not free themselves from their perception of the original matrix (iconic representation). In contrast, the seven-year-olds translated the visual image into a verbal rule that allowed them to make the transposition (involving symbolic representation); for example, "They get wider in one direction and taller in the other."

Evaluation of Bruner's theory.   There are important similarities between Bruner's three types of representation and Piaget's stages of cognitive development. But, there are some noteworthy differences between the two theorists as well. First, on a theoretical level, Bruner places greater emphasis on the role of language in cognitive growth. For Piaget, language is a distinct system, separate from logical thought, although language and thought develop hand in hand. For Bruner, thought is nothing more than internalized language. It is the child's increasing facility with language that allows him to solve complex problems like the conservation and the transposition tasks.

In addition, while Bruner proposes that the three levels of representation typically appear in children's thinking in a fixed order (the order being at least partially due to maturation), he also stresses that even young children may have all three modes available to them. It is more a matter of one mode predominating over the others. For example, as symbolic representation strengthens during the elementary school years, the enactive and iconic modes do not drop out of the child's repertoire, but remain (even in adulthood) and interact with the symbolic mode.

The primary rationale for placing Bruner more toward the middle of our unfolding/molding continuum has to do with his opinions on maturation and readiness. Although Bruner agrees that biological maturation is an important variable in the development of thought, he emphasizes the need for encouraging maturity by providing appropriate learning experiences; readiness is not something to wait for, but something to teach, or at least to nurture. At one point, Bruner (1960) made an even more controversial statement: "Any subject can be taught effectively in some intellectually honest form to any child at any stage of development" (1960, p. 33). He seemed to say that any child, regardless of age, is always ready to learn an aspect of a particular skill or subject matter. If we have tried to teach a child and have failed, it is not because of a lack of readiness, *but because of our own ineptness in matching the curriculum and the teaching strategies appropriate for the child's level of development.*

Based on his developmental work, Bruner made some specific suggestions for curriculum design and classroom instruction. Because his theory is both a developmental theory and an instructional theory, Bruner has done much to bridge the gap that sometimes seems to exist between psychology and education.

Hunt and Bloom

Like Piaget and Bruner, J. McVickers Hunt and Benjamin Bloom have each proposed theories that are having a great impact on education. However, Hunt and Bloom are not stage theorists to the extent of Piaget and Bruner. Rather than tracing the development of thought throughout childhood, they have focused on the significant period of early childhood. In addition, although they draw from the unfolding viewpoint by emphasizing neural development, Hunt and Bloom clearly tie neurological development to the nature of the child's preschool experiences. Thus, they fall slightly toward the molding end of our continuum.

The theories of Hunt and Bloom are variations of the "critical period theory" of development. The notion of **critical periods** grew out of animal research conducted by ethologists, such as Konrad Lorenz. In 1937 Lorenz described the process of "imprinting" in birds. He showed, for example, that there is a limited period of time shortly after birth during which the newly hatched gosling will attach itself to the first moving object it meets in its environment. Under natural conditions the young bird imprints an attachment to its mother, an event that has considerable survival value. But if another moving object, such as a human, is substituted for the mother, faulty imprinting will occur and the bird will adopt the substitute object as its mother. The significant aspect of imprinting for our purposes is that it is a type of learning that occurs during a very limited period of time in the early life of the animal. Furthermore, if the environment inhibits or prevents appropriate learning during the critical period, then the resulting faulty learning will be permanent or at least difficult to change.

HOW DO UNFAVORABLE EXPERIENCES AFFECT DEVELOPMENT?

Psychologist William Goldfarb has conducted a significant series of studies (1945, 1947) that highlight the effects of favorable or unfavorable experiences on child development. He compared the intelligence and behavior of children ten to fourteen years of age who had been adopted as young children. One group of subjects had lived in an orphanage until age three before they were adopted, while the other group was adopted at age one. The orphanage was clean and had adequate physical facilities, but could not provide the children extensive or prolonged contact with adults.

This lack of early stimulation apparently took its toll. The children who had spent the greatest amount of time in the institution (the children adopted at age three) were less intelligent than the one-year group and were described as being aggressive, unable to form meaningful social relationships, poor students who were restless and inattentive, and chronic troublemakers in comparison to the children who were adopted at age one.

This type of evidence is often cited in support of theories at the "molding" end of the theoretical continuum, since it suggests that experience plays a major role in shaping development. It is particularly important evidence to theorists such as Bloom and Hunt, as it emphasizes the importance of early experience on later behavior.

Many researchers have attempted to discover if there are such critical periods in the development of certain human abilities and traits. Bloom (1964), for example, analyzed many longitudinal studies in which data such as IQ scores and personality measures were taken on the same individuals at different times in their lives. A review of these studies led Bloom to conclude that for each intellectual or personality characteristic studied there was a period of relatively rapid growth, as well as periods in which little development occurred. He postulated that the environment would have its largest effect on the development of a characteristic during its period of most rapid growth.

In regard to intelligence, Bloom proposed that the period of most rapid growth is during the preschool years, with 50 percent of one's adult intelligence achieved by the age of four. Between the ages of four and eight another 30 percent of development takes place, with the remaining 20 percent occurring between the ages of eight and seventeen. If during the critical ages from birth to four years the child lives in an extreme environment, either deprived or enriched, it may affect development by about 2.5 IQ points per year. Moreover, losses in intellectual development suffered by a deprived preschool child are quite permanent and are difficult to recover, even if the child is placed in an enriched environment after age four. Likewise, the child who spends her early childhood years in an enriched environment is not likely to lose her intellectual advantage, even if exposed to less stimulating environments between the ages of four and seventeen.

Hunt (1961), in a similar version of the critical period hypothesis, attempted to integrate what is known about the functioning of the central nervous system with what is known about the development of intellectual skills. In his theory, Hunt relies heavily on the work of D. O. Hebb and other physiological psychologists who studied both the functioning of the brain in lower animals and the effects of early sensorimotor deprivation or enrichment on "intelligent" behavior in these animals. Hunt points to a large body of research indicating that laboratory animals deprived of normal sensorimotor experiences early in life show later deficits on various perceptual and problem-solving tasks.

Hunt argues that early experience affects neurological development. If the individual is deprived of important stimulation during early childhood, the central processes within the brain that mediate intelligent behavior will not become firmly established. Conversely, he argues (like Bloom) that providing the child with appropriate intellectual experiences during the critical preschool years might enhance intellectual development:

In the light of evidence now available, it is not unreasonable to entertain the hypothesis that with a sound scientific educational psychology of early experience, it might become feasible to raise the average level of intelligence as now measured by a substantial degree. In order to be explicit, it is conceivable that this "substantial degree" might be of the order of 30 points of IQ. (1961, p.267)

Hunt also extensively analyzes Piaget's theory and proposes that in order to maximize the neurological development of young children we need to match the learning experiences provided to the child with the child's own level of development, using Piaget's concepts to determine what that level is.

Bijou, Baer, and Bandura

Hunt and Bloom have done much to further the idea that the environment has a large impact on the development of children's skills and characteristics. Their research has been largely responsible for the push toward infant day care and preschool enrichment programs, such as Head Start, witnessed in the last decade. We will turn now to a group of theorists who take up the task of identifying in more precise ways the specific mechanisms through which the environment affects behavior. We refer here to **behaviorists** — learning theorists whose work is based on the early research of psychologists like Watson, Pavlov, Thorndike, and Skinner. Moreover, we are particularly concerned with one subgroup of behaviorists, those who follow the **applied behavior analysis** approach to understanding behavior. Applied behavior analysis is concerned with the application of principles of learning discovered in controlled settings, such as laboratories, to socially significant human problems found in classrooms, mental hospitals, prisons, and so on. The goal of applied behavior analysis is to develop a comprehensive set of principles based on rigorous research that will not only explain why we behave the way we do, but that will also yield practical and effective techniques for modifying the environment to maximize human development.

Since the early 1960s, many psychologists and educators have contributed to the growing field of applied behavior analysis. We have chosen to focus on Sidney Bijou, Donald Baer, and Albert Bandura as representatives of this position because they have provided the most comprehensive treatments of the principles of learning applied specifically to child development (Baer, 1973; Baer & Wright, 1974; Bandura, 1977; Bijou, 1968, 1976; Bijou & Baer, 1961, 1965).

In introducing behavioral theory, it is important to take note of how these theorists view the concept of "development." The majority of developmental theorists use a conceptual model of development that states behavior is directly related to age. In contrast, behaviorists use a conceptual model that states behavior is a function of experience. Children interact constantly with their environment. The sequence of interactions with the environment over periods of time causes developmental changes in behavior, not just the passage of time as reflected in age.

Let us look at an example that illustrates the differences between these two ways of looking at development. Suppose we visit a nursery school and observe that a little boy named Jimmy is particularly "selfish." He grabs toys away from the other children; he will not offer his toys to children who have none; and he throws a temper tantrum whenever the teacher asks him to share.

Now suppose that we visit the nursery school six months later and, to our surprise, we observe Jimmy playing cooperatively with the other children, even standing up for a child who has less than the others and admonishing the group to "let Billy have a turn now." What could have caused this dramatic change in Jimmy's behavior? Gesell and other psychologists at the unfolding end of the continuum might attribute the new behavior to a change in age or stage (for example, they might say that the child has passed from the "terrible twos" to the "trusting threes"). In contrast, Bijou, Baer, and Bandura would look more closely at the events in the environment that might have caused the child to *learn* cooperative behavior.

Let us examine now what some of those events might have been. Perhaps the teacher during those intervening months turned playtime into a structured learning experience for Jimmy. At first she may have prompted Jimmy to share by occasionally asking him to give his favorite toy to Billy; but in such a case guidance alone might have been insufficient to modify Jimmy's behavior. So the teacher may have needed to arrange some encouragement for sharing.

During the next playtime the teacher again may have asked Jimmy to share and then immediately rewarded him for extending the toy toward Billy by giving him an equally attractive toy in place of the original. At the same time, she could have hugged and praised him, indicating her approval of children who share, which eventually led to an increase in Jimmy's sharing.

This example is only one of the kinds of events that may influence behavior and the ways in which they may be arranged to promote learning. Because the principles of learning to be discussed in detail in Chapter 5 come directly from, or are at least consistent with, the theory of Bijou, Baer, and Bandura, we will not delve further into the specifics of the theory now. Suffice it to say that they would attribute the change in Jimmy's behavior to the complex sequence of interactions that took place between Jimmy's behavior and his environment during the intervening months.

We have placed Bijou, Baer, and Bandura on the molding end of our continuum, but to the left of Watson, because they do not deny the influence of genetic and biological factors or age on child development as Watson seemed to do. Their willingness to accept these factors is illustrated in the following quote from Bijou and Baer (1961):

The number and kinds of responses a child is capable of displaying at any point in his life are determined by his status in the animal kingdom (species characteristics), his biological maturational stage, and his history of interaction with his particular environment from fertilization on. (p. 15)

HOW EARLY IS THE DIE CAST?

A teacher soon forms impressions as to which students in his or her class are "good" pupils and which are not; even kindergarten teachers form such opinions before much academic instruction has taken place. Harold Stevenson's research group at the University of Michigan's Center for Human Growth and Development (Stevenson, Parker, Wilkinson, Hegion, & Fish, 1976) has conducted a study to see how accurate these early impressions are. The teacher ratings of 217 kindergarten children were confidentially kept on file and later compared with academic achievement test scores of the same children at the end of second and third grade. The kindergarten teachers were found to predict later achievement better than chance or random predictions, but were only moderately accurate overall; many of the early impressions formed of individual children proved to be inaccurate. Interestingly, teacher ratings turned out to be more accurate than the ratings of parents, and previous research suggests that the ratings of kindergarten teachers are generally more accurate than batteries of readiness tests, especially in choosing those students who are most in need of special academic instruction (Ferinden, Jacobson, & Linden, 1970). Still, early teacher ratings are only moderately accurate; children can change rapidly during the elementary school years. This suggests that you should discount rumors about children until you see how they are going to behave and learn in your unique classroom.

However, the major contribution of behaviorists has been *not* in describing how biological maturation and learning interact, but rather in identifying the ways the children learn to shape their behavior. Behaviorists, then, are placed toward the molding end of the continuum. More than any other theorists previously cited, they emphasize the need to directly encourage development by shaping the child's behavior, by setting up a sequence of behavioral objectives, and by gradually rewarding closer and closer approximations to the final desired behavior.

Behaviorists have criticized traditional developmental psychology, as exemplified by the unfolding theories of Gesell, Piaget, and Bruner (Baer, 1973; Bijou, 1968). They reject the use of age in combination with constructs such as "internalized thought" and "egocentrism" as explanations for changes in behavior. Furthermore, they attribute developmental changes during childhood to "the same environmental mechanisms that can and do produce behavior change in the adult organism" (Baer & Wright, 1974, p.1). The developmental processes that Piaget postulates as being unique to childhood and qualitatively different from the processes of adulthood are rejected by behaviorists in favor of the principles of learning, which much experimental research suggests govern the development of many behaviors at all age levels.

A Final Comment: The Authors' Place on the Continuum

No single theory discussed in this chapter comprehensively explains all aspects of human development; nor does any theory adequately pinpoint the complex interplay that takes place between a child's biological makeup and his or her experiences. This is to be expected because psychology is a young science and because human behavior is complex. Yet each theory has, we believe, something important to say about children and how they change over time.

If we were to place ourselves on the unfolding/molding continuum which we used in organizing these theories, we would probably fall to the left of Bijou, Baer, and Bandura. We find the applied behavior analysis approach to be the most productive for generating specific suggestions for modifying the classroom environment to promote optimal development in all children. On the other hand, we see considerable value in the theories of Piaget, Bruner, Hunt, and Bloom and believe that the teacher's attempts to promote learning by structuring the classroom environment must be tempered by a sound knowledge of the course of normal development in children. We believe that teachers can avoid considerable frustration, both for themselves and their students, by matching curriculum objectives and materials to the developmental status of the children they teach, on the one hand, and by knowing how to stimulate and guide development when necessary, on the other.

REVIEW 2-2

1. What does Piaget mean by the term *stage of development?*
2. What is Piaget's view of the role of maturation and learning in development?
3. List and briefly describe Piaget's four stages of development.
4. Describe the three kinds of representation distinguished by Bruner.
5. What is the meaning of Hunt's and Bloom's concept of critical period and its implication for education?
6. What is the view of Bijou, Baer, and Bandura on the role of maturation and learning in development?

SUMMARY

The behavior of children is different at different ages. These developmental changes are not fully understood by psychologists, but teachers need a general knowledge of them if they want to succeed in matching instruction to the needs of individual children.

The major theoretical views of development can be placed along a continuum ranging from "unfolding" theories to "molding" theories. At the unfolding end of the continuum, development theorists argue that development is guided by internal biological processes (maturation), with experience having little influence on development. Theorists at the molding end, in contrast, argue that experience is the most important process of development, with maturation playing only a minor role. Gesell, McGraw, and Dennis are examples of historically important unfolding theorists, while Watson was discussed as a prime exponent of the molding point of view.

Most modern developmental psychologists and educators, however, take less extreme points of view. Piaget and Bruner are important modern theorists who can be placed toward the unfolding end of the continuum. Both view maturationally determined developmental stages as the key features of development, but both see experience as playing an important role in development. Bruner sees the kinds of learning experiences created by teachers as more useful than does Piaget, and for this reason we placed him slightly to the right of Piaget.

Hunt and Bloom developed theories in which experience plays an even more important role in development. They see it as the most important factor in development; yet they view the age or developmental period in which learning takes place as being critical to development.

Bandura, Bijou, and Baer are placed the farthest to the right of any modern theorists. They regard experience as the key determinant of development. But, because they see maturation playing a role in development, we placed them to the left of Watson.

The authors have placed themselves between Bandura, Bijou, and Baer, on the one hand, and Hunt and Bloom, on the other. We feel that biologically determined processes of maturation play an important role in development, but that learning is the more important determinant. Moreover, we feel that teachers can play a very important role in guiding development at all age levels.

ANSWERS TO REVIEW QUESTIONS

Review 2–1

1. Developmental psychology is the branch of psychology concerned with the way individuals change as a function of age.

2. At the "unfolding" end of the continuum, theorists see an internal, predetermined process of maturation guiding development. According to this view, the teacher plays the role of a gardener who tends to developing plants, but who can do little to determine the direction of their development. Theorists at the "molding" end of the continuum, in contrast, see experience as determining the rate and course of development. The teacher plays the role of a potter in this view, helping to actively shape the development of the child.

3. Few current psychologists and educators adhere to a view of development at either extreme of the molding/unfolding continuum. Current theorists generally see both maturation and experience playing some role in development.

4. The term *maturation* refers to the processes of growth that are genetically determined, occurring independent of exercise and training. It is the most important principle of the molding point of view.

5. Developmental norms describe the average or "normal" age at which changes in behavior occur. They are important in the evaluation of development, but should not be taken too seriously

since variation in development is the rule and not the exception.

6. Learning is any relatively permanent change in behavior that is due to experience. It is the most important concept in the molding approach.

7. The longitudinal and cross-sectional methods are both ways of studying developmental changes in behavior. The longitudinal method does this by making multiple observations of the same individuals over long periods of time. In the cross-sectional method, different individuals who are different ages are observed once.

8. Arnold Gesell, Myrtle McGraw, and Wayne Dennis fall toward the unfolding end of the continuum; John B. Watson falls at the molding end.

Review 2–2
1. According to Piaget, a developmental stage is an age period in which behavior is qualitatively different from other age periods.

2. Piaget sees some role for learning in determining development, but views maturation as the most important process.

3. According to Piaget, children pass through four developmental stages:
   a. *Sensorimotor stage* (birth–2 years). The child has little or no language and cannot think in the normal sense.

b. *Preoperational stage* (2–7 years). Language and thought appear, but thought is immature.
c. *Concrete operational stage* (7–11 years). Thought becomes more mature, but is still concrete.
d. *Formal operational stage* (11–15 years). Thought is fully mature and the child can deal with abstract concepts.

4. Bruner distinguishes between three kinds of representation:
   a. *Enactive stage* (infancy and early childhood). At this stage, the child represents past experiences in motor acts.
   b. *Iconic stage* (preschool and early elementary ages). Images play an important role in knowing and thinking at this stage.
   c. *Symbolic stage* (late elementary school and thereafter). At this stage, symbols are used that do not need to be tied to concrete experience.

5. Hunt and Bloom believe that some periods of life are more important to the development of intelligence than others. Specifically, they see early childhood as most important. Their theories gave a big boost to early childhood education.

6. Bijou, Baer, and Bandura see a role for maturation in development, but see learning as the most important factor by far.

Chapter 3

The Normal Sequence of Development

In Chapter 2 we examined theories that account for change in children as they grow older. In this chapter, we will give you an overview of how children change by examining the characteristics and behaviors considered normal for children in various age groups, from early childhood through adolescence. It would be impossible to comprehensively discuss all the physical, the social-emotional, the moral, and the intellectual changes that occur during childhood. We choose, instead, to focus on the aspects that seem to have the most relevance for the classroom teacher, pointing out practical applications whenever possible. Later in the chapter we will consider the issue of "developmental readiness" and whether it is possible, or desirable, to accelerate the development of behaviors that normally appear at certain ages.

As you read the age-level descriptions that follow, be sure to keep in mind that our expectations of what is normal change with the age of the child. For example, five-year-olds who reverse letters when printing their names will not concern the teacher, since many five-year-olds reverse letters. In contrast, a child of ten who reverses letters will cause considerable concern, since most ten-year-olds do not have this problem. Similarly, first-graders who cry whenever they receive a poor mark do not surprise us, but high-school students who do the same thing might worry us.

What you expect of children at certain ages is important because expectancies, to a large extent, determine what you will teach and how you will teach it. As you walk into your first classroom, you will have a head start toward being an effective and happy teacher if you have some idea of what to expect from the particular age group you are working with. This is not to say that all children of one age *do* behave or *ought to* behave in the same way. Indeed there are wide individual differences among children—differences in what they have learned previously, in what they are ready to learn, in what they are interested in learning, and in how they learn best.

Although we believe that all teachers must respect individual differences, we also believe that a knowledge of the similarities often found among children of the same age can be helpful in formulating realistic teaching objectives and strategies and in establishing a climate in the classroom conducive to learning. In addition, if you know what is normal, you will be better able to identify truly exceptional children—children whose behavior is so different from the norm that special help is required to meet their needs.

THE PRESCHOOL YEARS: AGES TWO TO SIX

Between birth and six years, children grow rapidly, with perhaps the most dramatic changes occurring in their first few years of life. Although we do not mean to underemphasize the importance of the role the first two years of life play in laying the foundations for later development, we will focus on ages two through six. Relatively few infants, even today, are involved in formal educational programs. On the other hand, many children begin their school experiences at ages two, three, or four, and more and more teachers are becoming involved in preschool education, making a knowledge of preschool development important. So let us assume that you are confronted with a group of preschoolers. What characteristics and behaviors can you expect from them, and what kinds of changes can you expect to see before they reach age six and begin the first grade?

Physical Development

Although physical growth is slower and less spectacular during the preschool period than during infancy, many important changes occur. Preschoolers make steady gains in height and in weight, and the muscles, nervous system, and skeleton continue to mature. Paralleling their physical growth, children gain increasing control over the use of their bodies. In the United States many children are toilet trained between ages two and three, and most have learned to completely care for their own toileting needs by age four or five. As motor abilities improve, preschoolers become increasingly proficient in basic self-care skills such as eating, dressing, washing, and brushing their teeth. Because preschoolers enjoy learning "grown-up" behaviors such as these and because they have the necessary motor abilities to do so, it is important to encourage them to care for their own personal needs.

Motor coordination. Motor skills, however, develop unevenly during the preschool period. For example, the three-year-old may be quite proficient at walking, running, kicking, jumping, climbing stairs, and riding a tricycle. These activities require **gross motor coordination,** control over the large muscles of the body. In contrast, **fine motor coordination,** control over the small muscles, may lag behind. Thus it may be difficult for three-year-olds to button their shirts, draw, or string beads.

Both gross and fine motor coordination improve throughout the preschool period. For example, at five many children will be able to skip, balance on one foot, cut a straight line with a scissors, and copy a square—all things they were unable to do at age three. Nevertheless, the relative superiority of gross motor coordination still prevails. Many preschool programs take this into consideration by providing large-size pencils, crayons, scissors, and puzzles and by choosing activities that do not require fine motor coordination for long periods of time.

Preschoolers love to use their bodies and practice their new-found motor skills. Indeed, one of the most obvious characteristics of preschoolers is their seemingly endless supply of energy! Running, climbing, kicking, throwing, digging, and poking are just a few of their favorite activities. Because these activities are both enjoyable and educational, it is important to allow children plenty of physical exercise. But physical activities should be well-supervised and should be followed by rest periods or quiet activities, as young children are often unaware of their own limitations.

Attention span.   Preschoolers are easily distracted and have difficulty focusing their attention on any one activity for a long period of time, whether it is climbing the jungle gym on the playground or listening to a story in the classroom. Fortunately, attention span increases with age, and it is clear that learning plays a large role in its development. The teacher can help prepare the child for the requirements of the first grade by gradually increasing the time the child is expected to focus attention on classroom tasks. Of course the materials and activities must be interesting and appropriate for the child's level of functioning, since most of us have difficulty paying attention when we are bored or overly frustrated.

Social and Emotional Development

At age three, a child's immediate family, particularly the parents, is his or her primary source of social interaction. Three-year-olds are closely attached to their parents and depend on them for affection, approval, and guidance. After age three, however, the child's social world expands considerably. Adults outside the family become sources of satisfying interpersonal relationships—witness the kindergartener's love for his or her teacher! While the preschooler's closest attachments continue to be with adults, the influence of adults gradually diminishes as the child learns to play and work with other children.

Social interaction in play.   In order to better understand the growth of social competence, psychologists for many years have studied the development of social interactions in play situations. Barnes (1971), for example, described the changes in the way children play as they grow older. He found that the amount of time children spent in **solitary play,** playing alone and at a distance from other children, decreased steadily between ages two and five. **Parallel play,** in which children play *beside*, but not *with* other children, also decreased. In contrast, the time they spent in **cooperative play** increased. Formal games, drama, and activities directed toward some goal that involved cooperative play were common among the older children, with a "give and take" spirit similar to adult cooperation prevailing. It should be noted, however, that preschool play groups change quickly. Five-year-olds may cooperate with other children as they play, but many do not develop close and enduring friendships with their peers.

Emotional change and learning.   Occasional temper tantrums and outbursts of anger are characteristic of early childhood. Young children are still unable to control emotional outbursts in the face of frustration, loss of attention, verbal taunts, and physical hurt, all of which occur to some extent in a class of active preschoolers. One developmental trend that can be seen within the preschool period is the shift from generalized rage reactions to more directed aggression. Thus, temper tantrums, which are common in two- and three-year-olds, give way to direct aggressive attacks toward specific persons or objects, which are characteristic of four- and five-year-olds. (Sheppard & Willoughby, 1975)

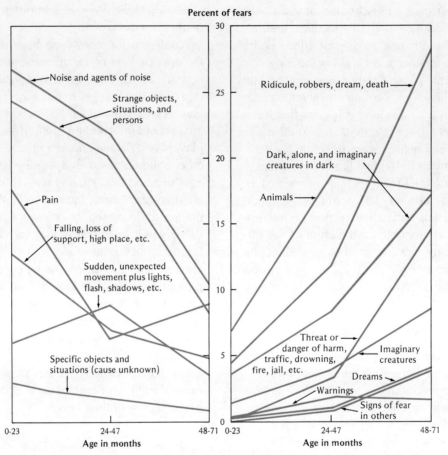

Figure 3–1. *Relative frequency of fears shown by children at different ages. (After Jersild &*
Holmes, 1935)

Fears are another aspect of the preschooler's emotional development that change rapidly at this age. Jersild and Holmes (1935) undertook an extensive study of developmental changes in children's fears from birth to nearly six years of age. (Figure 3-1 shows these changes graphically.) Fears of the "unknown" and of surprises rapidly decline in importance during this period while fears of real and imagined dangers become more prominent. This rapid shift in preschoolers' psychological makeup is repeated in many aspects of their social and emotional development. The vast majority of these changes are without serious consequences, however. If they are understood by the teacher, they cause no problems. They are, in fact, a major part of the joy of preschool teaching. But a key to understanding the emotions of children is to remember that it is normal for children to be "childish." It is usually uncommon for an adult to "behave like a four-year-old," but you can expect four-year-olds to do so.

The fears and emotional outbursts of young children should not lead you to despair. Learning to deal with one's emotions, as learning when aggression is appropriate and when it is not, is a large part of **socialization.** Psychologists define socialization as the process by which we learn the rules, expectations, and values of our culture.

There are at least two courses of action for the teacher to promote the young child's socialization as it pertains to aggression. One is to prevent situations that are likely to give rise to bad feelings from occurring in the first place. Making sure there are enough materials to go around, making your expectations clear, and avoiding frustrating tasks when the children are hungry, tired, or ill are just a few examples. Second, teachers can *teach* appropriate emotional expression to their students. Specific discussion of this topic follows in later chapters.

Sex-typing. In the last decade psychologists have taken an interest in the way children learn sex-appropriate behaviors. **Sex-typing** refers to the way children learn what it means to be a boy or girl in their society. Every society has expectations regarding the attitudes and behaviors that are "appropriate" for each gender.

Psychologists have discovered that children begin to learn at an early age what these expectations are. For example, Gesell (1943) found that by age three most children can apply the correct label "boy" or "girl" to themselves. By four they are not only aware of their own sex and the sex of others, but also show consistent preferences for toys and activities that society deems appropriate for their own sex (Maccoby & Jacklin, 1974).

The early onset of sex-typing has important implications for the preschool teacher, especially in light of many psychologists' opinions that many of our traditional sex-role stereotypes may not be particularly adaptive

and may even be harmful to children growing up today. Psychologists disagree how
sex-typing actually occurs, but most agree
that the models children are exposed to and
the extent to which children are rewarded
for sex-appropriate behavior are influential
factors (Money & Ehrhardt, 1972). Thus, it
seems wise for you to think carefully about
the kinds of sex-typed behaviors you may be
encouraging in young children.

Language and Cognitive Development

During the preschool years, children develop
an amazing ability to communicate. Psychologists label the initial stages of speech in
preschoolers **telegraphic,** because their
speech resembles a sparse telegram message
in which only essential words are included.

Two-year-olds typically have vocabularies of a few hundred words that they use to build telegraphic messages such as "give milk" or "baby go bye-bye." In contrast, the four-year-old uses, or at least understands, several thousand words and combines these words into complex sentences, exhibiting a workable knowledge of the rules of grammar. Four-year-olds understand how to form plurals and past tenses (although they may be unable to verbalize the rules and may make mistakes, like saying "dood" for "did" and "foots" for "feet"). They also use many adjectives, adverbs, pronouns, articles, and auxiliary verbs correctly and understand basic prepositions such as "in," "under," and "beside." This leads many psychologists to conclude that by age four most children have mastered the essential aspects of their language (McNeil, 1970). After age four further development occurs in vocabulary and in the use of more complex parts of speech, but the basics are usually mastered before kindergarten. It is important, then, to expose preschoolers to competent language models and to encourage them to verbalize and to ask questions about objects and events in their environment.

Teachers and parents often show concern about the preschooler's **articulation,** the ability to pronounce the sounds and words of a language correctly so that the child can be understood by others. Because preschoolers are still developing physically and because

they have had little practice in forming the sounds of their language, articulation problems are common. It is common for four-year-olds to substitute, omit, or add sounds in producing words. "Yewo for "yellow," "tree" for "three," and "sumber," for "summer" are just a few examples. Most errors disappear as children approach school age, although errors involving double or triple consonant blends like "str," "nth," and "fl" may persist through the early elementary years (Ainsworth, 1967). Extreme concern regarding articulation errors before age six is probably unjustified and may simply make matters worse. Of course if the child's articulation problems are so severe as to make his or her speech unintelligible, you should seek the help of a speech therapist.

A similar analysis can be made of stuttering in preschoolers. Two-, three-, and four-year-olds do not always speak fluently. They make false starts, pause, and repeat words and sounds, particularly if they are tired or excited. Again, this is probably more a function of the child's relative inexperience in speaking and should not generally be a cause of concern (Ainsworth, 1967).

As in language, rapid changes also take place in intellectual functioning prior to the start of first grade. You may recall that Piaget has provided us with some vivid descriptions of the preschooler's level of cognitive development. Although the preoperational child's thought is "internalized," it is not really logical in an adult sense. Preschoolers have difficulty classifying objects and events into conceptual categories. Their thinking is egocentric, which means that they are unable to see the world from another person's

TABLE 3–1

The Normal Pattern of Physical Development

Preschool 2–6 Years
Steady gains in height, weight, and coordination; very active with short attention span; fine motor coordination less developed than gross motor coordination

Elementary School 6–10 Years
Slower growth in size; improved strength, endurance, and fine motor coordination; activity level still high

Middle School 10–14 Years
Adolescent growth spurt in height and weight; secondary sex characteristics may appear; physical activity less prominent

High School 14–18 Years
Secondary sex characteristics have appeared; growth in size slows; physical maturity reached

point of view. Although four-year-old Susan may maintain that "Betty is *my* sister," she may also argue that "*Betty* doesn't have a sister." Preschoolers may also make mistakes in cause-effect relationships: "If I eat my breakfast, then the mailman will come." And on conservation tasks, preschoolers focus on only one dimension of the situation at a time. Given two rows of five pennies each, they do not realize that you can push the pennies in the second row closer together and still have the same number of pennies as in the first row. They are likely to say that the *longer* row contains more pennies, even though they can count correctly.

It follows directly from Piaget's theory that preschoolers need many opportunities to interact with their environment on a *concrete* level. They need to use their senses to directly experience the physical qualities of objects—the softness of fur, the smoothness of glass. They need to cause events by pushing, pulling, dropping, throwing, and shaking. Most importantly, they need to learn about measurement by actually measuring concrete objects, learn to count by counting concrete objects, and so on.

It is only through direct experience that young children come to realize that things can be classified qualitatively, that objects can be ordered quantitatively, and that events can be predicted. These are the kinds of cognitive abilities that lay the foundation for more complex mental operations which appear later in childhood. Fortunately, there is usually no problem in getting children to have these kinds of experiences. In fact, you may find yourself wishing they pushed, poked, and caused things to happen a little less frequently.

Moral Development

As children grow they begin to make judgments about what is right and wrong, good and bad, fair and unfair. Thus their behavior comes to be guided by standards of moral conduct or a sense of morality. Although moral development is intricately related to the child's social-emotional and intellectual status, it is receiving increasing attention as a topic in its own right.

Several psychologists have provided descriptions of the stages children go through in moral reasoning. In 1932, Piaget expanded his analysis of cognition to include moral reasoning. In *The Moral Judgment of the Child*, he described various experiments designed to elicit childrens' ideas about rules, moral responsibility, justice, and punishment. After interviewing many children of all ages, he came to distinguish between two broad types of morality in childhood. In the first stage of **moral realism,** characteristic of children approximately four through ten years of age, children have some conception of the rules of fair play. (Piaget's second type of morality, "moral relativism," is discussed in "The Middle School Years" section, later in this chapter.) Although children give up some of their earlier egocentric thinking and can follow someone else's rules once they are set down, their conception of these rules is rigid. Everything is "black or white"; there is no gray. Rules are rules and they cannot be broken or changed to fit the situation. Furthermore, during the preschool period in particular, children tend to judge the goodness or badness of an act by the consequences of the act instead of the intentions of the individuals involved. They judge the child who drops three eggs accidentally while trying to help mommy bake a cake "naughtier" than the child who drops one egg while rummaging in the refrigerator where he should not have been in the first place. After all, three broken eggs make a bigger mess.

More recently, Lawrence Kohlberg (1963, 1969) has proposed a three-level theory of moral development, with each major level having two substages. Like Piaget, Kohlberg emphasizes that the young child's moral judgments depend on the immediate consequences of the act, not on abstract principles such as trust, social obligation, or respect for authority. He calls the first level of moral reasoning **preconventional** or "premoral." Preschoolers up to the ages of six to eight may obey rules and conform to the standards set down by parents and teachers, but they do so in order to avoid punishment or to gain rewards. Moreover, when asked to judge whether a behavior is right or wrong, young children will make the decision on the basis of what the immediate consequences are likely to be: "You shouldn't beat up someone 'cause you'll go to jail"; or conversely, "You should love your brother 'cause he'll let you play with his toys."

Piaget's and Kohlberg's observations suggest that children before age four may be too egocentric in their thinking to comprehend the rules that others make at all. They are likely to interpret rules in any way they see fit. After age four, they may obey the rules, but they are unlikely to question them or to comprehend abstract moral concepts involving loyalty, trust, and respect. Still, even a rudimentary awareness that rules do exist and that predictable consequences follow when rules are broken seems to be a prerequisite for the more flexible and abstract moral reasoning that appears in later childhood.

HOW TOYS AFFECT SOCIAL DEVELOPMENT IN CHILDREN

Robert Quilitch and Todd Risley (1973) of the University of Kansas carried out a study that has interesting implications for our understanding of social development. They observed the social play of a group of seven-year-old children in a community recreation center where two different kinds of toys were available. Some toys were games that could only be played by two or more children (such as cards or board games), while others were toys usually played with individually (such as gyroscopes and modeling clay). Significantly, the children were observed to interact socially only 16 percent of the time when only individual toys were available, but interacted 78 percent of the time when only group toys were available. Our interpretation of norms of social development in children, then, must take into account the situation in which the children are observed. Different conditions can obviously produce different patterns of social behavior. Could you use this fact to intentionally encourage social interaction?

THE ELEMENTARY-SCHOOL YEARS: AGES SIX TO TEN

The early part of this period is an important transitional stage. New horizons open as the child goes off to first grade, and important changes take place in the child's cognitive abilities and learning style during the first and second grades. The later elementary years are a more stable time, with growth in most areas proceeding at a slower, but steady pace.

Physical Development

Between ages six and ten, children continue to grow in height and weight, although slower than in either infancy or in adolescence. The muscles, skeleton, and nervous system continue to mature and lead to increases in endurance, strength, and motor coordination. Both boys and girls improve in physical abilities such as running, throwing, catching, and jumping, and any differences between the sexes in these gross motor skills are slight during elementary school. In the early elementary school years, fine motor coordination still lags behind gross motor coordination, although by age nine or ten, children are adept at many fine-motor tasks.

Activity level is high throughout this period, and most children enjoy participation in physical activities. You will still find that students perform best when quiet activities are alternated with more strenuous activities. Happily, you will also find that they are increasingly able to concentrate on tasks requiring sustained attention.

Social and Emotional Development

Between grades one and four, children begin to associate more and more with peers of the same sex, their friendships become stronger and more enduring, and groups become more structured, cohesive, and influential. At six, play groups are still informal with boys and girls occasionally playing together. However, by about ten, children rarely associate with the opposite sex. They are likely to have one or two close same-sex friends, but can also get along well in larger groups. Cliques begin to form and peer approval becomes more important than adult approval.

Arguments are frequent, interests change rapidly, and competition for the approval of adults is keen. Fears that seem "childish" to adults are still prevalent, as is "rough-and-tumble" aggression.

Childrens' conceptions of sex-appropriate behavior also become clearer, although evidence suggests that boys become more sex-typed than girls during elementary school. When Ferguson and Maccoby (1966) asked ten-year-olds to indicate their preferences for traditionally "masculine" and "feminine" activities, girls showed more cross-sex preferences. Conventional social pressures influence children to think that it is sometimes acceptable for "girls to act like boys," but it is less acceptable for "boys to act like girls."

TABLE 3–2

The Normal Pattern of Social and Emotional Development

Preschool 2–6 Years
Close relationship with parents and teachers; some peer friendships emerging; early signs of sex-typing in behavior; frequent, brief displays of emotion; directed aggression

Elementary School 6–10 Years
Friendships with peers strengthen and become more enduring; formation of friendship groups; few friends of opposite sex; peer approval becoming more important than adult approval; sex-typing of behavior distinct

Middle School 10–14 Years
May show "adolescent emotionality"; "nonconformity" through strong conformity to peer groups; small cliques common; opposite sex friendships and dating emerge; same-sex friendships strong

High School 14–18 Years
Conformity less extreme; cliques becoming less important than dating and friendships; less strong emotional expression than previously, but still more than in adulthood

During the elementary years, children experience what psychologist Erik Erikson (1950) has called a crisis of industry versus inferiority. During the first years of school, children develop basic attitudes about work, responsibility, and their own competence as human beings. Children who are allowed to work independently, who are encouraged to persevere until tasks are successfully completed, and who receive praise and recognition for their own accomplishments are likely to develop a sense of industry. They de-velop an appreciation both for productive and meaningful work and for their own ability to succeed.

On the other hand, children who are prevented from doing many things for themselves and whose successes are ignored and failures ridiculed are likely to develop feelings of inferiority and aversions to responsibility and productive work.

Language and Cognitive Development

Although many remarkable changes in the child's use of language occur before and during the preschool years, several important changes occur after ages six to eight. Speech articulation improves, vocabulary increases, and language, both written and oral, diversifies. Children use a wider vocabulary and structure the words and phrases within their sentences in more creative ways. Several aspects of grammar that many children master between ages six and ten include (a) the difference between active and passive sentences (e.g., "The boy washes the clothes," versus "The clothes are washed by the boy"), (b) using a verb as a noun (e.g., "Jumping can be fun"), (c) using conjunctions such as "because" and "although" appropriately, and (d) applying double function words to people, as well as to objects (e.g., "sweet person" or "bright girl") (Palermo & Molfese, 1972).

According to Piaget (1954), first- and second-graders acquire more flexible thought processes to accompany their increasing language facility. In this period, children shift from the stage of preoperational thought to the stage of concrete operations. Thought becomes more socialized and children are better able to take another person's point of view. In addition, children are able to manipulate concepts internally in complex ways. They can classify objects and events according to similarities and differences and can deal with multiple classification systems. They begin to understand the principle of conservation and can use the logical operations necessary for solving math problems and for understanding cause and effect relationships.

A series of interesting experiments by Bruner and his associates at the Harvard University Center for Cognitive Studies highlight some important changes in intelligence that typically occur during the early elementary years. In a dissertation presented in 1963, Mosher examined the way children of different ages played the game of "twenty questions" in order to see how they reason and use information (Mosher & Hornsby, 1966). The experimenters classified the questions asked by the children by the implicit logic they used. Most questions could be classified as either unconnected "hypotheses" (guesses such as "Is it a bread box?") or "constraint" questions (connected questions that logically narrow down the alternatives, such as "Is it living?" or "Is it smaller than a bread box?"). As Figure 3-2 shows, the percentage of logical constraint questions rose from zero percent in six-year-olds to 75 percent in eleven-year-olds, while the percentage of hypotheses (guesses) dropped dramatically over the same age range.

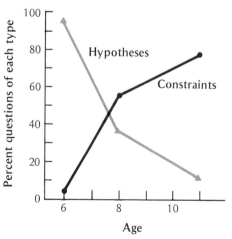

Figure 3–2. *Percent questions of each type asked by children of three ages in a game of "twenty questions." (From Mosher & Hornsby, 1966)*

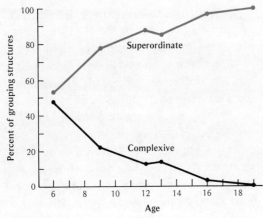

Figure 3–3. *Percent of two ways of grouping things together as being "alike." (From Olver and Hornsby, 1966)*

These data show that six-year-old children do not spontaneously use connected logic in solving problems. This does not necessarily mean that first-grade children could not learn subjects that involve complex logic if they were slowly and carefully taught, but it does suggest that complex subjects would be harder for them to learn. In other words, if you decide to teach symbolic logic, algebra, or the laws of motion to six-year-olds, you should have an exceptionally good reason for not waiting until they are a little older.

Another experiment by Bruner's group illustrates this change in conceptual sophistication in a different way. In his 1961 study, Olver asked children of different ages how the items in a list (e.g., banana, peach, potato, meat, milk, water, air, germs) were alike (Olver & Hornsby, 1966). He divided their answers into two categories: "superordinate" explanations that grouped the words under a single concept (such as, "Bananas, peaches, potatoes, and meat are all foods."),

or "complexive" explanations that linked the items in less efficient ways (such as, "Bananas and peaches are sort of yellow, and peaches and potatoes are almost round, and potatoes and meat are eaten together."). Figure 3–3 shows as expected that the use of efficient, superordinate concepts increases rapidly with age.

Taken together, these experiments demonstrate the dramatic changes in intellectual functioning that take place during the early elementary years and beyond. Fortunately, however, most of the essential educational skills and subjects that are taught in these years (reading, writing, spelling, and computing) are well-matched to the level of logical sophistication of young children. Still, it is necessary to understand these changes in order to appreciate the thinking and learning abilities of your students.

Although elementary students make impressive gains in reasoning, language, perception, and memory and they show curiosity and imagination, their thinking is still primarily tied to direct experience. Thus elementary-school teachers should use many *concrete* examples in teaching basic concepts. Piaget (1954) furthermore suggests that social interactions with peers help the child look at events from more than one perspective. Group projects in science, social studies, math, and art will help your students grow intellectually. Finally, you should get into the practice of carefully questioning your students in order to discover the extent of their understanding of basic concepts. There may be considerable variability among elementary students in their ability to deal with abstractions. Different children of the same age may be at very different levels in this ability. There may also be variability

FIVE TO SEVEN: A PERIOD OF TRANSITION

Psychologist Sheldon, White (1965) offers special evidence that the early elementary school years are an important transitional period for children. He reviewed many studies on learning in children and concluded that a shift occurs between ages five and seven in the child's performance on a variety of learning and perceptual tasks. Some of the shifts he described are summarized here:

1. There is a shift from tactual to visual exploration. For example, four- and five-year-olds will choose to play more with toys that offer tactual stimulation, like clay. Seven- and eight-year-olds prefer toys offering visual stimulation, like a kaleidoscope.

2. There is a shift from color to form dominance. When given a number of blocks differing both in color (red vs. blue) and form (triangle vs. square), four- and five-year-olds will sort on the basis of color, grouping the *red* triangle and *red* square together. Seven- and eight-year-olds will sort on the basis of form, grouping the red *triangle* and blue *triangle* together.

3. There is a decrease in form, letter, and word reversals. When asked to cross out all the letters "b" on a page of print, seven- and eight-year-olds will discriminate between "b," "p," and "d." Four- and five-year-olds may not.

4. At about age six, children are able to tell the left side of their body from the right side (although they may not be able to apply the concept of left and right to people facing them until later).

These are the kinds of abilities that will come in handy to the first-grader who is beginning to learn basic academics. Reading, writing, and arithmetic rely heavily on vision rather than on touching, on the perception of form rather than on color, and on left-to-right sequencing.

It is not clear what the cause and effect relationship is here. Do these particular abilities appear around age six because the child learns them in the process of learning to read, write, and do math in the first grade? Or does the natural emergence of these abilities around age six make learning academic skills possible, thus influencing the age requirements we set for formal school entrance?

---

within the individual child, as when a child grasps the concept of conservation as it applies to number, but not as it applies to weight or to volume.

Moral Development

As we said, both Piaget and Kohlberg suggest that the inflexible quality of moral reasoning found in preschoolers carries over into the elementary school. Children in the early grades are concerned with concepts of right and wrong, with fairness and taking turns. They are intolerant of rule-breakers, and they cannot conceive that sometimes it might be prudent to change the rules or that occasionally people break rules accidentally. Furthermore, Kohlberg has proposed that young children are motivated primarily to

behave morally out of fear of punishment or desire for rewards.

Kohlberg (1969) wanted to find the sources of childrens' moral judgments. He presented children of different ages with several stories in which the characters faced a moral dilemma, as illustrated in the story of Heinz:

In Europe, a woman was near death from cancer. One drug might save her, a form of radium that a druggist in the same town had recently discovered. The druggist was charging $2,000, ten times what the drug cost him to make. The sick woman's husband, Heinz, went to everyone he knew to borrow the money, but he could only get together about half of what it cost. He told the druggist that his wife was dying and asked him to sell it cheaper or let him pay later. But the druggist said, "No." The husband got desperate and broke into the man's store to steal the drug for his wife. Should the husband have done that? Why? (1969, page 379)

Kohlberg found that more than 90 percent of the responses made by seven-year-olds to stories such as this were preconventional; that is, they indicated a concern only for immediate punishment or reward. Examples of preconventional responses to the Heinz story included "You shouldn't steal the drug because you'll go to jail"; or conversely, "If you let your wife die you'll get in trouble."

Throughout the elementary school years, preconventional responses were most common. However, by age ten most children responded in ways that showed a concern for gaining the approval and avoiding the censure of other members of society, and the more abstract concepts of guilt, dishonor, and duty began to emerge in their responses.

In order to facilitate the transition to higher levels of moral reasoning, Kohlberg suggests that teachers encourage children to ponder moral dilemmas similar to those he uses in his studies. You should be aware, however, that the issue of moral education in the schools is controversial. It is difficult to distinguish between teaching children how to reason about moral dilemmas and teaching them specific moral values. This issue becomes even more complex when we consider that one's level of moral reasoning is not necessarily related to how "morally" one behaves.

REVIEW 3-1

1. What does it mean to say that our expectations for normal behavior are different for different age groups?

2. What is the value of developmental norms? Why do we need to be cautious in using them?

3. Describe the major physical changes that occur from ages two to ten.

4. What are the major social-emotional differences between preschool and elementary children?

5. Describe the major changes in language and cognition from ages two to ten.

6. How does the moral reasoning of children six to ten years of age differ from that of children two to six years of age?

THE MIDDLE SCHOOL YEARS: AGES TEN TO FOURTEEN

During the middle school years, we witness dramatic changes in all aspects of development. The famous adolescent growth spurt begins in this period and is accompanied by changes in how children perceive themselves and their relationships with others. In addition, a shift to more abstract reasoning occurs. In a sense, this period is similar to the early elementary years, since it is a time of important transitions.

Physical Development

Around age ten, both boys and girls reach a plateau in physical growth; they gain in height and weight, but the *rate* of growth is slow in comparison to other ages. The data in Figure 3–4, from a study by Tanner, Whitehouse, and Takaishi (1966), clearly show the pattern of the adolescent growth spurt as it pertains to height. The difference between the sexes is also apparent. You can see that the rate of growth begins to accelerate for most girls shortly after age ten and reaches a peak at age twelve. After twelve, the rate of growth gradually declines until age sixteen, when most girls reach their final adult height. In contrast, the onset of the growth spurt in boys usually begins at age twelve and reaches a peak at fourteen, with a decline in the rate of growth until eighteen. You can see also that the peak rate of growth is higher for boys than for girls. Although most girls are approximately two years ahead of boys in growth during this period, most boys will eventually be taller.

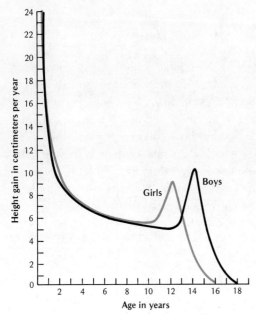

Figure 3–4. *The adolescent growth spurt. (From Tanner, Whitehouse, & Takaishi, 1966)*

The pattern of growth during early adolescence is similar for other bodily characteristics. Rapid gains in height are accompanied by gains in weight and in the development of the heart, lungs, and muscles. In addition, the reproductive system and the secondary sex characteristics begin to develop. Many girls reach puberty between ages twelve and fourteen, while most boys mature sexually somewhat later—usually between ages thirteen and fifteen. While girls are generally ahead of boys in all aspects of physical development, there is considerable individual variability. Some late-maturing girls may not develop sexually or physically until sixteen, while some early-maturing boys may begin the adolescent growth spurt at eleven, and vice versa. The problems that these differences in development can cause for some children are obvious.

Because the middle school years are a time of rapid physiological change for most young people, health and sex education become particularly important. An understanding of how and why these changes occur may alleviate many fears and the heightened sense of self-consciousness that are so common during early adolescence.

Social and Emotional Development

Much has been written about the emotional turmoil that accompanies the adolescent growth spurt. Adolescents are described as moody, unpredictable, selfish, intolerant, self-critical, insecure, and so on. Many young people do seem to experience a period of heightened emotional stress as they attempt to deal with (a) the physiological changes they experience, (b) the new, and sometimes inconsistent demands adults place on them, and (c) the changing relationships with their peers and family. However, the extent of the turmoil varies greatly from individual to individual and depends on how adults respond to them. Firmness, consistency, and clear expectations all are important in interacting with the adolescent. At the same time, it is important to encourage the gradual development of independence by giving the adolescent a voice in setting rules and making decisions.

Many adults find it difficult to allow adolescents more freedom in making decisions, since the decisions they *do* make may be in conflict with the standards of adult society. Every day we see examples of how preadolescents and young teens reject the values of their parents and teachers and follow the currently popular standards of their peers. Sometimes peer group conformity is reflected in relatively innocent fads in dress, music, and language or in hero worship or what seem to be rather silly initiation rites. In other cases, youngsters may conform to peer standards that are dangerous or antisocial like cheating, vandalism, or the use of drugs and alcohol.

According to experimental evidence, conformity to peer group standards peaks between ages ten and fourteen. In one study, Costanzo and Shaw (1966) measured con-

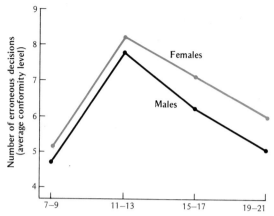

Figure 3–5. *Conformity measured by agreement with erroneous decisions. (After Costanzo & Shaw, 1966)*

formity by asking children to make perceptual judgments concerning the lengths of various lines. The correct response was obvious, but the researchers gave the subjects false information. They were told before responding on each trial that a group of their peers had chosen a different response. The number of times the subjects made erroneous judgments, the number of times they agreed with their peers, measured conformity. As Figure 3–5 indicates, subjects between ages eleven and thirteen conformed more than either younger or older subjects. The data also show that females conformed more than males at all age levels.

TABLE 3–3

The Normal Pattern of Language and Cognitive Development

Preschool 2–6 Years
Rapid shift from telegraphic to fully grammatical speech; articulation errors persist, but improving; stuttering may appear and go away before age four; thinking egocentric; logic and classification still immature; learn best through concrete examples

Elementary School 6–10 Years
Wider vocabulary; improvements in syntax; logic becomes more mature, but still concrete; thinking no longer strictly egocentric; wide individual differences and differences within individuals in conceptual development

Middle School 10–14 Years
Shift to being able to think in abstractions; solve intellectual problems more systematically; sex differences in intellectual functioning notable; only minor changes in vocabulary

High School 14–18 Years
Continued shift to adult cognition; no noticeable changes in language, except in vocabulary

members of the same sex, with little inter-mingling between male and female cliques. Toward the end of this period, several male and female cliques may merge together into a crowd. The crowd is larger and less cohesive than a clique; it serves to bring the sexes together in informal interactions. The activities of the crowd, such as weekend parties, set the stage for the development of heterosexual cliques and heterosexual friendships that develop later in high school.

Language and Cognitive Development

Around age eleven or twelve, many young people enter what Piaget calls the stage of formal operations. They can deal logically with objects and events they have never experienced and even with those they are not likely to experience in the future. They can speculate about philosophical, political, religious, and social issues. They can solve problems systematically by formulating hypotheses and testing each before reaching a conclusion. In short, critical thinking is now possible.

This transition to formal, adult thinking is demonstrated in one of Piaget's most famous experiments (Inhelder & Piaget, 1958). Children of various ages were shown a simple pendulum (made up of a string with a weight on the end) and were asked to discover what determined the period of the pendulum (the time required to make one complete swing). They were encouraged to vary the weight on

Conformity is not necessarily an undesirable aspect of growing up in our society. Conformity seems to be essential to healthy development. Moreover, many peer group standards are positive and not at all at odds with those of adults. Still, parents and you, as a teacher, should be alert to instances of excessive conformity and may need to encourage young people to develop questioning attitudes and to express themselves as individuals.

Studies show that the structure and function of adolescent peer groups change over time (Dunphy, 1963). During most of the middle school period, cliques prevail. Cliques are small, closely knit groups that provide their members with the opportunity to develop intimate friendships. At first, cliques are isolated and are made up of the string, the height from which the pendulum started, the push given to the pendulum, and the length of the string to determine the period.

Most children below age thirteen were unable to solve the problem, apparently because they did not understand the concept of holding all of the variables but one constant. Younger children varied several variables at once (added weight and pushed harder from a higher starting point), while those thirteen-years-old and older usually attacked the problem in a more systematic fashion. And with a little perseverance they discovered that only the length of the pendulum influences its period.

As with Piaget's other stages, the shift to formal operations takes place gradually over a period of years, but it does not seem to be inevitable. Evidence shows that some individuals never reach this level of abstract thinking, and that socioeconomic status and type of schooling influence the probability of reaching this stage more than the lower stages (Piaget, 1972). Thus, there is considerable interest in the U.S. in the development of middle- and high-school curricula that encourage the kinds of abstract reasoning abilities which Piaget describes.

We have little reason to believe that boys and girls differ in overall intelligence or in the ability to reason abstractly. Neverthe-

TABLE 3–4

The Normal Pattern of Moral Development

Preschool 2–6 Years
Moral rules interpreted rigidly, but are often misinterpreted to suit child's motives; transgressions of rules evaluated in terms of their consequences rather than motives; rules followed for personal gain

Elementary School 6–10 Years
More abstract conception of moral rules at later ages; shift from concern with direct personal gain to approval for good behavior

Middle School 10–14 Years
Shift to understanding relative nature of moral rules; evaluate transgressions according to motives rather than consequences; understand that rules can be changed; adherence to rules because they are necessary and it brings social approval

High School 14–18 Years
May see need for universal standards that transcend individual societies; may center standards on value of human beings

less, evidence shows that sex differences do emerge during the middle school years in regard to specific kinds of intellectual abilities. In a review of the literature on psychological sex differences, Maccoby and Jacklin (1974) found that at about age eleven, girls begin to score significantly higher than boys on tests of verbal ability. Girls excel at solving verbal analogies, comprehending written material, writing creatively, defining words, and so on.

At the same age, boys begin to show superiority over girls on tests of visual-spatial and mathematical ability.

These sex differences carry over clearly into late adolescence and adulthood. The causes are not yet firmly established, although it is unlikely that they are an inevitable result of simply being male or female.

Cultural expectations probably play an important role in the development of these sex differences. Perhaps we can increase the number of opportunities open to all children by placing equal emphasis on the development of verbal, mathematical, and visual-spatial abilities, or at least by avoiding arbitrary cultural stereotypes.

Moral Development

As children enter the stage of formal operations, they begin to deal with moral issues on a flexible and abstract basis. Using Piaget's (1932) terminology, they become **moral relativists.** They can see that a given behavior can be right in one situation and wrong in another situation, depending on the circumstances and the intentions of the individuals involved. They recognize that rules are made by people and that the rules can be changed.

Kohlberg (1963) found that at age thirteen, children gave **conventional** responses to his moral dilemmas. Children at the conventional level of moral reasoning recognize that adhering to the standards of one's family and society brings approval from others. Children also become aware of the necessity for rules and laws to maintain society and of the duty to uphold them. Examples of conventional responses to "Heinz's dilemma" include, "If you steal the drug you'll feel guilty for your dishonesty and lawbreaking"; and conversely, "You must do your duty to your wife; if she dies you'll never be able to look anyone in the face again."

THE HIGH-SCHOOL YEARS: AGES FOURTEEN THROUGH EIGHTEEN

Here again we see the cyclical aspect of development. While the late elementary years were a calm before the storm of early adolescence, we now return to another period of relative stability. Of course, *all* is not calm during late adolescence, since conflicts with authority and concerns over relationships with the opposite sex are common. However, many of the greatest developmental changes conclude during this time. High-school students consolidate their ideas about themselves and what they want to do in life, and begin to prepare themselves for adulthood.

Physical Development

At the beginning of high school, some girls and many boys still experience the adolescent growth spurt described earlier. Thus concerns over physical appearance and sexual functioning are common. In addition, eating and sleeping patterns are erratic. Interests in athletic activities may grow, particularly in males (another difference that appears to be changing), who on the whole now have more endurance and strength than females. By age eighteen virtually all students attain physical and sexual maturity and should adapt to their adult physical status.

Social and Emotional Development

We have seen that conformity to peer group opinions in experimental situations is less between ages fifteen and seventeen than between eleven and thirteen (Costanzo & Shaw, 1966). The same seems to hold true for everyday social interactions. As heterosexual cliques and individual dating relationships are established during high school, the peer group's influence diminishes. This is not to say that dramatic instances of excessive conformity do not occur in high school, but only that, on the whole, students are becoming more independent.

Emotionally, students still show freer and stronger emotional expression than adults, but they are rapidly becoming full adults in this area, too.

Language and Cognitive Development

Fortunately most adolescents (but certainly not all) have acquired the intellectual skills necessary to ponder the kind of questions that arise in searching for independence. According to Piaget, adolescent thought clearly resembles the thought of adults. Language does not change notably during this period, but vocabulary does continue to expand.

By eighteen, an individual reaches essentially maximum intellectual efficiency, and few further changes occur in the structure or quality of his or her thinking. While adolescents often have the "thinking power" of adults, they do not have the wide range of experience that adults have. They may not have the information available to them to use their reasoning abilities to the best advantage. It is not surprising, then, that in delving into societal and personal issues, adolescents sometimes arrive at impractical or improbable solutions.

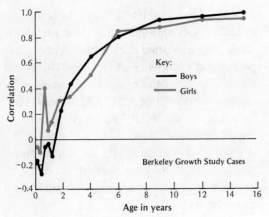

Figure 3–6. *Correlations of IQ scores at ages 16-18 with scores at earlier ages. (From Bayley, 1965)*

Moral Development

During late adolescence, some individuals reach the highest of Kohlberg's (1963) three levels of moral reasoning—the level of **principled** reasoning. Individuals at this level go beyond the conventional standards of the society in which they live. They may recognize the need for universal values that transcend particular societies and nations. These values generally center around respect for other human beings and the sanctity of the individual. At the principled level of reasoning, adolescents follow their own convictions and accept that these convictions may sometimes conflict with the values of society. It is likely that some of the young men who refused to serve in the Viet Nam War did so on the basis of principled moral reasoning.

But Kohlberg (1963) found that only a small minority of the responses given by sixteen-year-olds to his moral dilemmas could be classified as principled (e.g., "If Heinz didn't steal the drug he'd always condemn himself for not living up to his conscience."). Clearly, even in adulthood, many individuals fail to reach this state of moral reasoning. Unfortunately, we do not know why.

THE STABILITY OF INTELLECTUAL AND PERSONALITY CHARACTERISTICS DURING DEVELOPMENT

We spent considerable time discussing that people change as they grow older. This is a commonsense notion, but we hope that we fleshed out the bones of what you already knew. Like many commonsense beliefs, however, the opposite of the belief that people change with age is also something that we "know" to be true. We intuitively believe that people stay the same as they grow up. We say, for example, that a five-year-old with a quick temper "will be hard to live with when he or she grows up," or that a bright three-year-old "will be a scientist when he or she is an adult." These two views of development are not completely incompatible. Behaviors could show consistency and stability as they develop. But do they? Are intellectual and personality characteristics stable over time?

The important Berkely Growth Study (Bayley, 1965) sheds some light on this question. Researchers collected data on the development of a large group of individuals over the past twenty-five years. One of their major interests was to gauge the stability of intelligence over time. Figure 3−6 shows the relationship between IQ scores measured at sixteen to eighteen years of age with those measured at younger ages. Age is plotted on the horizontal axis of Figure 3−6 and correlation coefficients are plotted on the vertical axis. A correlation coefficient measures the strength of the relationship between two variables. As the coefficient increases (in either the positive or negative direction), it indicates a stronger relationship. As Figure 3−6 shows, there is little relationship between IQ scores measured at age two and those measured at ages sixteen to eighteen. The correlation does not become significant until at least age six.

This means that intelligence, at least as measured by IQ scores, varies until after age six and even after that. Figure 3−7 shows this fact in a different way. The raw scores on an IQ test of five boys who had the same score at age two are shown for each year until age twenty-five. As one can see, the course of intellectual growth for these five individuals varied considerably. Still, after age ten their relative positions remained unchanged.

These data suggest that intellectual development, at least to the extent that we are able to measure it, is quite variable and is difficult to predict before age six, and that an important degree of instability remains throughout childhood. Although it is much harder to measure changes in personality over time, the little evidence that we have suggests that personality characteristics are at least as unstable across early ages as IQ measures (Kagan & Moss, 1962).

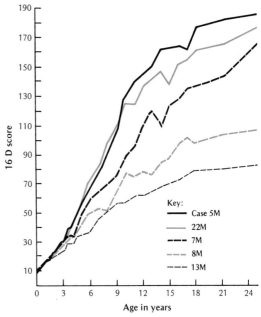

Figure 3−7. *Individual curves of 16 D scores (intelligence). (From Bayley, 1965)*

DEVELOPMENTAL ISSUES RELATED TO EDUCATION: ACCELERATION AND READINESS

Now that we know something about the behaviors that are normal for children of various ages, the question arises whether the normal course of development can be altered. In particular, there is much controversy over the issue of **acceleration:** Can we speed up the rate at which children acquire certain social, intellectual, and academic behaviors? In order to deal with the issue of acceleration, we must reintroduce the important concept of readiness.

Readiness refers to what can, and should, be taught at any given time in the development of the child. Or phrased differently, given the developmental status of the child, what is he or she *ready* to learn? Currently there are at least two opposing viewpoints regarding readiness (Clarizio, 1974). According to the **natural readiness** perspective, a child's readiness to learn depends on his or her own maturational time clock. Readiness to learn emerges naturally from within the child, as the child develops neurologically and psychologically.

Any attempts to teach children before they are naturally ready will lead to superficial learning at best, and may actually be harmful by dooming children to failure and frustration. The natural approach is implicit in this early statement of the concept of reading readiness: "To make any progress in reading, a child must have attained a mental age of at least six years . . . a mental age of six and one-half years more nearly insures success" (Harrison, 1939, p. 61). The natural readiness perspective has historically had a tremendous impact on education, particularly on teaching strategies in the preschool and elementary school and on the determination of formal school entrance requirements.

A second point of view is called **accelerated readiness** or "produced readiness" (Clarizio, 1974). According to this perspective, being ready to learn involves having the necessary prerequisite skills. Adults can play an active role in producing readiness by teaching the child the prerequisites necessary for successful learning. The notion of accelerated readiness is much less tied to maturational factors, although the child's neurological and physical status is not totally discounted. Instead, proponents of this view suggest that an undue emphasis on maturational time clocks within the child often results in postponing the teaching of behaviors that the child is capable of learning.

Glaser (1962) provides a good example of the accelerated approach in his concept of **entering behavior** discussed in Chapter 2 of this text. Entering behavior simply refers to the previously acquired behaviors that children bring with them to any learning situation. If the child's entering behavior includes the set of prerequisite skills and the motivation necessary to learn a given **terminal behavior** (the knowledge or skill that you want the child to learn), then the terminal behavior can be taught. If it does not, then the teacher's role is to arrange the learning environment so that the child acquires the necessary entering behavior first.

Perhaps the best way to examine these differing perspectives on readiness is to look at the research related to two basic questions. First, is it *possible* to teach age-related behaviors prior to their normal appearance? Second, is it *desirable?*

Is It Possible to Accelerate Readiness?

Much research directed toward answering this question has focused on whether young children can be taught to understand Piaget's concept of conservation. Several researchers report experimental results showing that conservation cannot be taught or that direct teaching leads to superficial learning. In one study, Smedlund (1971) used a balance scale to teach nonconserving children that two identical balls of clay weighed the same, even after the shape of one ball had been changed. After he trained these children, Smedlund presented them with a similar task, only this time, unknown to the children, he removed a chunk of clay from one ball as he shaped it into a sausage. The children, having learned conservation, predicted that the ball and sausage would weigh the same because only the shape had been changed. When they then saw from the scale that the ball weighed more, they immediately reverted back to their nonconserving responses (e.g., "The sausage weighs less because it's skinnier."). In contrast, a group of children who understood conservation to begin with (and presumably had acquired this understanding on their own, without training) "stuck to their guns" when confronted with this situation. They insisted that some of the clay must have been taken away. That the trained children evidently forgot what they had been taught in the face of discrepant information has been cited in support of Piaget's notion that training leads only to temporary and superficial learning.

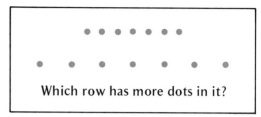

Figure 3–8. *Example of a number conservation task.*

But a number of other studies (e.g., Gelman, 1969) have shown that maybe it is *possible* to teach conservation in such a way that the resultant learning is both durable and generalized; that is, children can apply the principle to tasks other than the specific ones on which they were trained.

Gelman (1969) hypothesized that young children often fail on conservation tasks because they attend to irrelevant stimulus cues. For example, we know that on a typical number conservation task, such as the one shown in Figure 3–8, the nonconserving child will often say that the second row has more dots because it is longer. According to Gelman, the child fails to conserve because he or she attends to irrelevant stimulus cues, in this example the length of the row, and ignores the relevant cues, in this example the number of dots.

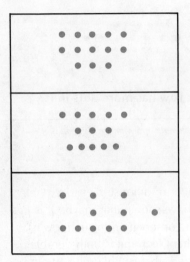

Figure 3–9. *Examples of the discrimination learning problems used by Gelman (1969) in teaching conservation.*

In the study, Gelman taught the children to attend to relevant stimulus cues in number conservation tasks by presenting them with a series of problems such as those shown in Figure 3–9. For each problem the child was asked either to point to two rows having the same number of items or to point to two rows having a different number of items. In order to make the correct discriminations, the child had to ignore the length of the rows and focus instead on the number of items in each row. Many problems like those in Figure 3–9 were given, one at a time, over a two-day training period. After each problem, the children were told whether they had answered correctly.

Gelman found that the children learned to make the correct discriminations over the course of training. Furthermore, posttests on standard conservation tasks were given after one day and then again three weeks after training. The children not only showed con-

servation of number on both the immediate and delayed posttests, but also showed considerable transfer or "generalization" to liquid and mass conservation tasks, tasks unrelated to the training they had received! In other words, they had learned a general rule about *quantity* being the relevant cue. They could apply this rule to liquid problems (ignore the size of the beakers and focus on the *amount* of liquid) and to mass problems (ignore the shape of the clay and focus on the amount), even though they had received no specific training using those materials.

A word of caution: Gelman's subjects ranged in age from four years nine months to six years. They were close to "normal" age for the acquisition of conservation. It is possible that many of the subjects were developmentally "ready" to learn conservation, and that Gelman simply helped them make the transition by providing training at just the right time. Still, Gelman's impressive results show that conservation is a kind of task, just like reading or math, that can be broken down into component skills and taught, if it is taught in this step-by-step manner.

Evidence on whether we can accelerate development also comes from studies (e.g., Durkin, 1975) on the effects of preschool education. We discussed the point of view that says that before age six, children are simply unprepared to profit from direct instruction in academic subjects such as reading, math, and writing. On the whole, the data simply fail to support this assumption. For example, O. K. Moore (1966) described his Responsive Environments Laboratory in which average two- and three-year-olds (as well as older children) are taught to read using a "talking typewriter" (a device that tells children what letters to type to spell

words). More recently, Delores Durkin (1975) published data showing that average children who began reading instruction at age four not only learned to read at that age, but also scored higher on tests of reading achievement given in grades one through four than control children who had had no formal instruction before the first grade.

This evidence supports the conclusion that children *can* learn before we ordinarily consider them to be ready to do so, if they are properly taught. The next issue to consider, therefore, is the *wisdom* of accelerating readiness.

Is It Desirable to Accelerate Readiness?

Should we teach academic skills to pre-schoolers or provide them with enrichment programs emphasizing exploration? Should we lower the age requirements for entry into the first grade? Is there any advantage to teaching children more in less time, so that they do not have to spend twelve years of their lives in formal school? Or are children growing up too fast as it is? Primarily, the answers to these questions require value judgments based on your own philosophy of education. But there is also some empirical data that bears on the subject.

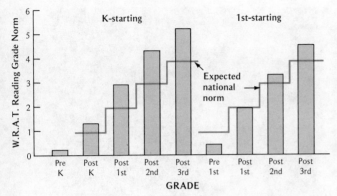

Figure 3–10. *Reading scores of kindergarten-starting children and first-grade-starting children.* (From Becker, Engelmann, & Thomas, 1975)

Torsten Husén's study (1967) is often cited as evidence against acceleration. Husén investigated math achievement and attitudes toward school as they related to the age of formal school entry in a cross-cultural sample of thirteen-year-olds. He found that age of school entry and achievement were unrelated; students who entered school at an earlier age did no better on achievement tests than did students who entered at a later age. Furthermore, students who entered at a younger age disliked school more than students who entered later. So the possibility exists that early school entrance does not inevitably lead to higher achievement in the end and that it may even have a harmful effect on the child's attitudes toward school.

In a similar vein, William D. Rowher (1971) proposed that some skills can be learned more rapidly in adolescence than in childhood and that postponing the teaching of those skills may considerably reduce the alienation we so often see in our schools. Finally, both David Elkind (1969) and Lawrence Kohlberg (1968), working from a Piagetian orientation, suggested that while

general intellectual stimulation is desirable during the preschool years, teaching aimed at "skills" or "content" will be of little benefit to the child. Elkind believes that there are "intellectually burned children" who have lost much of their motivation for learning by the third grade because they have been constantly shuttled from one academic activity to another.

The arguments of Rowher, Elkind, and Kohlberg are persuasive, even though the research evidence is insufficient. We *have* known children who, under intense parental and teacher pressure to achieve at an early age, have turned away from intellectual involvement. We *have* seen children struggle painfully with tasks they could probably have learned easily at a later age. And we *have* seen children fail at tasks they could not possibly comprehend or at tasks they had no interest whatsoever in learning.

But there is another side to the issue. It is clear that there are children who do *not* learn more easily later; there are many slow-learning children who may not learn later at all, because they lack the early experiences necessary to get off to the right start in school. The suffering for these children is great, to say nothing of the expense involved in helping them once they have started to fail. Accelerating the readiness of slow learners so that they can catch up to average children, then, would seem desirable even if the acceleration of average children serves no useful purpose.

An educational experiment conducted by Wesley Becker and Siegfried Engelmann of the University of Oregon (Becker, Engelmann, & Thomas, 1975) sheds important light on this aspect of the readiness issue. They worked with several groups of mostly disadvantaged children from kindergarten through the third grade in the evaluation of a highly structured educational program. Approximately half the students started reading instruction at the normal time in the first grade, while the rest started in kindergarten. This is unusually early, especially for disadvantaged children who often are below average in reading readiness. The results pictured in Figure 3–10 show that the kindergarten-starting group did in fact learn less than the first-grade-starting group during their first year of instruction. The kindergartners were younger and presumably less proficient in the entering behaviors necessary for learning to read. If we look at their gains over the second year of instruction, we can see again that the kindergarten-starting group gained slightly less than the first-grade starters. But if we look at their progress through the third grade, it appears that the kindergarten-starting group gained about as much each year as the first-grade starters from the second grade on. What may be more important is that since they had an extra year of instruction, the kindergarten-starting group was slightly ahead of the first-grade-starting group by the time they had both finished the third grade.

These results seem to suggest that it is unnecessary to wait until children are completely "ready" for reading instruction, that we can produce better learning by starting instruction earlier than is traditional. What must be kept in mind, however, is that this program was a very structured one. We cannot be sure that the same thing would happen in programs that were less oriented toward the careful sequencing of learning experiences in ways that were individualized for each child.

As mentioned earlier, the use of a structured approach to compensate for deficiencies from normal development is different from using structured teaching to accelerate development beyond the norm. We see no particular advantage to teaching three-year-olds how to read or nine-year-olds how to solve algebraic equations. But we see little harm in it either, as long as the learning experience is enjoyable for the child and the probability of successful learning is high. This is where entering behavior becomes so important. If children have the necessary entering behaviors for reading or solving algebraic equations, and if they are curious and enthusiastic about learning, as many young children are, then why not capitalize on this enthusiasm? We maintain that many of the "intellectually burned" children in our schools today have been burned not as much by structured curricula and pressure to achieve per se, as by pressure to achieve on tasks for which they have neither enthusiasm nor the necessary prerequisite skills.

REVIEW 3–2

1. How are changes in cognition reflected in changes in moral reasoning from ages ten to eighteen?

2. How does the role of peer friendships change from ages ten to eighteen?

3. What is the period of greatest conformity?

4. Describe sex-typed behaviors from ages ten to eighteen.

5. What is the meaning of the term *readiness* for teachers?

6. At about what age are intellectual and personality characteristics stable?

SUMMARY

This chapter describes the typical course of development from the preschool years to the high-school years. Although wide variations from this "typical" pattern are normal, understanding these changes is essential to effective teaching.

We discussed the child's physical growth in size, coordination, and activity level and mentioned ways of accommodating these changes in the classroom. We described changes in the social-emotional domain from high emotionality to mature emotions; from close parent ties and weak peer friendships, to strong peer relationships in middle school, and to more mature adult and peer relationships by high school; and we saw that sex-typing becomes more pronounced with age.

The most dramatic changes from childhood to adulthood, however, take place in language, cognition, and moral judgments. The major shifts from limited "telegraphic" speech to full use of syntax take place from ages two to four, with vocabulary continuing to be added through development. Cognitive changes take place throughout the "school-age" period, however, resulting in changes from an individual who can deal only in concrete thought processes to an adult who can understand abstractions. Morally, children move from individuals who mind because they are told to do so, to individuals who understand and apply the abstract principles of right and wrong. Despite the range of these changes, there is still a degree of continuity and stability in intelligence and other aspects of behavior, but it is usually not evident until after ages six to ten.

You as a teacher will be most interested in understanding the way children develop so that you can match your teaching to the level of growth of your students. You may at times, however, want to speed up the process of development. While this is possible, and is definitely necessary for slow-learning children, it is probably not justifiable for average children.

ANSWERS TO REVIEW QUESTIONS

Review 3-1

1. Since the typical behavior of children changes markedly over time, our view of "normal" behavior must take into account the age of the student. It would be normal for a five-year-old to reverse letters and to have a short attention span, because most five-year-olds have these characteristics. It would not be normal to see them in a ten-year-old, however.

2. Developmental norms give us standardized ways of measuring developmental progress, but since variability in the rate of development among children is very prevalent, only large deviations from the norm should be considered abnormal.

3. From ages two to six, the child gains steadily in size and weight, but this rate of gain slows from six to ten. Activity level declines somewhat and attention span increases slightly from two to ten. Both fine and gross motor coordination improve across this entire age span, but fine motor skills lag far behind gross motor skills until after age six.

4. Preschool children have close relationships with parents and teachers, with peer friendships beginning to develop in many children. In contrast, elementary children have stronger peer relationships, especially with children of the same sex. In addition, elementary children show more sex-typing in their behavior and fewer displays of emotion than preschoolers.

5. There are rapid changes from telegraphic to grammatical speech by about age three, with most changes beyond that point occurring in increased vocabulary and more complicated syntax. Thinking is still immature and very concrete during the preschool years, becoming more mature and less egocentric during the elementary years. Conceptual learning is still facilitated through use of concrete examples during elementary school, however.

6. During the preschool years, moral rules are viewed rigidly, but can be bent to suit needs of child. Violations of rules are judged by their consequences instead of their motives during this period. During the elementary years a shift begins to a more abstract conception of moral rules and concern with good behavior for its own sake rather than personal gain. This shift is usually completed by the end of the elementary period.

Review 3–2

1. At about age eleven or twelve, cognition usually becomes more abstract. At about the same time, children begin to see rules as arbitrary creations that can be changed. Later in this period a few very abstract standards of conduct (such as "justice" and "honor") may become particularly important.

2. During the middle school years, peer relationships become more important than ones with parents and other adults. The aversion to same-sex friendships dissolves and dating begins. Cliques dominate friendship patterns, continuing until high school when one-to-one friendships become increasingly more important.

3. Peer conformity gains importance in late elementary school and peaks in middle school. Thereafter, strict conformity declines in importance.

4. From the middle school years on, females may exhibit emotion more than males, will score higher on tests of verbal ability on the average, but lower on the average in mathematics and visual-spatial abilities. By high school more boys will take strong interest in athletics and generally have more strength and endurance. These differences vary greatly from individual to individual, however, and seem to be changing as views toward females change.

5. "Readiness" means having the entering behaviors that are prerequisite for learning some type of skill or knowledge.

6. Intellectual and personality characteristics can change throughout life, but IQ scores are somewhat stable after age six.

2

LEARNING, MEASUREMENT, AND SOCIAL PROCESSES

In the Introduction, a basic model of instruction was described, and in Part 1 we discussed theories of age-related changes and the normal pattern of development. If teachers are going to intervene in development to guide its course to any extent, they must have a specific understanding of the process of learning. This section will discuss the related topics of learning, intelligence, motivation, and memory. We will place learning in its social context and suggest productive ways of setting goals for instruction and for measuring progress toward those goals.

Chapter 4

Learning and Memory

As children grow, they develop their own unique personalities, learn skills, acquire attitudes, and master bodies of knowledge. Much of this learning takes place outside the classroom and is not the result of intentional instruction by either parents or teachers. Still, our society continues to place great emphasis on providing children with planned learning experiences within the classroom. In this setting, the key role of the teacher is to promote learning, to help children acquire basic information, skills, and attitudes.

We not only want children to learn, we want them to remember what they learn. And we want them to be able to **transfer** what they learn in one situation to others. For example, we would like students to use their knowledge of geometry when they learn trigonometry and to apply what they learn in automobile mechanics when they work with small engines. In this chapter, then, we consider learning, particularly as it relates to memory and transfer. Knowing how we acquire skills and abilities and how we receive, process, and remember information may help you plan classroom experiences that will have profound effects on your students.

DEFINITIONS OF LEARNING AND RETENTION

Learning is a complex process that we can study from many perspectives. Psychologists define **learning** as any relatively permanent change in behavior that is due to experience.

This definition has three important elements. First, the only way we can be sure that learning has occurred is to observe overt behavior or performance. Presumably the learning process is accompanied by internal events, such as chemical changes in the central nervous system, but existing technology does not permit us to observe these internal events directly. We must infer that learning has occurred on the basis of changes in performance. Of course, a child may learn a particular skill and then fail to use it because of lack of motivation or any number of other variables. Still, the only time you can be sure that learning has occurred is when you can see changes in overt behavior.

Second, only changes in behavior due to the individual's experience with his or her environment indicate that learning has taken place. Sometimes a child's behavior may change because of other factors — drugs, fatigue, and maturation are common examples. Generally we do not say that a child learns to focus his eyes, since this behavior results primarily from biological maturation. However, we do say that a child learns to throw a baseball or names the days of the week, because these behaviors require practice. The child who does not have certain kinds of environmental experiences will not acquire them.

Third, learning requires a permanent change in behavior. This does not mean that if we forget something, that we never learned it in the first place. This aspect of our definition means to emphasize that we can safely infer learning only after we observe several instances of the behavior change. For example, it is bad teaching practice to conclude that learning has taken place on the basis of what might have been a "lucky guess."

Again, the term *learning* generally refers to the initial acquisition of a new behavior. Beyond this time frame, we begin to deal with the process of memory. **Retention** refers to the extent that an individual can remember information or skills that he or she has learned at some previous time. The kind of learning involved, the strength of the original learning, the time since the learning took place, and other influences affect how well we are able to retain and use what we have learned. Much of the latter parts of this chapter are devoted to an examination of these factors.

VARIETIES OF LEARNING: GAGNE'S ANALYSIS

Psychologists have studied learning for many years and have discovered a number of principles that describe how learning, *in general,* occurs. For example, we can apply the principles of reinforcement (discussed in the following chapter) to teaching procedures that facilitate learning in a wide variety of situations. Still, you should be aware that there are *different kinds* of learning.

Learning to recite the alphabet differs from learning how to find the area of a triangle. And learning how to find the area of a triangle differs from learning to respect the rights of others.

Educational psychologist Robert Gagné has developed a useful way of analyzing different types of learning. In *The Conditions of Learning* (Gagné, 1970) and *Principles of Instructional Design* (Gagné & Briggs, 1974), he distinguishes between different types of learning and suggests how instruction can be designed to facilitate each type. Because Gagné's analysis is both logically sound and practical, we will look closely at his five major categories of learning—verbal information, intellectual skills, cognitive strategies, attitudes, and motor skills. (Part 4 of this book, particularly Chapters 10 and 11, will provide more detailed guidelines for instruction.)

Verbal Information

We usually expect students to learn a large number of labels and facts. Gagné refers to this as the learning of **verbal information.** We say that students have learned a *label* when they can consistently name an object or event. For example, filling in the names of the parts of the body on a diagram is an example of labeling. When students can use labels in sentence form to express a relationship between two or more objects or events, they have learned a *fact.* "The pancreas is located below the stomach"; "William the Conquerer invaded England in 1066"; "Two apples plus two apples equals four apples"; and "Tornadoes travel in a southwest to northeast path" are facts many of us have learned.

The learning of relationships between stimuli is essential to the learning of verbal information. For example, in teaching the class to name different kinds of birds, the teacher may hold up pictures of cardinals, orioles, sparrows, and other birds and ask the children to name each picture. Gradually the children learn to associate a name with each picture. In learning to state a fact, the units within the fact must be chained together so that, for example, the "Treaty of Versailles" becomes linked with "end of World War I," which in turn becomes linked with "1918."

Verbal information may be learned rapidly or slowly and only with much repetition. Usually learning is most rapid and retention is optimized when it is related to what the students already know. Psychologists refer to this as **meaningful learning.** This contrasts with **rote learning,** in which students simply memorize verbatim what they learn. They either do not understand what they learn, or what they learn is unrelated to what they already know.

American public schools have often been criticized for the excessive teaching of facts. To a certain extent, this criticism is justified. Facts learned in isolation are easily forgotten. Furthermore, being able to state a fact does not guarantee that the student understands the meaning of the underlying concepts. For example, a young child may make the factual statement "cats have fur" and at the same time label a cocker spaniel a cat. Nevertheless, knowledge of a large number of facts is necessary for further learning and for coping with everyday life. One of your jobs then is to decide what facts are important enough to teach your students in a meaningful way. Rote learning cannot always be avoided, but you can keep it at a minimum.

Intellectual Skills— *learning how*

Not only do students need to learn more than verbal information, they need to learn how to deal competently with different aspects of their environment; in Gagné's terms, they need to learn **intellectual skills.** The basic distinction between information and intellectual skills is one of *learning that* versus *learning how.* The student who knows *that* immunology is the branch of medicine concerned with protection from disease has learned a fact. The student who knows *how* to look up the meaning of "immunology" in a dictionary has learned an intellectual skill.

Intellectual skills make it possible for the student to think in terms of classes of objects and events, rather than working with a confusing blizzard of individual facts or instances. The student who can use a dictionary has learned an effective way for dealing with unfamiliar words.

We expect students to learn many intellectual skills in the classroom. Some, like counting, are simple; others, like diagramming sentences, are complex. Some, like reading or telling time, are used by nearly everyone; others, like designing a house or programming a computer, are used only by specialists. Regardless of the particular capability involved, you should always teach *concepts* and *rules* when you teach intellectual skills. All intellectual skills require your students to understand concepts and to follow rules.

Forming concepts.   Learning a **concept** means learning how to group ideas or things into classes on the basis of certain shared characteristics, even though individual members of the class may differ in noncritical ways. For example, the critical characteristics that define a square are four straight sides of equal length joined at right angles. In order to be sure that students understand the concept of "square" they must correctly identify positive as well as negative instances of the concept. For example, they must be able to indicate that circles, triangles, rectangles, and so on are *not* squares. Students must also be able to ignore noncritical features in identifying positive instances. For example, squares can be enormous, tiny, chartreuse, or violet, but it is not *necessary* for squares to have any of these characteristics. Thus the student learns that size and color have no bearing on squareness (see Figure 4–1). Concept learning clearly involves *demonstrating* the meaning of objects, events, and symbols, rather than simply stating verbal information.

From concepts to rules.   Once students have learned the basic concepts in any area, they can learn to combine these concepts into rules and use the rules to solve problems. **Rules** are verbal statements that tell the learner how to perform. "Width times height" is a rule that tells the student how to find the area of a rectangle; "i before e except after c" is a rule that tells the student how to perform a certain spelling pattern. Although rules can be formalized into verbal statements, it is unnecessary for the student to be able to state the rule. We can conclude that a rule has been learned if the student's *behavior* is consistent with it. Still, we often teach rules by (1) presenting the student with a verbal statement of the rule, (2) giving examples of the rule, and (3) asking the student to practice applying the rule in new situations.

Learning hierarchies. ⌐Sequential learning⌐ An essential aspect of most intellectual skills is that they are made up of prerequisite skills. In other words, students must understand basic concepts and rules before they can perform a specified skill. For example, in order to read orally, students must understand the concept of letters as symbols for sounds. They must identify individual letters by the sounds they represent, blend sounds together, and follow certain rules that specify whether vowels and consonants will be long, short, soft, hard, silent, and so on. These are only a few examples; perhaps you can think of additional prerequisite skills for oral reading.

In order to facilitate the acquisition of any intellectual skill, Gagné suggests that teachers develop a **learning hierarchy.** A learning hierarchy is a chart that shows the relationships between the prerequisites and the final skill to be learned. A learning hierarchy for subtracting whole numbers is presented in

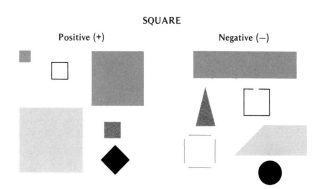

SQUARE

Positive (+)   Negative (−)

Figure 4–1. *Students must be able to identify both positive and negative instances of a concept before learning can be inferred.*

Figure 4–2. You may be surprised to see that such a simple skill has so many prerequisites (notice that many lower-level number skills are omitted and that the hierarchy starts with a knowledge of basic subtraction facts). Indeed, we often underestimate the number of prerequisites, or worse yet, overlook them entirely, causing children to struggle with skills they are unprepared to learn. Learning hierarchies can help teachers clarify the components of intellectual skills and plan appropriate sequence of instruction.

③ Cognitive Strategies

Just teaching verbal information and intellectual skills is a tremendous task, at which we are not always successful—witness the recent statistics showing that a frightening number of students receive high school diplomas without being able to read. Still, Gagné and most educational psychologists identify a third kind of learning that is of the utmost importance. Gagné uses the term "cognitive strategies"; others refer to creativity, learning to learn, productive thinking,

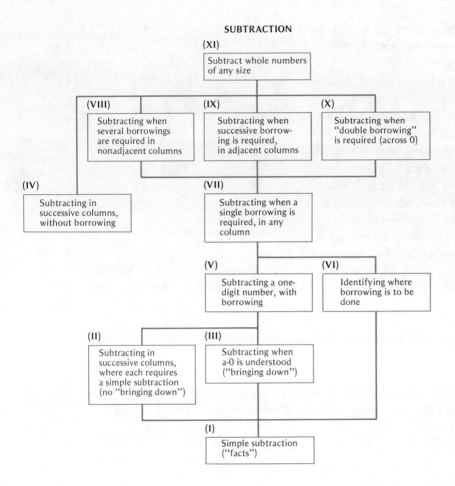

Figure 4–2. *A learning hierarchy for subtracting whole numbers. (From Gagné & Briggs, 1974)*

teaching oneself, and so on. We refer here to the type of learning that allows students not only to solve problems, but to solve problems they have never encountered before and to do so in novel ways.

To Gagné **cognitive strategies** are the skills we use in organizing our thought processes. Examples of cognitive strategies in-clude learning to listen, focusing attention, asking questions, formulating hypotheses, criticizing, and evaluating. You can do much to facilitate the acquisition of cognitive strategies. Indeed, special curricula have been developed to teach productive thinking and problem solving. Because this is such an important, and to some extent neglected topic, learning to think will be treated separately later in this chapter.

④ Attitudes

An **attitude** is "an internal state which affects an individual's choice of action toward some object, person, or event" (Gagné, 1974, p. 62). *Choice of action* is an important component of this definition, since the best way to measure someone's attitude toward something is to observe how he or she *behaves* in relation to it. Students who frequently forget their gym clothes and complain of feeling ill during gym classes have a negative attitude toward physical education. Students who spend their free time tutoring a classmate or driving a neighbor to the grocery store have a positive attitude toward helping others. We sometimes make inferences about people's attitudes based on what they *say* they like or dislike, but we can best measure attitudes by observing actual behavior.

Attitude learning falls into a separate category, because we learn attitudes in a slightly different manner than information, skills, and strategies. By themselves, verbal statements of what the student is to learn are usually unsuccessful in teaching attitudes. Verbal appeals to "keep America clean," "conserve energy," "be tolerant of others," or "stay away from drugs" generally produce poor results (Stuart, 1974).

Two other conditions appear more critical in the learning of attitudes. One is how successful students are in an activity or in their interactions with other people. A child who succeeds in learning to dance is likely to have a positive attitude toward dancing. A child who fails in learning to read is likely to have a negative attitude toward reading, even though the teacher proclaims daily the value of reading.

The second critical condition influencing attitude learning concerns the models the child is exposed to. We learn attitudes indirectly by observing the behavior of people who are important to us. Parents, teachers, peers, and public figures can exert a tremendous influence simply by acting in accordance with the attitudes they want to teach. In the classroom, teachers who exhibit kindness, fairness, competence, and a love for learning themselves are likely to influence their students to have positive attitudes toward school and other people.

⑤ Motor Skills

Gagné's fifth and final category of learning involves **motor skills,** activities which require a precise sequence of bodily movements. We can readily find examples of motor skill learning in the preschool and early elementary grades; learning to tie a knot, skip, ride a tricycle, and sharpen a pencil are just a few. But the learning of motor skills also occurs in the later grades and continues throughout adulthood. Swimming, playing the piano, typing, sewing, changing a tire, and driving a car all require the coordination of precise muscular movements. In some cases, motor and intellectual skills overlap; for example, writing is a skill that has both intellectual and motor components.

The conditions that facilitate motor learning depend somewhat on the particular skill involved. Sometimes it is best to master each

component of a motor skill separately before trying to execute the whole sequence (in learning to play the piano you usually learn to play with each hand separately before playing with both hands simultaneously). At other times, it is essential to begin practice with the whole sequence (such as learning a new swimming stroke or driving a car). In either case, demonstrations, practice, and feedback are necessary components of efficient motor skill learning. It is next to impossible to learn a complex motor skill unless we have the opportunity to observe someone demonstrate the skill, have a chance to try the skill ourselves, and receive feedback on how well we did.

In some cases, the feedback may be automatic and even internal. Tennis players can "feel" the racket hitting the ball, observe the ball sailing over the fence (instead of the net), and adjust their grip accordingly. But for most motor skills, particularly in the early stages of acquisition, feedback from others is also helpful: "You didn't keep your eye on the ball"; or "Toss the ball higher when you serve."

One characteristic that distinguishes most motor learning from verbal learning is that motor learning takes place more gradually, with improvements in speed and accuracy continuing over long periods of practice. Many professional athletes and musicians, for example, practice for years before reaching peak performance. Data from a study by Crossman (1959), reproduced in Figure 4–3, show that industrial workers continued to improve in the time required to make a cigar, even after seven years of experience. Furthermore, motor skills, once learned, are not easily forgotten.

1. Discuss the three elements of the definition of learning.

2. What is the difference between learning and retention?

3. Give several examples of verbal information and describe how verbal information is learned.

4. How does Gagne distinguish between intellectual skills and verbal information?

5. Define and give examples of concept and rule learning.

6. What is the purpose of a learning hierarchy?

7. Give several examples of cognitive strategies.

8. What two conditions are critical in the learning of attitudes?

9. Discuss how motor skills are learned.

LEARNING TO THINK, BE CREATIVE, AND TEACH ONESELF

Educators often propose that the ultimate goal of education is to teach children to think independently, to solve problems on their own. Using Gagné's analysis, we see that most problem solving requires the recall of relevant *verbal information* and performance of certain *intellectual* or *motor skills*. In addition, students must want to solve the problem to begin with—they must have a positive *attitude* toward finding a solution. These are necessary conditions for problem solving, but they are not sufficient conditions by themselves. Efficient *cognitive strategies* are also required. We refer here to the manner in which the individual approaches the problem and brings what he or she knows to bear on its solution. Perhaps you know peo-

ple who can recall facts and have the necessary motor and intellectual skills to solve problems, but whose thinking is so poorly organized that they are ineffective in dealing with everyday problems.

So we will begin this section stating that techniques of problem solving can be taught as important educational skills. Problem solving is important because we want children to be *lifelong learners.* We want them to know how to learn on their own and to enjoy learning long after they complete their formal schooling. Knowing how to approach and solve new problems is a critical aspect of continual learning, since each time we solve an unfamiliar problem we learn something new about the world in which we live.

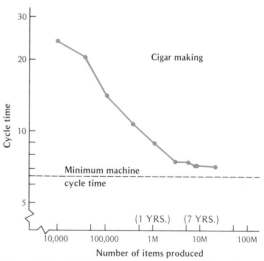

Figure 4–3. *Gradual improvement in the making of cigars over several years of work. (From Crossman, 1959)*

The Process of Problem Solving

Many psychologists, philosophers, and educators have attempted to analyze the steps people go through in solving problems. John Dewey (1910) proposed that problem solving involves five separate stages. We still do not know what takes place during problem solving, but Dewey's analysis seems remarkably useful even today. Dewey's first stage is *recognizing that a problem exists*. In the classroom, we often provide obvious clues to the existence of a problem. The student who is asked to write a term paper or to solve an algebraic equation on the blackboard is often painfully aware that a problem must be solved. But in everyday life the clues can be more subtle. We need to be "tuned in" to our environment in order to recognize the existence of a problem. We need to *hear* that peculiar rattle coming from under the hood of the car, or to *see* the leaves on our favorite plant turning brown, or to *feel* the hostility of our new next-door neighbor. Although these may seem obvious examples, it is clear that some people are much more sensitive to their environment than others.

Once we recognize that a problem exists, *the problem must be clarified and defined.* This involves reducing the problem to its essentials. For example, "The problem is that if I take this new job, I'll need dependable transportation, and I don't have enough money to buy a new car. The problem is *not* with the salary I've been offered, the fringe benefits, or the working conditions." Clarification helps you get started on the right track and prevents you from wasting time on irrelevant issues.

The next stage in problem solving involves *using relevant information to formulate possible hypotheses or solutions to the problem:* "I could get a loan from the bank, use my limited savings to buy a good second-hand car, use the subway, or turn down the job offer."

Once they have been proposed, *possible solutions must be tested.* In our example, it is likely that the individual would test the alternatives through logical reasoning. He or she would specify the pros and cons of each solution and attempt to predict what the outcomes and side effects of each would be. In solving other kinds of problems, one might actually experiment, that is, try out various solutions starting with one that seems most promising.

Finally, the learner must *evaluate the solutions and draw a conclusion based on the available evidence.* It is here that the learner learns something new—the problem and its solution is understood. If, at this stage, all solutions are unsatisfactory, the learner may need to redefine the problem or generate and test other hypotheses. Certainly not all problem solving would be conducted in this way, but Dewey's analysis serves to clarify the process of problem solving.

Teaching Students to Solve Problems

Students can be taught the skills involved in problem solving, either separately or in a sequence similar to the stages we just described. However, we have insufficient data to conclude that one particular teaching method is superior to any other. One commercially available curriculum, developed by Covington, Crutchfield, Davies, and Olton

(1972), is called *The Productive Thinking Program*. It is designed to teach fifth- and sixth-graders how to identify problems, sense gaps in information, search for information, generate ideas, and test, evaluate, and revise those ideas. Students learn these skills by working through a series of programmed instructional booklets at their own pace. The content of the booklets concerns the adventures of two children, Jim and Lila, who are amateur detectives attempting to solve various mysteries with guidance from their Uncle John. Students read about the frustrations Jim and Lila encounter and the steps they take in trying to solve the problems, and at the same time are asked to join with Jim and Lila in generating strategies and solutions.

Crutchfield (1966) reported that children who worked through the *Productive Thinking Program* scored significantly higher on tests of problem solving and creativity than control children. They generated twice as many relevant questions and ideas and came up with more creative solutions to problems. If complete programs such as this are unavailable in your school, you could, of course, develop your own unit on problem solving. This would be difficult for most teachers, though, because of the complex nature of problem-solving skills and the lengthy preparation necessary for writing adequate instructional objectives.

Others have proposed a very different kind of approach to teaching thinking skills. For example, Bruner (1960) and Suchman (1961) recommend **discovery learning,** that is, teaching children to think by presenting them with interesting problems and asking them to discover solutions on their own. The role of the teacher and curriculum materials is to occasionally guide the students in their search for a solution to stimulate them to ask questions.

Theoretically, children benefit from their own discoveries, developing an appreciation of the importance of systematic analysis and the thinking through of problems. They may also experience a feeling of **insight,** the feeling that comes to you when suddenly everything falls into place and a solution appears. Discovery learning has an important role to play in education, although the amount of teacher guidance required may vary considerably from student to student and situation to situation.

For example, you could have your high school math students discover how to convert inches into metric units for themselves instead of teaching it to them. You might give them rulers with both metric and English units and suggest that they measure objects of different lengths. The students could be left on their own at that point and allowed to discover their own formula for conversion. If the students had adequately mastered all of the mathematical concepts that are prerequisite to understanding the concept of conversion, most of them would solve the problem. Used at the right times and for the right kinds of problems, discovery

learning can be an enjoyable and effective way to learn. We will further discuss the advantages and limitations of this type of learning in Chapter 10.

Teaching children to be lifelong learners requires more, however, than learning to think. That is an essential part of it, but the ability to teach oneself also requires an independence of action and a love of learning. You can encourage these in your students by giving them as much freedom to direct their own learning as they can handle, by rewarding them for independent learning, and by demonstrating love of knowledge for them. You must not simply turn them loose and exhort them to learn for the sake of learning; rather, students should be turned loose only very slowly when you sense they are ready for independence.

Encouraging Creativity

Although many people prize creativity, few know what it is. Paul Torrance (1965), a research specialist on creativity, commented that even experts can rarely agree on a precise definition for creativity. Like Torrance, we favor a commonsense definition that stresses the everyday, useful aspects of creativity, rather than limiting it to rare flashes of genius among artists and scientists. We will define **creativity** in this text, therefore, as unusual and useful solutions to problems or the production of something new and enjoyable, such as works of art. This definition emphasizes that creative acts must be both novel and beneficial.

Society places a high premium on individuals who can deal innovatively with problems and create enjoyment, but how can you encourage creativity in your classroom?

Again, Torrance (1965) recommends a commonsense approach to creativity. His research suggests that teachers can effectively encourage creativity by respecting unusual questions and novel ideas, by occasionally allowing students to try creative activities (such as conducting scientific experiments or composing poetry) without any evaluation from the teacher, and by reinforcing creative behavior. In general, this means that you should accept novel ideas without criticism, suggest that your students try out novel ideas without the threat of failure, and reward their more successful efforts.

The importance of encouragement and reinforcement is illustrated in the following study (Torrance, 1965), which might be well subtitled "What You Reinforce Is What You Get." A large group of sixth-graders were randomly assigned to two groups. Both groups were asked to write a short essay on one of ten topics assigned to them, but one group was told that a prize would be award-ed for the essay that was neatest and most grammatical, while the other was told that only originality and interest would count towards the prize. The results showed that the originality group made almost three times the number of grammatical and mechanical errors, but they also received significantly higher ratings on interest and originality.

The results of this study not only suggest ways to encourage creativity, they also tell us that your students will give you what you ask for. If you encourage memorizing and parroting, memorizing and parroting is what you will get. If, on the other hand, you reward independent and creative thinking, both you and your students may learn something new.

THE EFFECT OF CREATIVE MODELS ON STUDENTS

We have tried to portray creativity and independent problem solving in this chapter as learned skills rather than as part of an individual's native intelligence. If this is so, is creativity influenced by modeling in the same straightforward way as other behavior? Terence Belcher (1975), a psychologist at Rhode Island College, conducted a study that demonstrates the effects of modeling on creativity. Two groups of fourth- and fifth-grade children were shown videotapes of an adult model who either described novel or unimaginative uses for tin cans. Two other groups read a pamphlet on creativity or received no treatment at all. When the four groups later took the Torrance Unusual Uses Test (which asks children to think of unusual uses for common objects), the group that viewed the creative models scored significantly higher than any of the other groups. These results suggest that you can influence creative behavior in much the same way as any other type of behavior.

REVIEW 4–2

1. Describe the five stages in problem solving.

2. Discuss the design and objectives of the Productive Thinking Program.

3. What is discovery learning?

4. How can teachers encourage creativity in the classroom?

MEMORY AND TRANSFER: LEARNING TODAY WHAT WILL BE USED TOMORROW

Learning, memory, and transfer are closely related processes. When an individual learns a skill, strategy, attitude, or bit of information, something is presumably stored in the person's memory. At a later time the individual may retrieve from memory storage what he or she has learned. If the previous learning can be recalled, retention has occurred. If previous learning cannot be recalled, forgetting has occurred. Finally, if learning in one situation has some influence, either positive or negative, on learning in another situation, transfer has occurred. We will look closely at these topics, first from a historical perspective.

Methods for Studying Memory

In 1885 Herman Ebbinghaus, a German philosopher and psychologist, published the first experimental study of learning and memory. In order to measure his own memory, Ebbinghaus first made many lists, each containing thirteen **nonsense syllables,** meaningless syllables composed of three letters such as "jal," "fip," and "tek." He started with a given list, memorized it, waited for a period of time to pass, and then relearned it. He used the difference between the time required to learn the list the first time and the time required to *relearn* it as the measure of retention.

By using many lists and many retention intervals, Ebbinghaus charted the effect of passage of time on his retention of meaningless material. You can see the results in Figure 4–4. There was a sharp drop in retention shortly after learning—after twenty minutes he remembered only 58 percent of the syllables. After approximately one hour, retention was 44 percent, and after one day, 34 percent. As the retention interval increased beyond one day, there was little further forgetting. After 31 days, Ebbinghaus still remembered 21 percent of the material.

You may question the importance of this study, given that Ebbinghaus focused on nonsense syllables and used only one subject, himself. The importance of the study lies not so much in the exact percentages obtained, but in that the *shape* of Ebbinghaus' curve accurately describes how forgetting takes place. Retention varies depending on the unique abilities of the individual and the type of materials to be memorized, but in general, people forget most rapidly right after learning, and at least part of what is learned is retained for long periods of time.

Ebbinghaus' creative approach to studying memory has had a tremendous impact on subsequent research. Current researchers sometimes use other methods to measure memory (see the feature on measuring retention) and other materials besides nonsense syllables. Still, the basic methods for studying memory today are similar to those developed so long ago by Ebbinghaus. In a typical study, experimenters ask subjects to learn some verbal information or skill under specified conditions. At a later time, retention is measured and compared with retention under different conditions.

Factors Affecting Memory

The efficiency of the memory process depends on the nature of the material, how much we try to learn at one time, how we

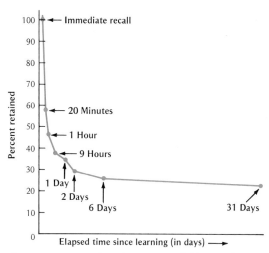

Figure 4-4. *Retention of nonsense syllables as a function of the retention interval. (After Ebbinghaus, 1964)*

organize the material and practice during learning, and what happens after we learn. Let's look more closely at some of these variables.

Overlearning.   **Overlearning** means learning beyond bare mastery. The student who repeats the Gettysburg Address over and over again, even after reciting it perfectly once, will show better retention than the student who stops practicing after one perfect recitation.

The importance of overlearning verbal information was shown in a classic study by Krueger (1929). Krueger asked his subjects to learn lists of twelve nouns under three different conditions. Under the first condition (bare mastery), they practiced the list until they could recite it once accurately. Under the second condition (50 percent overlearning), the subjects practiced the list for half as

THE MEASUREMENT OF RETENTION: THE THREE   Rs

In his famous study, Ebbinghaus used the method of relearning to measure retention. After learning a list of nonsense syllables, he waited a period of time and then relearned the list. In order to determine the percentage of the material retained or "saved" from one learning session to the next, he used the following formula:

$$\frac{\text{time for original learning} - \text{time for relearning}}{\text{time for original learning}} \times 100$$

For example, if the original learning required 10 minutes and the relearning required only 2 minutes, the formula would read:

$$\frac{10 - 2}{10} \times 100 = 80 \text{ percent retention}$$

Psychologists still use the method of relearning in studies of memory. But they also use two other methods in memory research today, methods more familiar to the classroom teacher. Recall involves measuring the extent to which one can reproduce what has been previously learned and is the method used in essay and completion tests. Recognition, on the other hand, requires only that the individual be able to identify what he or she has learned. Multiple-choice and matching tests are good examples of the recognition method.

In general, recognition is the most sensitive measure of retention and recall is the least sensitive. In other words, students might be unable to recite or write what they learned, but still be able to indicate some retention by picking out correct choices from a number of alternatives. Of course, recognition tests are not always "easier" than tests of recall. Sometimes the alternatives in a multiple-choice test are worded so poorly or are so similar that it is difficult for the student to identify the correct response.

It is impossible to say which method for measuring retention is better. Certainly recall, recognition, and relearning all have their place in education. Recall comes closest to guaranteeing that the student has learned the material. However, we simply do not expect students to be able to recall everything they have learned. We are often satisfied if students are able to recognize facts and relationships or if they are able to relearn material more efficiently at a later time.

many trials as it took to learn the list in the first place. Under the third condition (100 percent overlearning), the subjects mastered the list and then continued to practice it for as many trials as the initial learning required.

Krueger found that at retention intervals ranging from 1 to 28 days, retention was always greatest when 100 percent overlearning had occurred and least when bare mastery had occurred. Krueger also pointed out, however, that 50 percent overlearning was the most economical. Beyond a certain moderate level of overlearning, further practice does not appear to pay off in large gains.

Meaningful learning. Earlier in the chapter, we noted that it is possible to learn verbal information without understanding what you are learning or why you are learning it. This results in tedious learning. Furthermore, material learned through rote memorization is more difficult to remember than material learned in a meaningful way.

When we speak of meaningful learning, we refer to two aspects of the learning situation: the material to be learned and the response of the learner to the material. The material itself may vary in meaningfulness. In the United States, single English words (boy, table, telephone) are generally more meaningful than nonsense syllables. And English words that form a sentence (the boy is using the telephone on the table) are more meaningful than single English words. Thus, it is easier to remember poetry and prose than it is to remember lists of single words. And it is easier to remember single words than it is to remember nonsense syllables.

Nevertheless, the ways in which the learner *responds* to the material is the most important factor in influencing retention. Much of the material we ask students to learn and retain is potentially meaningful—poems, scientific principles, even isolated facts. But if students choose *not* to focus on the meaning of the material and instead learn it verbatim, meaningful learning cannot occur. Likewise, even relatively meaningless material can be made more meaningful if the student *imposes* some meaning on it.

A nice illustration of this last point is provided in a study by psychologists Raugh and Atkinson (1975) of Stanford University. These researchers wanted to develop a method for improving the retention of a foreign language vocabulary. They asked one group of subjects to learn the English translations of Spanish words by the *keyword method*. This method involved several steps. First the subjects were presented with a Spanish word such as *pato* (PAH-toh) and its English translation ("duck"). They were then given a keyword for the Spanish word. The keyword was an English word that *sounded* like all or part of the Spanish word. (The keyword for "pato" was "pot.") Finally, Raugh and Atkinson asked the subjects to form a mental image of the keyword interacting in some way with the English translation. For example, in the case of "pato" the subject might whimsically visualize a *duck* with a *pot* on its head. As you can see in Table 4–1, the keyword for *cebolla* (say-BO-yah) was "boy." In this case the subject might visualize a boy eating an onion (*onion* being the English translation of *cebolla).*

TABLE 4–1

Vocabulary Items and Keywords
Used in Teaching a Foreign Language

Spanish	Keyword	Translation
Charco	[charcoal]	Puddle
Arena	[rain]	Sand
Gusano	[goose]	Worm
Lagartija	[log]	Lizard
Rodilla	[road]	Knee
Prado	[prod]	Meadow
Cebolla	[boy]	Onion
Nabo	[knob]	Turnip
Payaso	[pie]	Clown
Trigo	[tree]	Wheat
Postre	[post]	Dessert
Chispa	[cheese]	Spark
Butaca	[boot]	Armchair
Cardo	[card]	Thistle
Carpa	[carp]	Tent

(From Raugh & Atkinson, 1975)

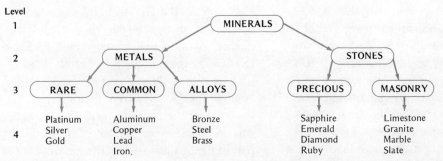

Level

1

2

3

4

Figure 4–5.   *The "minerals" conceptual hierarchy. (From Bower, Clark, Lesgold, & Winzenz, 1969)*

This may seem a cumbersome way to learn a foreign language. But Raugh and Atkinson found that subjects who used the keywords and mental imagery retained 88 percent of the words they had studied. In contrast, subjects who had simply learned the associations between the English and Spanish words in a rote manner retained only 28 percent of the words. These findings are surprising because logic tells us that the keyword group had to learn an extra association for each Spanish-English word pair. Apparently retention was enhanced because the extra associations *increased the meaningfulness of the material.* In situations such as this, you may teach keywords to your students to increase the meaningfulness of memorization; or better yet, you could encourage them to think of their own keywords so they could use the method in other situations.

It is not always necessary to make up artificial associations in order to increase meaningfulness. Sometimes material can simply be reorganized into more meaningful units and the units can be learned as clusters. A study by Gordon Bower and his colleagues shows the effectiveness of **clustering** as a memory aid (Bower, Clark, Lesgold, & Winzenz, 1969). Bower had undergraduates

memorize lists of words printed on cards. One group of subjects was shown cards, such as the one presented in Figure 4–5, with the words to be memorized (level-4 words) arranged in categories. Another group was shown the same words, but in random order. The subjects who memorized the words according to logical categories recalled two to three times as many words as those who memorized them in random order. Helping students to *see* meaning in what they are learning seems to pay off in increased retention. But, as before, you should strive to teach your students to do this on their own.

most effective

Massed versus distributed practice.   One research topic that has obvious educational implications concerns the *scheduling* of learning sessions. You may have found personally that "cramming" immediately before an examination is an ineffective way to learn or that it leads to poor retention. Psychologists refer to this as **massed practice** and have come to similar conclusions on the basis of

cramming

laboratory studies. In general, massed practice is less effective than **distributed practice,** in which practice sessions are shorter and separated by rest intervals (Underwood, 1949).

The advantages of distributed over massed practice are particularly clear when motor skills are to be learned. In an early study, Starch (1912) asked subjects to learn a coding task under differing practice conditions. The subjects were given a page of prose and a key showing each letter of the alphabet associated with a number. The coding task consisted of using the key to transcribe the prose into numbers. Although all subjects worked on the task for 120 minutes, the schedule of work times and rest intervals varied. One group of subjects (the 120-minute group in Figure 4−6) worked under conditions of massed practice, performing the entire task in one continuous sitting. The other three groups worked under conditions of distributed practice. The 10-minute group worked 10 minutes at a time, twice a day, for 6 days.

As you can see in Figure 4−6, the 120-minute massed practice group coded the fewest number of letters throughout the study, and the group with the shortest practice intervals (10 minutes) coded the most. Distributed practice in this particular motor skill facilitated performance.

The serial position effect.   We have seen that the conditions of overlearning, meaningful learning, and distributed practice lead to greater retention. But even under ideal conditions *some* forgetting is bound to take place. The human mind is simply unequipped to remember everything the individual experiences. Given this limitation, what

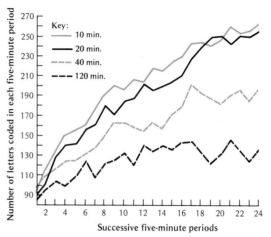

Figure 4−6.   *The effect of massed versus distributed practice on a letter-coding task. (From Starch, 1912)*

specific material is most likely to be forgotten? Psychologists have shown, for example, that subjects are more likely to remember the words that come *first* or *last* in a list. The material in the *middle* is most likely to be forgotten. This phenomenon is called the **serial position effect** (Underwood, 1949).

You can probably think of many examples of the serial position effect in your own life. If you cannot sing the entire national anthem, it is probably the middle part that you mumble through. Jensen (1962) conducted an experiment that shows how the serial position effect applies to classroom learning. He gave eighth-graders a spelling test on seven-letter words and college freshmen a test on eleven-letter words. Jensen was not interested in how many spelling errors the subjects made, but rather in the *location* of the errors within each word.

first & last material remembered; middle most likely forgotten.

HOW CAN I THINK STRAIGHT IN ALL THIS CONFUSION?

Environmental psychology is the branch of science that seeks to understand how the architectural and social environments we live in influence our behavior. A study conducted by Susan Saegert and two of her students in the Environmental Psychology Graduate Program of the City University of New York (Saegert, MacKintosh, & West, 1975) demonstrates the effects of the important environmental variable of crowding on learning and memory. Twenty-eight university students were asked to spend thirty minutes in the shoe department of a major New York City department store writing down brief descriptions of the shoes on display. Half of the students did this during a slack period of the day, while the other half wrote their descriptions during rush hour. Thirty minutes later, when the students were asked to recall characteristics of the shoes and the surrounding area, it was found that the crowded students recalled significantly less than the uncrowded ones. Perhaps the same thing happens in overcrowded or unruly classrooms.

Figure 4–7 shows that the highest percentage of errors occurred in the middle letter positions for both the eighth-graders and college freshmen. The subjects had little difficulty recalling the first and last parts of each word.

If you teach spelling, you might want to analyze your students' mistakes and compare your results with Jensen's. In general, encourage your students to overlearn the middle items in any verbal learning situation.

Theories of Forgetting

Meaningfulness is probably the single most important influence on retention. But even when meaningful learning occurs, some material is forgotten. Sometimes we are surprised to find that we have forgotten material we understood perfectly only a short time ago, but are still able to recall trivial, non-meaningful material learned in the distant past. Although psychologists have formulated many theories concerning the causes of forgetting, there is no single, easy explanation for this complex process. The theories described below each have some contribution to make to our understanding of forgetting.

Disuse theory.   According to the disuse theory, forgetting occurs when the individual fails to use what he or she has learned for some period of time. Presumably some sort of physiological memory trace is formed in the brain when learning occurs, and if this memory trace is not reactivated from time to time, it fades away. Disuse theory is one of the oldest theories of forgetting and on the surface seems reasonable. Certainly students should be encouraged to use what they have learned, to recall it periodically and apply it in new situations.

Actually, there is little experimental support for this theory. You may be able to think of examples from your own experience that are inconsistent with disuse theory. Have you ever known elderly people who had vivid memories of their childhood and adolescence, but who could not remember recent events? Have you had the experience of remembering some motor skill, such as riding a bicycle or skiing, which you had not practiced in years? Moreover, the following discussion shows that forgetting involves more than disuse.

Reorganization theory. Reorganization theory was first proposed by psychologist Frederic Bartlett in 1932 and concerns a special type of forgetting—that which occurs when one remembers part of what has been learned, but forgets many details. According to Bartlett, the memory trace does not just fade with time. It becomes changed or distorted so that we forget the details of past events and fill in the gaps with whatever makes sense to us at the present time. Inaccurate memories result because what we have learned is actively reorganized as time passes.

A study by Carmichael, Hogan, and Walter (1932) provides support for reorganization theory. These researchers showed ambiguous pictures, such as those shown in Figure 4–8, to their subjects and gave the subjects different word clues. For example, they told some subjects that the first picture looked like "curtains in a window"; others were told that it looked like "a diamond in a rectangle." Subjects were later asked to draw

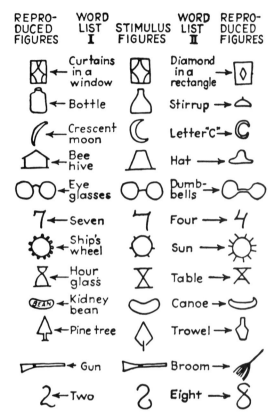

Figure 4–8. *Ambiguous drawings shown to subjects in a study that supported the reorganization theory of forgetting. (From Carmichael, Hogan, & Walter, 1932)*

what they had seen from memory. Their memories for the pictures were consistently distorted, as they reproduced figures resembling what they *thought* they had seen, rather than what they actually had seen.

Although reorganization theory is incomplete and inadequately explains certain aspects of forgetting, it provides description of a phenomenon with which we are all familiar. You will often see "reorganized" versions of what your students were supposed to remember; still, this aspect of forgetting has less relevance to the classroom than the following.

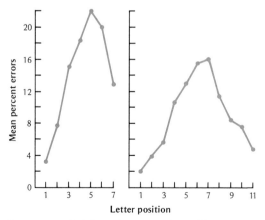

Figure 4–7. *Serial-position curves for spelling errors in 7- and 11-letter words. (From Jensen, 1962)*

Interference theory.   The theory that has the strongest experimental support attributes forgetting to interference from earlier or later learning. In other words, when asked to recall some skill or bit of information, we become confused by other skills or information we have learned.

Interference can be either retroactive or proactive. In **retroactive interference,** later learning "moves back" and interferes with the retention of earlier learning. Suppose you study for a history exam from 8:00 A.M. to 9:00 A.M. and then study for an economics exam from 9:00 A.M. to 10:00 A.M. At 10:15 A.M. you take the history exam and find that the concepts and terms for economics keep popping into your head when you need to recall the events of the American Revolution. Later learning has interfered with recalling earlier learning. What you need to do to minimize interference in this situation is to study history just before the history exam, or at least fill the time interval between studying and the exam with a different kind of activity, one that is unlikely to interfere with your recall of history. Sleeping would probably cause the least interference!

In **proactive interference,** earlier learning "moves forward" and interferes with later learning. Foreign-language students often experience proactive interference when they, for example, attempt to learn Spanish after learning French. They may be unable to recall the Spanish translation of an English word and instead recall the French translation, which they had learned at an earlier time.

Interference is greatest when the material learned is similar either to material yet to be learned or to material learned in the past. It is also greatest when the material lacks meaning for the learner. We can easily imagine that Ebbinghaus, who memorized many similar lists of nonsense syllables, encountered a great deal of interference. The implication here is that study time should be allocated so that highly similar types of learning are not practiced in close succession. In addition, interference can be minimized by engaging in meaningful, rather than in rote, learning.

The Nature of Transfer

Not only is proactive interference a cause of forgetting, it is *also* an example of **negative transfer**—what is learned in one situation has a damaging effect on what is learned in another situation. Teachers need to be alert to the possibility of negative transfer and should try to avoid it. Our concern here is with what can be done to reduce negative transfer by promoting **positive transfer.** How can we arrange instruction to increase the likelihood that learning which occurs in one situation will be helpful to the student in other situations?

Educators in the 1800s and early 1900s answered this question with the theory of **formal discipline.** According to this early theory, teachers could expect widespread positive transfer to occur as long as students were given many exercises to strengthen their "mental faculties." Educators recommended difficult subjects, such as the study of Latin and Greek, because they thought these courses would help students develop their powers of memory, reasoning, and concentration. Once these powers were de-

NOTE-TAKING: A WASTE OF TIME OR AN AID TO INCREASED RETENTION?

For many years, teachers have assumed that taking notes helps the student learn and retain the content of lectures. But we have never been very sure why this is the case. Furthermore, it can be argued that note-taking may actually *decrease* retention, since the student who is busy writing down everything the teacher says is less likely to pay attention to the *meaning* of the lecture.

What does research say about the value of note-taking? For one thing, taking notes does seem to increase retention, but the greatest increase comes if the student reviews those notes before taking a test on the content of the lecture. In one study (DiVesta and Gray, 1972), students who took notes while listening to a tape-recorded message and then reviewed those notes before taking the test retained more than students who just listened to the message. They also did better than students who took notes but were given no opportunity to review them. *One function, then, of note-taking is to provide the student with a method for storing information, so that the information can be rehearsed and recalled at a later time.*

Note-taking may also serve another function, as shown in a study by Fisher and Harris (1973). As before, students who took notes and reviewed them *again* retained more than students who took no notes or had no opportunity to review the notes they had taken. But, the most interesting finding was that students who reviewed their own notes also scored higher than students who took no notes and who were allowed to review a mimeographed copy of the lecturer's notes before the test. *Thus, note-taking in and of itself may serve an important function by leading students to reorganize and condense the lecture material*

into their own words. In transforming the lecture material, students "make it their own," increasing the meaningfulness of the material and facilitating retention (if notes serve only to provide students with a source for review, we would expect students who reviewed a copy of the *lecturer's* notes to retain as much as those who reviewed their *own* notes).

Of course the value of note-taking depends on many other factors (the quality of the notes taken, the speech rate of the lecturer, the difficulty level of the material covered, and so on). Given the experimental literature on this topic, we suggest the following *general guidelines* for using note-taking as an aid to increased retention:

(1) Before the lecture,
   encourage students to take notes, but discourage them from trying to mechanically transcribe the content of the lecture word for word.
(2) During the lecture,
   a. speak at the rate of normal speech.
   b. limit the number of new facts and concepts presented in a lecture.
   c. if the lecture material seems to be particularly difficult, divide the lecture into segments and have students record their notes *between* the segments, rather than during the lecture.
(3) After the lecture,
   a. give students time to review their notes and ask questions.
   b. encourage students to further condense and reorganize their notes as soon after class as possible.
   c. encourage students to review their notes while studying for the exam.

veloped, transfer to other disciplines and situations would occur automatically.

By the early 1900s many studies had examined this issue, and the results *did not* support the theory of formal discipline (Thorndike, 1924). Students of Latin were not superior in general reasoning abilities to students who had never studied the language. And mere practice in memorization did not increase the students' power of memory. Memory and reasoning abilities *can* be improved, but improvement does not necessarily come through the study of classical subjects. And transfer is not automatic, as the theory of formal discipline implies.

How, then, can transfer be facilitated? In *The Conditions of Learning* (1970), Gagné distinguishes between vertical and lateral transfer. In **vertical transfer,** learning in one situation allows the student to master more advanced or more complex skills in other situations. For example, students who can count and who understand the concepts of "plus" and "equal" can apply these prerequisites to learning a more complex skill — addition. *The key to promoting vertical transfer is to make sure that the students have learned the prerequisite skills.* In addition, learning should be meaningful, and the applications of current learning to later learning should be pointed out to the students. Students who do not understand what they have learned and have no idea why they have learned it will be unlikely to apply basic facts and concepts in more complex learning situations.

In **lateral transfer,** students apply what they have learned in one situation to other situations that are similar in complexity. Lateral transfer is apparent, for example, when students apply what they have learned in high-school driver's education to operating their own automobiles. It is also apparent when students use problem-solving skills acquired in school to solve real-life problems such as buying a house, choosing a job, or voting in a presidential election.

As is the case with vertical transfer, mastery of basic facts, concepts, and skills is essential for lateral transfer to occur. The student who was unable to parallel park in driver's education will probably be unable to parallel park in other situations.

Several other conditions are also important in promoting lateral transfer. *First, the original learning situation should be as similar as possible to the everyday situations in which the student will need to apply the learning.* That present-day educators recognize the importance of this principle is evident when one considers the current popularity of on-the-job vocational training, role-playing and simulation activities (such as when medical students practice diagnosing the ills of a device that simulates a body), field trips, and the like. *Second, students should be encouraged to practice applying what they have learned in a variety of slightly different contexts.* For example, home economics students should not only learn how to cook in a single classroom that resembles a real kitchen, they should practice cooking under many different conditions, using different recipes and a variety of cooking utensils. Of course it is not always possible to provide the student with a variety of "lifelike" experiences. In this case the teacher can still promote lateral transfer by pointing out possible applications and by encouraging students to anticipate situations in which they will need to recall and transfer what they are learning in school.

Positive transfer, then, is relatively easy to arrange if the above guidelines are followed. Since a primary goal of education is to provide students with skills, knowledge, and attitudes that they will use in novel situations *outside* the classroom, the concept of positive transfer is an essential one.

REVIEW 4-3

1. Describe the methods Ebbinghaus used to study memory and the results he obtained.

2. What does "overlearning" refer to?

3. What does the Raugh and Atkinson study tell us about improving meaningfulness in memorization?

4. Define "clustering" and discuss how it improves retention.

5. What is the difference between massed and distributed practice?

6. What did Jensen find regarding the serial position effect and spelling?

7. Compare the disuse theory of forgetting with the reorganization theory.

8. Define and give an example of retroactive interference.

9. Define and give an example of proactive interference.

10. How does transfer occur according to the theory of formal discipline? Has research supported the claims of its proponents?

11. Give several suggestions for promoting lateral and vertical transfer.

SUMMARY

Learning refers to any relatively permanent change in behavior that is due to experience. There are at least five different types of learning that teachers must be concerned with in the classroom: (1) First, acquisition of *verbal information* occurs when students learn facts and labels. (2) *Intellectual skills* are capabilities that allow students to deal effectively with many aspects of their environment. Concept and rule learning are types of intellectual skills. (3) *Cognitive strategies* are a special kind of intellectual skill that helps individuals manage their own thought processes during problem solving. (4) Students also learn *attitudes* in school. Experiences of success or failure and the models to which a child is exposed are critical in attitude learning. (5) Finally, *motor skills* are acquired in the classroom. They are usually learned gradually, through much practice and feedback.

Of the five types of learning, cognitive strategies are particularly important because they help the student apply knowledge systematically in solving problems. Problem solving can be seen as a five-step process: (1) recognition of the existence of a problem, (2) clarification of the problem, (3) formulation of possible hypotheses, (4) testing of the solutions, and (5) selection of the best solution. Considerable evidence indicates that students can learn efficient ways to solve problems so that they can continue to learn on their own, long after they complete formal schooling.

Learning is important, but we also want students to be able to remember what they have learned. Retention is maximized when students overlearn the material, when learning is meaningful, and when learning sessions are distributed over time. However, even under ideal learning conditions some forgetting will occur; in verbal learning situations the material in the middle is most likely to be forgotten. Psychologists are not sure how forgetting occurs. Disuse is probably one factor, as is the distortion or reorganization of memory which occurs as time passes. However, interference from other learning is the most likely cause of much forgetting.

Teachers should try to help students minimize forgetting. They should also help to maximize the likelihood that learning in one situation will transfer to other situations. Transfer does not occur automatically—we must promote it. Positive transfer is most likely to occur when the student has (1) learned prerequisite information and skills in a meaningful way, (2) learned in a situation that is similar to the situation in which the learning will be applied, (3) practiced applying the learning in a variety of contexts, and (4) anticipated future situations in which transfer will be required.

ANSWERS TO REVIEW QUESTIONS

Review 4–1

1. Defining learning as any relatively permanent change in behavior that is due to experience has three elements:

    a. We can tell that learning has taken place only when there are overt changes in behavior.

    b. Behavior may change as the result of fatigue, drugs, injury, and similar causes, but only those changes that result from experience reflect learning.

    c. Only relatively long-lasting changes in behavior are considered to reflect learning.

2. The term *retention* refers to the extent that learning is remembered over periods of time.

3. There are two types of verbal information according to Gagné, facts and labels. Labels are the names that we give to things, such as reading the letters d-o-g as "dog" or giving names to the parts of the heart on a diagram. Facts express a relationship between two bits of information, such as "Brooklyn is a borough of New York City," or "$2 \times 2 = 4$."

4. According to Gagné, the learning of verbal information is the learning of facts; whereas intellectual skills are used in other learning, such as learning how to find and use source materials in writing a term paper or using a slide rule.

5. When we learn a concept, we learn to group things together into classes on the basis of shared characteristics, even though there may be differences among the members of the class. Rules, on the other hand, are statements that tell the learner how to perform, such as "all words of the form consonant-vowel-consonant-e are pronounced with a long medial vowel and silent e."

6. A learning hierarchy is a chart that shows the relationship between the prerequisites and the knowledge or skill you want learned.

7. Cognitive strategies are types of intellectual skills that enable one to deal with situations and problems that have not previously been encountered, such as asking questions, evaluating evidence, and focusing attention.

8. Two critical aspects of attitude learning are the degree of success we experience and the models we are exposed to. If we observe models who seem to enjoy classroom learning and if we are successful in it ourselves, we will probably develop a positive attitude toward school.

9. Motor-skill learning takes place in much the same way as any other form of learning, except that it is usually more gradual and is often retained over longer periods of time.

Review 4-2

1. Dewey suggested that there are typically five stages in problem solving:
   a. Recognizing that a problem exists
   b. Defining and clarifying the problem
   c. Formulating possible solutions to the problem
   d. Testing possible solutions
   e. Reaching a conclusion

2. *The Productive Thinking Program* is an example of a highly structured program designed to teach the critical thinking skills necessary for a person to function effectively in situations in which no structure is provided, that is, to use independent problem-solving skills.

3. In discovery learning, the teacher presents the students with problems at an appropriate level of difficulty and encourages them to solve the problems on their own.

4. Teachers can encourage creativity by respecting new ideas and unusual questions, by allowing students to try out novel ideas on their own, and by reinforcing novel and useful solutions to problems.

Review 4-3

1. Ebbinghaus studied memory using himself as his only subject. He memorized lists of nonsense syllables and plotted a "curve of forgetting" that suggests that most forgetting occurs soon after learning and that information or skills remembered in this early period will be retained relatively well for long periods of time.

2. Overlearning refers to the extra learning that students do just after they have mastered material for the first time. Overlearning greatly facilitates retention in most cases.

3. The Raugh and Atkinson "keyword" technique suggests that rote learning can be improved by artificially increasing the meaningfulness of the material to be learned.

4. Clustering refers to the arrangement of the items of a list into logically related categories. This apparently facilitates retention through the improvement of meaningfulness.

5. In most cases, distributed practice in which learning is spread out over time is more effective than massed practice.

6. Jensen found that, as in research on memorizing lists of items, most spelling errors are made in the middle of words.

7. The disuse theory suggests that memory traces fade away with the passage of time; whereas the reorganization theory suggests that the traces are changed in order to make better sense.

8. Retroactive interference occurs when current learning interferes with the memory of previous learning, such as when studying for a chemistry test today interferes with our recollection of what we learned for a physics test yesterday.

9. Proactive interference involves the interference of earlier learning with the recall of later learning. For example, if you learn a list of phone numbers today, it may make it more difficult to recall a list of numbers learned tomorrow.

10. According to the theory of formal discipline, requiring students to learn subjects such as Latin and formal logic would strengthen their "mental faculties" and make the learning of other school subjects easier. Educational research has failed to support this claim.

11. In vertical transfer the learning of a basic subject facilitates the learning of a more advanced subject that is based upon it. It is facilitated by making sure that the basic subject has been mastered before going on to the more difficult one. Lateral transfer involves transfer to other learning situations of a similar level of difficulty. It is facilitated when the original learning situation is similar to the transfer situation, when learning occurs in a variety of different situations rather than just one, and when students are advised to anticipate the later situation.

Chapter 5

Learning and Motivation

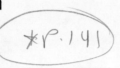

P.141

Teachers are in the business of guiding development. Our job is to see to it that children grow and learn as effectively as possible. And, while the best teachers respect healthy differences in the directions that growth and learning take, there are some ways in which we want virtually all children to develop. We want them all to learn to read, write, and calculate; we want them all to learn to live with others in society; and so on. While we must avoid choosing these directions autocratically, there are some goals, such as these, that nearly all segments of society share.

Few would dispute that the direction that growth and learning takes can be influenced to some extent by the child's environment. That a Chinese baby raised from infancy in a French home grows up speaking French and showing characteristically French behavior patterns is a good example of this point. We as teachers need to precisely understand how the environment influences behavior, so that we can sometimes intentionally change the course of growth and learning. That is to say, we need to fully understand the process of learning.

As in the previous chapter, we will define learning as any relatively permanent change in behavior that is due to experience. To this point, we have characterized learning as the storage of information in memory. Now we will expand our discussion of learning to include motivation. We will ask *why* students choose to learn what they learn or to behave in one way rather than in another. In this sense, learning includes "personality development" as well as strictly educational learning.

Over the past seventy-five years, psychologists and educators have derived several general *principles* of learning and motivation. These principles describe the relationship between events in the environment that we experience and the way these events affect our behavior. These relationships seem as reliable and as useful as any "law" in the physical sciences. And, just as the principle of moving objects developed by Newton allowed us to develop the practical techniques of mechanical engineering, so too have the principles of learning led us to develop practical and effective teaching methods. An educational program designed with these principles in mind can maximize learning, but a program that is inconsistent with the laws of learning is as likely to be effective as a rocket whose design is inconsistent with the laws of motion.

This chapter discusses the major principles of learning and gives some examples of their application. Keep in mind, however, that these are *general* principles. Later chapters discuss techniques based on these principles for use in specific situations.

POSITIVE REINFORCEMENT

The staff of the Laboratory Preschool at the University of Washington reported a case of a four-year-old girl who spent little time playing with other children (Allen, Hart, Buell, Harris, & Wolf, 1964). Her teachers designed a simple program to change this behavior. They encouraged peer play by systematically praising the child whenever she played with other children. Figure 5–1 shows the results of this program.

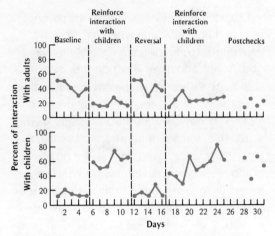

Figure 5–1. *Percentage of time spent by a preschool child interacting with adults and other children. (From Allen, Hart, Buell, Harris, & Wolf, 1964)*

Before the reinforcement program started, the child spent approximately fifteen percent of her time interacting with children and forty percent of her time with the teachers and aides. After the staff began praising her for playing with the other children, the amount of time spent with children rose to about sixty percent. In order to make sure that praise was actually responsible for the dramatic change in her behavior, the teachers discontinued praising her for social play and instead gave her attention when she was with adults. She spent much less time with the children after the teachers stopped praising her, but returned to her peers when praise was resumed. The amount of time spent with adults followed just the opposite pattern.

This example illustrates the principle of **positive reinforcement.** Each of us divides the world into things that are good, bad, or neutral. The term used in this book for "good" things is **reinforcer.** It is roughly synonymous with reward. Reinforcers may

be objects (such as money, gold stars, bicycles), things to eat (candy and cookies), or activities (such as playing basketball or having free time in school). Reinforcers are not always "pleasurable"—the opportunity to help others is a strong reinforcer for some people, even though it is not pleasurable in the traditional sense. Nor are the same things reinforcing to all people. There is, in fact, tremendous variability in this fundamental aspect of human personality. Some children can be reinforced by a scolding, while others find green peppers more rewarding than candy.

The principle of positive reinforcement states that when any behavior is followed by a reinforcer, that behavior will strengthen. In the example above, social interaction was followed by praise to the child and, as a result, social play increased. It is important to give the reinforcer to the child *soon* after the response occurs and to ensure that the reinforcer be made *contingent* upon the behavior. That is, the reinforcer should be presented consistently just after the target behavior occurs and should never be given when it does not occur.

The following classroom experiment gives us another good example of the principle of positive reinforcement (Kirby & Shields, 1972). Tom, a thirteen-year-old boy, attended the laboratory school at Humbolt State College in California. He scored in the normal range on intelligence tests, but did poorly in school largely because he was inattentive and worked very slowly. To increase his rate of working arithmetic problems, he was placed in a positive reinforcement program. For several days a teacher gave Tom a page

The teacher then asked Tom to work only two problems at a time and turn them in for correction. The teacher immediately graded the problems and strongly praised Tom when he answered correctly ("Great! You got them both right"). This procedure of grading and praising two problems at a time was repeated throughout the twenty-minute work period for two days. On the third day, the teacher asked Tom to complete four problems. On later days he was asked to complete eight problems, then sixteen. During this phase, the number of problems Tom completed correctly rose to 1.5 per minute, a gain of 300 percent. At the same time, the percentage of time he spent attending to his work rose from 50 to 100 percent during the reinforcement phase. As Figure 5–2 shows, the rate of correct responses fell when the reinforcement was discontinued for experimental reasons, but rose again when it was reinstituted.

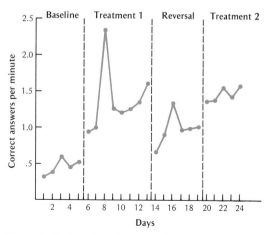

Figure 5–2. *Number of correct arithmetic answers per minute during the four phases of the experiment. (From Kirby & Shields, 1972)*

of multiplication problems and asked him to turn them in solved at the end of a twenty-minute work period. The teacher corrected and returned the problems the next day without comment in order to get an accurate picture of Tom's baseline rate of solving arithmetic problems. During this period, Tom correctly finished an average of one-half problem per minute.

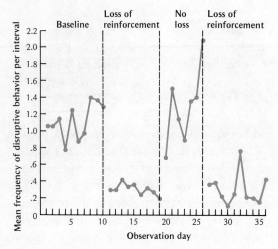

Figure 5–3. *Average number of disruptive behaviors by students in a psychiatric hospital school. (After Kaufman & O'Leary, 1972)*

LOSS OF REINFORCEMENT

The principle of positive reinforcement describes one way in which you can manipulate the classroom environment to strengthen a desirable behavior. The principle of **loss of reinforcement,** on the other hand, indicates how you can manipulate reinforcers to *decrease* the frequency of *undesirable behaviors.* The following example illustrates this principle.

A team of psychologists at the State University of New York at Stony Brook recently studied the use of loss of reinforcement in managing the disruptive behaviors of students in a psychiatric hospital school (Kaufman & O'Leary, 1972). The students in this school were adolescents with histories of deviant behavior, academic deficiencies, and high rates of disruptive classroom behavior. Though they were a group that was considerably more difficult to teach than most teachers will face, what we can learn from

this study is applicable to most regular classrooms.

During a ten-day baseline period, disruptive behavior occurred every twenty seconds on the average. These behaviors included being out of seat, talking, hitting, and so on. During the experimental phase, each student received ten plastic tokens (they were allotted to the students but kept at the teacher's desk to avoid stealing, throwing, etc.). The students could later exchange these tokens for candy, games, cosmetics, and so on, at the rate of one token per one cent of merchandise. About every fifteen minutes, the teacher went to each student's desk and told him or her that tokens had been deducted for rule infractions that had occurred during that period. If no infractions had occurred, the students were told that their total remained the same. The students got to buy merchandise only with their remaining tokens at the end of the class. As Figure 5–3 shows, this procedure reduced the frequency of disruptions from one every 20 seconds to one every 100 seconds, still a high rate, but much improved for this population.

Thus, the principle of loss of reinforcement states that a behavior will weaken if its occurrence consistently leads to the loss or elimination of reinforcers. Later (see Chapters 12 and 13), we will discuss a variety of useful classroom techniques based on this principle.

PUNISHMENT

The term **punishment** is used here in an everyday sense. There are many things in the environment that will weaken a behavior when they consistently follow that behavior.

Spanking a child for running into the street is a common example. Psychologists call these bits of the environment *aversive stimuli*. It is well to keep in mind that different things are aversive to different individuals and in different circumstances. A scolding may be punishing in some situations and reinforcing in others. And, just as all reinforcers are not pleasurable, many aversive stimuli are not "painful." A quietly spoken "no" can be very aversive (but, unfortunately it can often have just the opposite effect).

Physical or other strong forms of punishment are only rarely necessary or desirable in the classroom. They can only be justified in circumstances when other procedures have failed or when the behavior is so dangerous or so disturbing that it must be quickly eliminated. But, even in these cases, extensive consultation with other responsible individuals, especially the parents, would be required. Frequently this ethical requirement is required by law.

An unusual case in a Florida public elementary school provides an example of an apparently justified use of punishment (Lahey, McNees, & McNees, 1973). One of the teachers requested help from a psychologist to deal with a twelve-year-old who swore repeatedly, had facial twitches, and jerked his head at the rate of 150 times per hour. The boy resembled a few other cases reported in the psychological literature in which otherwise normal adults "involuntarily" blurted out obscenities. The boy had repeatedly been seen by physicians and psychologists, without improvements in his behavior. His parents were so embarrassed by his bizarre behavior that, except for school, they had kept him from outside activities for two years.

After consultation with the parents and other professionals, it was decided to use a form of punishment to reduce the frequency of this behavior. This was a serious step and was taken only because of the severity of the problem and because all previous treatments failed. The decision to use punishment is similar to the dentist's decision to use a drill or to the surgeon's decision to use a scalpel. It is sometimes necessary to do something unpleasant to correct a condition that is far more unpleasant. The method chosen, however, was believed the least aversive procedure that would be effective.

The teacher told the child that every time he said an obscene word he would be asked to leave the classroom and sit in a "timeout" room for a minimum of five minutes (five minutes plus one minute without shouting an obscenity in the room). The timeout room was a large, well-lighted closet that only contained a chair. The child had shown no signs of having a fear of being left alone in a closed room.

From then on, *each and every time* the child said an obscene word, he was placed in the timeout room and the door was locked. At first the teacher walked the child to the room every time he said an abscene word; later he only needed to be told to go. On a few occasions, however, she had to drag the child into the timeout room. The teacher was careful on these occasions to avoid saying anything to the child, especially a scolding, and even to avoid eye contact. She did this to avoid the possibility of accidentally reinforcing the child's bad behavior with her attention. The most effective reinforcer for disruptive behavior, unfortunately, is often just getting the teacher mad.

After three days of punishment, the number of times the boy swore fell sharply from more than 150 per hour to fewer than 15 per hour. During these first few days, the teacher spent a considerable amount of time sending the child back and forth from the timeout room, but the procedure quickly produced a noticeable improvement in the child. On the fifteenth day of punishment, the teacher stopped enforcing the contingency without saying anything to the child. There was little change in his behavior at first, but the frequency of obscenities shot up to 135 per hour on the second day of no punishment. Since this was partly an experimental program, it would have been desirable to extend this period for several days to observe the child's behavior without punishment. For ethical and pragmatic reasons, however, the teacher quickly reinstated punishment. The child's rate of tics and obscenities fell again rapidly and was at zero within five days. Since the behavior rarely occurred thereafter, the teacher was able to keep punishment in effect with little effort on her part. Figure 5–4 shows the results of the teacher's procedure.

The use of punishment in this case provided a successful and seemingly justifiable solution to a child's serious problem. Psychologists still disagree as to the advisability of punishment in less extreme situations, however. This is especially true for the question of physical punishment in childrearing. Some feel it is sometimes necessary; others feel it is not. This disagreement is largely based on two points. First, people *do not like* to be controlled by punishment. The child who is kept at his or her work by the threat of punishment will probably learn to dislike school. Second, some studies show that punishment, especially when it involves aversive stimuli that are physically painful, has several negative side effects. Punishment often causes the child to be aggressive, to dislike the person who administers the punishment, to become inflexible, and to cease engaging in behaviors similar to those punished even though they may be desirable (Bandura, 1969). The child who is ridiculed for reading poorly, for example, may yell back, ridicule other children, dislike and avoid the teacher, and refuse to read at all.

These potential side effects may turn out to be more a product of the method of administration rather than of the punishment itself. But until we know more about punishment, they must be kept in mind. We should also remember that the most dangerous side effect of all may involve the punisher. When punishment succeeds in eliminating an annoying behavior in a child, the punisher may be encouraged to use it in future cases of the child's bad behavior. This could lead the adult to use punishment more frequently and might be a major factor in the origin of some forms of child abuse.

For these reasons, and for other legal and ethical reasons, teachers rarely need to use any of the stronger forms of punishment. Most teachers rely heavily, however, on *verbal* punishment to maintain classroom control ("Don't do that! How many times do I have to ask you to stop that!"), usually without much success. The frequent use of criticism by teachers probably *causes* more misbehavior than it stops, and children certainly

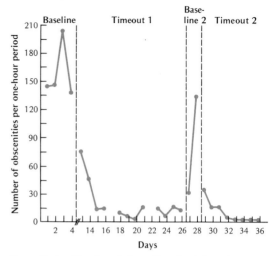

Figure 5–4. *Number of obscenities shouted per hour. (After Lahey, McNees, & McNees, 1973)*

do not like to be controlled by punishment of any type. Fortunately, all forms of punishment can usually be replaced with positive forms of discipline that are more desirable and considerably more successful.

In those rare cases when teachers must use punishment, they should also positively reinforce desirable behaviors that can take the place of the punished behavior. This will make the punishment procedure more effective and will likely reduce the negative side effects.

such as physical education class or public speaking, because of their whining complaints are being *taught* to be whiners. Children who are let out of staying after school because of their apologies and their promises to be good are not being taught to stop the behaviors they were punished for; they are being taught to weasel out of unpleasant things.

The principle of negative reinforcement, like the preceding three principles of learning, describes ways in which behavior changes as a result of what *follows* the behavior. These four principles, then, specify the ways in which the consequences of a behavior can influence its future occurrence. The following diagram illustrates the relationship between these four principles.

	Reinforcer	Aversive
Behavior makes it happen	Positive reinforcement (increase)	punishment (decrease)
Behavior removes it or prevents it from happening	loss of reinforcement (decrease)	negative reinforcement (increase)

NEGATIVE REINFORCEMENT

If a behavior consistently terminates something aversive or prevents it from occurring, that behavior will increase in strength. This effective way of modifying behavior is termed **negative reinforcement.** It is probably not justifiable in the classroom for ethical reasons, but you must be careful that you do not inadvertently strengthen unwanted behavior in this manner. Children who are let out of something that is aversive to them,

If a behavior leads to reinforcement, that behavior will be strengthened (positive reinforcement). If the behavior causes something aversive to happen, on the other hand, it will be weakened (punishment). If a behavior causes a reinforcer to be removed or prevented from occurring, that behavior will be weakened (loss of reinforcement), but if something aversive is removed or prevented from occurring by the behavior, it will be strengthened (negative reinforcement). Collectively, these four types of be-

havior-change principles are termed **operant** ✳
conditioning.

MODELING

We have a strong tendency to imitate each other's behavior. The procedure of intentionally presenting desirable behavior to others in hopes that they will imitate it is called **modeling.** The following are examples of classroom applications of the principle of modeling.

A research psychologist from the University of Illinois used a simple modeling procedure to produce rapid and pronounced changes in the behavior of "withdrawn" children (O'Connor, 1969). Preschool teachers frequently encounter children who stand timidly away from other children and shy away from normal interactions. One way to encourage these social isolates is to systematically reinforce social behavior and not reinforce withdrawn behavior. But this is a time-consuming procedure. The same goal was reached in this classroom experiment by showing a group of withdrawn children a film of a child watching a group of children at play. At first the child stayed at a distance, but gradually joined more and more into the fun of the interaction. Figure 5–5 shows that the group of children who watched this film engaged in social interactions more than five times as frequently after the film than before, while a matched group of isolates who did not see the film remained the same. Comparison with a normal group of children showed that the children who viewed the film rose to a level of social participation that was higher than the average for the normal group. This represents rapid improvement with little expenditure of the teacher's time. Films of this

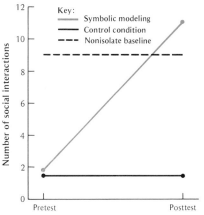

Figure 5–5. *Number of social interactions before and after viewing film of model. (From O'Connor, 1969)*

type, which deal with eliminating common behavior problems through modeling, are becoming more widely available through commercial sources as demand increases.

Another experimental demonstration of the effectiveness of modeling gives us a look at a different use of the principle. Administrators of a preschool program for children from low-income families decided to increase the use of adjectives in their young students' descriptions of objects and situations. A simple modeling technique was designed for this purpose (Lahey, 1971). The children were shown a series of eight colored boxes that each contained arrangements of several toys. The toys were colored differently and arranged in groups of one, two, or three identical toys. The teacher first asked each child to describe the contents of the first box, and then he described the contents in the second box. The child and the teacher alternated describing the toys in a similar fashion until the child had described four

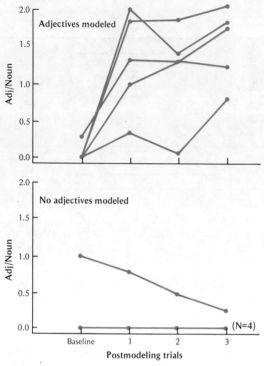

Figure 5–6. *Number of adjectives per noun used by children who heard adjectives modeled and by children who did not. (From Lahey, 1971)*

boxes. For one group of children, the teacher used adjectives of color and number in his descriptions ("I see two red cars, a green spoon, three black horses, and a blue cup."). In the other group, he used no descriptive adjectives in his descriptions ("I see some cars, a spoon, some horses, and a cup."). Figure 5–6 shows the effect of the teacher's modeling of descriptive adjectives. There was a marked increase for the five children who heard adjectives modeled, but there was no increase for the five children who did not hear them.

Modeling has still not been fully utilized in the classroom, but it can be useful with a wide variety of teaching and classroom management problems at all age levels. What the teacher can learn from this principle is that children often learn from what they see others doing. A bored, critical teacher can be a negative influence on children, while an enthusiastic, sympathetic teacher can be a good influence. As we will see in Chapter 8, however, the teacher is just one of the individuals that students imitate. Peers, parents, and the rest of society provide a variety of models for the student.

STIMULUS PAIRING

Psychologists call an object or event in the environment a **stimulus.** Stimuli can be reinforcing or aversive; they can cause behaviors to occur, influence ongoing behavior, or they can have no function at all ("neutral stimuli"). To the infant, most stimuli are neutral, but they acquire significance through learning. The function of any stimulus can transfer to any previously neutral stimulus if they are consistently *paired* (if they occur together). For example, if a teacher's praise has little reinforcement value for his or her children, it can be enhanced by frequently saying "good" or "that's right" while handing out reinforcers (food, tokens exchangeable for free time, etc.). This will pair the teacher's praise with the reinforcer and strengthen the reinforcement function of the teacher's praise. But, this principle can work against the teacher if he or she is unaware of it. For example, if cheating always stops when the teacher stands up (standing up is a stimulus to the students that stops cheating) and if the teacher always closes a book just before standing up (a stimulus that was neutral with respect to the behavior of cheating), the students will stop cheating when the book closes and never get caught. Their cheating will be stopped by a previously neutral stimulus because it was paired with a stimulus that had the function of interrupting cheating.

It is perhaps most important to understand the concept of stimulus pairing in dealing with emotional reactions to stimuli. The things that frighten us, anger us, or even reward us are often learned through stimulus pairing. John B. Watson and Rosalie Rayner (1920) provided an excellent example of this in their classic study of "Little Albert" discussed in Chapter 2. In this experiment a young boy was shown a white rat, which he initially found interesting and amusing. After Albert had looked at the rat for a moment, he was intentionally frightened by a loud noise, which produced an equally loud emotional reaction. Later, he was shown the rat several more times and each time the loud noise was paired with it. Watson and Rayner soon found that Albert was frightened by the white rat by itself in the same way that

A GOOD MEMORY: IT MAY RUB OFF ON OTHERS

As you learned in Chapter 4, there are many factors that contribute to efficient memorization and recall. One is the way that information is organized as it is being learned. For example, in memorizing lists of digits, it is better to group the digits into clusters than to learn them as individual units (282-379-121, rather than 2-8-2-3-7-9-1-2-1). The results of a study conducted by psychologists at California State University in San Diego indicate that students can be taught to use efficient grouping strategies simply by watching a model do so. A group of forty first- and second-graders and forty seventh- and eighth-graders were asked to memorize several series of digits after watching a videotaped model do the same. Half the subjects watched the model group digits, while the other half saw the model recall digits as strings of individual items. The group that watched the model use the efficient grouping strategy recalled digits more accurately when they were tested later. Their memory for digits was better because they had observed an efficient use of a memorization strategy. Could you apply the findings of this study in your classroom? (Franzini, Litrownik, & Choisser, 1973) he was frightened by the loud noise, even though he initially reacted to the rat in a positive way. Albert learned to fear the rat through stimulus pairing. Many similar emotional reactions have been learned by our students, and by ourselves.

STIMULUS REPETITION

A stimulus presented repeatedly or presented for a prolonged period of time will lose some or all of its stimulus function. This is a phenomenon that we know from common experience; we would rarely watch television if there were only one program, and even children eventually get enough ice cream. This simple principle, however, can be extremely useful in the classroom. For example, public speaking is an activity that produces fear in many children. It is a fear that can be lost, however, simply by giving a number of public talks. This is the principle of stimulus repetition in action. When we are repeatedly placed before an audience to give a talk, that stimulus will gradually lose its stimulus function (its ability to produce "fear": sweating, trembling, stammering, and forgetting).

This is an effective remedy for a fear of public speaking, but those of us who have taken it remember that it is also an unpleasant one. A variation on this treatment that is at least as effective and considerably more pleasant involves presenting the fear-producing stimulus in *gradually* larger doses. The

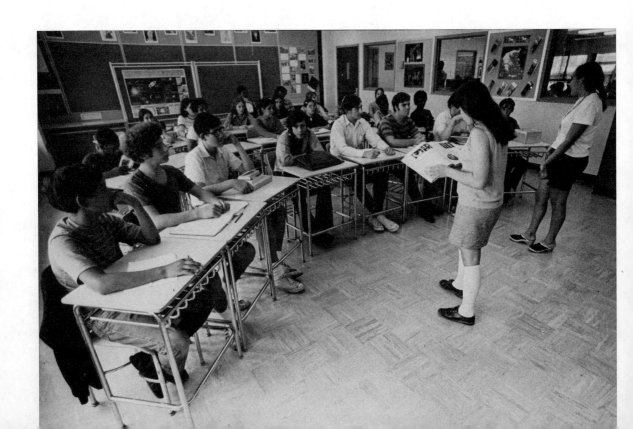

teacher might ask the child at first to give a short talk in front of the teacher alone, then the teacher plus one good friend, then a few more classmates, and so on until the child fearlessly speaks in front of the whole class. If the child begins to show fear at one of these steps, he or she could go back a few steps and begin the sequence again. The gradualness of the process is the key in applying this form of the principle to the classroom. When appropriately carried out, this procedure gives us an effective tool for painlessly reducing undesirable fears.

This principle can be applied to the fears of children (ones that may have been learned through stimulus pairing), but its proper use can often be tricky and complicated. Furthermore, since many educators consider the elimination of fears to be outside the domain of a teacher's normal duties, it should only be attempted after consultation with parents and under the supervision of qualified professionals.

Keep in mind that this principle, like all of the others we have discussed, can work against you if you are careless. Teachers who never change the format of their lectures will find that they will soon lose their ability to command their students' attention, and teachers who never vary their reinforcers may see them lose some or all of their value. Since the laws of behavior are always operating, we must plan our educational programs carefully so that we will be using these principles rather than fighting against them.

REVIEW 5–1

1. List and define the seven principles of learning described in this chapter.

2. List the potential negative side effects of punishment.

3. How could you accidentally use the principle of modeling to teach something that you do not want your students to learn?

After mastering these questions, review the examples to see how they illustrate the principles.

ADDITIONAL CONCEPTS IN LEARNING

The seven principles of learning discussed above describe some of the better understood ways in which the environment influences behavior. The following two concepts are related to most of these principles and increase their significance considerably.

Stimulus Control   => positive reinforcement

A stimulus can gain such decisive control over our behavior that we may tend to behave in one way in its presence and a different way in its absence. If, for example, a child only engages in disruptive behavior when the teacher is on the far side of the room, the child's disruptive behavior is under the stimulus control of the teacher's proximity. This is not to say that the child is "forced" to behave badly when the teacher is on the other side of the room, but only that the child's disruptions are more likely when the teacher is far away.

Stimulus control can be desirable and is, in fact, the aim of most education. For example, we want the child to learn to say "dog" in the presence of some stimuli (the word *dog*, pictures of dogs, etc.), and we want the child to do gymnastics when asked to do so, but not when asked to study.

In the classroom, you can teach stimulus control by using all but one (stimulus repetition) of the seven principles of behavior change. Your choice of a procedure will depend partly on what kind of stimulus control you need to teach and partly on convenience. Probably the most powerful and useful procedure for teaching stimulus control is reinforcing the child for desirable responses to a stimulus (saying "four" to "what is two plus two?") and not reinforcing undesirable responses. This is probably the teacher's most frequent task. When we said earlier that the teacher should see to it that the child speaks and writes often and that the teacher should give prompt feedback and reward in responses, this is what we meant. If this is done, the probability of a correct response to each question will increase rapidly.

You can also effectively teach through modeling by having the model exhibit the desired behavior in the presence of the appropriate stimulus, but not in the presence of other stimuli. For example, when Kermit the Frog says "one" to a picture of the number on "Sesame Street," his viewers are learning to make the same response to the same stimulus. This is a largely unexplored method of teaching stimulus control, but apparently a very important one.

The principle of stimulus pairing has some important applications in the teaching of stimulus control in some simple, but frequently used ways. Teachers use this principle whenever they hold up the letter "A" and pronounce its name, then hold up the letter "B" and say its name. By pairing the different names with the different letters, a discrimination among the letters is being taught (for best learning, however, the teacher will need to let the children practice the names while giving them appropriate feedback and reinforcement).

Extinction

When reinforcement consistently follows a behavior, the behavior will be strengthened. If, however, reinforcement is discontinued, that behavior will usually be weakened. The same holds true for any of the principles of learning we have just discussed. If the source of the behavior change is removed, the behavior will tend to return to its original state. In the case of punishment, for example, if a behavior is no longer punished, it will tend to return to its original strength (unless, for example, some other behavior has been reinforced to take its place). In the case of modeling, the newly learned behavior will return to its original reduced strength if the model no longer models it.

The following report provides a good example of the extinction of a positively reinforced response (Hall, Fox, Willard, Goldsmith, Emerson, Owen, Davis, & Porcia, 1971). It is an especially informative example in that the behavior that was extinguished was inadvertently "taught" to the student while the teacher thought he was punishing the behavior.

Mike was a fifteen-year-old boy who had been paralyzed since birth from the waist down and attended a junior high school class for the "educable mentally retarded." He argued frequently with the teacher over assignments and was described as "self-centered, belligerent, and spoiled." The psychologist who consulted with his teacher suspected that the teacher was unintentionally reinforcing Mike's disputes by arguing back and giving critical attention to his behavior. He suggested that the teacher try to remove any possible source of reinforcement for the behavior in hopes that it could be extinguished.

After a ten-day baseline period, which was used to obtain an accurate measure of the frequency of the behavior, the teacher changed his reactions to Mike's disputes. Whenever Mike argued with him, failed to carry out a request within ten seconds, or shook his head negatively while discussing assignments, the teacher stopped the conversation and walked to another part of the room. Whenever Mike followed the teacher's instructions to begin an assignment without a dispute, however, the teacher made a positive statement to or about him. As you can see in Figure 5–7, the frequency of disputes dropped dramatically when the teacher ignored them and praised compliance. In this example, extinction was a useful process. Instead of using punishment or loss of reinforcement to reduce Mike's disruptive behavior, the teacher simply removed its source (his inadvertent reinforcement).

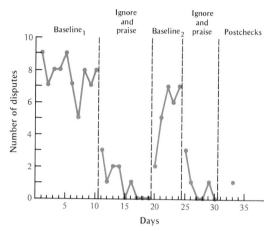

Figure 5–7. *Number of disputes between Mike and the teacher during the four experimental phases and a follow-up. (From Hall, Fox, Willard, Goldsmith, Emerson, Owen, Davis, & Porcia, 1971)*

Understanding the concept of extinction exactly doubles the significance of the seven principles of learning. Not only can a behavior be changed by using these seven principles, but in certain cases the teacher can also eliminate an undesirable behavior by removing its source. Extinction can, however, be undesirable as well. Often a desirable behavior will be taught and then lost when the source of the change is removed. In the cases reported in Figures 5–1 through 5–4, for example, the desirable behavior changes were lost during the periods of time in which the sources of those changes were temporarily removed. Unless studiously avoided, this can be a frequent occurrence in the classroom.

Because extinction is an unreliable phenomenon, it may not occur in every case. Whether this is desirable or not depends on whether you *want* the behavior to extinguish. Often you may not want a newly learned pattern of behavior to extinguish. For example, if you have spent nine months reinforcing a child for speaking in front of the class, you would not want that new behavior to extinguish in the next teacher's class. If the next teacher fails to reinforce the behavior (most teachers would automatically reinforce this to some extent), you will have to *protect* it from extinction. You can do this by gradually reducing the frequency and consistency with which you reinforce the behavior after it has been well learned. When you are first teaching a new behavior, you should reinforce it every time (or as much as you can). But, later you should not reinforce it every time or even in a consistent manner. [Gradually, reinforcement should become infrequent and random. This makes the response more resistant to extinction than if you drop reinforcement abruptly. You will also get fewer emotional reactions from students if you discontinue reinforcement gradually.] (In either case, however, when you decide to end reinforcement, do not reinforce your students by giving in to them if they get upset and ask you to reinstate reinforcement. If you do give in to them, your problems may just be beginning!)

REVIEW 5–2

1. Define extinction. Give two examples of it.
2. What are some of the factors that influence extinction?
3. Define stimulus control. Give two examples of it.

MOTIVATION

We sometimes ask why students do not behave as we think they should. Sometimes the answer we reach is that the children *cannot* behave appropriately. For example, we may decide that children who function intellectually at a very low level cannot be taught to do certain types of mathematics—it is beyond the limits of their behavioral repertoires. Another conclusion we frequently reach is that the child *does not know how* to behave appropriately. For instance, we may decide that a very disruptive child has never been taught to work quietly or to follow instructions, or that a very withdrawn child has had insufficient opportunities to learn how to interact with other children.

A third explanation we often accept is that although the child can behave appropriately and has learned to do so, he or she is simply not *motivated* to do so. For example, we may decide that a group of children who leave their math assignments unfinished do so because they dislike math, do not care if they receive a good grade, dislike the teacher, or are more interested in getting the attention of other children by showing off than in gaining the approval of the teacher. The motives of children are difficult to understand and to deal with properly. Yet in a very important sense, effective learning cannot take place unless students are "motivated" to learn. This section, therefore, will attempt to explain children's motives and to provide you with a strategy for dealing with them.

Types of Motivation

Intrinsic motives.   Do children have a natural motivation to learn? Many educators from

Plato to Piaget assumed that they do, and that there is something intrinsic to or included in the act of learning that automatically rewards children. Considerable evidence exists to support this point of view, surprisingly coming from studies of animals. Psychologist Harry Harlow, for example, learned long ago that monkeys who were housed in sterile and uninteresting laboratory cages spent long hours taking apart and reassembling mechanical puzzles (Harlow, Blazek, & McClearn, 1956). He also found that monkeys learned to press levers in order to open a window that let them see other monkeys, television sets, or electric trains. Berlyne (1950) found that even mice have a strong tendency to explore novel areas when part of their environment changes. Animals will look, manipulate, and learn without external rewards, especially when there is little stimulation in their environment.

Can we conclude from this information that children have a natural motivation to learn? The best answer to this question seems to be both "yes" and "no." Anyone who observes young children at play knows that they spend a great deal of time engaged in exploring and learning activities for which there are no apparent rewards. Much early learning seems to stem just from the child's natural tendency to push, pull, and fidget with everything in his or her environment (Bijou & Baer, 1965). Why is it, then, that we ever have trouble getting children to learn? Educators who emphasize the importance of intrinsic motivation suggest it is because adults *inhibit* the natural tendency of children to learn through their emphasis on formal regimented learning. Educators with this point of view see traditional

intrinsic motives stifled w/ formal regimented learning

THE ROLE OF POSITIVE REINFORCEMENT IN THE OPEN CLASSROOM

B. F. Skinner is America's leading advocate of positive reinforcement in the classroom and is also a leading critic of punishment. Research over the last two decades showing the effectiveness of positive reinforcement has led many advocates of open and humanistic education to loudly protest Skinner's view. They fear that we are developing such effective methods of controlling behavior that we may rob our children of both their freedom and their dignity. In the following quotes, Peter Madden (1970), who is a leading proponent of open humanistic education, develops an alternative view in which he sees Skinner and open education as allies.

"Some new teachers in open classrooms attempt a more passive role in which they offer a variety of attractive and interesting activities without giving children any sense of direction from above. These teachers refuse to use reinforcement because they view it as an imposition upon the students' freedom to pursue activities for their own intrinsic satisfaction. Unfortunately, the result is often chaotic classroom behavior. The children may respond to this situation by turning elsewhere in the environment for gratification, often to peers who tend to reward playing or similar behavior which provides instant and continuous reinforcement. . . .

"What these teachers apparently failed to understand was that control is not a process to be avoided but a tool which must be exercised in either a positive or a negative way. Having refused to systematically help children adapt to change through supportive means of control like positive reinforcement, they even-

tually had to regress to the traditional forms of structure and punishment, or negative reinforcement. . . .

"Advocates of freedom, says Skinner, have traditionally dealt with these individuals by stating that they have the right to behave in any manner they wish *if* they are willing to abide by the consequences of their actions. Proponents of dignity add that to take away an individual's option to behave as he wishes if he will be held accountable infers that he loses the right to be 'good' of his own accord. However, almost no one feels that freedom and dignity can or should be allowed to operate without accountability. For this reason, all the traditional aversive rituals and punishments are maintained despite their lack of effectiveness in dealing with individuals who abuse others in society while exercising their own freedom. . . .

"Skinner suggests that a greatly increased, well-organized use of positive reinforcement techniques may be the only way to reconcile any society's need for control with the individual's desire for freedom from aversive or punishing contingencies.

"In the schools, this means a virtual abandonment of the kinds of threats and punishments so familiar to every teacher and student. Teachers must develop new powers of observation and learn to note, record, and reward the good things children do rather than swoop down with vengeance upon their errors. The classroom atmosphere must become positive and loving, drawing out desired behavior with encouragement and rewards rather than stressing and punishing failure. While this sounds idyllic, it is a mere technical skill, part of Skinner's 'technology of be-havior.' After learning how to operate this way, teachers often respond, 'Why, that is nothing more than common sense.' Positive reinforcement may be merely common sense but in few classrooms today is it common practice! . . .

"If teachers view freedom of choice and self-direction as skills to be learned in small, sequential, reinforced steps rather than as the natural condition of American schoolchildren today, they find the path to creating and maintaining an open classroom much easier. . . .

"The effect is circular in operation. Positive reinforcement techniques will make possible the creation of an open classroom while the operation of the open classroom will, in itself, minimize the negative effects of control. The result can and should be the development of a humane classroom culture in which each child can learn not only to be free and inde-pendent but how to reconcile the demands of social living upon freedom." (pp. 103–106)

schools with structured curricula as special villains. This position suggests that when children are placed in loosely structured educational environments that respect their natural tendency to learn, learning will take place at its maximal rate.

As already discussed in Chapters 1 and 2, when we discussed open education and the unfolding view of development, this ap-proach to education is an old one, but it has recently been in vogue. Still, there is little data available with which to evaluate its ef-fectiveness. Reports from schools based on this philosophy, however, suggest that when children are allowed to learn *only* when they want to learn, little academic learning takes place (Neil, 1960).

The following statement by Gagné and Briggs (1974) on the topic of open education is particularly cogent:

Systematically designed instruction can greatly affect individual human development. There are hints in some educational writings (e.g., Frieden-berg, 1965; Silberman, 1970) of a belief that edu-cation would perhaps be best if it were designed simply to provide a nurturing environment in which the child and youth were allowed to grow up in his own way, without the imposition of any plan for the direction of his learning. We consider this line of thinking to be mistaken. Unplanned and undirected learning, we believe, is almost certain to lead to the development of individuals who are in one way or another incompetent to derive personal satisfaction from living in our society of today and tomorrow. A fundamental reason for instructional design is to insure that no one is "educationally disadvantaged," that everyone has an equal opportunity to use his individual talents to the fullest degree. (p.5)

In its less extreme form this approach has much to offer to educators, nonetheless. In-trinsic rewards in spontaneous learning can be enhanced by creating interesting and ex-citing learning circumstances, but there also are limitations in self-directed and self-moti-vated learning. Studying geometry theorems can be a terrific way to spend the afternoon for some children, but other children may need guidance and external rewards for learning them, while virtually every child will need some encouragement to practice basic arithmetic skills.

SELF-DETERMINATION OF REINFORCEMENT STANDARDS BY CHILDREN

What happens when children set their own standards for reinforcement? The teacher can set a reasonable standard, such as "You will get fifteen minutes free time when you have correctly answered all of the problems on pages seven through nine." But would children just let themselves off easy: "I get two hours free time for doing this problem." Some would, of course, but the performance of most children may surprise you. Confirming a number of recent studies, Felixbrod and O'Leary (1974) found that third-graders get as much work done when they set their own standards for reinforcement as when the teacher sets them. You might try this under some circumstances as a way of involving students in their own education.

Extrinsic motives. In contrast, it is abundantly clear that extrinsic or external rewards can be used to motivate children. Praise, raisins, and free time are a few examples. Teachers who succeed in motivating their students not only have the ability to make learning exciting, they also have a wide variety of external rewards at their command. It is particularly important to remember, however, that different children respond in different ways to the same rewards. If we are going to achieve enjoyable, efficient learning for all children, we must remember to individualize rewards as well as instruction.

Understanding Motivation

The following suggestions may be useful in dealing with students' motivation.

Understand motives in terms of the rewards for which a student is willing to work.
Consider the following situation: Two children misbehave during their second-period class. Whenever these children misbehave, their teacher reacts with shouts and criticism. In discussing this problem with other teachers, the teacher learns that although the children had been disruptive in their classrooms at the beginning of the year, they had settled down soon after. Searching for a solution, the teacher asked the other teachers how they reduced the disruptive behaviors. They replied that they simply ignored the children when they were disruptive and gave them positive attention when they were quiet. Being desperate, the second-period teacher decided to try the same approach. At first, little happened, but after ignoring the disruptive behaviors for a few weeks, they began to drop in frequency.

In such a situation, one can conclude that the teacher's attention, even though it was critical, was a reward for the disruptive behavior. Without intending to, the second-period teacher had been rewarding the children for bad behavior. We could say that the children had a "need for teacher attention," but it is enough to know that the shouts and criticisms were unintentional rewards and that removing them solved the problem.

To give another example, a teacher might have developed the following system for rewarding students. Each period begins with a stack of ten poker chips on each child's desk, with the rule that one will be removed for every violation of the classroom rules. At the end of the period, the students are allowed one minute of free time for every poker chip that is left in the stack. If the frequency of rule violations drops noticeably, we could conclude that a "need for free time" motivated the students to change their behavior; but again, it is enough to know that free time is an effective reward with these children.

We are frequently tempted to delve into difficult or impossible motivational questions that may distract us from more important issues. For example, the teacher in the first example may have wondered whether the children were motivated to gain attention because they felt unloved and were willing to take criticism if that was the only type of attention they could get, or did they dislike the teacher so much that they enjoyed seeing the teacher get upset? Such questions are fascinating and seem to be important to the understanding of the child, but they are generally useless in dealing with a specific classroom situation. First, these questions cannot be reliably answered. We cannot get inside children's heads to see what they are thinking; we can only make limited inferences. It is easy to test the hypothesis that attention is a reward by carrying out a "mini-experiment" in which attention is no longer given after disruptive behaviors, but we can only speculate as to *why* it is a reward. If you have tried to answer this type of question before, you know that a dozen individuals are likely to reach a dozen different conclusions. Further, we do not *need* to answer such questions. In this case, it was enough to know that the teacher's critical attention served as a reward in order to solve the problem.

When we ask profound motivational questions, we often take the wrong path in search of a solution. For example, a psychologist we know once visited a preschool classroom at the request of the teacher who was concerned about a four-year-old boy. He had not left his chair by the door of the classroom and had not spoken to any of the children or teachers in the two months he had been in the program. When the psychologist asked the teacher why she thought the child behaved in this way, she answered that she felt that he was insecure and frightened of the large group of children. She had, as a result of this analysis of the child's motivations, decided to try to make the child feel more at home by frequently spending time with him on an individual basis, bringing him toys and games, and even giving him extra snacks of cookies and juice. What did this teacher accomplish through these actions? Of course! In an effort to make the child lose his fears, she *rewarded* the child for acting fearful. The psychologist suggested that the teacher try ignoring the child when he sat in his chair by the door and give him lots of attention as soon as he made his first moves toward interacting more normally with the other children. The teacher agreed and called back four days later to say that it had been an unqualified success.

Use existing motives to teach new ones.
One of the primary goals of education is to prepare children for their future lives. Teachers often seek to teach motives to their students that will serve them well in later life.

At issue here is whether we would like children to continue learning without being told to do so, to seek and hold employment without being prodded, and to help others without the hope of personal gain. We will better be able to promote these goals if we focus more on what we want the children to *do* rather than on their motives. Instead of trying to change children's motives through discussions or preaching, the teacher can have the greatest influence by simply rewarding them for appropriate activities. If teachers give children interesting books and reward them for reading by warm and interested comments, they will likely both continue to read after they leave school and tell us that they enjoy reading. By using the child's existing motive for the reward of attention (or for free time, coins, etc.) the teacher can teach a new positive motive. If, on the other hand, the child is forced to read dull and boring material, is criticized harshly for minor mistakes, and is unrewarded for successes, the teacher will have taught the child to dislike reading. In general, the child who is rewarded for schoolwork will acquire a love of learning, while the child who is punished for it will learn an aversion to education.

Satisfy motives when the student's behavior is appropriate. The teacher plays an important role in seeing to it that the child's major motives are satisfied. This is particularly true of the need for attention. The child who is strongly rewarded by attention, but who does not get much of it, may develop some highly effective and highly undesirable ways of getting it. The teacher may need, therefore, to see to it that this child receives enough warm, personal attention. It is critically important, however, to give this attention

They want their pupils to continue to learn after their formal education is over because they enjoy learning, to perform useful work because they enjoy working, to be good citizens because they want to promote the common welfare. The methods teachers use to teach these motives are generally unsuccessful, however. Most frequently, teachers exhort children to adopt them through arguments based on reason, fear of divine or temporal punishment, or through personal affection.

(or any other type of reward) *at the right time*. Giving rewards at the right time is every bit as important as giving them in the first place.

If you have been following the line of reasoning in this chapter, you may be able to guess when the right time is. Reward children only when they behave in appropriate ways, not when they seek rewards in inappropriate ways. When children disrupt the classroom routine because they find the teacher's critical attention rewarding, the teacher must wait to give that attention when the children are behaving more appropriately—even if the teacher has to wait a long time to catch them being good (Madsen & Madsen, 1974).

Remember: different things are rewarding to different children. One of the major jobs of a teacher is to determine what things are rewarding to each child in the class. This is usually not much of a problem, as there are some things that are rewarding to most children, such as free time. But, children who need special rewards certainly come along frequently enough to warrant discussion. Many children are unmoved by good grades or gold stars, and the student who could care less about extra time in PE class but would love to earn some free time in the neighborhood poolhall is all too common. The authors have also learned from personal experience that there are some children who detest candy, but who would do anything for raw vegetables (a mother told us this after watching us try to modify her son's behavior with chocolate candy for two weeks!).

Sometimes a teacher can transform something into a reward for a child. For example, if a teacher notices that one of the children

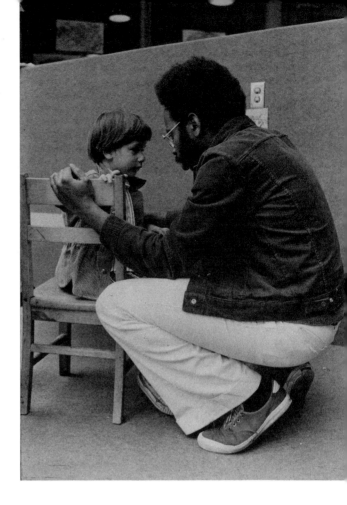

in the class is unrewarded by good grades, but is rewarded by the teacher's attention, the teacher could transform good grades into a reward by warmly praising the child whenever a paper is returned with a good mark. This method (based on the principle of *stimulus pairing* mentioned earlier in this chapter) provides teachers with another way of teaching new motives to their students.

Do not use the term "motivation" as a catch-all excuse for inappropriate behavior. Teachers frequently follow this pattern of behavior: Three new students come into a

139

WHICH BEHAVIORS SHOULD WE REINFORCE?

Proponents of structured approaches to education that rely heavily on positive reinforcement have recently engaged in a considerable amount of self-criticism. Much of the research in this area (but certainly not all) has been directed toward teaching children simply to "be still, be quiet, be docile." We need, instead, to reinforce those behaviors that will lead to competence and maturity. Psychologists Richard Winett and Robin Winkler (1972) have stated the problem this way:

"There is a strong need for extensive dialogues in our communities on just what kinds of human beings we want our children to be and to grow up to be. Such dialogues would determine what values and behavior we want our schools to transmit and reward. The second part of this dialogue would include discussion on how these objectives can be achieved so that school can become a rewarding, fulfilling experience for the child. The complexity of these questions in an age of rapid social and moral change is apparent, and the weight of their political, social, and economic significance is enormous. We suspect that there is no one solution for education's problems, but that different alternatives can be developed for different communities or groups within a community." (p. 502)

classroom with a reputation of being slow learners. After the teacher comes to know them, she might decide that they are intelligent, but that their poor backgrounds are slowing down their learning. If the teacher spends many afternoons tutoring them without any sign of improvement, however, she might be tempted to conclude that they do not "care" about learning, are afraid to try, or make some other such motivational diagnosis. This solution is an attractive one to teachers as it removes the responsibility from their hands and drops it back into the laps of the students: "We cannot be expected to succeed with children who do not want to learn in the first place." It may be true, of course, that the children fear failure or have other such feelings that interfere with learning, but we cannot know for sure and we cannot let our hunches in this area justify giving up on them. We must continue to look for teaching methods that will be successful.

The Hierarchy of Motives

It is fairly obvious that each person has many different motives and that each of these cannot be active at the same time. Only relatively recently, however, psychologist Abraham Maslow noted that these different motives seem to be organized in a coherent "hierarchy" (Maslow, 1954). This means that some motives are more basic than others. When a basic motive is active and unfulfilled, those motives that are less basic will, in effect, be "turned off." For example, a child who comes to school hungry will not be much affected by gold stars.

TABLE 5–1

Maslow's Hierarchy of Needs

Self-actualization:
displaying the needs of a fully functioning student or
human being; becoming the self that one truly is.

Aesthetic Needs	Aesthetic needs: appreciation for the order and balance of all of life; a sense of the beauty in and love for all.	Being and growth motives that spring from within, are gentle and continuing, and grow stronger when *fulfilled*.
Achievement, Intellectual Needs	Need for understanding: knowledge of relationships, systems and processes that are expressed in broad theories; the integration of knowledge and lore into broad structures.	
	Need for knowledge: having access to information and lore; knowing how to do things; wanting to know about the meaning of things, events and symbols.	
Affiliation, Social Needs	Esteem needs: being recognized as a unique person with special abilities and valuable characteristics; being special and different.	Deficiency or maintenance motives that are granted or denied by external factors, are strong and recurring, and grow stronger when *denied*.
	Belonging needs: being accepted as a member of a group, knowing that others are aware of you and want you to be with them.	
Physical, Organizational Needs	Security needs: being concerned that tomorrow is assured; having things regular and predictable for oneself and one's family and in-group.	
	Survival needs: a concern for immediate existence; to be able to eat, breathe, live at this moment.	

(From Maslow, 1954)

Similarly, children who have not been let out of their seats for several hours will care little whether they receive an A or a C on their worksheets. This is a simple but extremely important point. Although behavioral scientists disagree how to define the motives and where to place them on the hierarchy, most agree that we must satisfy our basic motives before the less basic motives will play any part in determining our behavior. Children must have food, clothing, and security before praise and report cards can motivate them.

Maslow's theory of the hierarchy of motives is illustrated in Table 5 – 1. It shows the motives Maslow thinks are most important in human behavior and the position that he gives to each. Again, other psychologists place different motives on the hierarchy, describe them in different words, and place them in different positions. What is most important, however, is the general concept of the hierarchy of motives. Following the terms used in Maslow's program for the moment, however, it suggests that a person with unfulfilled needs for love and belongingness would not be rewarded by success in school, since it ranks higher on the hierarchy and therefore would be dormant.

Achievement Motivation

Achievement motivation is another term that deserves special mention in any discussion of motivation in education. Psychologists coined this term to refer to individuals for whom success and its visible concomitants are especially important. Children who are said to have high achievement motivation usually are strongly rewarded by praise for their performances, good grades, special awards, and the like. Interestingly, research over the past twenty years suggests that children who have high achievement motivation usually have parents who have a very high opinion of them, expect success from them at an early age, and reward them with strong emotional praise for their success (McClelland, 1961).

It has also been found that birth order and family size also play some role in determining the reward value of academic success (Adams & Phillips, 1972). Firstborn children and children from small families are slightly more likely to be rewarded by academic and occupational success than others. This means that only-children have a special likelihood of being high achievers. It is interesting to note, for example, that every astronaut chosen for a mission in the early years of the manned space program was either a firstborn or an only child.

You should not conclude, however, that achievement is out of your hands. While the influences mentioned above are significant, there are many exceptions to the rule. History is filled with stories of last-born children from large families whose parents neglected them and turned out to be high achievers, but the odds *are* slightly against them. Most importantly, teachers can also respect, have

*P. 141

high expectations, and provide strong rewards for all of their students regardless of their birth order or size of their family.

REVIEW 5–3

1. How can a teacher determine a child's motives?

2. Give an example of using motivation as an *excuse* for allowing a child to engage in inappropriate behavior.

3. When should a teacher satisfy a child's motives?

4. What is the significance for teachers of Maslow's hierarchy of motives?

5. What roles do parents and teachers play in the development of "achievement motivation"?

SUMMARY

Behavior is influenced by the environment. The goal of educational research is to find out how it does its work so that we can harness its power to encourage growth and learning. Educators have long sought to do this and have become rather good at it. A thorough knowledge of the principles of learning, motivation, and development enables teachers to intentionally and effectively influence behavior. Four of the principles of learning we have discussed (the operant learning principles) show the importance of the consequences of a behavior for its future occurrences. One shows that we learn from observing others, and two describe the effects of repeatedly presenting stimuli or of pairing them. Supporting these seven principles and adding to their importance are the concepts of extinction and stimulus control. These concepts describe how learning can be reversed by removing the source of the learning and how stimuli can come to set the occasion for the occurrence of certain behaviors.

When we look for the reason behind children's behavior, we are often asking about their motivation. Understanding children's motives is essential to good teaching, but there are many pitfalls in trying to analyze motives. They can be best understood by finding out what children will work for—what is a reward to them. Keep in mind when asking this question that different children may have different motives. Once a child's motives are understood, the teacher can use existing motives to teach new ones. One motive that has been given special attention by educators is achievement motivation. This term refers to the fact that "success" in school or a career is more rewarding to some people than to others.

The teacher plays a special role in seeing to it that the child's basic motives are satisfied. This is particularly important in view of Maslow's theory that unfulfilled motives may interfere with the child's use of more socially important motives. But it is also important to remember that the teacher should not speculate about a child's inner motives as an excuse for inappropriate behavior. We too often say, "He could do it if he wanted to, but he just doesn't want to," and leave it at that.

Instead, we need to use the principles of learning and motivation to encourage children both to behave appropriately and to want to do so.

ANSWERS TO REVIEW QUESTIONS

Review 5–1

1. The seven principles of learning:
   a. *Positive Reinforcement:* If a behavior is consistently followed by a reinforcer, that behavior will strengthen.
   b. *Loss of Reinforcement:* If a behavior consistently results in a reinforcer being removed or prevented from occurring, that behavior will be weakened.
   c. *Punishment:* If a behavior is consistently followed by an aversive stimulus, that behavior will be weakened.
   d. *Negative Reinforcement:* If a behavior consistently results in an aversive stimulus being removed or prevented from occurring, that behavior will be strengthened.
   e. *Modeling:* Presenting the behavior of one individual for another individual to observe in hopes that it will be imitated (increase the frequency of the same behavior in the observing individual).
   f. *Stimulus Pairing:* The stimulus function of a stimulus can be acquired by a neutral stimulus if those stimuli are consistently presented together (paired).
   g. *Stimulus Repetition:* If a stimulus is presented repeatedly or for a prolonged period of time, it will tend to lose some or all of its stimulus function.

2. Punishment may cause the child to become aggressive, to dislike the person who administers the punishment, to become inflexible, and to cease engaging in desirable behaviors that are similar to those punished. The person who uses punishment may also be reinforced by its immediate effects on the child and thus become more likely to use punishment in the future.

3. Teachers often teach children to "do what they do, rather than what they say," without meaning to do so. For example, the teachers who yell and scream at their students as they are telling them not to yell and scream, may find that their students imitate them rather than abide by their requests.

Review 5–2

1. Extinction is the return of a changed behavior to its original state produced by removing the source of the learning (the contingent reward, the pairing stimulus, etc.). For example, if teachers have taught their children to talk too loudly by speaking too loudly to them, they can extinguish that behavior by no longer speaking too loudly. If they have encouraged them to throw spitballs by throwing a fit every time they did so, they could extinguish that behavior by ceasing to pay attention to it.

2. When attempting to reduce the frequency of an undesirable behavior through any means (extinction, punishment or loss of reinforcement), reinforcing another behavior to take the place of the undesirable one will increase the efficiency of the procedure and reduce the likelihood of undesirable side effects.

3. A stimulus is said to "control" behavior if the probability that the behavior will occur in the presence of that stimulus is higher than in its absence.

Review 5–3

1. The easiest way to determine a child's motives is to find out what works as a reward. Sometimes this will be praise or free time; sometimes it will be shouts and paddlings from the assistant principal. Trying to delve deeper than this into a child's motives is generally unnecessary and can often be misleading.

2. If a white teacher says that a child hates all white people too much to learn anything from him or her and does nothing more to try to teach the child, he or she is speculating about the child's hidden motives to excuse a lack of success in teaching.

3. A teacher should only satisfy children's motives when they behave appropriately. Satisfying a motive is the same as giving a reward, and teachers must be careful to give rewards only when they will reinforce desirable behavior.

4. Maslow's hierarchy of motives suggests that higher motives (e.g., high grades) will only be able to influence the behavior of children when their more basic motives (e.g., physical needs) are satisfied.

5. Both parents and teachers can encourage achievement by rewarding success and showing children that they have high expectations and a high opinion of them.

Chapter 6

Measuring Educational Potential

If all children entered school with the same abilities, interests, and levels of motivation, and if all students learned at the same rate, they could all be taught in exactly the same way. However, anyone who has ever been in a classroom knows this is not the case. Students *do differ* from one another in many ways. In order to successfully individualize instruction, therefore, you must know how to measure individual differences. We need to be able to measure what students can do and what they cannot do; what they know and what they do not know; what they feel and what they do not feel. In particular we need to measure (1) before instruction, to determine where and how to begin teaching, (2) during instruction, to determine whether to change materials and teaching strategies, and (3) after instruction, to evaluate our own teaching effectiveness. In this chapter, then, we will consider the concept of individual differences, including how to measure these differences and what might cause individuals to differ from one another. Finally, we will look closely at the measurement of one very important characteristic, intelligence.

DIFFERENCES BETWEEN INDIVIDUALS

Individuals differ from one another in many ways. In the typical classroom, students vary greatly in intelligence, motivation, past achievement, interests, and personality—all of these factors can influence the amount and type of learning that occurs. Consider a study, for example, that showed achievement (measured by grade norm scores) of a large group of ten-year-olds ranging from first- to ninth-grade levels (Hildreth, 1950). The teacher must be prepared to take this poten-

tial variability into consideration when planning and evaluating instruction.

Measuring Individual Differences

Whenever one measures the extent to which a group of students differ from one another, the result is likely to be a set of numerical scores. These scores must be summarized and interpreted before the information can be used in planning or evaluating instruction. Thus, we first need to consider some basic statistical concepts used in educational measurement.

Frequency distributions.   Usually the first step one takes in summarizing test data is to construct a frequency distribution. A **frequency distribution** is a list of scores, ranked from highest to lowest, that indicates how many individuals received each score. Many teachers use frequency distributions when grading tests by simply listing all possible scores and placing a tally by the appropriate score for each student. Table 6-1 presents an example of a frequency distribution for a set of twenty-eight scores on a 10-point test.

TABLE 6-1

A Sample Frequency Distribution

Score	Tally	Frequency
10	I	1
9		0
8	III	3
7	IIII	5
6	IIII II	7
5	IIII	5
4	IIII	4
3	II	2
2		0
1		0
0	I	1
		N = 28

CONSTRUCTING A FREQUENCY POLYGON

Frequency distributions are sometimes more meaningful when the data are presented in a graph] One type of graph you are likely to encounter and may want to construct yourself when summarizing test scores is a frequency polygon. The frequency polygon shown here is based on the data in Table 6–1. In constructing it, we first marked off equal spaces on the horizontal axis and labeled each mark with a possible test score. We then marked off the vertical axis in a similar manner and labeled each mark with a possible frequency (number of persons). The graph was completed by adding dots corresponding to the number of persons receiving each test score and by connecting these points with straight lines. The result is a visual presentation of how the test scores are distributed according to their frequency.

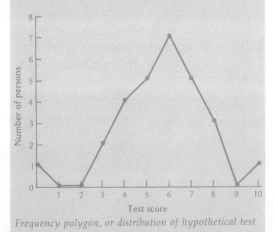

Frequency polygon, or distribution of hypothetical test scores.

As you can see, one student received a perfect score of 10, no students received a 9, three students received an 8, five students received a 7, and so on.

In the example in Table 6–1 there are only 11 possible test scores (ranging from 0–10) and only 28 students taking the test. But in actual practice you may give tests to larger groups and give tests with many more possible points. In this case, you may want to tally the scores according to class intervals, rather than listing each score separately. For example, on a 100-point examination the scores might be grouped into class intervals of 5: 96–100, 91–95, 86–90, and so on.

Mean. The **mean** is the average score, calculated by adding up all the scores and dividing the resulting sum by the total number of scores (N). For example, the sum of the scores 12, 16, and 20 is 48; dividing 48 by 3 gives us a mean of 16. Likewise, the sum of 2, 4, 5, 8, and 11 is 30; dividing 30 by 5 yields a mean of 6. [When you have many scores, it is useful to calculate the mean directly from a frequency distribution.] Although calculating the mean for a set of scores requires additional time and effort, you may find it worthwhile, since you then have a single number which is representative of how the group *as a whole* performed.

Range. Another statistic used in describing a set of scores is the **range,** defined as the highest score minus the lowest score. To illustrate, consider a group of scores on a 100-point examination where the highest score is 96 and the lowest score is 40. The range is 56. If the same exam was given to a second group with a resulting high score of

85 and a low score of 60, the range for this group would be 25. Computing the range is a simple way to determine the amount of variability in a set of scores. By **variability** we mean the degree to which the scores spread out or differ from one another. In the examples above there is much more variability in the first set of scores (with a range of 56) than in the second set (with a range of 25).

Standard deviations and the normal curve.
The range gives us some idea of how much variability there is in a set of test scores. It may be deceptive, however, since it takes into account only the two most extreme scores and ignores the distribution of scores in between. Thus, the standard deviation (abbreviated SD), which takes into account all of the scores, is the statistic most often used to describe degree of variability. The **standard deviation** is an expression of the average amount by which individual scores differ from the overall mean of the distribution. The smaller the standard deviation, the less variability, that is, *the more the scores cluster around the mean*. The standard deviation is a useful statistic because it allows us to see more clearly how one individual's score compares with the scores of other individuals who took the same test. In order to see why, we need to consider the concept of the normal curve.

In studying individual differences, psychologists have long subscribed to the notion that most physical and psychological characteristics are distributed *normally*. This means that if one were to measure a particular characteristic such as weight or intelligence

USING A FREQUENCY DISTRIBUTION WHEN CALCULATING THE MEAN

When computing the mean score from a frequency distribution, the following formula is used:

$$\text{Mean} = \frac{\Sigma fX}{N}$$
where Σ = the sum of
f = frequency
X = raw score
N = total number of scores

In order to obtain the mean from a frequency distribution, follow these steps:

(1) Multiply each raw score by its frequency (fX).
(2) Add the products to get a sum of the raw scores (ΣfX).
(3) Divide the sum of the raw scores by the total number of scores $\left(\frac{\Sigma fX}{N}\right)$.

These steps are illustrated below for a hypothetical frequency distribution.

X	f	fX
100	1	100
98	1	98
97	1	97
93	1	93
90	3	270
88	2	176
81	1	81
76	5	380
72	1	72
71	2	142
70	4	280
64	1	64
53	1	53
48	1	48
	N = 25	ΣfX = 1954

$$\frac{\Sigma fX}{N} = \frac{1954}{25} = 78.16$$

CALCULATING THE STANDARD DEVIATION

The standard deviation is computed using the following formula:

$$SD = \sqrt{\frac{\Sigma d^2}{N-1}} \quad \text{where} \quad \Sigma = \text{the sum of}$$

d = the difference between each score and the overall mean score

N = the total number of scores

In order to obtain a standard deviation, follow these steps:

(1) Compute the mean.

(2) Find the difference between the mean and each score (d).

(3) Square each difference (d^2).

(4) Add the differences squared to get a sum (Σd^2).

(5) Divide the sum of the differences squared by the number of scores minus one $\frac{\Sigma d^2}{(N-1)}$.

(6) Take the square root of the sum of the differences squared divided by the number of scores minus one $\left(\sqrt{\frac{\Sigma d^2}{N-1}}\right)$.

These steps are illustrated below. Note that we have calculated the standard deviation for two distributions. Each distribution has the same mean and range. Distribution B has a smaller standard deviation than Distribution A, however, since the scores in Distribution B cluster more around the mean.

Distribution A			Distribution B		
Raw Score (X)	Deviation Score (d)	Deviation Score Squared (d^2)	X	d	d^2
70	+20	400	70	+20	400
68	+18	324	56	+6	36
62	+12	144	54	+4	16
55	+5	25	52	+2	4
51	+1	1	52	+2	4
48	−2	4	49	−1	1
46	−4	16	47	−3	9
37	−13	169	45	−5	25
33	−17	289	45	−5	25
30	−20	400	30	−20	400
$\Sigma X = 500$		$\Sigma d^2 = 1772$	$\Sigma X = 500$		$\Sigma d^2 = 920$
$N = 10$			$N = 10$		

$$\text{Mean} = \frac{\Sigma X}{N} = \frac{500}{10} = 50 \qquad\qquad \text{Mean} = \frac{\Sigma X}{N} = \frac{500}{10} = 50$$

$$SD = \sqrt{\frac{\Sigma d^2}{N-1}} = \sqrt{\frac{1772}{9}} = \sqrt{196.8} = 14.1 \qquad SD = \sqrt{\frac{\Sigma d^2}{N-1}} = \sqrt{\frac{920}{9}} = \sqrt{102.2} = 10.1$$

in a very large sample of people, and if the scores were plotted in a graph (frequency polygon), the result would be a **normal curve,** such as the one shown in Figure 6−1. You can see from Figure 6−1 that most scores fall near the mean, with fewer and fewer scores falling toward either extreme end of the distribution. The normal curve is by definition bell-shaped and symmetrical, with the majority of scores falling close to the mean.

It is important to note that the normal curve is a *theoretical* distribution. In other words, it describes how we would expect scores to be distributed ideally, provided that a very large sample of scores is taken (a few individuals would score high, a few individuals would score low, and most would score somewhere in the middle). In actual practice we very rarely deal with large enough samples to obtain a distribution of scores that is perfectly normal. Still, many distributions found in real life are close enough approximations, so that we can use the mathematical properties of the normal curve to better understand the particular set of scores we obtain.

The relationship between the standard deviation and the normal curve is of particular interest to us. Returning to Figure 6−1, you can see that there is an exact relationship between the standard deviation (SD) and the percentage of cases that fall under various portions of the normal curve. For example, 34.13 percent of the scores fall between the mean and 1 SD *above* the mean. Because the normal curve is by definition symmetrical, an identical percentage of scores (34.13 percent) fall between the mean and 1 SD *below* the mean. In a similar manner, 13.59 percent of the scores fall

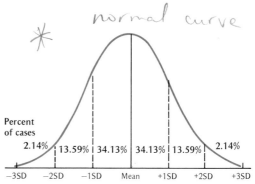

normal curve

Figure 6−1. *Standard deviations and the normal distribution.*

between 1 and 2 SDs above the mean, 13.59 percent fall between 1 and 2 SDs below the mean, and so on. Thus, if we are dealing with a set of scores that approximates the normal curve and if we know the mean and SD of the distribution, we can see how one student's score compares with the scores of others who took the same test.

Here are several guidelines for interpreting test scores using the mean and standard deviation:

(1.) The performance of a student who scores 1 SD *above* the mean is good, since we would expect theoretically only about 16 percent of the students to score this high. (Example 1: On a test with a mean of 100 and SD of 16, a score of 116 is 1 SD above the mean. A student who scored 116 did well in comparison with others who took the same test.)

(2.) The performance of a student who scores 1 SD *below* the mean is poor, since only about 16 percent of the students would score this low. (Example 2: On a test with a mean of 100 and SD of 16, a score of 84 is 1 SD below the mean. A student who scored 84 did poorly in comparison with others.)

(3.) The performance of a student who scores 2 SDs (or more) *above* the mean is excellent, since only about 2 percent would score this high. (Example 3: On a test with a mean of 100 and SD of 16, a score of 132 is 2 SDs above the mean and can be considered excellent.)

√(4.) The performance of a student who scores 2 SDs (or more) *below* the mean is very poor, since only about 2 percent would score this low. (Example 4: On a test with a mean of 100 and SD of 16, a score of 68 is 2 SDs below the mean and can be considered very poor.)

√(5.) If two groups of scores have the same mean, but different SDs, then a given score does not have the same meaning in each group. (Example 5: Test A has a mean of 30 and SD of 5. Test B has a mean of 30 and SD of 2. On Test A a score of 35 is 1 SD above the mean and reflects a *good* performance. On Test B the same score [35] is 2.5 SDs above the mean and reflects an *excellent* performance.)

It is important to keep in mind that these guidelines are not useful in *all* testing situations. In using teacher-constructed achievement tests in your own classroom, you may neither expect nor find that the resulting distribution of scores resembles the normal curve. This will likely be the case if you use a mastery learning approach and therefore expect to find a preponderance of perfect or near-perfect scores. The use of the mean and standard deviation in this case is inappropriate, since the scores are not normally distributed. Additionally, in a mastery learning approach you are not generally interested in comparing one student's score with the scores of other students; you are more interested in how that student stands in relation to some absolute criterion of mastery (we will discuss this type of testing in more detail in the following chapter). For the time being, remember that the statistical concepts introduced here are most useful in interpreting standardized intelligence and achievement tests that have been given to very large groups of individuals.

Sources of Individual Differences

In the process of measuring the extent of differences among your students, you might wonder what accounts for such variability. In Chapters 2 and 3 we discussed how one variable, age, affects how students behave; age may account for some of the variability you observe, even within a single grade level. But even children with identical birthdates may differ from each other in significant ways. We will now examine other variables that contribute to making each student unique.

Heredity.   It is clear that many physical characteristics, such as hair color, and many disorders, such as color blindness, are inherited. But what about intelligence and personality? Does heredity influence the ways we learn and the ways we behave? If so, to what extent? The answer to the first question is almost certainly yes. Heredity influences all aspects of human functioning, including intelligence and personality. However, the second question is much more difficult to answer. Psychologists and biologists are as yet unable to determine exactly *how much* of our behavior is determined by heredity and *how much* is determined by environmental experiences. Still, many researchers have tried to answer this question and, in the process, have shed some light on the contribution heredity makes to these kinds of individual differences.

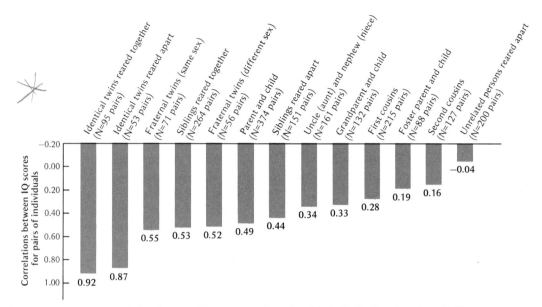

Figure 6–2. *Median correlations between IQ test scores for pairs of individuals. (Based on Burt, 1966)*

One way to study the issue of heredity and intelligence is to examine some characteristics of pairs of individuals who have differing degrees of genetic relationship. This was the approach taken by psychologist Cyril Burt. Although Burt's data have come under much critical scrutiny, his research program has had a major impact on theories of individual differences.

Burt obtained IQ scores from many British schoolchildren and their relatives and in 1966 published a major study based on these data. Burt's results are summarized in Figure 6–2. If anything in this figure gains your immediate attention, it probably is the very low correlation between the IQs of unrelated persons (−0.04) contrasted with the very high correlation between the IQs of identical twins (0.87 and 0.92). (Note that correlations near 0.0 indicate very little relationship or similarity between the pairs of scores, while correlations near 1.0 indicate

great similarity.) Thus, there is essentially no similarity between the IQs of unrelated persons and great similarity between the IQs of identical twins. Since identical twins come from one egg and one sperm and have essentially the same genetic makeup, some psychologists use these data to support the position that intelligence is determined by heredity.

Further support for this position comes from additional data illustrated in Figure 6–2. As the pairs of individuals tested become more closely related, their IQs become more similar. For example, the correlation for second cousins is only 0.16; for first cousins it is 0.28, for grandparent and child, 0.33, and for parent and child, 0.49.

One further point to be stressed has to do with Burt's data on children reared apart versus those reared together. If environment has an important influence on intelligence, one would expect that the IQs of genetically related children reared in the same home would be more similar than those of related children reared in different homes. To a limited extent, Burt found this to be true. The correlation for siblings reared together is 0.53, while the correlation for separately adopted or otherwise separated siblings who were reared apart is 0.44. On the other hand, the correlation for identical twins reared together (0.92) is only *slightly higher* than the correlation for identical twins reared apart (0.87) and both of these are *much higher* than the correlations for siblings reared together (0.53). Although the exact correlations vary from study to study, other researchers have reported results similar to Burt's (e.g., Newman, Freeman, & Holzinger, 1937; Erlenmeyer-Kimling & Jarvik, 1963).

Still, the issue of heredity and intelligence is far from settled. Some have been quick to point out the shortcomings of these studies (e.g., Daniels, 1973; Schwartz & Schwartz, 1974). One criticism raised is that environmental similarity tends to increase as genetic similarity increases. For example, identical twins have more similar environments than fraternal twins or other siblings. Identical twins are often dressed alike and are treated in a similar manner by parents, teachers, and peers. Thus, similarities in intelligence could be due to environmental, as well as genetic factors. Furthermore, even separately adopted identical twins reared in separate homes may have been intentionally placed by adoption agencies in environments uniform in income, child-rearing practices, and so on. Until researchers can show that identical twins reared apart were actually raised in environments that differed in *specific* ways, the twin studies must be interpreted with caution.

Even given the shortcomings of the twin studies, however, most psychologists agree that heredity does have a significant influence on intelligence. Can we say the same about the effects of heredity on personality? Does heredity also influence our "temperament," our "emotional stability," our typical ways of behaving? Again, twin studies have been used to attempt to answer this question, and in several cases the results have been positive. For example, Vanderberg (1967) found that identical twins were more alike than fraternal twins on measure of extroversion (friendliness) and introversion (shyness). Similar results have been found for overall activity level (Willerman, 1973).

There is also increasing evidence that a slight predisposition to schizophrenia, a severe personality disorder, may be inherited. In 1972 Gottesman and Shields published a detailed study of hospitalized schizophrenics who happened to be twins. In the twenty-two cases where the schizophrenic twin had an *identical* twin, eleven of the co-twins (50 percent) were also schizophrenic. In the thirty-three cases where the schizophrenic twin had a *fraternal* twin (developed from two different ova and sperm cells), only three of the co-twins (9 percent) were found to be schizophrenic. Thus, when the twins had identical genetic makeup, the probability was quite high that both would be schizophrenic (*if* one was schizophrenic; twins are no more likely to develop this problem than nontwins); when the twins did not have identical genetic makeup, the probability was much lower.

One hypothesis offered to account for the higher IQs of children from middle- and upper-income homes is that their parents take a greater interest in their children's schoolwork than do the parents of children from lower-income homes.

In evaluating the studies on heredity and personality, keep in mind that they are subject to the same criticisms as the twin studies on intelligence. *Identical twins tend to be raised in similar environments.* Thus, one cannot rule out the influence of the environment. In regard to the Gottesman and Shields (1972) study, remember also that even with identical twins, 50 percent of the co-twins *were not* schizophrenic. Was this because they were not exposed to the same environmental stresses as their schizophrenic twins? The answer to this is very possibly yes. In fact, the most popular theory today says that a weak predisposition to personality disorders can be inherited, but that this predisposition will never be expressed if the individual grows up and lives under favorable environmental circumstances (Coleman, 1976). This theory points out the important interaction that always occurs between heredity and the environment.

Learning. If heredity and environment interact, how does this interaction occur and what role does learning play in this process? Again, we cannot answer this question conclusively, but we have much evidence that intelligence, personality, and achievement are related to the kinds of learning the child experiences.

One important source of information on the effects of learning comes from cross-cultural studies. For example, psychologist Mary Ainsworth (1967) has described how mothers in America and Uganda differ in their child-rearing practices and how these differences affect infant-mother attachment and the development of "separation anxiety" in infants. In Uganda, infants are nursed until they are two years old; in addition they are physically close to their mothers for most of the day and are often strapped to the mother's back or straddled across her hip. Ainsworth found that infants in Uganda exhibit clear distress when the mother leaves them as early as six months of age. In contrast, American infants do not typically develop separation anxiety until twelve months of age, presumably because they do not spend the first year of their lives in such close proximity to their mothers. American infants, then, are less likely to notice their mothers' absence at a very early age and this difference is clearly related to the type of environment in which they are raised.

We need not, however, compare different countries in order to conclude that one's cultural environment exerts a tremendous influence on the growing child. There are subcultures within each country that have their own value systems and child-rearing practices. In the United States many studies have focused on ethnic and socioeconomic class differences in child-rearing practices among the many American subcultures. These studies have shown that middle-income mothers talk more to their infants and try to entertain them more than lower-income mothers (Tulkin and Kagan, 1972) and that middle-income parents are less likely to use physical punishment on their children (Allinsmith, 1960). Also, Kagan and Madsen (1971) have found that Mexican-American children are consistently more cooperative in a gamelike situation than are Anglo-American children, perhaps because the Anglo-American value system places greater stress on competition.

Evidence on the role of learning in producing individual differences also comes from studies dealing with the plasticity of intelligence. These studies have generally asked the question, "Can intelligence test scores be increased by providing the child with a more stimulating environment?" Although many studies related to this issue have been conducted, we will focus here on only two illustrative ones.

Skeels and Dye (1939) transferred a group of thirteen orphaned infants who were suspected of being mentally retarded from an orphanage to an institution for the mentally retarded. In the institution, each infant was assigned to an older, mildly retarded girl who, with help from the professional staff, served as the child's "mother." The "mothers" gave the children lots of tender loving care, playing with them and teaching them informally. A second group of twelve orphans remained at the overcrowded orphanage, where they received the minimal supervision and stimulation that was typical of orphanages in the 1930s. Both groups were tested before the study began and several years later. Surprisingly, the group raised in the institution showed an average gain of 32 IQ points, while the group that remained at the orphanage lost a mean of 21 IQ points. Evidently the stimulation the experimental group received from their foster mothers, even though those mothers were retarded themselves, did them a world of good. The results from a 21-year follow-up study (Skeels, 1966) were even more impressive. Most of the experimental group had left the institution and were leading normal lives, while many of those raised in the orphanage were described as retarded and were residents of state institutions.

A second, more sophisticated study that confirms the important influence of experience on intellectual development is being conducted by educational psychologist Rick

Heber and his associates at the University of Wisconsin (Heber, Garber, Harrington, Hoffman, & Falenger, 1972). In this study, twenty infants of poor inner-city mothers with IQs below 75 received high quality day-care and preschool experiences from infancy through kindergarten, while a similar group of children served as controls and received no enriched intellectual experiences. These children were chosen for the experiment because the majority of offspring of mothers with IQs below 75 become at least mildly retarded, probably due to heredity and lack of intellectual stimulation.

By the end of kindergarten, none of the children in the experimental day-care group had IQ scores in the retarded range and scored on the average 20 to 30 IQ points higher than the children in the control group. Most importantly, these gains have been maintained as the children have grown older. At nine years of age, all of the day-care children were still in the normal range of intelligence and scored a mean of approximately 20 points higher than the control children.

Considered together, the data on the role of heredity and experience in influencing intelligence strongly suggest that both factors play important roles. We are as yet unable to say which factor has the strongest role, but it is clear that carefully designed programs of enriched experience can have a powerful influence on intelligence, at least when they begin in early infancy. At present, this type of early childhood intervention is not considered a legitimate responsibility of public school systems, but as data emerge that

show the influence these programs have in *preventing* mental retardation, a redefinition of "schooling" may take place.

Birth order and family size. For many years, psychologists suspected that children are influenced by the size of their families and their relative positions within those families. Some studies, for example, have reported that firstborn children are more achievement oriented (Helmreich, 1968) and have a greater need for affection and personal relationships (Schacter, 1959) than laterborn children. There is especially strong evidence that *intelligence* is related to birth order and family size.

One convincing study was conducted by Lillian Belmont and Francis Marolla (1973). They studied an unusually large sample of subjects—almost 400,000 nineteen-year-old men in the Netherlands. As part of their examination for military induction, these men were given the Raven Progressive Matrices, a widely used intelligence test. For each subject, data were also collected on the number of children in the subject's family (family sizes of one child through nine children or more) and on his birth order position (first through ninth or more). Belmont and Marolla then examined the relationship between scores on the intelligence test and family size and birth order. The results presented in Figure 6–3 clearly show a birth order effect as described by the authors:

Within each family size (i) firstborns always scored better on the Raven than did laterborns, and (ii) with few inconsistencies, there was a gradient of declining scores with rising birth order, so that firstborns scored better than secondborns, who in turn scored better than thirdborns, and so forth (p. 1098).

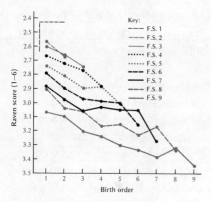

Figure 6–3. *Mean Raven class score by birth order within family size (F.S.) across the population (N = 386,114). Note that a score of 1.0 is high and a score of 6.0 is low. (From Belmont & Marolla, 1973)*

Figure 6–3 also shows the effect of family size:

In general, as family size increased, there was a decrease in Raven performance within any particular birth order position. The clearest example of this trend was among thirdborns, where those from three-child families did better than thirdborns from four-child families, who in turn did better than thirdborns from five-child families, and so forth (p. 1098).

Why is it that birth order and family size influence intelligence? In regard to family size, it might be that poor people tend to have larger families, and thus poverty, rather than large families per se, contributes to lower intelligence. However, when Belmont and Marolla controlled for income, they still found similar results. Even among professional and white-collar workers, the subjects from larger families obtained lower intelligence scores than those from smaller families. One reasonable explanation, therefore, is that parents with small families may be able to pay more individual attention to each child than parents with large families. A sim-

ilar explanation may account for birth order effects. Parents may unintentionally treat their first child differently than laterborn children. Perhaps they are more conscious of the child-rearing techniques they use or set higher expectations for the firstborn; certainly they can give that child their undivided attention, at least until a second child is born.

Sex. As you look around your classroom one of the most obvious differences you will see is that some students are males and some are females. You may also have some preconceived notions about differences in how males and females behave. The following are just a few examples of popular beliefs concerning sex differences: females are more social than males; males are more aggressive than females; females lack achievement motivation; males lack "maternal" tendencies; females excel in verbal abilities; males excel in mathematics; females are more compliant; males are more competitive. It is a difficult task for psychologists to determine which of these statements are accurate descriptions and which are cultural stereotypes. Furthermore, once we separate the myths from the facts, we face the even more difficult task of determining which sex differences are due to innate biological factors and which are due to learning and cultural expectations. Finally, we must consider the implications for education. Should males and females be taught differently? Should education aim to maximize the differences between the sexes or to minimize them? These are difficult questions that are likely to be debated for a long time. For the present, we need to focus on what little we know about how males and females do actually differ.

The most comprehensive source of information on sex differences comes from the book, *The Psychology of Sex Differences* by Eleanor Maccoby and Carol Jacklin (1974). In reviewing a large body of literature, these Stanford University psychologists found that only four sex differences are fairly well established: (1) After the age of eleven, females consistently score higher than males on tests of verbal ability; (2) from adolescence onward, males consistently score higher than females on tests of visual spatial ability; (3) after the age of twelve, males are superior to females in mathematical ability; and (4) at all ages, males are more aggressive than females, both physically and verbally.

Surprisingly, Maccoby and Jacklin found that a number of well-accepted beliefs about sex differences seem totally unfounded: Females are not more social or suggestible, nor do they have lower self-esteem or lack achievement motivation. Moreover, the authors questioned several popular notions (e.g., females are more compliant and cooperative, while males are more dominant and competitive), citing ambiguous findings or too little evidence to draw any conclusions.

In evaluating the work of Maccoby and Jacklin, keep in mind that their statements about sex differences are *generalizations* and nothing more. Females, *in general,* may excel in verbal ability and males, *in general,* may excel in math, but you are likely to encounter many exceptions to the rule. In addition many traits are situation-specific; that is, in certain situations females may indeed be more aggressive than males. Finally, we have a lot to learn about *why* males and females differ in these respects. Maccoby and Jacklin cite evidence that aggression and visual-spatial ability may have strong genetic components. For other characteristics, such as verbal and mathematical ability, learning and cultural expectations may play a much larger role. In either case, environmental experiences influence whether an innate predisposition will be expressed. Females who are encouraged to practice visual-spatial skills, for example, may indeed perform better than males who have not been encouraged to practice such skills.

Medical factors.   A discussion of the sources of individual differences would be incomplete without mention of medical factors. As with sex differences, differences in health and overall physical well-being can be related either to heredity or to the environment. Some medical conditions are clearly inherited (sickle cell anemia, for example). Others, such as lead poisoning or malnutrition, occur only under certain environmental circumstances. Regardless of the ultimate cause (heredity, environment, or both), medical factors in and of themselves are sources of individual differences in the classroom. In other words, medical factors may affect personality and achievement and also may influence *how* students learn and what they are capable of achieving.

Some medical conditions are relatively permanent and severe. Included here are physical and sensory defects, such as blindness, deafness, and cerebral palsy and chronic illnesses such as diabetes and heart disease. We might also include here certain types of mental retardation in which there is known brain damage. Children who have these obvious medical problems often need special learning environments and usually are eligible for special education services, described later in Chapter 12.

Individual differences can also be caused by medical conditions which are much more subtle than those mentioned above. Undetected vision and hearing problems, serious dental problems, severe allergies, inadequate sleep, malnutrition, and common childhood illnesses such as colds, are just a few examples of health-related problems which can affect a child's temperament, activity level, and alertness in the classroom. If such conditions become chronic, they may have long-term and far-reaching effects on the child's academic achievement, behavior, and even his or her level of intellectual functioning (Kennedy, 1975).

REVIEW 6–1

1. Define the following: mean, range, and standard deviation.

2. What is meant by a "normal curve"?

3. What do twin studies tell us about the role of heredity in determining intelligence?

4. Discuss two criticisms that have been made of the twin studies.

5. What is the most popular theory today on the cause of personality problems?

6. What do cross-cultural studies tell us about the effects of the environment on child behavior?

7. Describe the basic design of the Skeels and Dye (1939) study. What were the results?

8. What effects do birth order and family size seem to have on intelligence?

9. List four sex differences that are fairly well established in the literature.

10. Give examples of three different medical conditions and indicate how they might affect classroom behavior and achievement.

INTELLIGENCE

Having explored a few of the factors that can cause children to differ, we now turn to the topic of how these differences can be measured. We will first consider the measurement of intelligence because of its central importance in educational testing and because most of the principles of intelligence testing apply to the measurement of other characteristics as well.

The Concept of Intelligence and Its Use in Education

"Intelligence" is a concept that means different things to different people. Most of us agree that intelligence has something to do with being able to profit from experience, to learn efficiently, and to deal effectively with one's environment. But what exactly do these words mean? What do people who are able to profit from experience have that persuades us to call them intelligent? Some psychologists have emphasized that intelligence is a single type of mental process, a general capacity to think and reason which manifests itself in a wide variety of situations. Charles Spearman (1927), who formulated an early theory of intelligence, stressed this general aspect of intelligence. Other theorists have proposed that intelligence is made up of a number of distinct traits or abilities and have suggested that is it quite possible for a person to be strong in certain intellectual abilities and weak in others. One example of this viewpoint can be found in the work of L. L. Thurstone (1938) who postulated the existence of seven "primary mental abilities": (1) verbal comprehension, (2) word fluency, (3) number facility, (4) spatial relations, (5) rote memory, (6) perceptual speed, and (7) gen-

eral reasoning. J. P. Guilford (1967) provided an even more extreme example of this approach in his important text *Structure of the Intellect*, in which he proposed that intelligence is made up of 120 separate factors.

Both approaches to defining intelligence are probably valid to some extent. The authors of this text prefer to think of intelligence as a number of separate "intelligent skills," but this does not rule out the possibility of a general factor that contributes somewhat to each facet of intelligence. In the classroom, however, we strongly recommend that you think of intelligence primarily in terms of the wide variety of specific skills needed for coping and learning that each student either already possesses or needs instruction in.

Measuring Intelligence

For all the problems in defining intelligence, its measurement presents even more difficulties. To say that intelligence is a collection of mental abilities that individuals use in adapting to their environments is a theory that most experts would accept, but to specify what these abilities are and develop a test to measure them with precision is another, more difficult matter.

First, intelligence tests, as we shall see, must be designed to be administered under standardized conditions. The items consist of specific tasks such as defining vocabulary words, solving arithmetic problems, and putting together jigsaw puzzles, tasks that can be easily administered and objectively scored. But quick answers to short questions are only one aspect of intelligence. These items cannot tap all the resources that individuals use in adapting to their environment: Intelligence tests were never intended to measure the ability to solve complex, long-term problems, fine-motor mechanical aptitude, creativity, and many other variables which certainly contribute to success in everyday life.

Second, while most intelligence test items are designed to measure certain underlying mental processes (such as memory and abstract reasoning), which presumably operate when a person acts intelligently, they do so *indirectly*. Thus, the examiner must make *inferences* about the individual's mental processes based on his or her performance, and drawing such inferences can be very dangerous. Take, for example, a child who does poorly when asked to repeat sequences of digits (an item used to measure rote memory on many tests). The examiner may infer that the child has a poor memory and that this causes the child to have trouble learning in school. Is this inference justified? It may not be. Perhaps other factors interfered with the child's performance on the memory items — fatigue, hunger, boredom, distractions, anxiety, failure to understand the instructions, and a cultural background that never emphasized this type of skill are all possibilities. Also, might not the *kind* of memory process measured by the test be different from the kind of memory involved in learning the alphabet or recalling what you are supposed to buy at the grocery store?

The purpose of this discussion is to point out that *we cannot measure intelligence or its components directly.* "Intelligence" is an abstraction, an invisible quality assumed to be within a person. In attempting to measure it indirectly, we devise test items to measure some aspects of intelligent behavior and we draw inferences about "how much" intelligence a person has based on his or her performance on these items. Because there is considerable room for error in drawing these inferences, however, we must interpret intelligence test scores cautiously.

Another problem with the measurement of intelligence is that intelligence testing from the outset has been associated with the notion of *innate capacity* or *potential.* The original intelligence tests were designed to predict future success in school. Alfred Binet developed the first version of the Stanford-Binet Intelligence Scale in 1905, at the request of French officials who wanted an objective method for differentiating children who were intellectually "dull" (and thus unlikely to succeed in school) from those who had the innate capacity to benefit from ad-

vanced schooling. Much the same logic is still behind the use of intelligence tests in schools today. These tests are usually given to decide which children have the capacity to be placed in classes for the intellectually gifted or will require special education or should be guided toward vocational education rather than college preparatory courses.

Our analysis of intelligence tests raises two questions. First, do intelligence tests measure an individual's *innate* (inborn or inherited) potential for learning? Many people assume that IQ tests have this ability. When we speak of an "underachiever," for example, we think of an individual who has the inborn potential to do well in school, but who fails to use it. Tests of intelligence simply lack the ability to provide us with a pure measure of innate intelligence, however. They do give us information about an individual's capacity to perform in school and other settings, but as we have already discussed in this chapter, intelligence always reflects the *combined* influence of genetics, learning, and related factors. There is no way to separate, therefore, innate from learned capacity.

Second, how well do intelligence tests measure educational potential? On the whole, studies of the prediction of school success from IQ scores suggest that intelligence tests do only a fair job of predicting. Correlations between IQ scores and school grades and between IQ scores and achievement test scores generally range from 0.40 to 0.60 (Tyler, 1974). Although this is only a modest relationship, it is a consistent and reliable one. Furthermore, children with low IQs are more likely to drop out of school, while those with high IQs are more likely to complete high school and go on to college.

lack of opportunity

Intelligence test scores are only fair predictors of school success, but are the best single measures we now have for predicting school success in a large sample of children.

The real problems in using IQ scores as measures of potential arise when we begin to predict educational outcomes for *individual* children. We have already discussed the Skeels (1966) and Heber et al. (1972) studies which provide convincing data that IQ scores can be modified by placing children in enriched learning environments. Furthermore, a child who has never been exposed to jigsaw puzzles and colored blocks, a child who is unfamiliar with white, middle-class vocabulary, or a child who has received inadequate instruction in arithmetic is likely to be penalized on most standardized intelligence tests. The child will do poorly on the IQ test not because of a lack of ability, but because of a lack of opportunity to learn. What a child could know and does know can never be fully separated in IQ testing.

In summary, then, the IQ score *on the whole* is a fair but consistent predictor of the future school success of large groups of children, but it is even less useful in predicting the achievement of an individual child. Given these limitations, some psychologists, educators, and parents argue that intelligence tests should *never* be used in making educational decisions about children. We disagree with this position and believe that child psychologist Wallace Kennedy made an important point when he likened the blanket condemnation of intelligence tests to "throwing the baby out with the bathwater" (1973, p. 4). Intelligence tests have their limitations, but they are legitimate sources of information about individuals, as long as the following considerations are kept in mind:

(1.) An intelligence test is nothing more than a sample of behavior taken at a particular moment in time. Test scores (and the informal observations psychologists make while testing) *can* tell us something about how the child is currently functioning, and this information *can* help us in planning programs to fit the child's individual needs. Test scores *cannot* tell us why the child is functioning in a particular way; nor can they tell us whether he or she will continue to function that way in the future.

(2.) Many things can artificially lower an IQ score: The student may be sick, tired, or frightened or may find the test boring and irrelevant. The student may come from a subculture vastly different from the one the test is based upon, or the student who is overactive and distractible or anxious may score low on IQ tests because of these problems rather than low intelligence.

(3.) An IQ score *alone* should never be used in diagnosing a child as mentally retarded or in making any decision about the child's future education. Intelligence tests should always be used in conjunction with other tests and with information on the child's family background, health, school history, and so on. This is particularly important when evaluating minority group children.

(4.) When results from intelligence tests and other information are used in planning educational programs for children, the program should be carried out and the child should be reevaluated periodically. That is to say, the IQ score should only be taken as a *tentative* estimate of the child's ability to learn.

IS A HIGH IQ A GOOD THING?

Lewis Terman of the University of California at Berkeley conducted a study of individuals with very high IQ scores from childhood to adulthood, entitled *Genetic Studies of Genius*. The following description of the research program by Harvard University psychologist Richard Herrnstein (1971) outlines the major findings:

"The plan of the study was simple: find a large group of young children with exceptionally high I.Q.'s, record as many potentially interesting and useful additional facts about them as practicable, and then follow the course of their lives. Terman and his staff found slightly more than 1500 California children whose I.Q.'s averaged about 150. (Because they used different intelligence scales for some of the children, no precise average figure can be given.) This was no small achievement in itself, for an I.Q. of 150 or greater is a rarity, possessed, on the average, by the smartest child in a randomly selected group of about two hundred. Most of the children were between the ages of eight and twelve when chosen, but there were also some younger and some recruited in high schools.

"Right from the start the findings were informative. For example, highly bright boys were easier to locate than highly bright girls. And the disparity increased slightly with age, suggesting that whatever the I.Q. is, boys maintain it better than girls. For this reason, the final sample had 857 boys and 671 girls. The children, mainly from urban public schools, definitely did not represent the ethnic or social composition of their communities. Compared to the population from which they were drawn, there was an enormous (over tenfold) excess of the children of

fathers in the professions and an even more marked scarcity (only .013) of the children of laborers, echoing once again the correlation between I.Q. and social class. In addition, the sample contained an excess of Western and Northern Europeans and Jews, and a shortage of Latins, non-Jewish Eastern Europeans, and Negroes. . . .

"The children were non-representative physically as well as intellectually, ethnically, and socially. They tended to be taller, heavier, more broad-shouldered, stronger in hand grip, larger in the vital capacity of their lungs, and somewhat earlier in their sexual maturity than children in the general population. The physical differences, though not large, were large enough to counter the stereotype of the fragile bookworm. Not surprisingly, the gifted children did better in school than their classmates, but mainly in subjects—like reading and arithmetic—that seem to call on intelligence. In subjects like woodworking or sewing, the gifted children enjoyed no particular advantage. They most often liked precisely the subjects that the other children most often disliked, such as reading and arithmetic. At seven years of age the gifted children were already reading books at a higher rate than the average child of fifteen. And even in sports they outdid their classmates, knowing more about the games of childhood and knowing about them earlier. Finally, even in tests of "character"—honesty, tendency toward overstatement, trustworthiness, and the like—the gifted children showed their precocity. At nine or ten years, they had reached the "moral development," by those no doubt quaint standards, of the average child of thirteen or fourteen.

"Children with I.Q.'s of 150 or so are, then, special. But the big question is whether they mature into something special, for that would be the proper test of intelligence testing. Did the I.Q. make the difference it should have made? At last assessment, the sample had reached their middle forties, about thirty-five years after their selection for the study. The death rate in the sample had been less by a third than that in the general population, with fatal accidents quite uncommon. Childhood delinquency, criminal convictions, and alcoholism are all strikingly rare in the sample. More common, and benign, maladjustments are not so rare, with the women showing slightly more emotional trouble than the men. It may be a psychological burden to be so bright a woman in our culture, but this is pure speculation. In any event, not much can be made of the differences in minor mental disturbance between the sample and the general population.

"About 70 percent of the sample *finished* college, men ahead of women by a couple of percentage points. This should be compared with the 8 percent of their contemporaries in the general population who finished college (the 1930–1940 college generation). Out of the more than 1500 in the sample, only eleven did not finish high school, and of these, eight went to professional or trade school. Forty percent of the male college graduates earned law, medical, or Ph.D. degrees, and over half of all the college graduates have at least some postgraduate training. There are, proportionately, five times as many Ph.D.'s in the sample as in the population of college graduates in general. As expected, the sample excelled in college: 80 percent averaging B or better in their courses, and more than 35 percent graduating with honors (Phi Beta Kappa, *çum laude*, or the like). In addition to their academic degrees, the sample has earned a disproportionately large number of professional licenses—CPA's, Fellows of the American Board of Surgery, Fellows of the American Institute of Architects, and so on.

"The ten most common occupations among the men are not the common lot in our society: lawyers first, followed by college faculty members, engineers, physicians, school administrators or teachers, chemists and physicists, authors, architects, geologists, and clergymen. All told, over 85 percent of the working men became either professionals or managers in business and industry, with the first category the larger. At the other end of the occupational scale, only about 3 percent became semiskilled laborers or farmers, and virtually none unskilled laborers. The men are bunched at the top of the scale of occupations, just as they are at the top of the scale of I.Q. And the sample outperforms not only the population in general, but also the average college graduate. The run-of-the-mill college graduate has a 5 percent chance of becoming a semiskilled or unskilled laborer; the sample's college graduate has a chance of only .5 percent, a tenfold reduction. . . .

"In addition to everything else, a high I.Q. pays in money. The average professional or managerial man in the sample was earning about $10,500 in 1954, compared to a national average of about $6000 for those occupations. Even the semiskilled and clerical workers in the sample were outearning, by about 25 percent, the general averages for the same jobs. The total family income for the sample more than doubled that for white, urban American families of roughly the same socio-economic status. About 30 percent of the families in the sample earned more than $15,000 a year in 1954, compared to only one percent for ordinary families in the same general socio-economic class. The sample shows the economic advantages of a high I.Q., after discounting education, race, occupation, and geography. . . .

"Not just the economic facts of life were gathered. When the men were asked about their state of mind, almost 90 percent said that they were at least fairly content, and virtually half were finding "deep satisfaction" in their lives. Only 6 percent reported discontentment. The more prosperous men were generally the more contented. When the men were asked to estimate how well they were living up to their intellectual abilities, there was again a correlation between satisfaction and income. The average yearly wage of those who said they were "fully" living up to their capacities was almost $12,000, while the group least satisfied was making less than $5000 per year." (pp. 51–53)

Apparently a very high IQ is a desirable thing. But too much can be made of this study. First, keep in mind that these children come from advantaged families. Perhaps the factors that led to high IQs also led to success in life. Just because two variables are related does not mean that one *causes* the other. That is to say, high IQs may not cause success, rather they may be *both* caused by the *same* unknown factor.

Second, some of the very bright individuals in this study did poorly in terms of economic and personal success: A high IQ is no guarantee of a happy life. And, since very high IQs are very rare, it is obvious that most of the world's successful people have lower IQs.

Constructing Intelligence Tests

When someone sets out to design a standardized test of intelligence, there are a number of steps to follow. The researcher has a definition of intelligence in mind and devises test items related to that definition. But much more is involved before the test is ready for use. The researcher must establish the objectivity of the test items and the *reliability* and *validity* of the test as a whole. In addition, the test must be tried out on a *standardization* group. Let us examine briefly what each of these terms mean, keeping in mind that these steps of test construction apply to tests of achievement and personality as well.

Objectivity. By **objectivity** we mean that the test results must be as free as possible from the biases and prejudices of the person giving the test. This is a real advantage of standardized tests. Teachers, parents, and psychologists may gain much information by simply observing and interacting with the child on an informal basis. But the impression we get of a child in this way may be strongly influenced by our preconceptions and biases. We may be so close to the child that we cannot separate what we *want* to see from what is actually occurring. Objectivity in a test, then, is a desirable characteristic, and if our own subjective impressions are accurate, objective test items ought to confirm them.

In order to obtain objectivity, intelligence test items are constructed so that they can easily be administered in a standard way by anyone trained to give the test. Furthermore, clear-cut scoring criteria increase the likelihood that the score will be objective and accurate. On a test with ambiguous scoring criteria, it is easy to see that a child's score might depend more on *who* scores the test than on the child's performance.

Reliability.   Objectivity is closely related to reliability. **Reliability** has to do with the consistency of the test scores. To be reliable, a test must yield similar scores when given to the same individual on different occasions. It must also yield similar scores when different individuals grade the same test.

Perhaps several analogies will help you to understand this concept. There are many different ways to measure time, some more reliable than others. For example, a watch with a normal clockface is more reliable than a sundial. You can confirm this by asking a friend to glance at a watch with you. You are both likely to come up with similar measures—"The watch reads 2:17." But ask your friend to glance at a sundial with you. The measures of time each of you obtain will probably differ. This is because the sundial provides a much more ambiguous reading, making it unlikely that the measures taken by two different observers will be consistent.

Another way to determine the reliability of a measuring instrument is for a single observer to take separate readings on two different occasions. For example, you might measure the width of a room using a tape measure. Now try it again. Do your two measures closely agree? If so, you can conclude that your tape measure is reasonably reliable. If you were to measure a room twice by pacing it off and counting the number of feet, you would probably get less consistent, and hence, less reliable measures.

Reliability is important in testing because we want to be able to use the test results with some confidence. If a test does not produce consistent results, we cannot place much confidence in a single test score. There are several ways to determine test reliability.

One is to give the test (or alternate forms of the test) to the same individuals on two separate occasions and compare the two sets of scores. Another is to compare a group of individuals' scores on all the odd-numbered items with their scores on all the even-numbered items. Either way, the two sets of scores must be similar to ensure that we have a reliable test.

A number of factors can serve to lower the reliability of a test. Unclear scoring procedures, tricky test items, and confusing instructions for administering the test are a few examples. In addition, very short tests often are unreliable because they provide an inadequate sample of the behavior being measured. Although these are the types of factors test designers try to avoid to increase the reliability of their tests, you should remember that *no* test provides us with a perfectly reliable score. Temporary characteristics of the subjects (e.g., fatigue, illness) or the testing conditions (e.g., poor lighting, a fire alarm) contribute to **errors of measurement** and thus affect the reliability of a single test score. Some intelligence tests report a statistic called the **standard error of measurement** (see Sattler, 1974). This statistic allows us to predict the range of fluctuation for each student's score likely to occur as a result of chance errors of measurement. Thus, the individual's *true* score can be thought of as falling within some range of the *obtained* score.

Validity.   In our discussion of reliability, we said that being able to place confidence in a test score is very important. In order to do this, the test must not only be reliable, it must also be valid. **Validity** refers to how well a test measures what it is intended to measure. It is possible for a test to yield consistent scores, but at the same time be invalid for the purposes for which it was designed. For example, a written driver's examination may produce consistent scores when given several times to the same group of individuals. But it may be measuring something other than one's driving skill — perhaps it is measuring one's ability to read complicated test questions or one's attitudes toward automobiles as a means of transportation. If this is the case, the test is a reliable measure of something, but it is not a valid measure of driving skill.

ways to determine validity

As with reliability, there are several ways to determine a test's validity. One is to simply ask a number of experts to judge whether the test is a good measure of whatever was intended; if they agree, then we say that the test has **content validity**. In developing

content validity

the first version of the Stanford-Binet Intelligence Scale, Binet asked many teachers what children had to know in order to succeed in school and based the test items on their responses. When he completed the test, all could agree that it had content validity.

An even more critical component of a test is its **predictive validity**. This refers to how

predictive ability

well the test score predicts a person's performance on some outside, but related criterion. We have already seen that many intelligence tests are valid in this respect. IQ scores correlate modestly with various outside criteria such as school grades, achievement test scores, and level of occupational status. Predictive validity is particularly important for tests used in any kind of selection process. For example, we might develop a test for screening applicants for a teacher-

training program. To be useful, the scores on the screening test should adequately predict to some extent which students will successfully complete the program and become good teachers and which will not. If most students who score low on the test still become good teachers, we must conclude that the test is not a valid measure of teaching potential. Remember: even if the reliability of a test is high, it is useless if it is not valid.

Standardization. Before publishing a standardized test, legitimate test designers provide potential users with data on the reliability and validity of the test. But in order to be able to interpret the test scores, we must also have a set of **norms.** Norms are simply the scores obtained by a large sample of people, called the **standardization group.** The norms provide a standard against which we can compare the scores we obtain when we administer the test (if no one had ever taken the test, how would we know whether our scores are low, average, or high?).

norms

In standardizing a test, the test designer should administer the test to a *large* sample of people, a sample *representative* of the population for which the test is intended. In developing the screening test for the teacher-training program referred to previously, it would *not* be necessary to include high-school dropouts or medical doctors in the standardization group, since the test is not being designed for use with these populations. But, the standardization group should include a representative sample of teacher training applicants: males, females, whites, blacks, graduates from urban high schools, graduates from rural high schools, and so on.

After administering the test to the standardization group, the tests are scored and the scores are plotted from highest to lowest. Norms are then developed to tell us what scores are above average, average, and below average. The norms may be reported in a variety of ways: standard scores, percentile ranks, grade equivalents, stanines, mental ages, and so on. We will discuss these different types of scores later in the chapter when we deal with the interpretation of various intelligence and achievement tests.

Intelligence Tests and Their Interpretation

In this section, we will describe three widely used intelligence tests and discuss briefly how to interpret scores from these tests. Keep in mind that in addition to the three tests covered here, many other intelligence tests are used in American schools today. Some tests have been adequately developed and normed and some have not. Remember also that psychologists do not always agree on a definition of intelligence. Thus, different intelligence tests may be composed of different kinds of items. Do not be surprised, therefore, if a child taking two different tests receives two substantially different IQ scores.

The Stanford-Binet Intelligence Scale (Terman and Merrill, 1973).   You may recall that French psychologist Alfred Binet developed the first version of this intelligence test in the early 1900s. In 1916, Lewis Terman, an American psychologist, adapted

Binet's scale for use with American children. He called his test the Stanford-Binet Intelligence Scale in honor of the pioneering work of the Frenchman and in honor of the university with which Terman was associated. Although the Stanford-Binet has been updated several times since 1916, the test in use today is similar to those early scales.

The Stanford-Binet must be administered by a qualified psychologist to one person at a time. Although the test is designed for persons ranging in age from two to adult, for educational purposes it is used primarily at the younger age ranges (ages two to six). Testing generally takes about one hour. One important characteristic of the Stanford-Binet is that it is an **age-level scale.** In other words, test items are grouped according to age levels, with items becoming more difficult at each succeeding age level. In administering the test, the examiner starts at an age level slightly below the child's chronological age (e.g., with an eight-year-old child the examiner might start at the six- or seven-year level to maximize the probability of the child

TABLE 6–2

Samples of Test Items at Various Age Levels on the Stanford-Binet Intelligence Scale

Age Level	Sample Items
2 years	Given blocks and a model, build a four-block tower
	Given a paper doll, point to the parts of the doll's body
3 years	Given pictures of common objects, name each one
	Given paper and pencil, copy a circle
5 years	Given pairs of pictures, tell whether the pictures are alike
	Given simple vocabulary words, define them
7 Years	Given a verbal analogy, solve it (e.g., we sleep on beds, we sit on _____)
	Given a sequence of five digits presented orally, listen and repeat them
10 Years	Given abstract words, define them
	Given a picture of piles of blocks with some blocks partially hidden, count them

achieving success early in the test). If the child responds correctly to those test items, the examiner proceeds to the next age level and so on, until the child misses all items at a single age level. At this point the examiner stops the test. See Table 6–2 for a description of some test items given at various age levels (remember these are just a sample; in actuality, there are six items at each level).

Scoring of the Stanford-Binet has traditionally been based on the concepts of **mental age** (MA) and **chronological age** (CA). Chronological age simply refers to the actual age

of the child in years and months. Mental age is somewhat more difficult to understand and is based on how high the child progresses on the age-level scale of the test. A key assumption of the test is that, for example, a child of seven years who passes all items through the seven-year level *and some* of the items at the eight-year level is "more intelligent" than a child of seven years who passes all the items through the seven-year level, *but* fails *all* the items at the eight-year level. In this example the first seven-year-old has passed some items which the *average eight-year-old child* in the standardization sample passed. Thus, his or her mental age will be greater than the chronological age. The second seven-year-old has not passed any items usually passed by older children. However, the child has passed all items the average seven-year-old child passes, so that the MA will equal the CA. We might also consider a third seven-year-old who fails items that the average six-year-old passes. In this case, the MA is less than the CA.

We can now introduce the concept of the intelligence quotient or IQ. The word "quotient" is used here because intelligence test scores have traditionally been based on the *ratio* between a child's mental age and his or her chronological age. Using this formula, the IQ is determined by dividing the MA by the CA and multiplying by 100 (scores are multiplied by 100 simply to remove the decimal point):

$$IQ = \frac{MA}{CA} \times 100$$

If the MA and CA are equal, the child's IQ will be 100, exactly average:

$$IQ = \frac{8 \text{ years}}{8 \text{ years}} \times 100 = 1.0 \times 100 = 100$$

If the MA is greater than the CA, the child's IQ will be greater than 100, above average:

$$\text{IQ} = \frac{10 \text{ years}}{8 \text{ years}} \times 100 = 1.25 \times 100 = 125$$

Similarly, if the MA is less than the CA, the child's IQ will be less than 100, below average:

$$\text{IQ} = \frac{6 \text{ years}}{8 \text{ years}} \times 100 = .75 \times 100 = 75$$

The latest revision of the Stanford-Binet (1973) uses a somewhat different IQ formula. The test manual contains normative tables that list the IQs for particular MAs obtained by people of particular CAs. Because of statistical reasons, beyond the scope of this text, the IQs obtained using the traditional formula may differ somewhat from the IQs obtained using these tables. But the basic idea is still the same: The IQ score reflects how well a child performs in relation to children of the same age in the standardization group.

A final word about the use of the Stanford-Binet: One distinct disadvantage of the test is that it yields only one IQ score. Returning to Table 6–1, you can see that the test items tap different kinds of skills and information (although, on the whole, the test is composed of mostly verbal items), yet in the report written by the psychologist, only one overall score will be given. It is impossible to determine the child's relative strengths and weaknesses from this one IQ score. This information *can* be obtained, but only if the psychologist does a very subjective and time-consuming analysis of the kinds of items the child tended to pass or fail. Sattler (1974) has provided a scoring system for sorting the items into seven categories based on what the items supposedly measure: language, memory, conceptual thinking, reasoning, numerical reasoning, visual-motor skills, and social intelligence. This system is relatively unproven, however, and is advised against in the manual of the Stanford-Binet. Such judgments must necessarily be based on inferences made by the psychologist.

The Wechsler Intelligence Scale for Children-Revised (Wechsler, 1974). In the late 1930s, David Wechsler, a psychologist at Bellevue Hospital in New York City, decided that there were a number of shortcomings in the Stanford-Binet and set about to develop his own intelligence scale. Initially Wechsler was concerned with the measurement of adult intelligence. The first scale he developed, the Wechsler-Bellevue Intelligence Scale (1944), was designed for this population. The present-day version of the Wechsler-Bellevue is called the Wechsler Adult Intelligence Scale (WAIS) and is widely used in testing adults. Shortly after publishing the adult scale, Wechsler developed an intelligence test for children, which was updated in 1974 as the Wechsler Intelligence Scale for Children-Revised (WISC-R).

The WISC-R is similar to the Stanford-Binet in that it is an individual test, requiring at least an hour to administer. In addition, it includes many items that are similar to those on the Stanford-Binet. However, the similarity ends here. The WISC-R is designed only for children between the ages of six and sixteen, and the procedures for administering and scoring the test are quite different.

First and foremost, the WISC-R is not an age-level scale. Instead of arranging items according to age level, all items of a given *type* (i.e., supposedly measuring the same kind of ability) are grouped into subtests. *Within each subtest* items are then arranged according to difficulty level. The examiner begins with the easiest items on the first subtest, continues with that subtest until the child fails a certain number of items, and then goes on to the second subtest, repeating the procedure until all ten subtests have been given.

A second distinguishing feature of the WISC-R is that each of the ten subtests is designated as being either verbal or performance oriented. While scores on all subtests contribute to the overall or Full Scale IQ, it is also possible to determine a Verbal IQ and a Performance IQ. A listing of the subtests composing the Verbal and Performance Scales, as well as a brief description of the kinds of responses required, is presented in Table 6 – 3.

In scoring the WISC-R, mental ages are not obtained. Instead, the examiner determines the child's raw score for each subtest. The raw scores are then converted into **standard scores.** Standard scores express the individual's distance from the mean or average score in terms of the standard deviation of the distribution. The particular standard score used on the WISC-R is called a **scaled score.** Scaled scores on the WISC-R subtests have a mean of 10 and a standard deviation of 3. You should also note that the subtest scaled scores reflect the child's performance in relation to the mean of the child's own age group. Thus, a child of ten who obtains

a scaled score of 13 on the Vocabulary subtest has scored 1 standard deviation *above* the mean for ten-year-old children in the standardization sample. A child of six who obtains a scaled score of 4 on the Picture Completion subtest has scored 2 standard deviations *below* the mean for six-year-olds.

One advantage the WISC-R has over the Stanford-Binet is that it provides separate standard scores for each of the ten subtests. Thus, one can see immediately where the strengths and weaknesses of the child lie. For example, a child who receives scaled scores of 14 and 15, respectively, on the Vocabulary and Similarities subtests has a strength in these verbal areas. The same child may have a scaled score of 6 on the Arithmetic subtest; this can be identified as a relative weakness. The WISC-R, then, can give you more information than just a single IQ score, but we must be careful again not to put *too* much faith in these measures of ability. Because each of the subtests is more limited and based on a smaller sample of behavior than the full scale, their reliability is much lower and their validity is more questionable (Wechsler, 1974). Remember, the predictive validity of full IQ scores in predicting school achievement is only fair; the predictive validity of the subtest scores is even less impressive. If a student scores very low on the verbal subtests, therefore, this can be used as *one bit of evidence* that, when combined with other kinds of evidence, can be used in developing an understanding of the student's intellectual functioning. Patterns of strengths and weaknesses on the WISC-R should never be accepted as *facts* that are more important than other sources of information, but they can provide useful insights when used in the proper manner.

*TABLE 6–3

Subtests on the WISC-R

Scale	Subtest	Order of Administration of Subtests	Type of Items
	Information	1	Given a question, recall a general fact
	Similarities	3	Given two concepts, use a higher order concept in describing how both are alike
VERBAL	Arithmetic	5	Given an orally presented word problem, solve it without pencil and paper
	Vocabulary	7	Given a vocabulary word, define it
	Comprehension	9	Given a question requiring practical judgment and common sense, answer it
	Picture Completion	2	Given an incomplete picture, point out the part that is missing
	Picture Arrangement	4	Given a series of pictures, put them in the right sequence to tell a story
PERFORMANCE	Block Design	6	Given a picture of a block design, use colored blocks to reproduce it
	Object Assembly	8	Given a jigsaw-type puzzle, put the pieces together to make a picture of an object
	Coding	10	Given a key which matches numbers to geometric shapes, fill in a blank form with the shapes that go with the numbers

Overall (Full Scale) IQ scores are calculated on the WISC-R by totaling the ten subtest scores and converting them into an IQ score by use of a table. In addition, separate Verbal and Performance IQs (based on the sum of the five Verbal and Performance subtest scores, respectively) are obtained in a similar manner. On the WISC-R, the Full Scale, Verbal, and Performance IQs are called **deviation IQs.** The same is true of the revised Stanford-Binet, which no longer uses the formula based on chronological and mental ages. Deviation IQs are actually another kind of standard score; in this case, they are standard scores with a mean of 100 and a standard deviation of 15 (see the feature on WISC-R scores and their relationship to the normal curve). Regardless of the type of IQ score used, however, its meaning is the same; it states how many "intelligent" things an individual can do relative to other individuals of the same age.

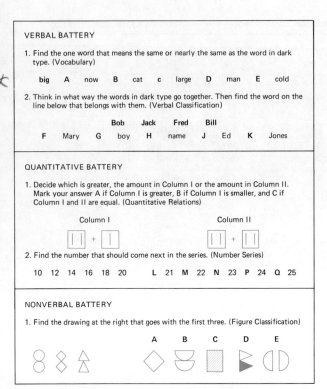

Figure 6–4. *Practice exercises illustrating typical items from the Cognitive Abilities Test, Multi-level Edition (1971).**

Cognitive Abilities Test, Multi-Level Edition (Thorndike & Hagen, 1971). This test, unlike the Stanford-Binet and WISC-R, is a *group* intelligence test. This means that it may be administered to many individuals at the same time. In addition, it may be administered by classroom teachers, provided that the instructions in the examiner's manual are studied beforehand and followed carefully during test administration.

Like many group intelligence tests, the CAT is a multilevel test. This means that it consists of a series of levels, with each level

*Adapted with modifications from the Examiner's Manual for the COGNITIVE ABILITIES TEST, Multi-Level Edition, copyright © 1971 by Houghton Mifflin Company. Printed with permission of Houghton Mifflin Company.

designed for a particular grade (the CAT can be administered to grades 3–12). For any given level, items are arranged into subtests and subtests are grouped into batteries. The CAT has three batteries, with each battery designed to test the student's ability to reason using different kinds of symbols. The Verbal Battery emphasizes verbal reasoning and consists of four subtests (Vocabulary, Sentence Completion, Verbal Classification, and Verbal Analogies). The Quantitative Battery emphasizes numerical reasoning and consists of three subtests (Quantitative Relations, Number Series, and Equation Building). Finally, the Nonverbal Battery emphasizes spatial reasoning and consists of three subtests (Figure Analogies, Figure Classification, and Figure Synthesis). Approximately one hour is required to administer each battery; it is recommended that a separate testing session be scheduled for each battery.

In Figure 6–4, several practice exercises for the three batteries of the CAT are illustrated. You should note that all items are multiple choice. Students record their responses on special answer sheets. Note also that the instructions in Figure 6–4 have been abbreviated. In actual use the examiner reads more detailed instructions aloud (while the students read along silently) and the students work through several practice exercises before beginning each subtest.

The CAT can be scored either by hand or by machine. The normative score obtained on this test is called a Standard Age Score (SAS). The SAS is a standard score with a mean of 100 and a standard deviation of 16, equivalent in meaning to the deviation IQs obtained on the Stanford-Binet and WISC-R. On the CAT separate Standard Age Scores are obtained for each of the three batteries.

INTELLIGENCE TEST SCORES AND THE NORMAL CURVE

It is very important that we look closely at how intelligence test scores relate to the normal curve. Remember, for the WISC-R, subtest scaled scores have a mean of 10 and a standard deviation of 3. Performance, Verbal, and Full Scale IQs have a mean of 100 and a standard deviation of 15. As the following diagram shows, on a *theoretical* basis 68.26 percent of the population should have WISC-R IQs between 85 and 115 (±1 standard deviation); 13.59 percent should have IQs between 115 and 130 (+2 stan-

dard deviations), 2.14 percent should have IQs between 130 and 145, and only .13 percent should have IQs over 145. (Note that the exact figures for the Stanford-Binet IQs are slightly different, since the Stanford-Binet has a standard deviation of 16, instead of 15). Most achievement and personality scores are also reported in standard scores that only have meaning when related to the normal curve. To interpret them, you need only to know what the mean and standard deviation of that type of standard score is.

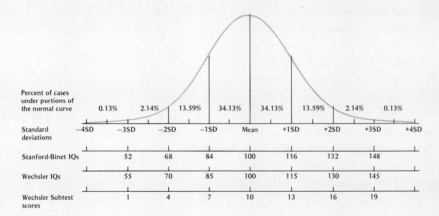

In the WISC-R manual, data are presented to show that the percentages of scores falling under various portions of the normal curve in the actual standardization sample are very close to what is expected theoretically. These data are presented in the table to the right, along with the classification system used by Wechsler to describe the various IQ ranges.

IQ Range	Classification	Percent of Standardization Sample
130 and above	Very Superior	2.3
120–129	Superior	7.4
110–119	High Average	16.5
90–109	Average	49.4
80–89	Low Average	16.2
70–79	Borderline	6.0
69 and below	Mentally Deficient	2.2

Thus, it is possible to see how a student compares with other students of the same age in verbal, quantitative, and spatial reasoning skills. For example, a ten-year-old student who receives SASs of 80, 100, and 114 on the Verbal, Quantitative, and Nonverbal batteries, respectively, has evidenced a rather uneven pattern of development. The Verbal score is more than 1 standard deviation below the mean for ten-year-olds. In contrast, the Quantitative score is average and the Nonverbal score is almost 1 standard deviation above average.

In concluding this chapter, a few points should be made regarding the relative merits of individual and group intelligence tests for educational purposes. Group tests, such as the CAT, have the advantage of being less costly and easier to administer and score than individual tests. As a result, they are often used as part of a school system's routine testing program and may be given once a year to an entire school population or several grade levels. In group testing, however, there is significantly less opportunity to gain the cooperation of individual students and to note interfering factors such as fatigue, illness, and anxiety. In addition, students who have difficulty reading, following oral instructions, or concentrating amid distractions may be penalized to a much greater extent on a group test than on an individual test. For these reasons, group intelligence tests are probably best used as screening tools to identify students who might benefit from more extensive individual testing. Finally, remember that intelligence tests, whether group or individual, should *never* be used in isolation when making important educational decisions about individual students.

REVIEW 6-2

1. What do we mean when we say that intelligence is an abstraction?

2. Are intelligence tests good predictors of school success?

3. Do intelligence tests measure innate potential?

4. Discuss three considerations that should be kept in mind when using intelligence tests for educational purposes.

5. Define reliability, standardization, content validity, and predictive validity.

6. Why is the Stanford-Binet referred to as an "age-level scale"?

7. Calculate the IQ of a child with an MA of 6 and a CA of 8 using the traditional formula.

8. Describe how the items are arranged on the WISC-R.

9. Describe the different kinds of scores available from the WISC-R.

10. What are the advantages and disadvantages of group intelligence tests, such as the CAT?

SUMMARY

Because students differ from one another in many ways, teachers must be knowledgeable in measuring individual differences and interpreting test scores. The first step in summarizing test data is to construct a frequency distribution. From a frequency distribution you can calculate the mean, or average score, which describes how the group as a whole performed. You may also be interested in the range, the difference between the highest and lowest scores obtained on a test. The range tells us how much variability there is in a distribution of scores. Another measure of variability is the standard deviation, which reflects how much the scores cluster around the mean. Psychologists have found that many physical and psychological characteristics are distributed normally; that is, if scores are taken from a large sample, most scores will fall near the mean, with fewer and fewer scores falling toward either extreme end of the distribution. There is an exact relationship between the hypothetical normal curve and the standard deviation. This relationship helps us to see how one score compares with other scores on the same test. Statistics such as the mean and standard deviation are necessary for the interpretation of standardized achievement and intelligence tests given to large groups of individuals.

Studies of identical twins and other pairs of related and unrelated persons have shown us that individual differences in personality and intelligence are, to some extent, related to hereditary factors. However, heredity necessarily interacts with environmental experiences in determining our actual behavior. The importance of the environment is shown in cross-cultural studies and studies on the plasticity of intelligence. For example, increases in intelligence test scores can be obtained by placing children in more stimulating learning environments.

Intelligence is also related to birth order and family size. Firstborn children generally score slightly higher on intelligence tests than laterborn children, and children from small families generally score higher than children from large families. There seems to be little difference between males and females in overall intelligence, although certain kinds of sex differences are fairly well established: males are better in math and visual-spatial skills, females are better in verbal abilities, and males are more aggressive. Even these differences are slight, however, and do not mean that any male or female student cannot excel in any area of ability. Finally, individual differences in intelligence, achievement, and personality are sometimes related to medical factors, both readily apparent conditions such as blindness and chronic heart disease and more subtle conditions such as inadequate nutrition and dental problems.

Intelligence tests are one type of measurement tool frequently used in education. Because there is much disagreement over how to define intelligence, intelligence testing is controversial. In general, you should remember that intelligence tests are simply samples of behavior taken under standardized conditions. They can tell us something about how a child is currently functioning, but they cannot tell us why the child is functioning that way. Although IQ scores are fair predictors of school success on the whole, inferences about the ability of individual children should be made only with extreme caution.

In developing intelligence tests, test designers are concerned with reliability (consistency of the test scores over time) and validity (how well the test measures what it is intended to measure). They also provide norms to be used in interpreting scores. Norms are based on the performance of a large, representative standardization group.

The Stanford-Binet Intelligence Scale is a widely used individual intelligence test. It is referred to as an age-level scale because the test items are arranged according to age levels, with the items at higher levels more difficult than the items at lower levels. The test yields two types of normative scores: a mental age, which indicates the age level at which the child is functioning intellectually, and the IQ, which is a quotient indicating the relationship between mental age and chronological age. The Wechsler Intelligence Scale for Children-Revised (WISC-R) is another widely used test. On the WISC-R, items are arranged according to subtests, with each subtest measuring a somewhat different type of ability. Scaled scores are obtained on each of the 10 subtests. In addition, verbal, performance, and full-scale IQs can be obtained. The mean IQ on both the Stanford-Binet and WISC-R is 100, with a standard deviation of about 15.

The WISC-R and Stanford-Binet are both individual tests and are quite costly and time-consuming to administer and score. For this reason many school systems also use group intelligence tests, which can be administered by the classroom teacher to a large group of students at one time. Group intelligence tests, such as the Cognitive Abilities Test, can help classroom teachers learn more about the strengths and weaknesses of their students. However, the scores must be interpreted with caution, since many factors which might interfere with testing and cause a child to score poorly (such as illness, anxiety, or difficulties in reading or following instructions) are more difficult to detect in a group testing situation.

ANSWERS TO REVIEW QUESTIONS

Review 6–1

1. The mean is the average score, calculated by adding up all the scores and dividing the resulting sum by the total number of scores. The range equals the difference between the lowest and the highest score and is a measure of variability. The standard deviation is also a measure of variability, but it reflects the average amount by which individual scores differ from the overall mean of the distribution.

2. If scores from a large sample are plotted from high to low according to frequency, we often find that the scores are distributed normally; that is, most of the scores fall near the mean, with few scores falling at the extremes. The normal curve is symmetrical and bell-shaped.

3. Researchers have found that as genetic similarity increases, similarity in intelligence test scores increases.

4. Identical twins are treated more alike than other pairs of children; thus the role of the environment cannot be ruled out. In addition, even identical twins reared apart may be raised in very similar environments.

5. A predisposition to personality disorders can be inherited, but whether this predisposition is ever expressed depends on the environment.

6. Different cultures stress different values and use different child-rearing procedures. Consequently the behavior of children raised in separate cultures is sometimes quite different. Environment has a clear effect on behavior.

7. Skeels and Dye transferred 13 children from an understaffed orphanage to an institution for the retarded, where each was assigned to an older retarded girl who served as "foster" mother. A control group remained in the orphanage. The experimental group gained considerably in IQ, while the control group lost.

8. Firstborns score better on intelligence tests than laterborns. Children from small families score better than children from large families, regardless of social class.

9. a. Females excel in verbal abilities.
   b. Males excel in math abilities.
   c. Males excel in visual-spatial abilities.
   d. Males are more aggressive than females.

10. Subtle problems such as inadequate nutrition, dental problems, and common childhood illnesses may affect the child's ability to concentrate and learn. If these conditions are long-lasting, they may have far-reaching effects on the child's self-concept, achievement, and intellectual skills.

Review 6-2

1. Intelligence is generally thought of as an abstract, invisible quality within a person that cannot be measured directly. We must make inferences about mental processes based on overt behavior during the testing session.

2. On the whole, children who do well on intelligence tests do well in school. The correlations range from 0.40 to 0.60.

3. To a large degree, test items measure what the child has already learned and not what he or she is capable of learning, given ideal conditions.

4. a. Such tests provide us with a sample of behavior; they can tell us something about the level at which the child is currently functioning, but cannot tell us why.
   b. IQ scores should never be used alone in making educational decisions about a child.

c. When educational decisions are made in conjunction with other test data, testing should be repeated at a later date to reevaluate the child's progress.

5. Reliability refers to how consistent the test scores are across time. Validity refers to how well the test measures what it was designed to measure. Standardization is the process involved in obtaining normative scores to be used in test interpretation; the test is given to a large, representative sample under clearly specified conditions.

6. It is an age-level scale because the test items are arranged according to age level, with the items becoming more difficult as the age increases.

7. $IQ = \dfrac{MA}{CA} \times 100$. If MA is 15 and CA is 10, IQ is 150.

8. Items are arranged according to subtests, with each subtest presumably measuring different kinds of abilities. Item difficulty increases within a given subtest.

9. The WISC-R yields scaled scores on each of the 10 subtests. The scaled scores are standard scores with a mean of 10 and a standard deviation of 3. These scores allow one to make comparisons between the child's performance on different subtests. Scaled scores from the five verbal subtests are summed and the sum converted to a verbal IQ. Scaled scores from the performance subtests are summed and the sum converted to a Performance IQ. Finally, all subtest scores contribute to the Full Scale IQ. The IQs have a mean of 100 and a standard deviation of 15.

10. They are relatively inexpensive, easy to administer, and can be administered by the classroom teacher. But it is hard to note interfering factors such as anxiety, illness, and reading difficulties. Also, they are limited to multiple-choice questions.

Measuring Educational Progress

Intelligence tests are considered to be scholastic *aptitude* tests; that is, they supposedly predict the student's *potential* for school success. In contrast, achievement tests are designed to measure directly how far students have progressed in academic achievement. We have seen that this distinction is not always clear — intelligence tests measure to an extent what the student has learned in school. Still, it is not the goal of intelligence testing to measure skills and information taught specifically in school, as is the case with achievement testing.

There are many reasons why evaluation of academic achievement is an essential aspect of education. From the teacher's point of view, achievement tests can provide information which is helpful in planning and carrying out instruction. Furthermore, test results can assist the teacher in evaluating the effectiveness of specific teaching methods and curricula used in the classroom. From the students' and parents' point of view, achievement test scores also provide important feedback on relative strengths and weaknesses. Finally, achievement test scores give school systems feedback, revealing where students in one system stand in relation to students in other systems and, hopefully, motivating administrators to improve existing instructional programs and to implement new programs.

There are many ways to evaluate student achievement. We have chosen to separate the different kinds of achievement testing into two overall categories: (1) commercially available standardized achievement tests, and (2) teacher-constructed achievement tests. Most teachers use both kinds because each has its own advantages and disadvantages.

STANDARDIZED ACHIEVEMENT TESTS

Like standardized intelligence tests, standardized achievement tests are usually developed by professional test designers who provide the potential user with data on the reliability and validity of the test, as well as norms for interpreting the test scores. The tests are constructed to measure academic content which is common to most school systems and which is not likely to change so that the test can be widely used without yearly revisions. Some tests are designed to measure academic achievement in a specific area, such as mathematics or foreign languages. The most widely used tests, however, are *batteries,* which measure achievement in many different areas such as reading, mathematics, language, social studies, science, and study skills. These batteries are typically given once or twice a year to an entire school population or to certain grades as part of the system's testing program. This is the type of standardized achievement test we are most concerned with here.

The Design and Administration of Standardized Achievement Tests

Some test batteries are designed only for use with students in a narrow range of grade levels, but most are designed so that they can be administered to the majority of students in a school system, regardless of grade level. In other words, the test battery may have different levels, with Level I designed for the primary grades, Level II for the intermediate grades, Level III for the middle

[handwritten margin notes:] 1. meas. one specific area 2. batteries meas. several areas

TABLE 7–1

Widely Used Achievement Test Batteries

Battery	K	1	2	3	4	5	6	7	8	9	10	11	12	13	14
California Achievement Tests: 1970 Edition	x	x	x	x	x	x	x	x	x	x		x		x	
Iowa Tests of Basic Skills	x	x	x	x	x	x	x	x							
Iowa Tests of Educational Development										x	x		x	x	
Metropolitan Achievement Test: 1970 Edition	x	x	x	x	x	x	x	x	x	x					
SRA Achievement Series	x	x	x	x	x	x	x	x	x	x					
Sequential Tests of Educational Progress (STEP)—Series II				x	x	x	x	x	x	x		x	x	x	x
Stanford Achievement Test	x	x	x	x	x	x	x	x	x	x					
Stanford Test of Academic Skills (TASK)									x	x	x		x	x	x
Tests of Academic Progress (TAP)										x	x		x	x	

(From Anastasi, 1976)

school grades, and so on. The actual test items (and their degree of difficulty) vary from level to level, but the basic procedures for administration and the general types of skills and content measured are similar for each level. Thus, it is possible to administer the same basic test at different points in the child's schooling. Table 7–1 lists a sample of widely used achievement batteries and shows the grade levels for which each is designed.

Just what kinds of achievement do standardized batteries measure? It is likely that you have taken several batteries during your own school career and have some recollection of their typical content. To refresh your memory, let's examine briefly the content of one widely used test, the *Comprehensive Tests of Basic Skills* (published by CTB/McGraw-Hill, 1973). The CTBS is available for use in kindergarten through grade twelve and takes from three to four and a half hours to administer, depending on the

grade level. For grades two through twelve, separate scores are obtained in six major categories: Total Reading, Total Mathematics, Total Language, Reference Skills, Social Studies, and Science. Total Reading is further broken down into Vocabulary and Comprehension; Mathematics into Computation, Concepts, and Applications; and Total Language into Mechanics, Spelling, and Expression. The content of these subtests is tied specifically to skills and information taught in most schools. For example, on the Reference Skills subtest, items involve alphabetizing and the use of the card catalog and library reference books. The language subtests deal with identifying mistakes in spelling, punctuation, capitalization, and so on. The CTBS, like most other batteries, avoids content idiosyncratic to certain school systems, such as coastal ecology or state history.

In administering achievement test batteries it is important to keep in mind that the tests are standardized. This means that the person giving the test (typically the classroom teacher) must adhere closely to the instructions for

HOW TO GIVE A STANDARDIZED ACHIEVEMENT TEST

It is very probable that at some point in your teaching career you will be expected to administer a standardized achievement test. Although each test has its own specific instructions for administration, there are a number of general rules that need to be kept in mind, regardless of the test. Bruce Tuckman (1975), in his book *Measuring Educational Outcomes: Fundamentals of Testing,* has made several particularly helpful suggestions which are reproduced in full here:

(1) *"Familiarize yourself before the testing date with all instructions for administration.* This means reading the Teacher's Directions for Administering carefully and completely so that you know exactly what to do. For example, some standardized achievement test batteries come with practice tests that are to be given a few days before the actual testing. Had you not read the directions thoroughly you might not have known about this and hence might have overlooked it.

(2) *Make sure all students have everything they need to take the test and no more.* Students must have number 2 lead pencils, test booklets, and answer sheets. They should not have books or papers out other than scratch paper when allowed.

(3) *All information called for in the Pupil Information Box must be filled in by the student.* This information typically includes name, date of birth, grade level, sex, teacher, school. For younger students, the teacher is usually requested to fill in this information.

(4) *All test instructions, both general and specific, must be clearly given by the teacher to the students exactly as called for in the directions.* For example, students are told to mark only one answer for each item and to erase an answer completely if they decide to change it. Giving more or fewer instruc-

tions may cause variability in student performance and render the norms unusable for that testing.

(5) *Time limits must be adhered to exactly.* Standardized achievement tests are almost always timed tests. The test Directions tell you precisely how much time is allowed per test. Use a watch with a second hand to be sure that students start and stop each test exactly on time. If students complete a test ahead of time, they may not go on to the next test. If time runs out before they are finished, they must stop nevertheless.

(6) *Make sure that all students know how to take the test.* Answer any questions by reading again appropriate instructions. Make sure, particularly, that all students know how to mark their answer sheets.

(7) *Monitor the test taking from various points in the room.* Check that all students are following directions. Be available for questions about procedures.

(8) *Make sure the students take the testing seriously.* The students should not be frightened by testing but they must take it seriously. Teachers should prepare but not scare students by explaining its purposes to them in advance. They will be more likely to take it seriously if you take it seriously but calmly and positively. Give it the same importance as you would your own final exam. Show that you feel the results will help students; do not show annoyance with the administration for wasting your time. The students will sense your feelings and will behave accordingly." (pp. 383–385)

If you follow Tuckman's suggestions, you will increase the likelihood that the test scores obtained will be accurate reflections of your students' level of achievement.

administration set forth in the test manual. Any departure from the standardized test conditions may affect the scores of the students involved and make interpretation of the scores difficult. Remember also that most test batteries require more than an hour or two to administer and thus disrupt, to some extent, the normal school schedule. In addition, these batteries often cause considerable concern for parents and students alike, making their administration a potentially difficult experience for everyone involved. The classroom teacher, therefore, plays an important role in helping to minimize the disruption caused by standardized achievement testing and to maximize the likelihood that the tests will yield valuable information.

The Interpretation of Standardized Achievement Tests

Standardized achievement tests are often scored by a computer scoring service provided by the test publisher. In this case, the teacher will receive summary report sheets on which various types of scores are reported for each student. The actual number of correct answers (raw scores) are generally not reported. Instead, the scoring service converts the raw scores to various kinds of normative scores so that the scores of the students can be compared with the norm. In cases where teachers or counselors score the tests themselves, norms are usually available in the test manual to convert raw scores to normative scores. In either case, you must be able to interpret the scores obtained.

Grade equivalents are one type of normative score you are likely to encounter. Grade equivalents describe a student's performance according to grade levels. Let's suppose you are a third-grade teacher and one of your students receives a grade equivalent of 5.8 in reading comprehension. This means that the student received the same raw score on that particular subtest as the *average* child in the eighth month of the fifth year of school in the standardization sample. A second child obtains a grade equivalent of 2.0. This child has earned the same raw score as the *average* child just beginning the second grade.

A second type of normative score frequently used in achievement testing is the **percentile rank.** Keep in mind that percentile rank *does not* refer to the percentage of items the student answered correctly. It refers, instead, to the percentage of students in the standardization group who scored *lower than* the student in question. Typically the percentile rank shows the standing of a student in relation to students of the same *grade level* in the standardization group. Thus, a ninth-grader who obtains a percentile rank of 63 has scored better than 63 percent of the ninth-graders in the standardization group.

The last type of score we want to consider is the **stanine.** Stanines are normally distributed standard scores ranging from 1 to 9 (the term stanine is an abbreviation of "standard nine"). When interpreting stanines it may be helpful to think of the scores being divided into nine separate groups, with a certain percentage of the standardization sample falling into each group. Stanine 1 is the lowest group, Stanine 5 is the middle group, and Stanine 9 is the highest group. Thus, a student who earns a stanine score of 9 falls into the highest group, with approximately 4 percent of the standardization sample scoring that high. The percentage of cases that fall within each stanine is shown in Table 7–2,

TABLE 7–2

The Interpretation of Stanines

Stanine	Percentage of cases in each stanine	Description
1	4	Lowest level
2	7	Low level
3	12	Well below average
4	17	Slightly below average
5	20	Average
6	17	Slightly above average
7	12	Well above average
8	7	High level
9	4	Highest level

along with the descriptive terms suggested by Tuckman (1975) for interpreting each stanine.

When you interpret grade equivalents, percentile ranks, and stanines remember that these scores may be based on either *national* or *local* norms. The norms provided in the test manual are generally national norms; that is, they are based on a large group made up of representative students from all over the United States. Thus, the use of national norms allows you to compare the achievement of your students with the achievement of students *in general.* But this may not always be the most useful comparison. Your instructional objectives or those of your school system may differ somewhat from the objectives of most schools. Or perhaps you are not using standard textbooks or are teaching skills and content in a different sequence than what is commonly followed. In these cases, local norms may yield more

useful information on your students' achievement. Local norms may be based on the
scores of students in your state, school system, school building, or even your own
classroom. In using local norms, then, you
are comparing your students with students
who have probably had similar instructional
programs. Many school systems are now
supplying teachers with scores based on
both types of norms. This practice should
increase the amount of useful information
obtained from standardized achievement
tests.

TEACHER-CONSTRUCTED ACHIEVEMENT TESTS

We have already mentioned several disadvantages of standardized tests. They generally cover very broad topics and are sometimes inappropriate for what you may want
most to measure—the learning of the *specific
content* taught in your own classroom. In
addition, standardized tests are relatively
expensive and are usually *not* designed to be
administered frequently to the same group of
students. For these reasons, you will probably want to design and administer your own
achievement tests.

Frequent evaluation of student achievement is an essential aspect of good teaching.
Teachers who give only midterm and final
exams risk finding that a fair percentage of
their students do not have a good understanding of the material covered and, at that
point, are hard pressed to do anything about
it. If tests are given more frequently, it is often possible to discover *why* students are
having trouble and to intervene in some way
to facilitate learning.

Conversely, frequent testing may also help
you to prevent a situation in which students
are not being challenged by instruction. Either way, you will be in a position to improve instruction only when you are aware
of how your students are progressing, and
such awareness comes primarily from frequent testing.

Of course, teacher-made tests must be
more than just frequent to be good measures
of progress; they must also be reliable and
valid measures of the behaviors you are
trying to teach. This primarily means that the
test items should reflect your own instructional objectives. If your intention in teaching a social studies unit on the Civil War is
that students learn to recognize the names,
locations, and outcomes of important battles,
then test items on the dates of those battles
or the generals who fought in them are not
valid. This point cannot be overemphasized:
In order to construct a good achievement
test to be given *after* instruction, you must
have a clear idea of what you expect your
students to learn *before* instruction ever
begins. This means that you must be skilled
in writing instructional objectives, the topic
to which we now turn.

INSTRUCTIONAL OBJECTIVES

Instructional objectives are simply statements that describe the goals you expect the
student to reach when you complete instruction. Robert Mager (1962), whose book
Preparing Instructional Objectives has become a classic in teacher-training programs,
defines objectives in this way:

A learning objective may lead you to choose a field trip as a relevant learning experience for your students.

Mager, '62

An objective is an *intent* communicated by a statement describing a proposed change in the learner — a statement of what the learner is to be like when he has successfully completed a learning experience. It is a description of a pattern of behavior (performance) we want the learner to be able to demonstrate. . . . I cannot emphasize too strongly the point that an instructor will function in a fog of his own making until he knows just what he wants his students to be able to do at the end of instruction. (p. 3)

Most instructors have some conception of what they want to teach when they begin a unit of instruction. But unless these ideas are clearly thought out (and preferably written down), it is easy to get sidetracked while teaching. Writing out objectives will help both *you and the students* to choose the most relevant learning experiences for each goal (e.g., films, lectures, field trips, term papers, or homework exercises). Furthermore, if achievement tests are based on the objectives (and hopefully what you actually tried to teach), they are more likely to be fair and valid measures of what the students have learned under your direction. Finally, objectives have the additional benefit of clearly communicating to the student exactly what is expected, leading to more efficient use of the student's time.

Writing Instructional Objectives

Mager (1962), Vargas (1972), Gagné (1970), and others in the field of instructional technology emphasize three important steps in writing meaningful instructional objectives. First, *specify the terminal behavior expected of the student.* In specifying the terminal behavior, the emphasis should be on observable performance, that is, on what students must be *doing* when they exhibit achievement of the objective. Avoid general terms such as "appreciate," "know," and "understand" since they do not clearly communicate the behavior expected of the student. In contrast, terms like "point to," "list," "solve," "give examples of," and "separate into categories" describe types of terminal behaviors that can be more readily observed.

Second, *specify the conditions under which the terminal behavior is expected to occur.* In the following example the terminal behavior is clearly specified, but the conditions are not: "The student will write, in alphabetical order, a list of words." This objective could be improved by adding more details: "Given a list of ten proper names starting with different letters of the alphabet, the student will write the names in alphabetical order." Likewise, "The student will multiply any two, two-digit numbers," could be improved to read: "Without use of a calculator or slide rule, the student will multiply any two, two-digit numbers." The purpose of adding such details is to ensure that the objective will not be misinterpreted or confused with other similar objectives.

Third, *specify the level of performance acceptable for mastery of the objective.* In other words we must answer the question, "How well does the learner have to perform in order to conclude that he or she has met the objective?" Levels of acceptable performance may be stated in a number of ways. In some cases we are concerned with the number or percentage of correct responses: "Given pencil and paper and ten, three-digit subtraction problems, the student will solve 90 percent of the problems correctly." In other cases, we may also be concerned with time limits: "Given a 250-word business letter, the student will type the letter in less than 5 minutes with fewer than 6 errors." Finally, we may be concerned with some other characteristic related to precision or accuracy: "Given a sample of steel, the student will determine the percentage of magnesium in the sample to within 1 percent of the actual value."

It may be apparent to you that it is easy to write objectives as specific as those above for certain content areas, but for others it may be extremely difficult. It may also be obvious that within any given content area many *different kinds* of objectives are appropriate. At times, simple recognition or recall of specific information is the goal. At other times, we may be more concerned with applying information to new situations, with drawing conclusions, with making value judgments, with creating something original, and so on. In general, it is much easier to write specific objectives when simple recall is the behavior desired of your students. It is more challenging to write objectives when we are concerned with teaching higher level cognitive processes, such as those involved in creativity or critical thinking, or when we want to teach values and attitudes.

One system that you may find useful in classifying and writing different kinds of objectives is in Benjamin Bloom's *Taxonomy of Educational Objectives, Handbook I: Cognitive Domain* (Bloom, Engelhart, Furst, Hill, & Krathwohl, 1956). Bloom and his colleagues developed a system for categorizing objectives into three domains: (1) the **cognitive domain,** which includes objectives for recalling knowledge and developing intellectual skills, (2) the **affective domain,** which includes objectives for developing appreciation, interests, attitudes, and values, and (3) the **psychomotor domain,** which includes objectives for developing manipulative and motor skills. Within each domain, objectives can be arranged in a hierarchy of categories ranging from simple to complex. Table 7–3 is based on Bloom's taxonomy for the cognitive domain. In it we have included sample objectives that fall into each category of the taxonomy (keep in mind that, given space limitations, these objectives are stated in rather general terms).

TABLE 7–3

Bloom's Taxonomy of Educational Objectives: The Cognitive Domain

Categories of Objectives	Sample Objectives (the student will be able to . . .)
Knowledge (recalling or recognizing facts, concepts, rules)	Define the term "archeology" List four Central American countries
Comprehension (understanding facts and concepts by summarizing, interpreting, translating, etc.)	Indicate which states have the highest and lowest per capita incomes given a bar graph Give an example of "loyalty" from his or her own experiences
Application (using facts and concepts to solve *new* problems)	Use *Robert's Rules of Order* in conducting a class meeting Determine the amount of calcium in a sample of drinking water
Analysis (identifying component parts of a whole and their interrelationships)	Distinguish between the main and subordinate themes in an unfamiliar literary passage Recognize the persuasive techniques used in a political campaign speech
Synthesis (integrating components into a new whole)	Write an original musical composition Develop a proposal for reducing litter on the school grounds
Evaluation (judging or comparing ideas, procedures, products, etc.)	Indicate which of three poems best conveys a feeling of hopelessness and why (there is no "right" answer) Discuss the differences between the Chippewa and and Sioux Indian cultures and cite reasons why you would choose to live in one or the other

WRITING INSTRUCTIONAL OBJECTIVES IN THE AFFECTIVE DOMAIN

Most of the instructional objectives you use in your classrooms will probably be *cognitive* objectives; that is, they will specify what knowledge and intellectual skills you want your students to master. But virtually all educators agree that there is much more to education than teaching students to recall and apply information in solving problems. Students learn emotions, attitudes, and values in school, just as surely as they learn facts and intellectual skills. And many educators agree that this *affective* (or emotional) aspect of education has been neglected for too long.

This is not to say that teachers have shown no interest in furthering the affective development of their students. Indeed, objectives such as "the student will develop an appreciation for English literature" have long been recognized as educationally valid. Instead, the problem seems to lie in writing affective objectives behaviorally, so that instructional experiences which help students reach the objectives can be more systematically designed and evaluated.

As with cognitive objectives, affective objectives ideally should be written in sufficient detail so that we can clearly tell when the objective has been met. In the affective domain, this is difficult to do because we are dealing with emotions, attitudes, and values that cannot always be observed directly and that can be interpreted in different ways by different people. Consider the objective, "The student should learn to appreciate good music." What do we mean by *good music*? (classical music, jazz, pop,

country rock?) And what must students do to show *appreciation*? (Indicate on an attitude questionnaire that they like good music, listen when music is played in the classroom, answer test questions about musical composers, buy record albums, attend concerts, join the school choir?) Finally, *to what extent* must they show appreciation? (Give good music a rating of 7 on a 10-point rating scale, smile and show enthusiasm while listening to music, buy one record album, attend seven concerts?) Hopefully, you can see that specifying and measuring attitudes, values, and emotions is not an easy task!

We have a long way to go in developing systems for writing worthwhile affective objectives. You may find it helpful to start with a book by Krathwohl, Bloom, and Masia (1964), *Taxonomy of Educational Objectives, Handbook II: Affective Domain.* In this book, the authors propose that affective objectives can be classified along a continuum, ranging from simple to complex. At the simplest level, *receiving,* the student is required to merely attend to or to be aware of some phenomenon. A sample objective at this level might be "The student develops an awareness of aesthetic factors in architecture." At a slightly higher level, *responding,* the student must go beyond mere awareness and actively do something with or about the phenomenon ("The student develops a positive attitude toward school by completing homework."). Next, we have the *valuing* level, at which students respond to a phenomenon with consistency and with feeling, implying that they find worth in the phenomenon ("The student develops an appreciation for helping others by doing volunteer work on a regular basis at a community agency.").

At the fourth level, *organization,* the students begin to bring their values together into a system and look at the interrelationships between values ("The student identifies the characteristics of a political ideology he or she admires."). Finally, at the highest level, *characterization,* the students organize their values into a system or philosophy of life that affects how they behave in many different situations ("The student develops the habit of approaching problems in an open-minded and objective manner.").

It should be noted that the classification of objectives into various domains is done for the sake of convenience. Many educators find it easiest to write objectives when they consider affective goals apart from cognitive goals. But in actuality, attitudes and values often go hand in hand with knowledge and skills. Thus, students who experience success in learning to read are likely to value reading as a pastime, while those who experience failure are likely to develop a negative attitude toward reading. The implication here is that while you may write separate affective objectives for your students, these objectives will often need to be tied to the cognitive learning experiences you are providing in the classrooms.

Finally, remember that you need to be very cautious in writing affective objectives. There are some attitudes and values that are considered desirable by virtually everyone in our society. More often, however, we are less concerned with promoting specific values and more concerned with teaching students how to explore their own values and the values of others. The primary purpose, then, in using affective objectives should not be to *grade* students on their values and interests, but rather to obtain information that will help you to guide students in their own personal growth.

One common criticism of instructional objectives is that they tend to be "trivial." This is probably because it is so much easier to write objectives that measure simple recall of knowledge than it is to write objectives at Bloom's comprehension, application, analysis, synthesis, and evaluation levels. But, Bloom's taxonomy shows us that it is *possible* to write meaningful, and yet specific, objectives that tap higher-level intellectual skills. Furthermore, although instructional objectives add structure to learning, their use need not necessarily lessen "spontaneity," "creativity," or "individuality" in the classroom. By being flexible in designing and using objectives, teachers can allow for individual interests and ability levels, and at the same time facilitate learning and its evaluation.

It is unnecessary and even undesirable for all students to work on the same objectives or for all students to reach a given objective in the same way. Further, it is seldom necessary for every teacher to take on the time-consuming task of writing his or her *own* objectives for every unit of instruction. Many publishers now provide instructional objectives to accompany their textbooks and teaching materials. School- or district-wide curriculum committees are another source of instructional objectives. And of course student input should not be ignored. The preparation of instructional objectives is far too important a topic to be covered adequately in a brief section in a text of this type. We strongly recommend, therefore, that you study a text such as Dick and Carey's *The Systematic Design of Instruction* (1978).

Writing Test Items

Let us assume that you have written objectives for a unit of instruction and have chosen to evaluate student progress by means of a paper and pencil test. How would you actually go about constructing the test items? You will find that you have many types of items to choose from, each with its own advantages and disadvantages.

In general, we can classify test items into two major types: supply items and choice items (Bloom, Hastings, and Madaus, 1971). **Supply items,** such as completion and essay items, require the student to construct his or her own response. In contrast, **choice items,** such as true/false and multiple-choice items, require that the student select the correct response from a number of given alternatives. For any test, the type(s) of items you choose will depend on a number of variables including the following:

(1.) The amount of time you have to devote to test construction (completion and essay items are generally the easiest and least time-consuming to write).

(2.) The time you have to devote to scoring and the degree of objectivity desired (multiple-choice and true/false items can generally be scored more quickly and with more objectivity).

(3.) What you want to measure (for recall of basic concepts and facts, completion or choice items will often be adequate; for higher level cognitive processes such as synthesis and evaluation, essay items are often more appropriate).

Regardless of the type(s) of items you use, you will want them to be reliable and valid measures of whatever you have tried to teach. With this in mind, we will summarize some basic guidelines for writing effective test items. For a more detailed discussion of the "do's" and "don'ts" of item writing, you may want to refer to a basic text on educational measurement. Ebel (1972), Gronlund (1976), Nunnally (1972), Stanley and Hopkins (1972), and Tuckman (1975) are all good sources.

Completion items. Completion items are constructed so that the student must fill in a blank to complete a sentence. In writing completion items, keep the following rules in mind:

(1.) *Avoid giving too many clues to the answer the student must supply.* This means being very careful in the vocabulary that you

choose. It also means making the blanks equal in length and using grammar that does not give the student a hint to the correct response.

Poor: An angle exceeding 90 degrees but less than 180 degrees is called an _____ angle. (The correct answer is "obtuse.")

Better: An angle exceeding 90 degrees but less than 180 degrees is called a(an) _____ angle.

(2.) *Avoid ambiguous items for which more than one answer is correct.*

Poor: General Lee surrendered to General Grant in _____. ("1865," "Virginia," and "Appomattox" might all be considered correct.)

Better: General Lee surrendered to General Grant in the town of _____.

(3.) *Avoid multiple blanks, unless you clearly communicate the information called*

*for and can use them without chopping up
the sentence excessively.*

     Poor: The city of _____
               is located on the _____
               River and is the capital of
               the state of _____.
               (The correct answers to the
               second and third blanks
               depend on what the
               student writes in the first
               blank. "St. Paul" followed
               by "Mississippi" and
               "Minnesota" would be
               correct, but so would
               "Albany" followed by
               "Hudson" and "New
               York.")
     Better: The city of St. Paul is
               located on the _____
               River and is the capital of
               the state of _____.

True/false items. If well written, true/false items can provide a satisfactory measure of the student's ability to recognize factually correct and incorrect statements. Remember, however, that when students guess on a true/false item, they have a fifty percent chance of being right. In addition, it is difficult to write true/false items that are challenging and yet not subject to many interpretations. The following rules may prove useful.

(1.) *Avoid qualifiers such as "never," "always," "impossible," "seldom," "usually," and "may."* The first three qualifiers imply an absoluteness seldom found in nature, and thus signal the student to answer "false." Perceptive students also will tend to answer items using the last three qualifiers "true."

Poor: Giant pandas are never out-
           side of China. T F
Better: Giant pandas are native to
           China. T F

(2.) *Ask only one question at a time.* If you ask more than one, you confuse the student. You also have no idea which aspect of the item students responding incorrectly failed to understand (they may be misled by irrelevant insertions).

Poor: Dwight D. Eisenhower, a Republi-
           can and the thirty-fourth President
           of the United States, served as a
           general during World War II. T F
Better: Dwight D. Eisenhower served as a
           general during World War II. T F

(3.) *Make sure that the correct answers to the items are neither exceedingly obvious nor exceedingly unclear.* This means avoiding statements taken word for word out of the textbook (with possibly a "not" added to make the item false). On one extreme, statements pulled blindly from the text may be trivial; on the other extreme, they may be unclear when taken out of context.

Poor: Research has shown that children
           are influenced by television. T F
Better: Research has shown that children
           who watch "Sesame Street" regular-
           ly score higher on number recogni-
           tion tests than those who do
           not. T F

Multiple-choice items. A multiple-choice item consists of three separate parts: the introductory statement or question (referred to as the "stem"), three or more incorrect alternatives (referred to as distractors), and the correct alternative. Although multiple-choice items are less influenced by guessing than true/false items because there are more alternatives, they are even more difficult to write. If you follow these basic rules, you may find the task easier:

(1.) *Make sure the distractors are totally incorrect, and yet plausible.* If you use distractors that are highly unlikely, the item will not discriminate between students who really understand the concept and those who do not. It will help if you try to identify common errors that students make and use these as a basis for the incorrect alternatives. Note that in the first example below, the three distractors border on absurdity; the three men cited were American presidents, not inventors. In the second example the student must at least choose between four inventors. The last example is best, since the choice is between four inventors of communication devices.

Poor: The telephone was invented by
   a. Abraham Lincoln
   b. George Washington
   c. Alexander Graham Bell
   d. John Quincy Adams
Better: The telephone was invented by
   a. Eli Whitney
   b. Orville Wright
   c. Alexander Graham Bell
   d. Cyrus McCormack
Best: The telephone was invented by
   a. Thomas Edison
   b. Guglielmo Marconi
   c. Alexander Graham Bell
   d. Samuel Morse

(2.) *Do not give unnecessary clues to the correct alternative.* Try to make the four alternatives similar in length, complexity, and sentence structure (in striving for clarity, there may be a tendency to make the correct choice longer and more detailed; this should be avoided). It also means _not_ using a word or phrase in the correct alternative that is closely associated with a word or phrase used in the stem.

Poor: Which response most clearly gives one meaning of the word "adjust"?
   a. To move into just the right position for proper use
   b. To order
   c. To record
   d. To categorize
Better: Which response most clearly gives one meaning of the word "adjust"?
   a. To move into proper position
   b. To place in correct order
   c. To make a record of
   d. To place into categories

(3.) *Write the stem and alternatives as simply and as concisely as possible.* Students taking a multiple-choice examination have a lot of reading to do! Excessively technical vocabulary, awkward sentence structure, and unnecessarily lengthy items may cause the test to be a measure of the students' deciphering skills, rather than of their knowledge of the subject matter.

Essay items. All essay items are similar in that they give the students the opportunity to express themselves in writing. However, essay items can vary greatly in their scope and structure. Some require that the student supply short responses of a sentence or two; others call for longer more detailed answers and make it necessary for students to spend considerable time organizing and expressing their thoughts. In addition, essays may be designed to measure any of a number of cognitive skills. These may range from simply reproducing a factual definition (which is quite easy to score objectively) to justifying one's own opinions (which may be much more difficult to score objectively). The key to writing good essay items is to specify beforehand as clearly as possible what you want the students to do, as the following guidelines indicate:

(1.) *Introduce the item with a key word that describes the type of behavior expected of the student.* If you are using Bloom's taxonomy of cognitive objectives (refer to Table 7–3), you may want to consider these words, which roughly correspond to the behaviors called for at each level of the taxonomy:

For: Knowledge (recall)
  Use: state, define, list, identify, give the meaning of
For: Comprehension
  Use: give an example of, summarize, interpret, translate, discuss
For: Application
  Use: predict, relate, determine, apply, explain in terms of
For: Analysis
  Use: distinguish between, compare, contrast, infer, identify the interrelationships between
For: Synthesis
  Use: create, develop, suggest, produce, formulate
For: Evaluation
  Use: criticize, defend, cite reasons why, justify, judge

(2.) *Add enough details so that the student has some framework within which to write.*

Using an appropriate key word is necessary, but is usually insufficient to give students a clear idea of what to focus on.

Poor: Discuss the Watergate Scandal.
Better: Discuss the coverup of the Watergate Scandal focusing on (a) the motivations of its major participants and (b) the reasons for its failure.

(3.) *While writing the item, try to anticipate the kinds of responses the students may give. Then revise the item if necessary and develop a tentative plan for scoring it.* Once you have given the item and have read a few actual responses, you may have to change your scoring criteria somewhat. Still, if you try to specify beforehand what you expect in an answer and doublecheck to make sure that this is what the question asks for, you will find that the scoring of essay items is greatly simplified.

(4.) *In scoring essay items, first read a reasonable sample of the answers; then assign points for various parts of the desired answer, being as consistent and fair as possible in grading.* For example, if the student is asked to *predict* and *explain* three possible outcomes of a given course of action, the item could be assigned a total of six points (one point for each prediction and one point for each explanation). Or you might decide to give full credit for an answer containing three predictions, but only two *well-reasoned* explanations. Regardless of the particular criteria used, it will be helpful to jot them down and refer to them as you read each response. Scoring will also be simplified if you focus on scoring one particular item for all students, rather than completely scoring each test before going on to the next.

Basing Achievement Tests on Instructional Objectives

In designing a test based on the objectives for a unit of instruction, it is sometimes possible and even desirable to use the objectives themselves as test items. For example, if one objective in a literature class is to compare and contrast two authors' viewpoints on marriage, an essay item can be stated as such. In other cases, it is more appropriate to develop test items that fit, but are not identical to, the objective. This is particularly important when the objectives are more general, or when it seems necessary that the student respond to more than one item before it can be safely concluded that the objective has been met.

The type of test items developed to measure each objective will depend to a large extent on the complexity of the objective. Returning to Bloom's taxonomy, we find that at the knowledge and comprehension levels, completion, multiple-choice, matching, true/false, and short-answer essay items are most often adequate to measure attainment of the objectives. These types of items are well suited to the measurement of recall, recognition, and interpretation of facts and concepts. At the higher levels, particularly for synthesis and evaluation objectives, longer essay items and exercises involving the creation of *new* ideas are more often appropriate. Regardless of the particular types of items involved, it is important to remember three points when constructing an achieve-

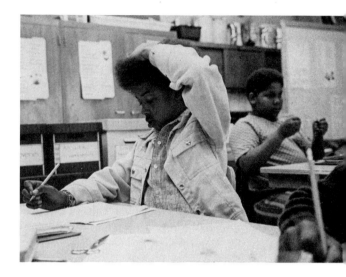

ment test: (1) Make sure that the number and complexity of test items is appropriate for the amount of time you give the students to take the test; (2) include enough test items to adequately sample the objectives being measured; and (3) develop scoring procedures that are as clear-cut as possible (this is much easier if criteria for acceptable performance are stated as part of the objectives).

The length and format of the test will depend to a great extent on the particular objectives involved and the types of items included. Length and format will also depend on how often you test, and how often you test will depend on your philosophy of teaching. If you prefer the mastery learning approach introduced in Chapter 1, you will probably give relatively short biweekly, weekly, or even daily tests on a limited number of objectives. You may also develop alternate forms of the same test to be taken by students who fail to achieve at an adequate level on the first test. Although this approach initially involves a considerable investment of the teacher's time and effort, we believe that the payoff will be worthwhile. (You might want to look ahead to Chapter 11 for some hints on how to use frequent tests both as teaching tools and as evaluation procedures.)

CRITERION-REFERENCED TESTS

Grading and interpreting the results of achievement tests based on instructional objectives can be accomplished in several ways. In some school systems traditional grading systems are no longer used. Instead, parents and students receive periodic feedback in the form of "report cards" that list general objectives for each school subject. The teacher simply checks which objectives have been achieved and which the student is currently working on.

It is also possible to combine a more traditional grading system with objective-based achievement tests. One way to do this is to develop tests with a specified number of points (test items might be weighted differently depending on the importance of the objectives being measured) and to use some *absolute standard* in assigning letter grades to test scores (for example, 90–100 percent = A, 80–89 percent = B, 70–79 percent = C, 60–69 percent = D, and scores below 60 percent = F). This method compares the performance of each student against some absolute criterion of proficiency chosen by the teacher, not against the performance of other students. *All* students who master 90 percent of the objectives receive an A, regardless of

how well other students in the class perform. When tests are based on instructional objectives and when test results are interpreted in a manner similar to that described above, they are referred to as **criterion-referenced tests.**

It is possible to interpret the results of teacher-constructed achievement tests in such a way that they become **norm-referenced tests.** This would occur when a grade assigned to a student's test score is dependent on how *other students* performed. For example, the scores might be "curved," so that a small percentage of the class receives As and Fs, a larger percentage receives Bs and Ds, and the majority receives Cs. In general, this is a much less desirable way to interpret the results of teacher-constructed achievement tests, and it certainly is not well suited to a mastery learning approach. It is the standardized achievement tests that are most often used as norm-referenced tests, in the sense that the grade equivalents, percentile ranks, and stanines reported are normative scores obtained by comparing a given student's performance with the performance of other students. We have seen that this type of information is useful in making general comparisons. But, criterion-referenced testing in the classroom can yield information that is valuable in diagnosing and remediating individual student weaknesses on specific instructional objectives and still allow you to "grade" the student only in comparison to his or her own potential, rather than in comparison to others.

In this chapter we have suggested several important guidelines for using teacher-constructed achievement tests: (1) Base your test items on specific instructional objectives, (2) test frequently, and (3) assign test grades

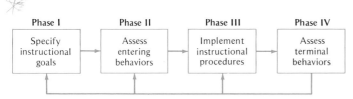

Figure 7–1. *Glaser's model of an instructional system (1962).*

according to how the student performs in relation to some absolute standard of competency. If you take this approach to the evaluation of student achievement, we believe you will find that testing becomes much more than an isolated part of what goes on in the classroom. Instead, it becomes an integral component of the total instructional process. This is what is meant by the concept of **systematic instruction.** According to this concept, teaching is a process made up of a number of distinct, yet interrelated components. All of the components must work together if teaching is to be truly effective. In Chapter 1 we introduced you to one particular model for making instruction systematic—a model developed by psychologist Robert Glaser (1962). We return here to Glaser's model in order to illustrate the important role teacher-constructed achievement tests play in the total instructional process.

As shown in Figure 7–1, the first phase of Glaser's model is the specification of instructional goals, that is, the objectives you want the student to reach. Once the goals have been identified, you are in a position to gather data on the entering behaviors relevant to these goals. Entering behaviors may be assessed in a number of ways. Teacher-constructed achievement tests can be used at this point, as can standardized tests of intelligence and achievement, attitude questionnaires, and less formal assessment techniques such as observational checklists and rating scales. The point here is that information from a variety of sources can be integrated to form a picture of the student's performance prior to instruction. This information allows you to make systematic decisions about the kinds of curriculum materials and teaching techniques needed during Phase III—the phase in which the actual instruction is implemented. You can see that in Glaser's model the instructional procedures must be individualized to meet the needs of the student identified during Phase II.

Once the instructional procedures have been carried out, we move into a critical phase of teaching—performance assessment or the assessment of terminal behaviors. Glaser has referred to this phase as the "quality control" component of teaching. In other words, we must have some measure of the student's progress toward the goals specified in Phase I. At this point in the teaching process, achievement tests based on instructional objectives become critical, not only because they allow you to measure how far the student has progressed, but also because they allow you to identify weaknesses in the *total* instructional process as it has been carried out to this point.

Glaser's model assumes that most, if not all, students can achieve some prestated level of mastery on any given unit of instruction, provided that the instruction is adapted to fit the needs of the individual student (note the difference between this assumption and the assumption of normality—that a few students will achieve a high level of mastery, a few will achieve a low level, and most will fall somewhere in between). By assessing terminal behaviors in Phase IV, the teacher knows if the student has achieved the desired level of mastery. If mastery has been achieved, the teacher can proceed to the next unit of instruction, starting the process over again with the specification of new instructional goals. If mastery has not been achieved, the teacher's role is to identify the problem and remediate it. This involves returning to one or more of the previous phases and making the needed adjustments. The adjustments may be minor—perhaps the student simply needs more practice using the same basic instructional procedures. On the other hand, you may find that you need a totally different teaching approach. Or you may find that your assessment of entering behavior was inaccurate or incomplete, requiring that you collect additional data and adjust the instructional procedures accordingly. Or you may even find that the goals of instruction were inappropriate for a particular student. The point is that achievement testing is most clearly justified when test results are "fed back" into the total instructional system in an effort to facilitate learning for individual students.

REVIEW 7–1

1. Discuss several characteristics of standardized achievement test batteries.
2. Give an example of each of the three most commonly used standardized achievement test scores and explain what each means.
3. Describe the differences between local and national norms.
4. Why is frequent achievement testing useful?
5. List three advantages of using instructional objectives.
6. List three steps in writing instructional objectives.
7. What are the identifying characteristics of objectives in *each* category of Bloom's taxonomy for the cognitive domain?
8. What is the major difference between "supply test items" and "choice test items"? Give two examples of each.
9. What is the basic difference between criterion-referenced and norm-referenced tests?
10. Describe Glaser's model of an instructional system in terms of its four component phases.

ISSUES IN TESTING

The last two chapters have been based on two assumptions: (1) that measurement of student behavior is an essential aspect of good teaching, and (2) that formal testing is a useful measurement technique. We believe that these assumptions are valid, but we are also aware that there is considerable controversy over the use of tests in education. This is because tests have historically played such an important role in determining the futures of students. Test scores influence the kind of education students receive, the career opportunities open to them, the perceptions they have of their own self-worth, and so on. As long as tests continue to play such an important role in education, teachers have the responsibility to seriously examine the philosophical and ethical issues involved in testing. Thus it seems appropriate to conclude our discussion of educational measurement by raising some concerns regarding the uses and abuses of intelligence and achievement tests.

Using Tests in Grouping

The ultimate purpose of testing should be to provide information that will help those involved in the educational enterprise enhance the development of individual students. Unfortunately this does not always occur. Critics of educational testing have been quick to point out that tests have been used too frequently to the *detriment* of the individual. There has been a great deal of controversy, for example, over the use of tests to assign students to groups, whether this grouping involves ability groups within a single classroom or to special tracks or classes within a total school system.

The first issue that must be raised here concerns whether grouping is a worthwhile educational practice. This is a difficult question, which we cannot answer for you. On the plus side, some educators argue that narrowing the range of individual differences a teacher must deal with allows the teacher to provide better instruction for all students. On

the minus side, others argue that students placed in lower groups or classes will inevitably suffer from the stigma attached to such groups, and that the harmful effects of grouping on those students is great enough to outweigh any potential advantages. Regardless, some form of grouping is being used in many schools today. Thus, we need to consider how to lessen the detrimental effects that testing in conjunction with grouping can have on students.

One of the greatest hazards in grouping is that students may be placed erroneously in special classes because of an overemphasis on standardized test scores. Psychologist Jane Mercer (1971) studied this phenomenon in a California school system and found that Mexican-American and black children were overrepresented in classes for the mentally retarded. She suggested that many low-income and minority-group children who are *not* mentally retarded are more likely to be identified as such because the standardized tests used in making placement decisions are culturally biased toward the white middle class.

Even if the tests used with a particular cultural group are appropriate, that is, if they were standardized on and designed for use with that group, you should remember that it is poor practice to place too much emphasis on a single test score. We have seen that IQ scores and achievement scores change with time and depend on the testing conditions and the learning experiences of the child. We also know that intelligence and achievement are only two factors that enter into school success. Other factors such as the student's health, motivations, interests, special aptitudes, and family background must be taken into account.

The points to emphasize here are that in making grouping decisions, one must make sure that the tests chosen are appropriate, that the scores are not given too much importance, and that information other than test scores is considered. When the decision involves major changes in the student's education, such as placement in a special class, it is also essential that (1) several professionals be involved in the decision-making process, (2) that the test results be clearly communicated to the parents and student, and (3) that the parents and student be given alternative courses of action from which to choose. *We can never be completely sure that a particular grouping decision is in the best interest of the student, or if grouping is appropriate at all.* But by allowing parents and students to participate in the decision-making process and by periodically evaluating the student's progress once the decision is made, we can lessen the likelihood that testing will have a detrimental and irreversible effect on the student.

Tests and Record Keeping

Another area in which there is potential for the abuse of tests is the issue of the individual's right to privacy and possible violations of that right that may occur when test data are improperly collected and disseminated. We have emphasized that test scores should be treated with caution because of their potential for influencing students' lives. Regrettably, this has not always been the case. Schools have failed to adequately explain their testing programs to parents and students. Sensitive, and sometimes educationally irrelevant, test scores have been obtained and released to potential employers, the po-

lice, and others without the knowledge and consent of parents, and secrecy in maintaining school records has prevented parents from even knowing what kinds of information schools keep on their children and from challenging the accuracy of this information.

In response to this state of affairs, the Russell Sage Foundation held a conference in 1969 on the ethical aspects of school record keeping. The purpose of the conference was to develop guidelines that would help schools set reasonable policies in regard to administering tests and maintaining the confidentiality of test scores (as well as the confidentiality of other information such as the child's health history, family background, and teacher reports of misconduct). We will summarize here several of the conference's recommendations and urge you to seriously consider them.

1) *Collection of Test Data*
   a. In the case of ordinary standardized and teacher-constructed *achievement* tests, it should not be necessary to obtain written consent from parents before the tests are administered. However, representatives of the parents (e.g., the local school board) should give approval for school-wide achievement testing programs. In addition, reasonable attempts should be made to clearly explain to parents and students the types of achievement tests to be used, their purposes, and the meaning of the test scores.
   b. In the case of individual intelligence and personality tests and any tests used for research purposes, testing should not

begin until written, informed consent has been obtained from individual parents. Informed consent means that the parents give their approval after receiving complete information on how the test data will be administered, how it will be used, how and for what time-period records will be kept, and who will have access to the records.

(2) *Maintenance of Test Data*

a. School records containing sensitive data (such as scores on intelligence and personality tests, family background information, verified teacher reports of misconduct, etc.) should be kept under lock and key in the care of a designated administrator.

b. Parents should have access to such records and should be able to challenge the accuracy of the information contained in them through a formal hearing process.

c. Schools should destroy school records containing sensitive information when the student leaves school, unless good reasons for maintaining them can be demonstrated.

(3) *Dissemination of Test Data*

a. Schools may, without written parental consent, share school records containing sensitive information with other school personnel in the same district who have a legitimate educational interest in the child. However, all school personnel should indicate in writing what that interest is when checking out the file.

b. Schools should not share in any form such records with individuals or agencies outside the school district, except with written consent from the parent, specify-

ing to whom the records are to be released.

Remember that these points are *suggested* guidelines for schools to follow. Many states have since passed state *laws* concerning the confidentiality of school records and test scores. It will be necessary to familiarize yourself with the specifics of laws in your own state, as they may vary somewhat from the Sage Foundation recommendations.

Tests and Grading Policies

It has been standard practice in American schools for many years to summarize a student's level of achievement on a particular test or in a given course of study by assigning letter grades. Furthermore, many schools have used and continue to use a highly competitive grading system based on the normal curve. Thus, a few students receive As (indicating an outstanding performance), a few students receive Fs (indicating a dismal performance), and most students receive Bs, Cs, and Ds (indicating varying degrees of mediocre performance). In this type of grading system, grades are assigned to each student *in relation to his or her peers.* Thus, grades as a source of information can be used by colleges attempting to select the most promising candidates for higher education and by employers attempting to select the most competent employees.

It has been argued that society benefits when schools provide such evaluative information to industry and higher education. Certainly those who achieve excellence are rewarded and the processes of selection and admission are simplified. Furthermore, it is difficult to deny that the larger society in which American students must learn to function as adults is highly competitive. But, many educators believe that harm is done to the majority of students under such a system and argue that it should be abandoned.

A key flaw of this system, critics point out, is that grading systems based on competition among students inevitably produce "winners" and "losers." The losers are often those students who begin their school careers lacking the basic prerequisites necessary for school success. As early as the first grade, they begin to receive low grades and they develop feelings of inadequacy as a result. Other detrimental side effects of highly competitive grading systems include (1) the excessively high levels of anxiety created in many students, particularly those who are motivated to go on to college and are thus pressured to achieve top grades; (2) the cheating and dishonesty found among students who are pressured to achieve, but find themselves unable to "make the grade" on their own; (3) the tendency to just "get by" found among students who are less motivated to achieve; and (4) the tendency to view grades and test scores rather than enjoyable learning experiences as the most important aspects of education.

Detrimental side effects such as these have led some educators to propose that all types of testing and grading should be abandoned. Others (and we fall into this category) favor retaining tests and grades as legitimate sources of feedback to teachers, students, and parents, with the stipulation that *less emphasis* be placed on competition among students. We have seen in this chapter that there are alternatives to norm-referenced testing and grading. Indeed, if you use instructional objectives, frequent performance assessment, and individualized instruction systematically as Glaser (1962) and Gagné and Briggs (1974) have proposed, the emphasis on norm-referenced testing in the classroom lessens. Instead, the student's performance is compared against some absolute standard of proficiency (did he or she master the objectives?) or against his or her own previous performance (how much has the student improved?).

This is not to say that all competition among students can be eliminated; it is not clear that this could or should ever be accomplished. But by tying grades to how much the student has improved or to his or her absolute level of competency, we can give the student feedback and at the same time avoid the detrimental effects of grades based on the normal curve.

Accountability in Education

We have dealt in some detail with the use of tests as part of the teaching process, that is, with how tests can help the teacher plan and monitor instruction on a day-to-day basis. However, tests are also used to assess overall educational outcomes. In other words, they are used to give parents, school districts, and state and federal governments feedback on the effectiveness of school programs in meeting relatively long-range goals. As the costs of supporting public education skyrocket, and as taxpayers become more and more disillusioned with the results of public schooling, this type of overall educational assessment is becoming more and more common. Parents and legislators are asking, "Are we getting our money's worth? Are students really learning what we want them to learn? If not, why not, and what can be done about it?" Moreover, schools are finding that they must provide answers to these difficult questions or face further erosion of public confidence and loss of financial support.

We refer here to the issue of **accountability,** a term borrowed from business and introduced into education in the 1960s by Leon Lessinger. In a general sense, educational accountability refers to holding schools responsible for what the students learn, just as people hold a business responsible for the products it sells. In a more specific sense, accountability means that school systems, under directives from local school boards or state legislatures, must do three things: (1) adopt instructional objectives that clearly state the goals the system intends to reach for student achievement, (2) employ outside or independent consultants to assess and make public the degree to which the students in the school system achieve these goals, and (3) use the information from this assessment to modify the school system in an attempt to narrow the gaps between prestated goals and actual achievement (Lessinger, 1973).

As you might imagine, few educators disagree with the general notion of accountability. There is little doubt that schools ought to be held accountable for student progress. But there is considerable controversy over what constitutes student progress, how it should be measured, who within the school system should be held accountable, and what the

implications of accountability will be. For example, it has been argued that only a small portion of what students learn in school can be readily transformed into instructional objectives and measured using currently available tests. Thus, teachers fear they will be evaluated on the basis of how well their students perform on tests that do not reflect the full amount of learning that has occurred in the classroom. Related is the fear that accountability will lead teachers to "teach to the test" and to emphasize rote drill at the expense of providing innovative and exciting learning experiences in the classroom. And what about schools in poverty areas, where the student population achieves considerably below national norms, and where factors beyond the teachers' control, such as poor housing, family pressures, and inadequate educational facilities, interfere with the students' ability to learn? Will these factors be considered in an accountability plan?

These complex issues will not be resolved overnight, but educators are making gradual progress toward implementing accountability in ways so that the best interests of student, parents, administrators, and teachers are served. One way is through the notion of *joint accountability* (Dyer, 1973), which involves a recognition that teachers alone cannot be held responsible for their students' achievement. Instead, the entire school staff is jointly responsible to the community for the quality of education provided. And the community is responsible to the school for providing financial and moral support necessary for effective instruction. Further, accountability plans are being developed that take into account more than just measures of student achievement. For example, a plan developed by educator Henry Dyer (1973) looks at education as a system, with four groups of variables that must be measured: (1) the input, or the entering characteristics of the students, (2) the educational processes, or the instructional procedures used in the school, (3) the surrounding conditions, or the conditions in the home, community, and school that are beyond the control of the teacher, and (4) the output, or final characteristics of the students.

Finally, it has become apparent that accountability goes hand in hand with a mastery learning approach to teaching. As more schools adopt this approach and become more comfortable in specifying instructional objectives, using individualized instruction, and developing criterion-referenced tests, we are beginning to see that accountability can work. Granted, it is a big job for schools working in cooperation with community members to decide what their overall mission and specific objectives ought to be. In addition, we do have a long way to go in developing objectives that comprehensively cover all aspects of cognitive, affective, and psychomotor learning. But, as Lessinger points out:

There are and should be larger objectives in education that are difficult to define and impossible to measure as the consequence of any given program. . . . But the fact that many results of education are subjective and not measurable in the "hard," scientific sense should not deter personnel from dealing precisely with those aspects of education that lend themselves to precise definition and assessment. (1974, p. 32)

NATIONAL ASSESSMENT

For a number of years a large-scale program to assess the educational achievements of students in the United States has been underway. Called the National Assessment of Educational Progress (NAEP), this federally funded program is based on the assumption that educators will be able to make wiser educational decisions if they have accurate information on the skills, knowledge, and attitudes of American students. To this end, committees composed of specialists and lay persons began in the early 1960s to identify sets of objectives in ten subject areas: art, career and occupational development, citizenship, literature, mathematics, music, reading, science, social studies, and writing. A variety of test exercises to measure specific objectives in each area were then developed. The plan of NAEP is to assess student achievement by giving the exercises in a given subject matter periodically to a representative sample of students chosen from schools all over the country. The actual testing began in 1969 and continues today. Each year, achievement in two subject matter areas is assessed and data are published describing the achievement of American students.

Thus in the 1970s, we are seeing a renewed commitment to improving our schools by clearly thinking out just what the outcomes of education should be and developing new techniques for measuring these outcomes. There is a recognition that there is a great deal we do not know about how students learn, how teachers teach, and how

NAEP uses a criterion-referenced approach to testing. The test exercises are tied to specific objectives and test results are summarized according to the percentage of students at various ages passing each exercise. Two examples of test exercises given to nine-, thirteen-, and seventeen-year-olds in the writing assessment are shown below, along with the percentage of students passing the items at each age level (from Mellon, 1975).

	Age 9	Age 13	Age 17
Record a telephone message	31%	67%	79%
Fill in a personal information blank	16%	26%	61%

Thus, we can see that 31 percent of the nine-year-olds tested could fulfill the requirements of the message recording exercise but only 16 percent could adequately fill in a personal information blank. Among thirteen- and seventeen-year-olds, the percentages were considerably higher.

You can see from the examples above that NAEP is designed to give us *descriptive* information on what American students, in general, know and can do. Scores are not assigned to individual students, nor are the results summarized for individual schools, school districts, or even states. NAEP results are not to be used in comparing how one school stands in relation to another nor in measuring a school system's effectiveness, as might be done in an accountability plan.

Does this mean that the usefulness of NAEP is limited? Not at all! Descriptive data on the educational attainments of American students give teachers and administrators a starting point from which to make decisions about educational reform. Also, as the assessment continues, each subject matter area will be retested, so that changing patterns in achievement levels can be detected. Finally, the approach NAEP has used in identifying objectives and in designing exercises to measure those objectives is highly innovative. State Departments of Education and school systems are finding that they can use NAEP's approach to assessment as a model in devising accountability plans on the local level.

For students wishing to learn more about national assessment, NAEP publishes a *General Information Yearbook,* as well as individual reports on the yearly assessments. Much of this information is available in university libraries. In addition, the book *What Is National Assessment?* by Frank Womar (1970) gives a more detailed explanation of the actual procedures used in implementing this exemplary program.

achievement can be measured. But, at the same time, there is a commitment to utilize what we do know about these processes to improve the quality of education for all students:

In principle, the American educational commitment has been that every child should be educated to his full potential. But this commitment has been voiced in terms of resources provided such as teachers, books, space, and equipment. When a child has failed to learn, school personnel have too often assigned him a label—"slow," or "unmotivated," or "retarded."

Accountability for results is a movement to stimulate the schools to assume a revised commitment—that every child shall learn. Such a commitment must include a willingness to change a system which does not work, and find out which does: To seek causes of failure in the system and its personnel instead of focusing solely on students: In short, to hold the school systems accountable for results in terms of pupil learning rather than solely in the use of resources. (Lessinger, 1973, p. 9)

REVIEW 7–2

1. Make several suggestions for ensuring that tests are used ethically in making grouping and placement decisions.

2. What was the purpose of the Russell Sage Foundation Conference?

3. What are possible negative side effects of grading based on competition between students?

4. In implementing an accountability plan, what three major courses of action must school systems undertake?

✲ SUMMARY   whole thing

Unlike intelligence tests, achievement tests are designed to measure understanding of academic content and skills taught specifically in schools. Standardized achievement test batteries yield normative scores for a number of different academic areas. Such batteries are typically given once or twice a year to students at all or selected grade levels. Scores are used in comparing the achievement of particular groups of students with national or local levels of achievement. Scores are typically reported in the form of grade equivalents, percentile ranks, or stanines.

Standardized achievement tests are not designed to be administered frequently to the same class; nor are they the best tools for measuring specific content and skills taught in a given classroom. Thus, teachers usually construct their own achievement tests. Frequent testing can help the teacher pinpoint strengths and weaknesses of individual children, particularly when the tests are based on the teacher's own instructional objectives.

Well-written objectives have three components: (1) the terminal behavior, expressed in terms of observable performance, (2) the conditions under which the behavior is to be exhibited, and (3) the level of acceptable performance. Ideally, the teacher will use many different kinds of objectives. Bloom's taxonomy provides a system for classifying objectives according to the behavior being measured. Within the cognitive domain there are six categories ranging from simple to complex: knowledge, comprehension, application, analysis, synthesis, and evaluation.

Once you have specified instructional objectives for a unit of instruction, you are in a position to develop test items to measure mastery of those objectives. There are four types of items widely used in achievement testing. Completion and essay items are "supply" items in the sense that students must construct their own responses. They are usually the easiest items to write, but the most difficult to score. True/false and multiple-choice items require that the student select the correct response from a number of given alternatives. They are easier to score objectively, but are more difficult to write.

The length and format of achievement tests based on objectives will vary depending

on how often you test and on the particular objectives covered. In general, you should develop clear-cut scoring procedures, include sufficient items to adequately sample the objectives, and match the time you give the students to take the test to the number and complexity of the item.

When teacher-constructed tests are interpreted in terms of the number of objectives or items passed in comparison to some absolute standard, they are criterion referenced. In contrast, they are norm referenced if a student's score depends on how other students performed. Criterion-referenced tests are more compatible with a mastery learning approach and are an essential aspect of systematic instruction.

Finally, we have considered a number of controversial issues surrounding the use of intelligence and achievement tests in education. It is clear that test scores continue to have a powerful influence on the lives of students. Because of this you should carefully examine your own attitudes toward testing, keeping in mind that the ultimate purpose of testing is to help enhance the growth of individual students.

ANSWERS TO REVIEW QUESTIONS

Review 7–1

1. (a) They are accompanied by data on test reliability and validity, as well as norms for interpreting scores.

(b) They are designed to measure academic content and skills common to most school systems.

(c) They provide separate scores in such areas as math, reading, language, study skills, science, and social studies.

(d) They must be administered under standardized conditions.

2. (a) A grade equivalent of 3.5, for example, means that the child received the same raw score as the average child in the fifth month of the third grade.

(b) A percentile rank of 94 means that the child scored better than 94 percent of the students of the same grade level taking the test.

(c) A stanine of 4 means that the child scored in the next lowest group below the middle of 9 groups. The score is slightly below average.

3. National norms are based on a large sample representative of students from all over the United States and are used to compare the achievement of students in a given school system with the achievement of students in general. Local norms may be developed for students within a given state, school system, school building, or single classroom and are more useful for making comparisons with students who are likely to have had similar instruction.

4. Frequent achievement testing aids the teacher in diagnosing individual students' problems and reveals whether students are being challenged enough by the material taught.

5. (a) Objectives help the teacher design meaningful achievement tests.

(b) Objectives help to communicate clear expectations to the students.

(c) Objectives help the teacher to select the most meaningful learning experiences for a given unit of instruction.

6. (a) Specify the terminal behavior expected of the students in terms of observable performance.

(b) Specify the conditions under which the behavior should occur.

(c) Specify the minimal level of performance acceptable for passing the objective.

7. (a) Knowledge objectives measure recall and recognition of facts, concepts, and principles.

(b) Comprehension objectives measure the ability to interpret, summarize, paraphrase, and give examples.

(c) Application objectives measure the use of facts, concepts, and principles in solving new problems.

(d) Analysis objectives measure the ability to identify components of a whole and their interrelationships.

(e) Synthesis objectives measure the ability to put components together to make a new whole.

(f) Evaluation objectives measure the ability to compare and judge ideas.

8. Supply items require that students construct their own responses, whereas choice items require that students select correct responses from a number of alternatives given to them. Completion and essay items are of the supply variety; true/false and multiple-choice are choice items.

9. In criterion-referenced testing, a student's performance is compared with some absolute criterion established by the teacher. In norm-referenced testing, a student's performance is compared with the performance of other students.

10. Glaser views the total instructional process as having four distinct, yet interrelated phases: (a) specifying instructional objectives, (b) assessing entering behavior, (c) implementing instructional procedures, and (d) assessing terminal behaviors. All phases must be tied to one another if instruction is to be fully effective.

Review 7–2

1. (a) Tests should be appropriate to begin with. This means that they must be reliable and valid for the purposes for which they are being used.

(b) Test scores should be placed in proper perspective; too much emphasis should not be placed on single scores and information from other sources should be considered.

(c) The meaning of the test results should be clearly communicated to parents and students.

(d) Whenever possible, alternative courses of action should be formulated based on all the data obtained.

2. The conference intended to develop guidelines for schools to use in determining how testing programs should be ethically administered, including how the confidentiality of test scores might be maintained.

3. For students at the bottom of the curve, competitive grading begins a vicious cycle of failure which has drastic effects on the students' self-esteem and future learning. Students may also feel excessive anxiety and pressure to perform and may turn to dishonesty or just give up when they can't perform.

4. School systems must (a) adopt instructional objectives that state the goals they intend to reach, (b) employ outside consultants to assess and make public the degree to which the system achieves these goals, and (c) use the information to modify the school system in an attempt to narrow the gap between prestated goals and actual student achievement.

3

SOCIAL ASPECTS OF EDUCATION

This part of the text is about the relationship between schools and society. We will discuss the fact that each classroom and each school comprises a "society" of its own and look at some of the ways that schools influence society. In Chapter 8 we will describe the ways that different styles of leadership used by teachers affect the behavior of their students and look at some of the characteristics of student peer groups. We will examine the factors that lead to high group cohesiveness and morale and examine the practice of creating classroom groups based on academic ability. In addition, we will discuss the effects that teachers' expectations have on the learning and behavior of their students. In Chapter 9 we will examine the effects that schools have on society. Particular attention will be paid to the educational problems of the disadvantaged and the role of schools in helping this segment of the population.

Chapter 8

Social Factors in the Classroom

Whenever an individual is in a group (which is almost always the case), his or her behavior can be fully understood only by understanding the influence of the group on the individual. The ways in which "mobs" can be moved to perform acts of violence foreign to the individuals in those mobs is a powerful illustration of this notion. Another example of this influence can be found in our hesitation to speak in front of large groups of people. The behavior of a thirteen-year-old boy at an all-male birthday party compared to an all-female party offers another good example.

People exist in social groups and must be understood in that context. Students live in the "societies" of their classrooms, their peer groups, their families, and their cultures. We cannot fully understand the educational process unless we understand the impact of groups on the behavior of individuals.

SOCIAL CLIMATE OF THE CLASSROOM

One of the best studied social determinants of the behavior of schoolchildren is the "climate" of the classroom group. We do not have to look at children in classes long to see that these groups can differ significantly. Some are tightly controlled by the teacher and allow little input from the students. In others, no one seems to really be in charge, with many different activities and conversations going on simultaneously. Still others seem to spend a great deal of time making decisions as a group, with the students' opinions carrying as much weight as the teacher's. Which of these climates of classroom organi-

zation is the best? Should teachers direct classroom activities according to their own plans (they are the experts after all)? Should teachers adopt a laissez-faire attitude and let each little "flower" bloom in his or her way? Or should we help our students set goals and policies for themselves as a group through democratic procedures? Which climate is best?

One answer to this question is easy to come up with: None of these *extreme* views is appropriate for the classroom. Teachers should neither be dictators, nor should they install voting machines and let students make all decisions, nor patiently sit and watch the little "monkeys" swing from the chandeliers. A style of leadership that falls somewhere in between these extreme points encourages learning most effectively, and is best liked by students (Lippitt & White, 1943).

Giving Direction to Learning

The notion that teachers should provide structure and direction to classroom activities without being harshly authoritarian is given sharper focus in a study by University of Georgia educational psychologist Paul Torrance (1971). Twenty-four activity groups of six five-year-olds each were randomly assigned either to a condition in which the teacher gave structure to their activities or one in which the teacher left their activities unstructured. In each case, their task was to build a "dream castle" out of construction materials. Twelve groups were given no more instructions than this and were left alone to work out their own plan of attack. The teacher suggested to the other twelve groups that they first draw pictures of a dream castle and then decide together whether to construct a castle that looked like one of the pictures or to combine the features from all of the drawings.

The social behavior of the children under the two conditions of leadership from the teacher was recorded and appears in Figure 8–1. The children who were given little structure in their activities exhibited less planning and cooperation, more verbal and physical aggression, and were more likely to leave the situation than the children who were given structure. Similar reactions to unstructured leadership styles or climates have been found with older children (Lewin, Lippitt, & White, 1939).

It is important, therefore, for teachers to provide structure and direction to learning, but it is equally important that they do so in ways that avoid being seen as harsh, unfair, and dictatorial. Teachers can easily avoid these negative reactions by providing structure in the following ways.

Clearly state reasonable objectives for learning.   The first step in providing direction to learning is to tell the students what you expect of them. The more clearly this is done, the more effective it will be. This is one of the reasons we have already devoted much time to discussing ways to prepare clear instructional objectives.

It is also important that these objectives be fair. One step that can be taken in this direction is to give students some democratic voice in the selection of objectives and methods of evaluation. In our college-level classes, for example, we ask students to help select some of the more optional content of the course and allow them to vote on the number of tests they will take in addition to the final examination (one, two, or three).

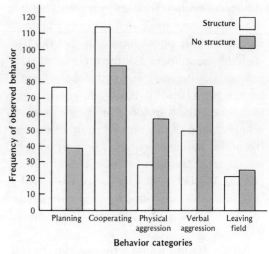

Figure 8–1. *Frequency of selected categories of behavior observed in groups of five-year-olds with and without task structuring. (From Shaw, 1976)*

This gives them a voice in determining content and evaluation procedures and starts the quarter out on a positive note. It also gives us a chance to perform some theatrical teaching. After they have voted for three tests (every class we have ever taught has overwhelmingly selected this option), we hand out an already printed syllabus that lists the dates of the three tests. This gives them a powerful demonstration that behavior is often more predictable than they think.

Know the subject matter.   Teachers who know their subject matter and communicate it clearly and simply will have students who learn effectively and who cause little trouble.

Give students personal feedback.   An important element of classroom structure is the feedback that teachers give. It should be personal, respectful, and clear when the students are wrong, and positive when they are right.

Hold to rules firmly and consistently.   Once reasonable rules and standards have been established, it is important that they be adhered to consistently and firmly. It is desirable to give students a role in choosing these guidelines, but only the teacher can enforce them.

Have positive feelings and expectations for your students.   Good teachers need not be constantly jovial or say something positive about every student's efforts. Rather, they can provide corrective feedback without criticizing and be generous with their praise only when a student has done well according to the expectations for that individual. A positive approach is more important in the early grades. A study conducted at the New School for Social Research in New York City (Firestone & Brody, 1975) showed that kindergarten and first-grade teachers who were judged to be positive in their interactions with children produced higher achievement in their students than other teachers. A similar study showed that disadvantaged first-grade children who were consistently told by their teachers that they would do well in school showed consistently higher achievement than children who were not given this expectation (Rappaport & Rappaport, 1975).

Focus on both the needs of students and the goals of teaching.   Other studies have looked at leadership (Shaw, 1976). Some "good" leaders do a good job of getting the work goals of the group accomplished, while others do a good job of meeting the needs of

the members of the group (making sure that each member gets a chance to talk and that the goals of the group reflect each member's views). Both styles of leadership are important, but they lead to different results in the classroom. Obviously it is important to focus on getting the "job" of learning accomplished, but it is also important to attend to the human needs of the classroom group. You will need to be both a goal- and a person-oriented leader.

Communication in the Classroom

The quality of communication among teachers and students in the classroom is closely related to the social climate. It is exceptionally important that you think in terms of keeping "lines of communication" open. Provide students with opportunities to contribute to policy setting and to give you feedback on your teaching in a way that encourages profitable communication. Many students—and parents—avoid giving their thoughts or may stay silent in large groups. This makes small group or individual meetings necessary. Similarly, you must ask for ideas and opinions in a way that genuinely means "tell me what you think." A hostile opening line like, "If you aren't satisfied with the way things have been, speak up now!" will get you nowhere. "I would like to spend some time with you now sharing thoughts about next week's poetry unit" would probably work a bit better. Another way to encourage communication is to communicate well yourself. Your students will speak their

THE SOCIAL CLIMATE OF THE CLASSROOM

One of the most frequently cited studies of social factors in working with children concerns the "climate" or style of leadership exhibited by the adult leader. The investigators, social psychologists Lewin, Lippitt, and White (1939; 1943), organized four after-school clubs for eleven-year-old boys. Adult leaders of the clubs used different styles of leadership in order to see how the children would react to them.

Two clubs had *authoritarian* leaders who strongly directed the activities of the members, with one authoritarian leader being harsher than the other. The third club had a *democratic* leader who let the boys determine their own actions, but who took an active role in helping them reach decisions. The fourth group had a *laissez-faire* leader who exerted no actual leadership over the group, but let each member go his own way.

The behavior of the boys under these three styles of leadership varied widely. The authoritarian leaders produced a great deal of anger and aggression among the boys, but they accomplished a great deal in their work activities, at least when the leader was present. The boys did not enjoy the groups, however, and disliked their leaders. The laissez-faire group, on the other hand, floundered a great deal and moved in different directions. They got into minor squabbles and found little enjoyment in their activities. The democratic group seemed to fare the best overall. They got along with each other and enjoyed the group more than the others, but still accomplished a great deal.

Studies of styles of leadership conducted in classroom settings since this original study generally confirm its findings. In a review of this research, Anderson (1970) found that there was little difference in the quality of learning in authoritarian and democratic classrooms, but that morale was higher under democratic leaders. Some studies, in fact, found that students who set their own standards for academic performance achieved better than when the teacher set the standards (Lovitt & Curtiss, 1968). These findings suggest that it is healthy to inject some degree of democratic decision making into the classroom.

minds more readily to you if you model an open, honest, and easy style of communication with them.

Keep one more thought in mind on this topic. When you become the principal or the superintendent of education, remember to keep the lines of communication open then. Schools and school systems are societies, too.

The Peer Group

Both inside and outside the classroom, one of the most powerful social influences on children's behavior is the peer group. As discussed in Chapter 3, peers exert considerably less influence than parents during early childhood, but in late childhood and early adolescence, a child's peers are among the strongest forces in determining his or her behavior. By and large, we are unaware of the influence that our friends have on our behavior, and they are unaware of the power that they wield. Occasionally, peers will intentionally set out to change someone's behavior, but in most instances we think of "peer pressure" as a natural and automatic process. Since we tend to imitate the behavior of others, we naturally imitate our circle of friends. As peers become more important to children, they become increasingly powerful models for their behavior. The rapid way in which fads, styles of dress, and slang expressions spread among teenagers gives us a vivid picture of the power of imitation.

Peer groups also enforce their norms and standards for conduct through reactions to each individual's behavior. Again, this is usually an unconscious process, a natural result of reactions of peers to one another. The member of a peer group who shows up in a "slick" (or whatever the current term happens to be) outfit will be greeted with positive reactions, but the "square" who dresses like his grandfather may not be well received.

Cohesiveness

The groups that exert the strongest control over their members are the most tightly knit, or *cohesive*. Cohesive groups are ones that are attractive to members and satisfy their needs. Such groups have a much stronger ability to enforce their norms than ones that are less attractive to their members. The more students want to belong to a group, the more their behavior will be influenced by it, particularly if they are low-status members of the group. Interestingly, high-status members are allowed more freedom to be idiosyncratic (Hollander, 1958), perhaps because their position in the group is more assured.

It is highly desirable in most cases for classroom groups to be cohesive. Classroom groups are less likely to be cohesive than the groups that students naturally form outside the classroom because the classroom group is formed artificially rather than according to the students' likes and dislikes. Still, most classrooms develop a useful degree of cohesiveness. The more cohesive the group becomes, the more likely that achievement and enjoyment will be high, and truancy, conflict, and misbehavior will be low. This is primarily because children are more likely to adhere to the "norms" of groups that are high in cohesiveness (Festinger, Schacter, & Back, 1950).

To a great extent, cohesiveness is an uncontrollable process that teachers can hope to understand, but can exert little influence on its development. However, there are some minor but important ways that you can contribute positively (or negatively) to cohesiveness. The following discussion describes the key characteristics of cohesive groups.

The members like one another. Groups will not develop cohesiveness unless the members like one another. If most members of the class dislike one another, no sense of belongingness will develop in the group. Cohesiveness results when the group develops a feeling of "us" versus "they," and this obviously cannot happen in a disorganized, unfriendly group. If you play a part in the assignment of children to the various classes, you will deal cohesiveness a murderous blow if you intentionally put together a group that you know will not "get along" (remember, however, that children do not always share the prejudices of their parents!).

Psychologists who are especially interested in group processes are called *social psychologists*. These researchers have studied the variables that determine the liking patterns of students and have concluded that the following are most important:

(1.) *Physical attractiveness.* At all school age levels and beyond, the individuals that are best liked, other things equal, are the best looking ones (Bany & Johnson, 1975). This includes facial characteristics, body build and shape, style of dress, and so on. This is only one part of the equation, but children who are attractive have a head start on being well liked.

(2.) *Likable behavior.* The most important factor, of course, in determing whether children will be well liked is their behavior. Students who are withdrawn or overly aggressive will not be highly desired companions. Those whose behavior grossly violates convention will similarly be viewed as unlikable. On the other hand, students who are outgoing, warm, and cooperative will be easy to like. Friendship also comes more easily to those who excel in sports, school politics, and other extracurricular activities (Bany & Johnson, 1975).

It has also been found that students who do well in their school work will be viewed positively, especially in the later grades. Educational social psychologist M. E. Bonney (1943) has found that capable primary-grade students are about as equally regarded as incapable ones, but that they become better liked from about the fifth grade on.

(3.) *Reciprocal satisfaction.* If friendships are to endure, they must be mutually satisfying. In simple terms, this means that friends must accept one another's faults and swap compliments ("I really like your haircut," or "She let you kiss her on the first date? What happened next?"). When friends stop giving positive feelings to one another, their friendships begin to weaken.

(4.) *Similarity.* Friendship ties form more easily among individuals who are similar in appearance, ethnic background, and interests (Shaw, 1976). In elementary classrooms, boys who were interested in the same activities were found to be more likely to form informal groups (Sherif & Sherif, 1953), and black and white children of the same age levels stated preferences for associating with members of their own racial and ethnic groups, and, indeed, showed this preference in their social behavior.

Teachers can obviously do little to strengthen the effects of similarity, but if they have substantial reasons for doing so, they can *reverse* its effects somewhat. A group of educational psychologists at the University of Tennessee (Williams, Cormier, Sapp, & Andrews, 1971) conducted a study to see if teachers could encourage the amount of social interaction between black and white junior high school students attending classes that had a 50–50 racial balance.

The target children in the study were the six blacks and whites who showed the least interracial interaction in each class. Their teachers were taught to give social reinforcement (praising, listening to, touching) to these racial isolates when they were interacting with a member of the other race, but to otherwise interact with them as little as possible. The results showed marked increases in the amount of interracial interaction as a result of this simple intervention.

Teachers should make every effort not to adopt such procedures in an arbitrary fashion, however. This type of intervention is not clearly within the rights of the teacher. Looked at positively, it is "humanistic education" of a very effective sort, but many members of the community will see it as irresponsible and immoral "social engineering." You should seek the opinion of both other experts and the community before adopting such procedures. Some may see this precaution as unnecessary and see no possible objection to such interventions. But would they feel the same way if a teacher unilaterally decided to use the methods in reverse to *decrease* the amount of interaction between ethnic groups?

Classes that contain likable students, then, will tend to be more cohesive. It must be strongly emphasized, however, that the preceding discussion does not mean that only classes composed of candidates for the year's "most popular" award will be cohesive. The class need not be composed of the most popular students in the school in order to be cohesive; it is only necessary that the students in that class *like one another*. Many classes that are made up of low-status students on a schoolwide basis form tight and satisfying friendship patterns.

Such friendships are, unfortunately, about as predictable as the weather, and just about as difficult to influence. Some recent research (Drabman & Lahey, 1974) suggests that teachers can intervene to help some of the least well-liked students, however. But it is a step that should be taken with care. A first-grade girl enrolled in a small private school in Florida was referred to a psychologist because of her frequent disruption in the classroom and her poor relationships with other children. The psychologist suggested that the teacher give Charlotte a gold star and praise for being good each time her behavior had been acceptable for fifteen minutes.

The teacher was apprehensive that this special attention would have serious negative side effects. She feared that the other students would react negatively to the target child because of her special status, or that they themselves would misbehave in order to get the teacher's attention, or worse yet, that both reactions would occur.

The teacher did agree, however, to implement the positive reinforcement program to see how it worked. In order to quickly detect any occurrence of the type of side effects that concerned the teacher, observers came into the classroom on a daily basis to monitor the frequency of misbehaviors by the target child, the frequency of misbehaviors by the other members of the class, and the social relationships between the class and the target child. These were monitored by recording the number of positive and negative statements made by members of the class to this child and by asking the children to list their favorite members of the class at regular intervals (a technique discussed later in this section). As Figure 8–2 shows, the target child's frequency of misbehaviors was initially higher than the average for the rest of the class. When the teacher reinforced her for good behavior, however, the target child's misbehaviors fell below the class average. When the treatment stopped in the third phase, the high rate of misbehaviors recurred, but went back down when reinforcement was begun again in the final phase.

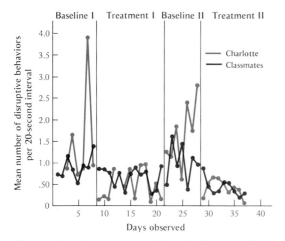

Figure 8–2. *Mean number of disruptive behaviors in each 20-second interval for Charlotte and her classmates. Positive reinforcement was given during the treatment phases, but not during the baseline phases. (From Drabman & Lahey, 1974)*

Moreover, the negative side effects that the teacher feared failed to develop; rather, the reverse was true. The program developed to help the target child's misbehavior seemed to have two other positive effects. First, when the target child improved, the rest of the class not only failed to get worse, they got slightly better. Second and more important, the target child's social standing improved as a result of the procedure. The frequency of positive statements directed to her increased and more students said they liked her when she received the added attention from the teacher (or perhaps it was because her behavior improved).

Giving extra attention to a student will not always be beneficial. The attention given to the "teacher's pet" can sometimes put that student in a more difficult position rather than an improved one. Perhaps the reason that the intervention just described and ones like it were successful in raising the likableness of the student was that the extra attention given to her was given *fairly*. It was clear to the class that her behavior needed improvement and that she only got extra attention when she earned it. This dimension of fairness may be important in determining students' reactions to extra attention given by a teacher.

Cohesive groups have many rather than few well-liked members. Cohesive groups are characterized by friendship patterns in which the members like a large number of the other members. This contrasts with groups in which there are a few highly liked members that everyone wants to be friends with, but who only like their own small circle of friends, or with classes that are composed of several tightly knit cliques (Schmuck, 1966).

The problems of conflict and frustration that can occur in such groups are obvious, but there is probably little that teachers can do about it. There is a way in which teachers can inadvertently contribute to this problem of broken up groups, however. Research on the establishment of subgroups by authority figures suggests that if teachers establish *permanent* high- and low-ability groups within the classroom, they will encourage the formation of several jealous cliques rather than one broadly based friendship group (Shaw, 1976). Such groupings are often desirable for instructional purposes, but they should be formed only when necessary and only kept separate for relatively brief periods of time. Whenever possible, without harming instruction, in other words, the class should be kept together as a single unit.

The group satisfies the members' needs. Not only do the individual members in a cohesive group satisfy one another's needs for friendship, the group as a whole also meets the needs of its members. In schools this means that the classroom *should* be a *place* where good things go on. It is a place where good discussions occur (both ones that are relevant to the subject matter of the class and ones that are not), where after-school baseball games are organized, where dates to basketball games are arranged, and where exciting and meaningful learning goes on.

The teacher's contribution to this aspect of cohesiveness is obvious. Teachers have a responsibility to see to it that the learning tasks and classroom discussions are meaningful and exciting, but can do little to see that everyone gets a date for the prom!

The members of cohesive groups frequently interact with one another. Groups cannot be close knit and enjoyable if their members never get a chance to interact with one another in informal ways. Increased social interaction is one of the benefits that come to teachers who organize their basic learning times efficiently enough so that there is time left over for more informal types of academic discussions. These types of discussions are not only good times for learning; they also contribute to the cohesiveness of the classroom by providing times for a type of social interaction. Discussions need not always be conducted with the entire class at one time, but if small groups are formed, they should not be permanent (the members could be formed and reformed into many small groups during the year to give them broad social exposure to one another), and they should not always consist of individuals of the same level of academic ability.

The importance of frequent social interaction provides another good reason for using free time at the end of the period as a positive reinforcer. When the students have earned free time through good academic work and good behavior (which they generally will after you have used this approach for a while), they can have time to build friendships and cohesiveness.

Cohesiveness is only one contributing factor in good education, but it is an important one. Classes that form a single cohesive group, or at least come close to this desired state, are desirable places to be, where learning is efficient. Classes with low cohesiveness can be unhappy places, where time and emotion is wasted on petty quarrels and dissatisfactions.

Research suggests that classroom groups can be *too* cohesive, however. Shaw and Shaw (1962) found that second-grade study groups that were formed of children who all liked one another did better initially on learning spelling lists than did groups formed of children who were not friends, but did less well in learning as time went on. The teachers reported that the highly cohesive groups spent an increasing amount of time in off-task social activities than did the low cohesive groups, which probably accounts for the decline in learning. It is rare, however, that a teacher has a classroom group that is so cohesive that unproductive social interaction cannot be kept to a reasonable level.

THE PRESSURE TO CONFORM

The pressure that groups place on us to conform was made very clear in a classic experiment by Solomon Asch (1956). The experimenter brought a group of eight college students into a room for a supposed study of "perceptual discrimination." One of these students was a real subject, but unknown to him, the other seven were accomplices of the experimenter. The students were shown a "standard" line, and then a set of several other lines of varying length. After each of the eighteen sets were shown, the students were asked to individually say aloud which line equaled the standard in length.

The items were easy, and on the first few trials everyone agreed on the correct choice. Soon, however, the seven accomplices began unanimously choosing lines that clearly did not match the standard in length on two thirds of the trials. This uniform agreement among the other "subjects" placed a heavy pressure on the real subject in each group to conform by choosing what he knew was the incorrect answer. About half of the subjects conformed on two or more of these trials, with approximately one fourth of the real subjects conforming four or more times. All the real subjects, even those who did not conform, found the experience to be uncomfortable.

Do you ever conform to the group, even when you know the group's action is incorrect or one that you do not want to do? Is this pressure to conform greater for children and adolescents?

Group Morale

The morale, or sense of satisfaction, of a group is closely related to its cohesiveness. The morale of low-cohesive groups is generally low as well. But, for many independent reasons, the morale of cohesive groups can also be low. Since group morale is obviously related to the goals of education, it is a topic that deserves mention.

Some of the same variables that determine cohesiveness also influence group morale, such as successful friendships within the groups, but most of the determinants of group morale originate in the actions of the teacher and other school officials. In other words, the things that lead to high morale are the things that make a classroom a pleasant place to be. Morale will be low if the teacher is harshly critical and sets impossibly high standards for behavior, but will be high if students enjoy their work. Morale may plummet if the principal eliminates recess for the last two months of the school year to make up for days lost because of snow, but might be high during a mock trial in civics class.

Fortunately, the kinds of actions on the part of the teacher that lead to good morale are the qualities that we have already ascribed to effective teachers. Effective teaching is, in fact, synonymous with building good group morale.

The strong influence of groups on its members can be beneficial, especially if the norms of the group are consistent with the goals of the school. We tend to be cynical about the norms of children's groups, but most children want to learn in school, be liked by the teacher, and so forth. Groups, through the tendency of members to imitate one another and their power to use reinforcement and punishment, can exert strong pressure on their members to conform.

Peer groups may not always be positive for children. They can frustrate members ("You can't be on our team!"), and they can create "role conflicts" by pressuring members to do things that their families or teachers are pressuring them to avoid. Furthermore, some children just have a hard time fitting into the group, and may need some help from the teacher or school psychologist on their social skills.

Sociometry of Peer Group Structure

Peer groups are considerably more complicated than they appear at first glance. In an informal but important way, peer groups have just as much internal structure as do parent-teacher organizations who elect presidents and vice-presidents and follow *Robert's Rules of Order*. Whether an individual is a leader or follower in a peer group has a great deal to do with how much the group influences his or her behavior and how much influence he or she has on the group.

One good way to understand the organization of peer groups is to step back and look at something that is far afield from education. Scientists who study animal behavior, for instance, tell us that monkey colonies are organized into a "dominance hierarchy." The monkey at the top of the hierarchy is given first choice of sleeping spots and of mates, is allowed to eat first, and so on by monkeys that occupy lower rungs of the ladder. Monkeys in the middle are submissive to those above them, while they dominate those who are below. A monkey who deviates from this established hierarchy is met with immediate violence.

Peer groups of children and adolescents are organized in similar ways. Not only are there leaders and followers, but each member of the group occupies a specific spot in the hierarchy. Those children who are the highest in the dominance network are the ones who are the most powerful models for the rest of the group. The belief among teachers that "bad behavior is contagious" is especially true when the bad behavior is started by a member with high status in the peer group.

Teachers can quickly learn about the structure of the groups in their classrooms by using a simple technique of **sociometry.** Sociometry is the measurement of the structure of groups. We will sometimes need to get a picture of the structure of the groups in our

classrooms so that we will know which children will be most influential and which children will be most influenced by the group. We can literally get a "picture" of this structure by using the simple technique of the sociogram. In doing this sociogram, teachers ask each member of their classes to list the two or three students who are their best friends or that they like the most or that they would want to take along on a trip to the moon (be careful to ask the kinds of questions that will give you the information that you are seeking, as different questions may lead to different results). Figure 8–3 shows how this information is then turned into a diagram of the social structure of the class.

Each student's name is placed in a circle and an arrow is drawn from each student's name to the circle of the students that he or

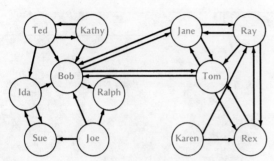

Figure 8–3. *Hypothetical sociogram of a class showing two friendship groups that are related through the mutual friendship of the leaders.*

she lists as friends. Students who are particularly popular and have leadership status in their group appear in the middle of clusters of circles as a result. Students who have low social standing in the group appear at the outside of the sociogram with few arrows drawn to them. The hypothetical class in Figure 8–3 reveals two major social groups within the classroom that are related only through the mutual friendship of the leaders of those two groups. This sociometric technique allows teachers to determine objectively which children rank highest and lowest in the eyes of their peers. You should keep in mind, however, that students' responses to sociometric questions will not always accurately reflect true friendship patterns.

Ability Grouping

Schools have long sought to improve the quality of education by assigning children to classroom groups in ways that are thought to facilitate learning and adjustment. One common method is to group children according to their learning characteristics, a

method known as ability grouping or tracking. In many high schools, some students are assigned to advanced classes, while others are assigned to lower-level courses such as "practical math" and "business English." At the elementary level, the children are divided according to assumed ability into grades 1A, 1B, and 1C.

This, as we have said, is a widely practiced procedure that has been experimentally evaluated many times. Do our practices conform with our knowledge? Do research studies suggest that ability grouping is a good thing? Marvin Shaw provides an excellent discussion of this topic in his book *Group Dynamics* (1976) which suggests that ability grouping is an indefensible practice. We should make it clear that we are talking about relatively permanent groupings that assign students to different classrooms on the basis of assumed differences in ability, not the informal subgroupings that teachers create for brief periods of time within the classroom for instructional purposes.

Ability grouping or tracking has been practiced in the United States since 1897, when the St. Louis school system began grouping elementary schoolchildren. The rationale for grouping suggests that the members of homogeneous groups will form friendships more easily because they are similar in interests and ability; that the less able members will not suffer loss in self-esteem because of an inability to compete with the brighter students in ungrouped classes; and that teachers will find it easier to teach children whose level of learning is similar. These arguments are plausible and compelling and have led to the adoption of the practice of grouping for nearly a century.

That grouping has withstood the test of time is a tribute to our inability to profit from research rather than the benefits of the practice, however. As pointed out by Shaw (1976), a large-scale study by Goldberg, Passow, and Justman (1966) provides an excellent evaluation of grouping. In a two-year study of 2,219 normal fifth-grade students ranging from below average to gifted in IQ scores, the researchers reached the following conclusions: Achievement was lower in most basic school subjects (reading, vocabulary, arithmetic, and social studies) when the students were in homogeneous ability groups than when they were ungrouped. Ability grouping similarly failed to lead to higher self-esteem, and, in fact, self-esteem dropped over the two-year period in the children who had been placed in the lower ability groups. Interests and attitudes toward school were unaffected by grouping, however.

These results are consistent with most findings in a large number of studies of the value of grouping conducted since 1920. As an added benefit, researchers find that teacher attitudes toward teaching are more favorable in ungrouped schools (Goodlad, 1960).

TEACHER EXPECTANCY EFFECTS

In 1968, Rosenthal and Jacobson published a book entitled *Pygmalion in the Classroom*. In it they stated a hypothesis that has extremely important implications for the social relationships between teacher and student. Without being aware that they are doing it, Rosenthal and Jacobson believe that teachers create a "self-fulfilling prophecy" by causing children whose ability they think is low to do poorly in school. Teachers do this, these authors suggest, through subtle actions that discourage the child's performance by giving these students less attention or by assigning them unchallenging work. At the heart of their book was an experiment in which teachers were led to believe that some students in their classes would improve markedly in performance during the school year. The experimenters told the teachers that a psychologist had given the children a test of "late blooming ability," and gave them a list of children who were supposed to improve during the year. At the end of the year, the children were retested and the experimenters found that the children the teachers expected to improve actually made small but significant gains in IQ scores compared to the other children in the class. This experiment has had a strong impact on educational thinking and has been the subject of many follow-up studies. Later investigations, however, have not consistently replicated the results of the original investigation.

A study by psychologists at Syracuse University is representative of the more recent investigations (O'Connell, Dusek, & Wheeler, 1974). In this study, two second-grade and two fourth-grade teachers were told that their children were taking a test that would predict academic improvement. They were each asked to list the students that they felt would do the best and the poorest on achievement tests at the end of the year and were also given a list of the children that the "test" predicted would show the highest degree of improvement. Actual achievement tests given at the beginning, middle, and end of the school year showed that the expectations built up by the psychologist through the fake test scores did not bias the teachers in any way. At least it did not bias them in a way that affected the children's test scores. The children that the teachers were told would do well during the year did no better than they had done all along. On the other hand, the teachers' predictions as to which children would do well on the achievement test proved accurate both during that school year and during the next school year. The psychologists concluded that since the teachers predicted the achievement of the children during the next school year as accurately as during the current one, their own expectations as to which children would do well on the achievement test were not biasing the way they interacted with the children; they simply were good predictors of which children would do well on achievement tests. An alternate explanation, however, is that the teachers' own expectations did influence the way the children behaved, and did so to such an extent that the effect continued into the next year. The reason that the expectations built up by the fake test scores given to the teachers by the psychologist did not affect the children may simply have been because the teachers did not believe in the "test" given by the psychologists.

When all of the experiments on teacher expectancy effects are looked at as a whole, clear conclusions cannot be reached. We simply cannot tell whether teachers' biases toward children influence the way they act toward the children and their academic performance. This is a possibility, however, that

teachers must take every care to avoid. This is especially true if you feel you have some degree of prejudice towards certain ethnic groups or children who behave in certain ways, since it is possible that your reactions to these children may create a "self-fulfilling prophecy" for their school performance.

REVIEW 8–1

1. What are the advantages of providing structure to the learning activities of your students?

2. What are the advantages of allowing your students to democratically assist you in the selection of classroom goals and procedures?

3. List six characteristics of effective leadership for teachers in providing structure to learning.

4. Give an example of an action by a teacher that would inhibit communication in the classroom.

5. How do peer groups "enforce" adherence to their norms?

6. How does cohesiveness affect adherence to group norms?

7. What factors contribute to high cohesiveness in groups?

8. What factors help determine whether an individual will be liked?

9. How can teachers contribute to high group morale?

10. What is a sociogram? How is it constructed?

11. Is ability grouping, or tracking, an effective method of school organization? Why or why not?

12. What does the term *teacher expectancy effect* refer to?

SUMMARY

Individuals are influenced by the groups they are in. Both inside and outside the classroom, the formal and informal groups to which students belong can powerfully promote, or inhibit, the goals of education. The influence that classroom groups will have over students is determined in large part by the style or climate of leadership and by the degree of cohesiveness and morale.

A democratic style of teacher leadership that gives considerable direction to learning seems most beneficial for students and teacher alike. This leadership style is promoted by a clear statement of reasonable instructional objectives, competence in the subject matter and clear communication of ideas, giving personal feedback to students, having positive feelings and expectations for them, focusing on both the needs of the students and of instruction, and by consistently and firmly holding to classroom rules. In addition, it is necessary to keep the lines of communication open among teachers, students, and parents.

At all school ages, peer groups exert a powerful influence on students' behavior, particularly during late childhood and early adolescence. This influence is especially strong if the group is cohesive and has high morale. Cohesiveness will be high when the students like one another, when each member has many friends in the group, when the group satisfies the members' needs, and when the members interact frequently.

Friendship patterns is the most important of these factors. The forces that influence a person's likableness as a friend include physical attractiveness, exhibiting likable behavior, having a reciprocally satisfying friendship, and the similarity of the interests and backgrounds of friends.

Group morale is closely related to cohesiveness, but is also influenced by the fairness and reasonableness of classroom demands. Teachers can have some impact on cohesiveness, but are particularly important in determining the morale of classroom groups.

Schools have long tried to maximize the nature of classroom groups for instructional purposes by grouping children according to their assumed ability. This practice makes good sense in theory, but has not proved beneficial in practice.

Although many aspects of the group psychology of the classroom cannot be completely controlled by the teachers, they are still the key factors in the social structure of the classroom. One potentially important factor in the social relationship between teacher and child is the teacher's expectations for the child's performance. Although the data are incomplete at present, it is possible that teachers may create a self-fulfilling prophecy by unintentionally leading children to perform in the way that they expect.

ANSWERS TO REVIEW QUESTIONS

1. The social interaction of students is better when learning tasks are structured than left entirely up to the students, and learning is often better as well.

2. Democratic styles of leadership tend to produce about the same amount of learning as authoritarian ones, but the group morale is generally better.

3. An effective style of leadership for teachers includes these characteristics:
   (a) clearly states learning objectives
   (b) knows the subject matter and explains it clearly and simply
   (c) gives students personal, respectful corrective feedback when wrong, and praise when correct
   (d) is firm and consistent in enforcing rules and standards, but gives students a voice in adopting rules and standards
   (e) is generally positive in his or her attitude toward students and his or her expectations for them

4. Asking for ideas with a request like, "If you have any complaints, spit them out now!" will probably lead to little constructive communication. The same might be true of, "We will have a discussion of the grading policy in the school auditorium Saturday at 8:00 A.M.

5. Usually without knowing they are doing so, peer groups influence our behavior through our tendency to imitate other group members, and through their reactions, positive and negative, to our actions.

6. Cohesive or tightly knit groups exerted stronger power over the behavior of their members.

7. Highly cohesive groups
   (a) have members who like one another.
   (b) have broad rather than narrow patterns of friendship.
   (c) satisfy the needs of their members.
   (d) allow frequent interactions among their members.

8. Factors that contribute to an individual's likability are
   (a) physical attractiveness
   (b) likable behavior

(c) reciprocal satisfaction with friends

(d) similarity of interests and backgrounds to friends

9. Teachers contribute to good group morale by being good teachers, that is, by making learning meaningful and efficient and the classroom a happy place to be in.

10. A sociogram is an illustration that describes the friendship patterns in a group such as a classroom. It is constructed by asking each student a question such as "Name your three best friends." Arrows are drawn from each child's name to the names of his or her friends, forming a picture of the friendship patterns.

11. No. Ability grouping or tracking does not lead to improved academic achievement, but often results in lowered esteem for those in the lower groups. In addition, teachers report more positive attitudes toward ungrouped classes.

12. Teacher expectancy effects are possible biasing influences of the preconceptions held by teachers about their students' ability on the actual classroom performance of these pupils. The research is equivocal, but we may unintentionally lead students to learn poorly because we *think* they will learn poorly.

The Influence of Schools on Society

The relationship between schools and society is a two-way street. Society builds schools and influences them in many obvious and subtle ways. Schools, on the other hand, work an influence on society. It is important that we examine that relationship in some detail if we are to present a view of the psychology of instruction that transcends the walls of a single classroom or school.

Not only does society build schools and pay teachers' salaries, it also sets the goals and direction for education. We often lose sight of this last fact because most people seem indifferent toward schools. When the public does express its opinion toward schools it often appears negative and destructive in character, such as when parents march on school libraries and demand the removal of certain books because of their "objectionable" contents, when they bring lawsuits against biology teachers for teaching evolutionary theory, or when violence breaks out during antibusing demonstrations. But in spite of these incidents, schools would not exist if it were not for society.

Society's most direct influence on education, however, is through its **subcultures.** The term "subculture" was coined to express the fact that the cultures of most countries are made up of many smaller cultures. This is especially true in the United States where the population can trace its origin to immigrants from many different countries (although American Indians were surely here first, many anthropologists believe they migrated here from Asia). These many smaller cultures that make up the American culture are subcultures.

As each of us grows up, we are closely in touch with our own subculture. Our family, be it Italian, Irish, English, Chicano, or whatever, reflects the knowledge, values, and skills of our subculture. The neighbors and friends that we have the most contact with are more likely to be members of our own subculture than of others. Through this contact, our subculture leaves an indelible imprint upon us. Through their educational process, the skills in which children will be most proficient, and the value that they place on educational achievement will reflect, in part, their subcultures.

Until relatively recently, subcultures came one to a school. Each school district was designed to include only blacks, high-income whites, or some other homogeneous group. It sometimes involved drawing school boundaries in some pretty absurd shapes, but it was done nonetheless. Today, for both legal and voluntary reasons, schools often contain a mixture of subcultures. This can often be a problem since the diversity in patterns of behavior will be more extreme in such schools than in ones with more homogeneous student bodies.

It carries with it an important advantage, too, however. Both teacher and pupils are given the opportunity to learn to live better in a diverse and pluralistic society. We can learn from each other in heterogeneous schools, provided prejudice and animosity do not get in the way, and place our own subcultures in a broader perspective as a result.

DO SCHOOLS CHANGE SOCIETY?

Although it is certainly true that society influences schools, is the obverse also true? Does the process of education *change* students in a way that alters the nature of society? To answer this question, and to understand why we even asked it, we need to place it in historical context. Americans decided in the early 1900s to pay for mandatory public education for all children. To take on such an enormous task they had to have a good reason. And they did. They wanted to bring fuller meaning to the American ideal of equal opportunity for every person. It was obvious by then that the nation's economy would continue to industrialize and that formal education was essential for an individual to obtain a desirable job. If only the rich could afford a satisfactory education, then only their children could aspire to high paying jobs and positions of leadership. This contradicted the American notion that any

child could grow up to be a doctor, lawyer, or president. As a result, state legislatures passed laws setting up public education. Every American child then had an equal right to "life, liberty, and the pursuit of happiness" regardless of his or her parents' ability to pay for an education. But is it true that public education lessened inequalities?

Our best answer to this question seems to be yes and no. Public education has had some influence on our lives, but not as much as we would like. Christopher Jencks of the Harvard University College of Education recently published his controversial views on this topic (Jencks, 1972).

Jencks' argument goes like this:

(1.) The quality of teaching has little to do with the amount of learning that goes on in the classroom. Based on Coleman's now famous survey of schools in the United States (Coleman, 1966), Jencks concluded that there is little relationship between the "quality" of a school and the average achievement test scores of its students.

(2.) The amount of schooling that individuals receive partly determines how much they will earn during their lifetime, but other important factors exert an influence as well. The individual who finishes college will, on the average, earn more than the one who does not, and the high-school graduate will usually earn more than the dropout. Similarly, the quality of the school will make some difference, but Jencks believes that these educational variables are far less important than other determinants. The qualities that individuals "bring with them" to school or to work—their family and social background,

THE COLEMAN REPORT

The Civil Rights Act of 1964 funded the U.S. Office of Education to authorize sociologist James S. Coleman to conduct a large-scale study of educational achievement in the United States (Coleman, 1966). Coleman designed the study to determine the extent to which advantaged and disadvantaged groups differed in educational attainment and to isolate the causes for those differences. Over a period of two years, data were collected from 4,000 schools, 60,000 teachers, and 600,000 students. The findings clearly showed that American blacks attained a lower level of educational attainment at all grade levels, and that the differences increased with age. This part of the findings was expected, but the analysis of the causes of this lag resulted in unexpected conclusions. It was anticipated that the large differences in quality between the largely segregated schools serving blacks and whites would be related to the lack of educational attainment among nonwhites. Coleman found, however, that regardless of the quality of the institution, as measured by variables such as the educational level of teachers, school budgets, pupil-teacher ratios, and so on, the educational attainment of blacks still lagged far behind whites. The only variable reliably associated with higher achievement in blacks was the percentage of whites in the school. When blacks attended predominantly white schools, their achievement levels were significantly higher than when they attended segregated schools.

These data were introduced to the Supreme Court and were key evidence in the decision that said "separate but equal" educational facilities could not exist. If attendance in predominantly white schools was the only factor that would increase the educational achievement of blacks, then a school system that was segregated could not by definition provide equal educational opportunity for nonwhites.

In public statements made in 1976, at the height of antibusing demonstrations in major American cities, Professor Coleman reversed his position on forced desegregation. He said recent studies have shown that *forced* desegregation does not result in increased educational attainment for blacks, since it results in whites leaving public school systems in greater numbers. Such "white flight" leaves schools segregated in reality, even though they are integrated by law. These issues are still controversial. If you were a justice on the Supreme Court, or a member of a local school board, how would you cast your vote? Would you leave segregated schools as they are, or would you attempt to integrate them?

a lackluster academic record. Partly because of this, he took a job as a sales representative for a small and struggling photocopy company. He liked the company and its ideas, and so he worked hard and bought its stock which was low priced at the time. The company continued to grow and the gentleman was frequently promoted, so when the company changed its name to Xerox, he found himself rather well-off financially! This type of story will always be with us and, unfortunately, so will the opposite type. The physicist who gets his Ph.D. at a time when there is an oversupply of physicists may wind up driving a taxicab instead, and the architect who is just starting out in the middle of a building slump may find herself collecting unemployment checks. It is also a fact that some intelligent members of our society become well-to-do plumbers, while others become modestly paid teachers.

The impact of these uncontrollable factors is easy for us to see in examples such as these, but their importance is far greater in all our lives than we realize. We normally think, for example, that rich parents pass on their wealth (and their ability to make more wealth) to their children and that poor parents pass on their poverty to their children. This is partially true, but not as much as we once believed. The children of parents in the top fifth of income are only about one-third as rich as their parents, and the children of parents in the bottom fifth are only one-third as poor as their parents. This is partly because some of the children of the rich fail to acquire the same level of income-producing skills as their parents, and because some of

what they learned from peers, and their heredity—are, in Jencks' opinion, a stronger force in determining an individual's adult income than the quality of the school. The most important factors in determining an individual's income are out of the individual's control—in other words, just plain luck. Financial success is strongly influenced by factors that simply cannot be predicted.

The following story is a good case in point. One of the authors knows a man who worked his way through college by working in an apple orchard. He was unable to devote much of his time to his studies, so he earned the children at the lower end of the economic scale stay in school longer than their parents did. But it is also partly because of those factors that are out of their control, such as choosing a profession that has a lower income potential than their parents or in being able to get into a union.

The most convincing data on the importance of chance factors, however, comes from Jencks' study of brothers. He found that brothers in the United States differ in yearly income by an average of $5,400. That is a huge difference, especially when you consider that the mean difference between *randomly selected individuals* is only $6,000 per year. Even though brothers share approximately the same background, heredity, and educational levels, their incomes are only slightly more similar than randomly selected individuals. The role of uncontrollable factors is powerful indeed.

Jencks' conclusions, though thought provoking, are equivocal for a number of reasons. First, Jencks based his conclusions on data collected during the early 1960s. Our knowledge of teaching procedures has increased greatly since that time, so much so that a study of the relationship between teaching quality and achievement conducted today might produce different results.

Second, Jencks judged the quality of a school as a whole (rather than studying the effectiveness of individual teachers), using variables such as the class size, size of the school budget, and the number of teachers with advanced degrees. Since each school had some good and some poor instructors who canceled each other out in taking a school average, and since the investigators did not look at the actual teaching skills of the teachers, the study could have been conducted in far more informative ways.

Also, Jencks based his analyses on differences across the entire scale of both income and educational achievement. This can be misleading since the factors that produce a $3,000 difference in income, for example, are far less important to the individual who earns $40,000 than to the one who earns $4,000. Similarly, the changes in teaching strategies that produce an improvement of three grade levels is far more important to the individual who leaves school barely literate than to the person who leaves reading at the high-school level.

Jencks does make one point that seems as undeniable as it is important, however: Many of the variables that determine an individual's income *are unrelated to his or her competence.* Schools can remove some of the restrictions that keep individuals from having a free choice in deciding what occupation they will enter and what income they will have, but there are *other* variables that are at least as important.

Moreover, poverty is a *relative* rather than an absolute condition. People feel poor because they have less than most other people, not because of the amount they have. Most of the poor in the United States have more money than the upper-middle class of Asian and African countries. They are truly "poor" only in relationship to others in the United States today. Education can help a larger proportion of individuals move into the "middle-income" bracket by making society more skilled and wealthy as a whole, but it cannot eliminate poverty. No matter how wealthy we are as a group, there will still be some proportion of individuals who are poor in this relative sense. Schools should not and cannot be held entirely responsible for the "poverty cycle"; it is an economic and political condition as well.

Even if we accept Jencks' argument, it does not entirely overrule the possibility that schools can affect society for the better. Public education plays an important role in seeing to it, for example, that members of specific ethnic groups are not prohibited from high paying occupations because of their lack of skills. We may always have poverty, but schools can help ensure that skin color does not play an important part in determining who will be poor. In a larger sense, schools will help determine if, and in what ways, societies will survive. We must have increasingly superior skills and knowledge if we are to cope with an ever more befuddling and complicated world. Moreover, they will help determine the quality of life. Future studies of the effects of schools on society should focus less on income than on satisfaction with life.

The Relative Importance of Inheritance in Educational Attainment

Another important but troubling analysis of the effects of education on society was published in 1971 in *The Atlantic Monthly* by Richard Herrnstein, professor of psychology, also at Harvard University. Herrnstein's thesis differs from Jencks' in several important ways, but both agree in their controversial conclusion that schools may play only a limited role in the elimination of poverty.

Herrnstein begins by reviewing the evidence for the heritability of intelligence. Although this is an unsettled issue, most psychologists believe, as we mentioned in Chapter 6, that genetics play *some* role in determining IQ test scores. Herrnstein is more emphatic—he believes inheritance plays a major role in the determination of intelligence. If success in occupations depends in large measure on intellectual skills, and if income and social standing depend greatly on occupational success, then it follows that income and social standing depend in some major way on the inherited intellectual differences among people. Again, the key to Herrnstein's argument is his controversial assumption that intelligence is an almost totally *inherited* characteristic, when most psychologists argue that quality and quantity of education, the type of environment in which the child grows up, and chance factors dilute the influence of inheritance to a great extent.

Herrnstein answers these arguments in a forceful way. While he grants that environmental variables play important roles in determining social standing and income, he believes they play increasingly less important roles in modern American society. Because of our democratic and egalitarian beliefs, we spend our tax money on programs designed to reduce social inequality among American citizens. Aid to Dependent Children is designed to free mothers of low-income groups from the necessity of working while their children are of school age; school desegregation is designed to let all children attend schools of equal quality; federal subsidies to school lunch programs help ensure proper nutrition; medical and dental services are offered to the children of the poor through

Head Start programs, and so on. Social action programs have certainly not been uniformly successful in assuring equal quality of life for all citizens of the United States, but Herrnstein argues that great strides have been made, and will continue in the future. As schools improve, more children will be exposed to the experiences that lead to full intellectual development. This will lead to higher average intellectual abilities for the population, but Herrnstein argues that it will only make things *relatively worse* for those at the lower end of the social scale.

The poor, Herrnstein believes, are at the bottom of the social scale partly because of inheritance and partly because of environmental and chance factors. But as the environment improves for more individuals, the extent to which social standing is determined by inheritance will *increase,* since the extent to which it will be determined by environmental variables will decrease. If environments are made similar, only genetic factors will be left to vary. This means that families who are the top of the scales of social standing because of their higher intellectual skills will remain there indefinitely (unless there is a radical reorganization of society), since they will pass their skills on to their children through inheritance. Similarly, the poor will consistently pass their lower level of intellectual skills to their offspring.

To Herrnstein, then, the schools can do nothing to improve the upward mobility of the poor. If anything, better education will only increase the degree to which inheritance determines social standing. If improved education has any impact on the intellectual

skills of the population, it would be to *increase* the difference between the poor and advantaged. The "genetically superior" children might benefit from improvement in education more than the "genetically inferior" students, thus increasingly the distance between their levels of intellectual skill. This argument is very provocative, but it is certainly not one that all social scientists would accept.

The Role of Inheritance in Racial Differences in Intelligence and Achievement

Educational psychologist Arthur Jensen of the University of California at Berkeley has taken a strong position on the role of inheritance in determining the intellectual and achievement differences between whites and nonwhites in the United States (Jensen, 1969). Jensen believes that genetics play, by far, the most important role in determining intellectual skills, and expands his argument in an attempt to explain racial differences in intelligence. He believes that blacks and whites in the United States have widely different intelligence test scores because blacks are genetically inferior. As previously discussed, this extremely controversial position has been attacked by many social scientists.

Most importantly, it seems impossible to determine the relative importance of inheritance and environment in a society that still shows obvious prejudice toward nonwhites. But Jensen's argument that is most directly related to our present discussion concerns the value of compensatory education for the poor (Jensen, 1969). In the following statement, he draws support for his hypothesis that blacks are genetically inferior from his claim that special educational programs for black disadvantaged children have been unsuccessful. Since Jensen believes compensatory education programs such as Head Start *have not* worked so far in increasing the educational achievements of blacks (a conclusion that we will discuss later in this section), he assumes that they *will never* work.

Compensatory education has been practiced on a massive scale for several years in many cities across the nation. It began with auspicious enthusiasm and high hopes of educators. It has unprecedented support from Federal funds. It had theoretical sanction from social scientists espousing the major underpinning of its rationale: the "deprivation hypothesis," according to which academic lag is mainly the result of social, economic, and educational deprivation and discrimination—an hypothesis that has met with wide, uncritical acceptance in the atmosphere of society's growing concern about the plight of minority groups and the economically disadvantaged.

The chief goal of compensatory education—to remedy the educational lag of disadvantaged children and thereby narrow the achievement gap between "minority" and "majority" pupils—has been utterly unrealized in any of the large compensatory education programs that have been evaluated so far. (pp. 2–3)

Jensen is right, we believe, in saying that the success of compensatory education programs for disadvantaged children tells us a great deal about the relative importance of environmental interventions in their intellectual skills. But, is Jensen correct in saying that education programs designed to improve the intellectual skills of the disadvantaged have never worked? The following section takes up that question.

COMPENSATORY EDUCATION FOR THE DISADVANTAGED

The key issue in this controversy is how successful has the educational system been in helping the disadvantaged in our society to have a greater range of occupational choice through improved educational skills. Students from families below the federal poverty guidelines, many of whom are from minority groups, are likely to have serious educational problems. On the average, they learn slightly more than half the material expected of them in each year of school (Becker, Engelmann, & Thomas, 1975), and they tend to fall farther behind each school year. This does not mean that every child from a disadvantaged background will do poorly in school. Like any other group, they will be characterized by great differences among individuals. Some will not only be successful in school, but will be spectacularly successful. Still, on the average, disadvantaged students will do far less well than children from middle- and upper-income families.

Theories of the Educational Problems of Disadvantaged Children

For the past twenty years, there has been a considerable amount of interest in the educational problems of the disadvantaged. This interest was particularly spurred by President Johnson's "war on poverty," whose administrators, like many Americans, assumed that

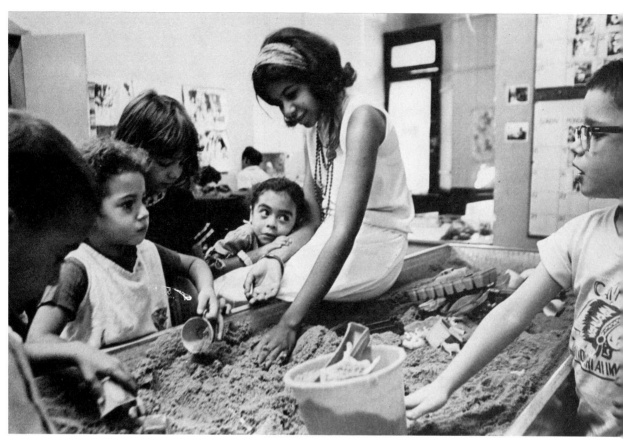

Preschoolers in a Head Start classroom

schools would play an essential part in breaking the "poverty cycle." It is clear today that schools have failed to break the poverty cycle through increased achievement for the disadvantaged (as have other antipoverty programs). Is it at all possible that they can do so? Is there something that schools can do to allow the disadvantaged to achieve at the national average?

The approach we take to this problem will depend in large measure on the way we view the problem. Over the years, several major approaches to the education of the disadvantaged have developed.

Cultural deprivation theory.   During the 1950s and 1960s the predominant point of view was that individuals from low-income backgrounds had difficulty in school because their culture deprived them of the experiences necessary to become successful. It was believed that the homes of the disadvantaged provided inadequate intellectual stimulation and a lack of encouragement for studying. This point of view faded in respectability as educators and psychologists gradually realized

CULTURAL RELATIVITY, OR DOES THE EARTH REVOLVE AROUND THE SUN?

When Albert Einstein formulated the General Theory of Relativity, he was interested in problems encountered in measuring moving objects. But since that time, the basic concept of relativity has found application in many diverse areas. Whenever we measure or evaluate something, it is always *in relationship* to something else. As is mentioned in the text, when we evaluate a culture, it is not according to some absolute standard of good or bad, but relative to some other culture, usually our own. If we encounter a culture that is less interested in drama and dance than our own, for example, it is tempting to say that it is *deficient* in the value it places on the performing arts. It would be more accurate to say, however, that the two cultures have *different* attitudes towards theater and dance. Since our judgment is only relative, it might be that both cultures have less interest in this area than some other third culture of which we are not yet aware. Deficiency is only a relative concept.

This is a rather difficult notion to completely accept, but the following illustration from elementary-school science helped one of the authors (BBL) to better understand the concept of relativity. Does the earth revolve around the sun, or does the sun revolve around the earth? Every student of astronomy from the third grade on knows that the Alexandrian astronomer Ptolemy thought the sun moved around the earth in a large circle made up of smaller circles, called epicircles, but that Copernicus set us all straight by discovering that the earth moves around the sun. The answer, then, is that the earth revolves

around the sun. Right? But, according to the principles of relativity, that answer is *wrong*— the correct answer is that *both* answers are correct. How can that be?

I had always thought that humans would someday travel far enough out into space to see that Copernicus was right. By stopping the spaceship so that it was stationary, the passengers could see the earth revolving around the sun. But that is the problem. There is no spot in space that is *stationary*, except *relative to something else*. If our spaceship is stationary relative to the sun, the sun will appear to stand still while the earth moves around it. If, on the other hand, the spaceship is stationary relative to the earth, the earth will appear to stand still while the sun moves around it. The earth and sun move relative to one another, but we cannot meaningfully say that one revolves around the other. There is simply no fixed spot in space in an absolute sense from which to make that judgment. In much the same way, we should only compare cultures in a relative way. It makes sense to say that two cultures are different from one another, but not that one is superior to the other in

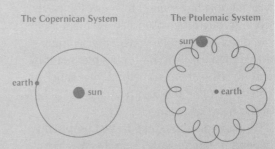

Figure 9—1. *Illustration of the solar systems conceived by Copernicus and Ptolemy.*

some absolute sense. This is the concept of *cultural relativity.*

Incidentally, we continue to use the Copernican system not because it is more accurate, but because it is so much simpler than the Ptolemaic system. Astronauts have found, however, that the Ptolemaic system is slightly more accurate in predicting the location of the planets for space shots. Using computers to handle the enormous calculations, our astronauts travel in a solar system in which the sun is assumed to revolve around the earth!

the prejudice involved in it. Major assumptions in the theory rested on stereotypic views of the home lives of the poor, lives unknown to most academics. The cultural deprivation theory assumes that if a person is not raised in a white middle-class home, that person is culturally deprived. A Chinese girl may do poorly in a French school because it is operated according to different patterns and standards than the ones she has encountered in her home, but that is not to say that she comes from a deficient culture. A French girl might equally do poorly in a Chinese school; they both cannot come from deficient cultures. It is simply that each girl's culture differed sharply from that of the school. Similarly, the subcultures of the poor in the United States (poor whites, poor blacks, poor Chicanos, etc.) *differ* from the subcultures of the middle class, but they are not necessarily *deficient* subcultures.

In the early 1960s, the Head Start program was begun to *compensate* for the alleged deficiencies in the culture of disadvantaged children. By bringing children into an intensive preschool and kindergarten program before they entered the first grade, educators hoped to create an intellectually stimulating and motivating environment outside the home that would enable them to do school-work equal to children from middle- and upper-income families. Initially, the results of Head Start programs looked promising. Children who participated in such compensatory programs performed much better during the first grade than did other disadvantaged children. Longer-term studies, however, consistently revealed that the intellectual and academic gains that these children showed during first grade faded by the time they reached third grade. From that point on, they performed, as a group, at the same low level as other children from disadvantaged backgrounds.

This is not to say that the Head Start program failed completely. Enormous amounts of necessary nutritional, medical, and dental care have been given under the auspices of this program. In educational terms, however, the program did not meet its original goals. Still, it was an important beginning. Through it, we became less prejudiced in our view of disadvantaged children. Instead of viewing them as deprived and trying to duplicate middle-class experiences for them in a preschool program, the focus has shifted to more sophisticated studies of the ways in which disadvantaged children differ from children who are successful in school, and to attempt to find effective ways of dealing with those differences.

Linguistic deficiency theory.   Until recently, one of the most promising theories concerned the language of the disadvantaged. Sociolinguist Basil Bernstein (a sociolinguist is a specialist who combines the disciplines of sociology and linguistics) speculated that a primary reason that disadvantaged children have trouble in school is their language (Bernstein, 1970). He believed that it was not sufficiently complex to deal with the sophisticated type of thinking expected in school. In studying lower-income British children, he noticed that they used a language that he characterized as more "restricted" than the language of middle- and upper-income children, which he characterized as "expanded." The disadvantaged children used shorter sentences, fewer adjectives and adverbs, and less complex patterns of speech. Studies of the language of disadvantaged children in the United States generally tended to confirm his observations, and language soon became a major focus of compensatory preschools. Some researchers believed, for example, that one of the major reasons for the difficulties encountered by black children in school was that they spoke an inadequate and inaccurate version of English.

This theory met with much the same criticism as the cultural deprivation theory, in that it contained too much fruitless and misleading prejudice and insufficient facts. It is one thing to indicate that two groups speak *different* languages, but it is something quite different to say that one group is *deficient* in their language because they do not speak the same language. The belief that black children make a lot of "mistakes" in using the English language is a good case in point. The linguistic deficiency theorists believe this is one of the primary reasons that black children do poorly in school. American sociolinguists such as Labov (1970), however, pointed out that black children speak their dialect just as accurately as white children speak theirs. Neither group makes a large number of "errors" in using their dialect; they just speak different, equally sophisticated dialects.

Ironically, the strongest arguments against this theory came from sociolinguistic research. Labov (1970) and Houston (1970) pointed out an important fact that early researchers overlooked. When in the presence of high-status adults, disadvantaged children tend to be inhibited in their language much more than middle- and upper-income children. Under these circumstances, they appear to use a reduced and contracted form of their language. When studied in a more natural situation, however, such as in the presence of their families or peers, they use a language that is every bit as rich and complex as that of middle- and upper-income children. More recently, psychologists Marwit and Neumann (1974) pointed out that even though black children in the United States speak a somewhat different dialect than do white children, they are able to comprehend white English as well as white children. This is perhaps because black children live in a culture that is dominated by white groups, and it is necessary that they understand both languages. This fact argues strongly against the linguistic deficiency theory.

TEACHER PREJUDICE TOWARD THE SPEECH CHARACTERISTICS OF MINORITY STUDENTS

New York City educators conducted a study that suggests the unconscious prejudice many of us have toward children from minority subcultures may affect our judgments as teachers. Sixty-two experienced white teachers were asked to assign grades to the oral answers of twelve ninth-grade boys to typical school questions. Unknown to the teachers, the boys' answers were made up by the experimenters and were only read by the boys. All the teachers heard the same answers, except that some heard them read by six white students, while others heard the answers read by six black students who spoke a black dialect. Significantly higher grades were given by the teachers to the answers when they were spoken by white students than when spoken by black students. Some teachers were more influenced by this bias than others, but the effect was found for teachers at all ages, for both sexes, at all years of teaching experience, regardless of the grade they taught most frequently or the percentage of black students usually in their classes (Crowl & MacGinnitie, 1974).

Cognitive styles hypothesis.   A theory that is widely accepted today suggests that disadvantaged children have difficulties in school because their cognitive (intellectual) styles are different from children from middle- or upper-income families. The term *cognitive styles* is used to suggest that they go about learning or solving intellectual problems in different ways. For example, psychologist Donald Meichenbaum from the University of Waterloo in Canada (Meichenbaum & Goodman, 1969) and Jerome Kagan (1966) of Harvard University believe that disadvantaged children are more likely to respond impulsively to school problems without giving themselves enough time to think. Other research suggests that disadvantaged children are more likely to think of objects in terms of their surface features (color, shape, and number), whereas middle-income children are more likely to think in terms of conceptual qualities (its name and defining characteristics) (Nelson & Klausmeier, 1974).

We need a great deal of additional information before we can accept or reject this hypothesis, but already it has had a great deal of influence on our educational practices. The "Sesame Street" television series is based largely on the cognitive styles hypothesis. The intellectual exercises on that program are designed to teach disadvantaged children to think in styles that are more compatible with the white middle-income school system.

Direct instruction approach.   One of the dominant approaches to disadvantaged children today maintains that we simply do not know why they have educational problems. Until we find out, we need to find educational methods that will result in the greatest amount of educational success for them. Regardless of why a group of individuals are having problems in learning, we can best help them by improving the conditions of learning so that they can learn at the same rate as most other individuals. This approach

program for the disadvantaged. Instead of working with the children only during the preschool years, Project Follow Through funded experimental teaching programs that gave the child intensive education from kindergarten through the third grade. Researchers hoped that this longer-term intervention would have more lasting results, hence the name "Project Follow Through." Of the many programs supported throughout the country under this concept, seven large-scale programs have been evaluated intensively by independent research organizations over the past several years. They range in design from highly structured programs consistent with the philosophy of this textbook to unstructured programs developed more along the theoretical views of Jean Piaget. Although all the results are not in, existing evidence supports the two programs that use approaches consistent with this book.

To date, the most successful programs have been the direct instruction models developed by Don Bushell at the University of Kansas and Wesley Becker and Seigfried Engelmann at the University of Oregon. Although there are some differences between these programs, their views are similar to those expressed in this book. They place particularly high emphasis on a clear specification of the learning tasks and on positive reinforcement. Their teachers were well trained in the use of these techniques, but otherwise the programs *could* be replicated in any classroom serving disadvantaged students.

The results obtained by these two experimental programs are extraordinary. The achievement scores in reading for the children in the University of Kansas Follow

is most consistent with the philosophy of this textbook: There are many reasons why children are different but we can help them most by respecting their differences on the one hand, and by helping to make learning as meaningful and efficient as possible for them on the other.

EXPERIMENTAL EDUCATION PROGRAMS FOR THE DISADVANTAGED: PROJECT FOLLOW THROUGH

When it first became evident that Project Head Start was not fulfilling its original goals of lifting the educational achievement of disadvantaged children, the Office of Education of the United States Department of Health, Education, and Welfare proposed a very large-scale and important experiment. They asked researchers in education and related fields to design a new type of educational

TWO FACES OF POVERTY IN GEORGIA

Poverty wears two faces in Georgia. Large numbers of urban poor live in Atlanta and other cities, and large numbers are scattered throughout the rural areas of the state. The same is true, of course, for nearly every state in the union.

These two groups of poor people share common problems of lack of discretionary income, lack of medical care, and high exposure to crime, and often share a common subcultural heritage as well. Many of Atlanta's poor can remember when they or their parents left an unproductive farm to look for a better life in the city. Yet, for all their similarities, the environment and everyday stress of these peoples differ sharply. The urban poor may face crowding and industrial pollution, while the rural poor may be forced to contend with isolation and dust.

Certainly, these individuals will differ in ways that schools must learn to accommodate, but do the same basic educational strategies apply to both disadvantaged groups? The results of two experimental education projects conducted in Georgia suggest that they do.

A group of psychologists from Emory University and educators from the Atlanta Public Schools worked together in a program to increase the educational achievement of disadvantaged urban children (Rollins, Mc-Candless, Thompson, & Brassell, 1974). They held workshops on the use of positive reinforcement given for good academic performance and provided follow-up consultations with the teachers. In an Appalachian school system, a school psychologist from Georgia State University teamed with local officials to set up a similar program of workshops and consultation on the use of educational objectives and positive reinforcement (Matheny & Edwards, 1974). The results showed strong improvements when children in both programs were compared with disadvantaged children whose teachers were not in the programs. The mean gain in grade levels of reading for the Atlanta group was .71, compared to .42 for the children not in the experimental program (the control group). The largest gains were 1.18 years of achievement (1.0 is "average" for the general population), which was found for second-graders, the youngest group in the study. Mean gain in grade levels for arithmetic for the experimental group was .66, compared to the control group. The Appalachian group showed mean gains in reading achievement of .95 years. Even larger gains (more than one grade level of achievement per year) were found for disadvantaged children in the experimental education program of the Fernald School in Los Angeles (Feshbach & Adelman, 1974).

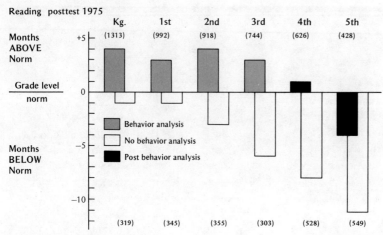

Figure 9–2. *Mean achievement in reading for children in the Kansas Follow Through Project and a comparison group of children who were not in Follow Through. (From Bushell, in press)*

Through program (Bushell, in press) appear in Figure 9–2. Presented with these data are the mean achievement scores for a matched group of disadvantaged children who attended regular school classes. These children showed the typical pattern of progressive decline in achievement from kindergarten to the fourth grade. Such children enter kindergarten slightly less prepared than their middle-income peers, so they learn slightly less. They enter the first grade slightly more behind than when they entered kindergarten, so they do even less well in the first grade. By the time they enter the second grade, they are considerably behind and second grade is consequently a much harder task for them than first grade. The cycle of entering each school year further behind than the previous continues, and the child's achievement spirals further downward. This is a primary cause for the high dropout rate

among disadvantaged children, and the frustration that it produces seems a major contributing factor in discipline problems, and perhaps even in the high rate of crime among such individuals.

The achievement data for the children in the Kansas Follow Through program, however, are in sharp contrast to this pattern. Each year, they have been at or above grade level in reading. Not only did they achieve better than other disadvantaged children and not show the pattern of progressive decline, they generally achieved at a rate *higher than the national average.* At the end of the third grade, Project Follow Through ends and the children go into normal fourth-grade classrooms. It is revealing to see that their achievement continued to be higher than the national average at the end of the fourth-grade year, a year in which they did not receive any type of special educational support, but dropped markedly during the fifth grade. In one sense, this indicates a "failure" of the Follow Through Program to produce *lasting* gains in educational competence, but viewed differently, it is more proof of its effectiveness. The disadvantaged children in the Kansas program (and the Oregon Program that found nearly identical results) continued to learn well as long as they were in top quality classrooms, but soon dropped off when they left them. The implication is that we must provide the disadvantaged with excellent education *throughout* their school careers if we are going to have lasting effects on their lives. However, it should be added that these children had already achieved functional adult literacy (a fourth-grade reading level).

We have neglected disadvantaged students far too long. We have given them the worst teachers, the worst schools, and the most shopworn textbooks. We have come close to giving up on them as educationally hopeless. If we instead give them our best educational efforts, schools might truly help change their futures. There is much that schools cannot do, but they are partially responsible for the overall competence of society's members and for the values and beliefs they hold. Even if there are limits on what schools can accomplish, their power should not be underestimated either. It is essential, therefore, that schools and society work in partnership to determine what the nature of schools will be like.

SUMMARY

Schools were created to give every individual a better chance to succeed in life. They succeeded to some extent in doing so, but critics argue that heredity and chance factors limit the impact of schools. This critical view has not been uniformly accepted, however.

REVIEW 9–1

1. What is a subculture?

2. What was the intended purpose of mandatory education in the United States?

3. Summarize Christopher Jencks' conclusion on the role of schools in equalizing occupational opportunity.

4. What is Herrnstein's position on the role of education in creating greater social equality?

5. According to Jensen, why do minority groups in the United States tend to score lower on IQ and academic achievement tests?

6. What is the "cultural deprivation" theory of the academic problems of disadvantaged children? What prejudice is inherent in this theory?

7. What is the "linguistic deficiency" theory? What are the main criticisms of this theory?

8. What is the "cognitive styles" hypothesis?

9. What is the "direct instruction approach" to the education of the disadvantaged?

10. Can disadvantaged students learn at the same rate as the national average? Give evidence for your answer.

Our best evidence of the ability of schools to reshape society comes from recent successes in education for the disadvantaged. Theories have suggested that the disadvantaged did poorly in school because of "cultural deprivation," linguistic deficiencies, and differences in cognitive styles, but none of these theories is widely accepted. The direct instruction approach has found, however, that the disadvantaged can learn effectively if the conditions of learning are made favorable.

ANSWERS TO REVIEW QUESTIONS

1. A subculture is a culture that makes up part of a larger culture. For example, the Italian, Chicano, and black subcultures make up parts of the American culture.

2. Public education for all was created in order to give every citizen a better opportunity to "pursue happiness" through work.

3. Jencks feels that the quantity and quality of education is only weakly related to the acquisition of intellectual skills. Furthermore, he believes that intellectual skills have less to do with occupational success than "chance" factors; therefore, he concludes that schools can do little to influence occupational success.

4. Herrnstein believes that heredity is the most important determinant of intellectual skills, but that environmental factors (such as education) play some role. If schools and other aspects of the environment become similar for everyone, however, genetics will become relatively more important in determining intellectual skills. If all individuals grow up in equally favorable intellectual environments, the only differences will be caused by genetic differences. This will mean, he theorizes, that genetics will be the strongest determinant of social standing, resulting in a decrease in social mobility.

5. Jensen feels that the difference in IQ and academic achievement between whites and non-whites is due to inheritance.

6. The "cultural deprivation" theory suggests that disadvantaged children perform less well in school than whites on the average because their cultures *deprive* them of some of the experiences necessary for full intellectual development. It is prejudiced in assuming that a culture that does not prepare children to deal effectively with the dominant culture is *deficient*, rather than merely *different*.

7. The "linguistic deficiency" theory states that disadvantaged children speak an incorrect version of English that is not complex enough to allow for effective thinking. Current viewpoints suggest, however, that these individuals speak a dialect that is different from Standard English, but not less complex. Because their dialects are different, minority students give the impression of making grammatical mistakes, but they speak their dialects as correctly as middle-income students speak theirs.

8. Many specialists in minority-group education now feel that minority students have difficulty in schools because some of their thinking patterns are different (but not deficient) from those of the majority population.

9. The "direct instruction approach" is not concerned with theories as to why disadvantaged students do poorly, but is concerned with more effective methods of teaching them.

10. The Oregon and Kansas Follow Through Projects, among other educational programs, suggest that the type of teaching procedures described in this text may lead to effective learning for disadvantaged children.

4
APPLYING BASIC PRINCIPLES IN THE CLASSROOM

We have now discussed the characteristics of children at different age levels, individual differences among children, social influences on learning, methods of planning and evaluating instructional goals, and some basic principles of learning—all within a theory of instruction that seeks to maximize meaningful achievement, happiness, and independence of action. Part 4 of this textbook will discuss some additional *specific* ways in which you can apply the information you learned in Parts 1 through 3.

We have divided this section on practical applications into a chapter on preschool instruction and basic educational skills (such as reading, arithmetic, and composition), and a chapter on content subjects that primarily involve the understanding and memorization of written material (such as history, social studies, and science). In discussing basic educational skills (Chapter 10), we begin by describing some of the different curriculum approaches used today and then show how you can use the principles of instruction with these approaches. Chapter 11's discussion of content instruction will focus primarily on broad methods of teaching. The controversies concerning content curricula have much less relevance to the way the principles of instruction are applied in teaching content subjects, so we will not discuss them in this text. In addition, there is so much variety in the subject matters of different content courses, that our discussion of applications will necessarily be less specific than in Chapter 10. We will attempt, however, to give you enough information to apply the procedures mentioned in Chapter 11 to any area of content instruction with relatively minor alterations.

In addition, this section will include a chapter on exceptional children (Chapter 12) and one on the subject of discipline (Chapter 13). In Chapter 12 we will discuss the concept of exceptionality, some types of exceptionality, and the changing role of teachers in dealing with such children. The final chapter will discuss some general issues and principles of classroom discipline and will describe some specific techniques that may help your own methods of discipline.

Chapter 10

Teaching Basic Educational Skills

We now turn our attention to what we try to teach our students. The goals of education are different at different age levels and for different kinds of instruction. The major objective of preschool education is to prepare children for the first grade, while a primary goal of the early elementary grades is to teach the basic skills of reading, writing, and arithmetic. And, the primary objective of late elementary and secondary instruction is to teach educational content—the ideas and concepts of history, science, and so on.

This breakdown of educational objectives by age level is basically accurate, but today, more than ever before, these different types of instruction have become mixed across ages. It is common today for content instruction to begin in kindergarten and to find basic reading instruction going on in high school. We will discuss these topics, therefore, partly according to age-group, but mostly according to different kinds of instruction. We will look at basic skills instruction in this chapter and focus on content instruction in the next. We will describe many of the types of learning that children must master in these chapters, but we place major emphasis on how you can apply the basic principles you have now learned to *teach* knowledge and skills. Because of the somewhat different types of learning involved in basic and content instruction, the discussion in this chapter will be most directly related to the concepts of learning and motivation discussed in Chapter 5, while the next chapter will be linked most directly to the discussion of learning and memory in Chapter 4. All of the preceding chapters are related in one way or another, however, to both the present chapter and the following one.

PRESCHOOL EDUCATION

Literally, the term *preschool* means education that takes place before schooling begins. What specifically constitutes preschool instruction, however, differs greatly depending on the goals that different school systems have for this period and the different types of children the school systems serve. School systems that believe that children should be mature before academic instruction begins, for example, or programs that serve largely disadvantaged children may spend the preschool years, including kindergarten, helping children become "ready" for learning subjects such as reading and arithmetic. Other preschool programs commonly begin academic instruction in kindergarten. We will use the term *preschool education,* therefore, to refer to instruction that precedes formal academic instruction, regardless of the age span it encompasses.

Early education provides many benefits. Children can be involved in a variety of enjoyable activities and adventures unavailable in the home, parents can have more time for themselves, and preschoolers will usually be better prepared for the first grade. Absolute readiness is certainly not a goal every child can attain, but it should be a principal focus of every preschool program. This means that preschool teachers need to devote much of their time to the identification and remediation of any deficits in social and educational entering behaviors for starting the first grade.

Objectives for Preschool Instruction

The following list highlights some of the most critical general areas of entering behaviors that children need for success in most first-grade classrooms (therefore, these are the kinds of skills that preschool children need to learn). Another way to look at these general objectives is as a list of the ways potentially successful first-graders behave. As you learned in Chapter 7, the following list is too vague in general to serve as specific instructional objectives. It is intended only as a general listing.

(1.) Attend to the teacher or activity; do not just "look around" the class inappropriately.

(2.) Volunteer to participate (Hops & Cobb, 1974).

(3.) Interact appropriately with peers and teachers.

(4.) Communicate effectively with language.

(5.) Have the intellectual/educational entering behaviors for first-grade work. These include the discrimination and naming of letters, counting, knowledge of basic concepts, and so on.]

The specific list of entering skills that your pupils need to master depends largely on the first-grade program they enter, but this list covers most of the obvious ones.

Some examples will give you a better understanding of how you can apply the principles of instruction to preschool learning. One of the most general goals of preschool programs is to help children get into the routine of being "students," a topic which has been researched extensively at the experimental Turner House Preschool of the University of Kansas. The preschool serves children primarily from low-income urban families. The educational strategies developed at Turner House are relevant, however, to most preschool children (Risley, 1967). Their philosophy is summarized in the following quote: *Turner House*

Some of the behavior we tried to teach the children at first may seem trivial. For example, we spent considerable time teaching them to say good morning to their teachers. This may not seem the stuff from which successful scholars are made. However, the child who says "good morning" cheerfully and consistently when he arrives at school will dispose most teachers quite favorably toward him—our own teachers testified to this during the experiment—and the credit he gains may survive a good deal of academic bumbling later in the day. This credit is useful, because it may make the teacher more likely to praise approximations of learning in the child. A similar rationale lay behind several other "social" projects, such as teaching the child to be quiet in some work situations and to converse in others, and to raise his hand and wait to be recognized before speaking in group discussions (Risley, 1967, pp. 30–31).

While the program works toward specific goals, it is not rigid or coercive. The staff works to accomplish the goals through the appropriate use of prompting, shaping, and positive reinforcement. It is a preschool that the children enjoy and benefit measurably from attending. The staff is intent on helping to prepare their children for the first grade, but they set a *minimum* number of necessary rules restricting the behavior of the children. In many instances, however, it is in the children's best interest to intervene and change their classroom behavior. Suppose, for example, that some of your children spend most of their time by themselves or standing near the teachers. A group of master teachers at the Laboratory Preschool of the University of Washington found that the reinforcing value of the teacher's attention can be brought to bear easily and effectively on this problem (Allen, Hart, Buell, Harris, & Wolf, 1964).

A preschool teacher described Ann, a four-year-old, as a social isolate who was afflicted with "nervous tics" and who spent little time playing with other children. The teacher decided to give Ann warm personal attention each time she saw her playing with other children, but not when she was alone or near the teacher. This simple procedure produced rapid and pronounced increases in the amount of social play. Similar positive results using the teacher's positive attention have been found in teaching children to play cooperatively (Hart, Reynolds, Baer, Brawley, & Harris, 1968). Similarly, by paying attention to aggressive preschool children when they played in ways that were not verbally or physically aggressive markedly reduced the amount of both kinds of aggression (Brown & Elliott, 1965). The skill of reinforcing children when they behave appropriately and subtly ignoring them when they do not takes some practice, but is easily acquired in time. The key is to learn to be immediate and consistent with your reinforcement.

✳*Classroom communication.* Language communication is another vital concern of preschool teachers. Many children, especially those from economically disadvantaged backgrounds, use very limited language in the classroom. The secret is to encourage them to use the full range of their language repertoire. One useful procedure, developed by psychologist Todd Risley (1967), led to the following solution. A preschool teacher decided to work individually for a short time each day with a boy who was extremely nonverbal. First, the teacher assessed his use of language. Each day the teacher asked the boy five questions of the type, "What did you see on the way to school?" for thirteen days. The boy's average reply was only 1.5 words in length. The teacher then tried to prompt longer answers by asking, "What else?" This did not help, so she began asking more logical questions. If he said "a doggie," the teacher asked, "What kind of doggie?" Expanded answers were reinforced in a natural way as the teacher continued the conversation ("Oh! That's a nice kind of doggie."). The teacher might ask what the dog was doing and so on, reinforcing only sentences that were increasingly long and understandable. Soon the boy used sentences

of a 7.5-word average length and used approximately 200 words in each 10-minute session.

✳*Learning to take turns.* One perennial problem for preschool teachers, and a significant developmental task for children, is learning to take turns. Judi Komaki at the Georgia Institute of Technology developed an excellent method to deal with this concern (Komaki, 1976). It is an excellent procedure because it works well and it requires little involvement of the teacher in the children's affairs.

Her demonstration experiment was conducted using preschool classes of three-, four-, and five-year-olds in a private suburban preschool. The focus was on the "water play" table, which Komaki arranged so that only one child at a time could play with water toys in a small tabletop pool. In the first phase, a baseline frequency of taking turns was measured in all three classes. Taking turns meant the player letting a child waiting in line behind to play with the water and toys within 3.5 minutes of starting to play. During this first phase, the teacher intervened and asked the player to let the next child play after 3.5 minutes passed and praised all spontaneous instances of taking turns. As Figure 10–1 shows, this routine resulted in virtually no sharing (the teachers were unable to reinforce the behavior of sharing because it rarely occurred).

During the next phase, teachers taught the children to time their own playtime and to

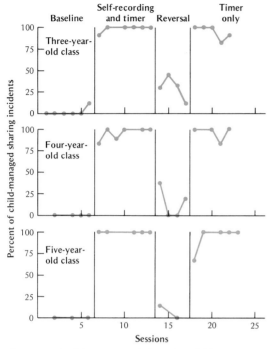

Figure 10–1. *The percent of times that children spontaneously shared the water table within 3.5 minutes without intervention from a teacher in 3 preschool classes. (From Komaki, 1976)*

reinforce themselves for sharing. The children used a three-minute sand timer to time their play at the water table. They were told that if they left the table right away (within thirty seconds) when the sand ran out, they could put a sticker next to their name on a "good sharers" chart. The children waiting in line were also asked to remind the player when the time was up. Figure 10-1 shows that this self-administered procedure produced large increases in the frequency of sharing, with the children sharing appropriately almost all the time. When Komaki discontinued the procedure for a few days in the third phase, the turn taking was greatly

MOLLY GOES TO TWO KINDERGARTENS

Molly is a bright, well-liked child who has just turned six. During the past nine months, Molly attended a highly structured, academically oriented kindergarten program that utilized many individualized learning materials in a well-organized instructional and recreation program.

But when summer came, Molly went to a new summer kindergarten program. Her previous school did not have a summer program, so since Molly very much enjoyed spending her mornings in school, she started in a new school which was designed according to an unstructured, open education format. After she attended the new program for a few days, her mother asked her if she liked it as well as her previous kindergarten. She replied, "Well . . . , I like my new school best because you can learn about anything you want, and you can play if you don't want to work, and because I'm the only one there who knows what sounds letters make. But I liked my old school best because it was fun, too, and we learned a lot more, and because I had a nice teacher." Would you rather teach in her new or old kindergarten? Which one would you want your own children to attend? Could you combine some elements from each school? (Recall the discussion of "open" and "programmed" philosophies of education in Chapter 1 and the "molding-unfolding" dimension of theories of child development discussed in Chapters 2 and 3.)

reduced, but became frequent in the last phase in which just the timer (without the good sharers chart) was employed.

This kind of self-administered technique is worth its weight in gold: It works, it requires little work from the teacher, and it teaches students something about controlling their *own* behavior. Interestingly, Komaki pointed out that although developmental changes in taking turns occur at these ages in most children, the procedure worked equally effectively in all three age-groups.

Teaching concepts and skills. Skillful teaching, as we have just described, can be used to prepare the general behavior of your children for the first-grade classroom. Conceptual and intellectual skills seem much more difficult to teach, however. They are more complicated, but they really do not pose a different kind of problem. The first step is to decide what concepts and skills you want to teach. This decision will be based largely on your view of the nature of intellectual development. You may wish to follow the ideas of Bruner or Piaget, as discussed in Chapters 2 and 3, or you may choose another approach (such as the "molding" theory of Bereiter & Englemann, 1966) based on your preschool curriculum course.

After you choose cognitive and intellectual goals, the next step is to teach these skills and concepts in the most effective way. This requires a good knowledge of how to maximize learning, but is relatively simple to do. A group of researchers in Atlanta, for example, trained aids with an average third-grade education to teach cognitive skills to disadvantaged preschool children (Roberts & Ayllon, 1974). One of the deficits found in many of the three-year-olds was the receptive use of prepositional concepts; that is, they were often unable to correctly follow instructions based on prepositions, such as "Place the block *on* the table," or "Place the key *under* the cup," and in other ways failed to comprehend prepositions. In response to this difficulty, the aids were trained to ask the child to place a small wooden figure of a boy on top, in, under, behind, or in front of a box. If the child responded correctly within ten seconds, he or she was praised and reinforced. If he or she was incorrect or failed to respond, the aid modeled the correct response while verbally stating the prepositional relationship. This procedure was repeated many times with excellent results. Several children who were correct on prepositions less than 50 percent of the time were taught to respond correctly over 80 percent of the time within a few days. You can adopt this general procedure to teach any concept or cognitive skill.

Organization of the Preschool Learning Environment

Because preschool children, by definition, are not "grown-up," a great deal of the teacher's time is spent in supervising and organizing their activities. Moving a group of preschoolers from lunch, to the bathroom, and to their cots for naptime can unnerve most teachers. What can be done to help teachers with this problem? Are there strategies of classroom organization that allow teachers to spend less time supervising and more time teaching? A study carried out in the Turner House Preschool by faculty and students of the University of Kansas compared two general strategies they called the "zone defense" versus the "man-to-man" defense (LeLaurin & Risley, 1972).

In the man-to-man strategy, each teacher is responsible for a specific group of children regardless of where they are and what they are doing. In the zone strategy, each teacher is responsible for all the children that are in a particular area or activity. In this study, the amount of time it took to get forty children from lunch, to the bathroom, to the area where shoes are removed, and settled in for naps was compared when these two methods were used by three teachers. The man-to-man strategy kept the children away from appropriate activities two to three times longer than the zone strategy. This was mainly because the man-to-man strategy requires every child to wait in an activity area until the last child is finished. The "reward" for being quick is to have time on your hands— the kind of boring time that leads to pushing, shoving, and screaming. In the zone strategy, however, as soon as a child finishes one activity area he or she can go on to the next. The same line of thinking can be used to reduce inefficiency in many other areas of preschool teaching. Could these same concepts also be applied to an open fifth-grade classroom?

Preschool Education in Perspective

Although preschool education does, in a sense, take place before formal schooling begins, the preceding discussion suggests

that it is far from an unimportant "baby-sitting" period. On the contrary, good preschool instruction can make the difference between an easy or difficult adjustment to elementary school. Intelligent children with good social skills who do not attend kindergarten usually catch up to those children who do without any great difficulty, but pre-school experience generally makes the first grade easier for all children, and much easier for those who would have started the farthest behind. Even excellent preschool instruction, however, cannot give disadvantaged and other children with educational deficits the ability to learn at completely normal rates (Engelmann, 1970). As discussed in Chapter 9, it can help, but such children require excellent instruction throughout their years in school.

REVIEW 10–1

1. List five general objectives for preschool instruction.
2. Why is the "zone defense" superior to the "man-to-man defense" in managing preschool children?

BASIC EDUCATIONAL SKILLS

At some point during kindergarten or the first grade, the child is considered ready to learn formal educational material and "real" instruction begins. This decision depends largely on the progress of the individual child, but is also dictated by the philosophy and curriculum of the school. This first formal instruction can take many different forms, but at some point early in the process the teacher faces the ultimate teacher's question, "How am I going to teach all these kids to read?"

READING INSTRUCTION

Reading is second only to spoken language in its importance to the further education and development of the individual. A prior mastery of reading is essential to learning virtually every academic subject area, to the securing of the great majority of responsible occupations, and as a vehicle for information and recreation. It is also one of the most complicated sets of skills that the child has to acquire, and is probably the most difficult to teach. Thus, it is understandable that more children have problems with reading than with any other aspect of education.

The first and most important thing to understand about reading is that it is not a single skill, but a *complex set of many different skills*, each of which must be treated separately. The global term *reading* encompasses everything from knowing letter names to the ability to paraphrase silently read passages. Different approaches to reading instruction distinguish different numbers of skills and treat them in different ways, but from all viewpoints, reading is a complicated series of skills which are built one upon another.

Table 10–1 presents a partial listing of these skills, stated in fairly broad terms. This is by no means presented as a final or authoritative list, but merely will give you a flavor for its diversity. This lesson will become more meaningful as the chapter progresses.

TABLE 10-1

Partial List of Reading Skills

Prereading Skills
Letter discrimination (visual)
Letter-sound discrimination (auditory)
Letter names
Eye movements from left to right, top to bottom

Oral Reading
Reading single words
Reading strings of words in sequence (phrases,
    sentences, paragraphs, etc.)
Reading with appropriate inflection and pauses
Reading at appropriate rate

**Comprehension (of Orally or Silently Read
    Material)**
Stating the "meaning" of a word
Pointing to the object labeled by a word
Paraphrasing a passage
Answering questions about a passage
Following directions given in a passage

Major Approaches to Reading Instruction

At the present time, there are a number of different approaches to reading instruction. These approaches recommend teaching strategies that differ greatly from one another, but, unfortunately, even extensive research has failed to demonstrate the consistent superiority of any one approach. As traditionally practiced, all the approaches succeed with most children but fail with a large minority of them. This chapter will describe and discuss the major approaches to reading instruction and then go on to describe some ways that the principles of instruction you learned in Parts 1 through 3 can be used to improve the teaching of reading.

Word-attack approaches. The initial emphasis of all approaches to reading instruction is to teach the child how to read words. The word-attack approaches attempt to teach this as a generalizable skill of pronouncing the sounds of letters and letter combinations. For example, children who have learned the word-attack rule for "silent e's at the end of a word" should be able to pronounce TINE and PANE with "long" vowel sounds and TIN and PAN with "short" vowel sounds, even if they have never seen the words before. This is the goal of the word-attack approach. If children can be successfully taught a small set of rules for pronouncing letter combinations, they should be able to pronounce any word they see. This frees the teacher from having to teach each of the ten thousand or so words in the elementary school reading vocabulary as single units.

There are some problems with this approach, however, at least in theory. Word-attack approaches are excellent for teaching a child to read a language such as Spanish which is phonically regular, but the English language is notoriously diverse in its phonic structure and replete with words that are not pronounced "according to the rules." The range of pronunciation found in the words *bough, rough, cough,* and *through* is a good example.

An interesting attempt to evaluate the regularity of pronunciation in English was made by the Southwest Regional Laboratory for Educational Research and Development (Berdiansky, Cronnel, & Koehler, 1969). Researchers analyzed a set of 6,092 words of one and two syllables taken from reading materials for grades one through three. They determined that a total of 166 different rules would be required to correctly pronounce 90 percent of these words. Since these rules are fairly complex and abstract, teaching 166 different rules represents a monumental task. Even at that, the children would be unable to pronounce 10 percent of their reading vocabulary.

Teaching 166 rules is obviously out of the question. Most word-attack approaches, therefore, attempt to teach only the most widely applicable rules. This strategy cuts the number of rules down to a workable number, but still leaves over fifty percent of all words as "irregular." One word-attack text lists 5,000 elementary level words, 40 percent of which are regular according to the set of rules that the student is taught. This is hardly a desirable solution. But, as

mentioned above, all approaches to reading instruction work to some extent, in spite of their drawbacks.

There are two basic types of word-attack approaches, the **phonics** and **linguistic** approaches. In spite of heated controversy, these approaches differ only in the specific tactics they recommend. Most phonic approaches teach letter-sound patterns beginning with single letters working towards words, whereas the linguistic approach deals with intact words. Confusing the issue are a few reading programs labeled "phonic" that actually use mostly intact words.

Whole-word approach.   Because of the problems in using a word-attack method of

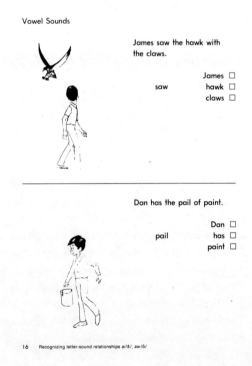

Word-attack approaches to reading. Above: the phonics method in an intermediate grades workbook. Right: the linguistics method in a third-grade workbook

reading with an irregularly pronounced language, many educators recommend that *all* words be memorized as individual units ("sight words"). This frees the child from having to learn a large set of difficult rules and from the confusion of trying to read words that are sometimes regular and sometimes not. On the debit side, it requires the child to learn a huge number of individual responses.

As mentioned above, no hard and fast choice can now be made between these methods. This is primarily because children who learn by the whole-word method seem to learn some word-attack skills as a by-product, and children who learn by word-attack methods usually acquire large sight vocabularies. This is not, however, something that can be counted on. The frequency of reading problems with both approaches is too high to be tolerated as they have been traditionally taught.

Eclectic approaches. Because neither the whole-word nor the word-attack approach has had a record of uniform success, most specialists in the field of reading advocate eclectic approaches that combine both whole-word and word-attack training. For example, Dolores Durkin (1970), of the University of Illinois, recommends an approach in which a whole-word method is used initially, with word-attack skills being introduced after the child masters a small sight vocabulary. Other reading specialists recommend other combinations of the approaches. Most recently published reading materials follow this middle course.

REVIEW 10–2

1. Why is reading an important skill?
2. What does it mean to say that reading is a "complex set of many different skills"?
3. What are the major approaches to reading instruction? Define them.
4. Compare and contrast phonics and linguistic approaches.
5. What are the major advantages and disadvantages of the word-attack and whole-word approaches?
6. What does research have to say about the relative effectiveness of the major approaches to reading instruction?

Applying the Principles of Instruction to Teaching Reading

A distinction should be made at this point between the various approaches to reading instruction and the *techniques of teaching* children how to read. The approaches determine *what* skills the children should be taught, while the techniques of teaching determine *how* they should be taught. Any of the approaches to reading instruction can be used within the framework of the principles of instruction discussed in this book. Regardless of the approach taken, the teacher must analyze each reading skill into clearly defined behaviors, measure entering behavior, arrange for the students to engage in the target behaviors frequently, give corrective feedback or reinforcement after their performance, require mastery on each skill before progressing to the next, and allow students to progress at their own rate. Any of the currently available reading programs can be modified to conform with these principles.

A WAY TO DETECT SEXISM IN ELEMENTARY READERS

Many psychologists and educators have recently suggested that our attitudes about "appropriate" male and female roles are passed on to each new generation in subtle ways. In the classroom, two important sources of sex bias are the teacher's behavior and, surprisingly enough, the elementary reader. University of Florida educator H. Thompson Fillmer (1974) prepared the list to the right to help evaluate the sexual bias in readers.

It might be an interesting project to apply this test to two sets of readers, those published in the 1950s and those most recently published. What differences do you see?

CHECKLIST FOR EVALUATING SEXISM IN READERS

Go through each book you are planning to use for the points listed below:

	Male	Female
1. Number of stories where main character is:	____	____
2. Number of illustrations of:	____	____
3. Number of times children are shown:		
—In active play	____	____
—Using initiative	____	____
—Independent	____	____
—Solving problems	____	____
—Earning money	____	____
—Receiving recognition	____	____
—Inventive	____	____
—Involved in sports	____	____
—Being passive	____	____
—Fearful	____	____
—Helpless	____	____
—Receiving help	____	____
—Shown in quiet play	____	____
4. Number of times adults are shown:		
—In different occupations	____	____
—Playing with children	____	____
—Taking children on outings	____	____
—Teaching skills	____	____
—Giving tenderness	____	____
—Scolding children	____	____
—Biographically	____	____

5. Ask these questions:
—Are boys allowed to show emotions?
—Are girls rewarded for intelligence rather than for beauty?
—Are there any derogatory comments directed at girls in general?
—Is mother shown working outside the home? What kind of job?
—Are there any stories about one-parent families? Families without children? Are babysitters shown?
—Are minority and ethnic groups treated naturally instead of stereotypically?

To understand how this can be done, we now look at the three major strategies of organizing reading instruction.

Basal readers.   Most of us learned to read using **basal readers.** These are series of graded books of prose reading material usually purchased as a set for grades one through six. They provide the teacher with a series of passages that are written in a consistent style and that gradually increase in the difficulty of vocabulary and writing style from one book to the next.

Proponents of this approach see basal readers as providing flexible raw materials that teachers can use in a variety of ways to fit the needs of the students and their own teaching styles. Because the readers are unstructured, they allow innovative and effective teachers to develop their own methods of instruction. Teacher's guides are usually provided that suggest teaching exercises, but these can be used as the teacher wishes.

Critics of basal readers suggest that it is difficult to apply sound principles of instruction to them. Because one book is usually assigned to each grade level, it is often difficult to provide reading material that matches each student's needs. The basal approach assumes that all second-grade students, for example, are ready to read in the second-grade book. This assumption can often have tragic consequences. The child who just began to catch on to the first part of the first-grade book at the end of the school year may feel defeated when he or she receives the second-grade book on the first day of the new school year. (This is exactly the type of problem that the principles of individualization and mastery learning attempt to avoid.) Basals need not be used in this inflexible

way, of course, but it is sometimes difficult to use them to meet the individual needs of the students.

Efficient and effective teaching is also made difficult when all instruction on reading the passages (on new phonics patterns, for example) is read aloud by the teacher. When the teacher addresses the entire class at one time (or three or four reading subgroups, at best), individual needs of students are necessarily ignored. And, because these series do not include workbooks, it is difficult to actively engage the students in the learning process and to provide them with frequent feedback on their progress except for reading aloud.

It is not simple to teach effectively using basal readers. But if you arrive in the fall and learn that you must use these materials, do not despair. Remember that you probably learned to read using the basal readers. They are good educational materials that with some modification you can use to effectively teach all your students.

An elementary-school teacher recently wrote an article for an educator's magazine describing how he individualized a basal system (Schmidt, 1974). First and foremost, he used the basal reader less than was ordinarily intended and used supplementary materials instead. His main reasons for using basal readers were that they contained high interest, well-graded passages and that his students would return to them when they entered the fourth grade in any case. The main changes he implemented were designed to allow students to work more independently. This allowed them to progress more at their own rate and gave him more time to evaluate each child's individual strengths and weaknesses.

Among the modifications were vocabulary cards and comprehension questions that were prepared for each story in the basal reader. Answer sheets for the comprehension questions were available to the students at a central location so they could correct their own work, and students were paired to give feedback and reinforcement to one another on the vocabulary cards and their oral reading. The teacher also frequently visited the school system's curriculum supply office and obtained supplementary workbooks from another reading series to provide even more active, self-paced learning. As a result, the teacher increased free time which he used to hold frequent individual conferences and help sessions with the students.

Although this is only one teacher's strategy for using basal readers, it suggests some of the more important ways that they can be supplemented. In general, the key needs are to increase individualization and active learning.

Programmed reading instruction.   Two decades ago, a new approach to education promised to revolutionize reading instruction. It offered the teacher a method that was designed with the principles of instruction we have discussed fully in mind. Using these "programmed" materials, the teacher would be able to individualize instruction, allow mastery learning, and provide immediate feedback with less effort than was required in using the basal approach. The new approach was so oversold to teachers, however, that it became a fad and collapsed when it could not fulfill all its promises.

Recently, however, programmed reading instruction has been coming back to take a more realistic position among the various approaches to instruction.

The essence of this approach depends on the active involvement of the student. After a small amount of oral instruction, the child learns to read by performing a series of carefully sequenced exercises. For example, in early reading instruction the children might look at a picture of a dog and then circle the word "dog" from among several alternatives. The children then look at the correct answer, thus providing themselves with immediate feedback on the correctness of their response. Later they might answer several comprehension questions based on the passage they just read silently. A major effort is made in the design of programmed texts to ensure that each step (or "frame") is built upon previous ones in such a way as to increase the probability of correct responses.

Advocates of programmed instruction argue that this approach improves the conditions of learning for each child with very little work from the teacher. It is a highly structured approach that allows students to progress at their own rate. Critics argue that it is expensive (because the children write their answers in the books, they can only be used once), and that it is boring for both the teacher and the student. Students, they argue, find it boring because they have to sit for long periods working by themselves in a highly directed activity, and teachers find it dull because the programmed texts do most of the teaching for them.

The recent revival in interest in programmed reading instruction has occurred only because teachers have developed ways

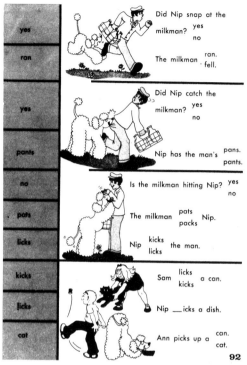

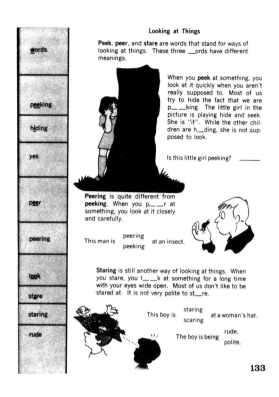

Pages from the Sullivan Programmed Reading Program.
Above: first-grade reader. Right: third-grade reader

of using it that make it both more interesting and more effective. First and foremost, many teachers enjoy the free time that programmed texts give them and put it to use spending more individual time with their students. This allows them to do an even better job of diagnosing and meeting each child's needs. One study found, for example, that teachers who use programmed materials spend an average of 68 percent of their time in individual work with pupils, while teachers who use lecture-oriented approaches (as with basal readers) spend an average of 3 percent of their time in individual student contact (Goebel, 1966).

The following classroom experiment illustrates one way of improving student interest in working in a programmed reading book. Psychologist Gary Holt (1971) evaluated the use of a programmed reading series with a class of twenty-one average first-grade children. The Sullivan Reading Program (published by Behavior Research Laboratories and Webster-McGraw-Hill), which is typical of currently available programs, was used in this study.

The teacher spent the first four fifty-minute reading classes teaching the children how to use the programmed materials. The children received reinforcement whenever they complied with the teacher's instructions and used the materials properly. During the next fifteen days, the students used the programs as described in the teacher's manual. The children looked at each problem, made a written response, then uncovered the correct answer and compared it with their own. No reinforcement (other than the immediate feedback provided by seeing the correct answer) was given during this period.

Positive reinforcement was then introduced for the next twenty days. During this period, the children could earn reinforcement by completing an agreed-upon number of pages. When a child had completed the pages, he or she was shown a drawing of stick figures engaged in enjoyable activities, such as playing outdoors, painting, watching filmstrips, and so forth. The child was free to choose any of these activities and engage in them for five minutes before returning to work. As the child entered the activity area, a five-minute timer was set to time his or her "vacation." The children were also free to choose to continue working in their reading books, which they occasionally did. At first, the children were required to complete ten

pages to earn five minutes of playtime, with the requirement being gradually raised to fifteen, twenty, thirty, and finally to forty pages for five minutes of playtime. Figure 10–2 shows the results of this classroom experiment.

During the preliminary phase in which there was no reinforcement contingency, the children read from 285 to 1,088 words in the program during each 50-minute class. After reinforcement was introduced, however, the number of words read per session rose from about 1,000 to 8,737 words, an increase of over 800 percent. When the researchers briefly discontinued contingency during sessions 36 and 37, the rate of progress fell dramatically, but rose again when they reintroduced reinforcement.

The children's progress was so rapid, in fact, that they completed fourteen workbooks during the seven-week program, the equivalent of two academic years of reading materials. More importantly, their scores on the California Achievement Test showed an av-

Figure 10–2. *The effect of positive reinforcement on reading. (From Holt, 1971)*

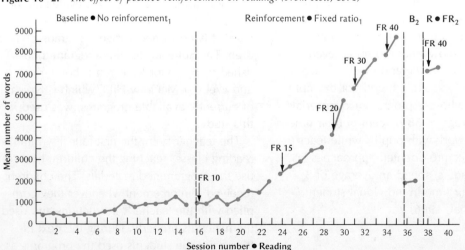

erage increase of 3.0 years in comprehension and 2.25 years in vocabulary. Very substantial improvement, indeed, for a seven-week program for first-graders!

You must be extremely careful, however, that the programming and reinforcement techniques employed in this study work for your particular group of children. There are many ways in which they might need to be modified. You may need to increase the number of days you spend in teaching the children how to use the program; you may need to start with a smaller requirement of pages and increase the number more slowly; you may find that other reinforcers are more effective with your children; and so on. The two most likely problems that can develop with this approach are cheating (looking at the correct answer before writing a response) and sacrificing accuracy for the sake of speed. This did not happen in the experimental study cited above, but it does happen fairly often in the classroom. You can try to head off and control these problems by frequently visiting each child as he or she works through their programs. During these times, the child can be asked to read aloud a few previously completed frames and then to read the next frame with you. Good performance on these spot checks can be reinforced verbally or with stronger reinforcers.

NO-COST REINFORCERS FOUND IN EVERY CLASSROOM

Many studies in which reinforcement is used to improve academic skills cited in this text use reinforcers that are not feasible in most classrooms. Either they cost a significant amount of money (on a teacher's salary!), or they do not conform with school rules on snacks, eating in the classroom, and so on. There are, however, many effective reinforcers found in every classroom that cost nothing and will not spoil appetites or even cause cavities. Researchers Thomas McLaughlin and John Malaby (1972) discovered a whole list in a successful study of the use of reinforcement in the classroom. They allowed fifth- and sixth-grade disadvantaged children to earn points for good behavior and schoolwork that could be traded for *privileges*. These included time to play sports, write on the board, play games, listen to records, and see the classes' laboratory animals. They also included sharpening pencils, coming in the classroom early, being on committees, special projects, and seeing the grade book. These privileges proved to be successful reinforcers, cost nothing, and made little extra work for teachers. In the same light, one of the author's first-grade teachers asked the children to volunteer old toys for the classroom's "prize box," a method that worked very successfully. Who says you never get anything for nothing? In truth, some of the best reinforcers in life are free!

Combined basal-programmed workbook systems.   A compromise between the basal and programmed approach seems to be the most popular current approach. Packages or "systems" that include correlated basal readers, programmed workbooks, and sometimes audio-visual aids are prepared as an integrated unit. Recently, publishers who originally dealt only in basal or in programmed approaches have introduced this type of package. Early indications are that this will be an extremely popular approach, and depending on the way it is implemented, it will probably prove to be effective as well. It is most effective using the methods described above for both basal and programmed materials.

Experience approach.   There is another important approach to reading instruction that has gained little acceptance as a comprehensive method, but over the years has been frequently used as an effective supplementary technique. This approach suggests that children learn best when they learn skills and knowledge relevant to their own lives. It is most often referred to as the *experience approach* (Lee & Allen, 1963). In early reading instruction, the children might learn to read the names of other children or the names of objects in the room (window, desk, chair, etc.) as sight words. Later, they would read prose passages that they themselves had dictated to the teacher (or an older student volunteer) about interesting events in their lives. Because of this, students often find the stories intrinsically interesting. But because the approach is unsystematic and time-consuming, it should probably only be used as a supplement or as a break in routine. Alternatively, you can enhance the intrinsic interest of reading materials by taking the time to find out what interests your students and then adopting (begging, borrowing, etc.) materials that match these interests. Either way, this is an important consideration, as recent research shows that comprehension is noticeably better when children read about preferred topics than ones they are uninterested in (Dorsel, 1975).

Role of the teacher in reading instruction.   No approach to reading instruction will produce enjoyable and efficient learning if the teacher coldly goes through the motions of teaching. On the other hand, any of the approaches described above can be used effectively by a skillful and enthusiastic teacher. What is important is that you create conditions that favor learning. We have focused primarily on how the principles of learning and motivation apply to reading instruction, but that is only part of the picture. Being a "skillful and enthusiastic" teacher requires an integration of all the content in the first three sections of this book.

REVIEW 10–3

1. List the three major curriculum approaches to reading instruction.

2. What is the major difference between the *basal* and the *programmed* approaches in terms of the students' activities? What is the major difference between these two approaches in terms of the teacher's duties?

3. How could you reduce student boredom associated with programmed exercises?

4. What is the *experience* approach to reading instruction? What is the best use for this approach?

5. How important is the interest level of reading material for reading instruction? Relate this to what we know about meaningfulness in memory.

SPELLING AND COMPOSITION

A major focus of elementary education is on teaching children to communicate through written language. In learning to read, children learn to understand what others have said in written language, while we teach children to express themselves in writing by teaching them spelling and composition.

Spelling

The important issues in teaching spelling are closely tied to issues in reading instruction. Most major approaches to elementary curriculum view spelling and reading as related skills that can strengthen one another when taught in a coordinated fashion. If you decide to take a word-attack approach to reading, you will probably teach your students to spell using letter-sound patterns. If you choose a whole-word approach to reading, your spelling instruction will probably stress the memorization of whole words. Similarly, if you use a programmed method for reading, you may wish to adopt a correlated spelling program from the same publisher. This consistency in approach is not only natural for most teachers, but is probably beneficial for the students.

Regardless of the approach you take in spelling instruction, there seems to be fairly widespread agreement about the importance of practice in learning to spell. Teachers from diverse points of view provide time for their pupils to study spelling lists, take practice tests, and receive feedback on their test performances. The following classroom experiment illustrates one way of improving the amount of learning that results from this type of practice.

This study was carried out with a group of average and above-average fourth-graders in Washington state (Lovitt, Guppy, & Blattner, 1969). The teacher in this classroom gave daily spelling tests (you may not wish to give them this frequently), but the principle tested in this study would apply to a less frequent testing schedule. The same list of words was tested each day for a week. Every child took every test regardless of his or her score on preceding tests. Data were collected on the performance of the children over an eleven-week period. Section I of Figure 10–3 shows the mean number of papers that contained no errors during these first eleven weeks.

Next, the teacher changed the rules so that any child who scored 100 percent on any test did not have to take any other test on that list for the rest of the week. Instead, the children could engage in whatever appropriate classroom activity they wished, as long as it did not disturb the rest of the class. When this change went into effect, the mean number of 100 percent correct papers rose rapidly. When the rules were modified slightly again in Phase III to allow the entire class to engage in a joint free-time activity when everyone in the class had gotten 100 percent on a list of words, the rate of perfect papers rose slightly again. The nice feature of this procedure is that the students learned more in less time, had more time to engage in social interaction, and the teacher had *fewer* papers to grade.

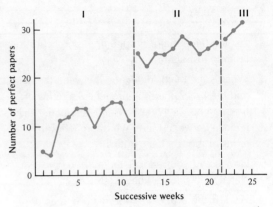

Figure 10–3. *Number of perfect (100 percent correct) papers scored by the students during the three successive experimental conditions. (From Lovitt, Guppy, & Blattner, 1969)*

Composition

Once children can spell some words, they can learn to express themselves in written language. This is a process that begins in primary grades, with learning to write a complete sentence, and continues into college, and sometimes beyond. As important as it is, however, this is a subject that receives much less emphasis in the classroom than reading, spelling, and mathematics. This lack of emphasis may result from composition not being a subject that appears on standardized achievement tests which most elementary students take at the end of the term. Composition is also a difficult subject to teach and few structured curriculum aids are available. We spend a great deal of time lecturing to students about rules of grammar, transition sentences, topical analysis, and the like, but how can you teach a student to write a "good" paragraph?

Part of the problem seems to be that we often fail to communicate what we expect of the student. Perhaps this is because we only vaguely understand what we want ourselves. A good paragraph is "well organized," is "not trite," shows "variety of imagery," and so on. In other words, it is a skill for which it is difficult to write clear instructional objectives.

Composition is a good example of an area for which clearly stated objectives can never encompass all the goals of instruction. Perhaps a certain amount of the "art" of putting thoughts into words is too subtle and subjective to ever be expressed in precise objectives. It is ironic: It is difficult to put into words what it means to effectively put ideas into words.

This does not mean that instructional objectives have no role in teaching composition. On the contrary, it is precisely where instructional objectives are the most difficult to define that they provide the greatest benefit. We might be able to get by with intuitive objectives where the goals of education are clear (as in teaching young children to print letters), but we are likely to find ourselves in a muddle when we teach complex and subtle skills without the benefit of clear objectives. In the case of composition, we cannot put every objective into clear and precise terms, but we can state many of the more basic objectives in a way that will be beneficial to both teacher and students.

A study of the use of objectives in teaching composition provides us with a good example (Maloney & Hopkins, 1973). A group of average fourth-, fifth-, and sixth-graders in a composition class were told to put more variety into their paragraphs. Specifically, they were told that they would receive one reinforcement point for each *different* adjective, action verb, and sentence-beginning they used in their writing. Compared to when they did not have specific objectives and feedback, the number of different words and constructions increased by approximately 75 percent. More importantly, two graduate students in literature who were not informed about the nature of the experiment independently rated the paragraphs that were written when objectives and feedback were provided as much more "creative." There are, of course, many aspects of creative writing that are too subtle to teach in this way, but the creative use of instructional objectives can be a big help.

MATHEMATICS INSTRUCTION

Another major academic goal of elementary education, second only to reading and language arts, is to give children a basic foundation and a working knowledge of mathematics. As with reading, mathematics curriculum issues have been and continue to be complicated and controversial. It is this state of disagreement among the "experts" that makes the choice of an approach to follow a difficult one.

Curriculum Approaches

One of the major decisions in mathematics curriculum is the same as one issue we discussed for reading instruction. Should the teacher use a formal textbook, programmed instruction, or a series that combines texts, workbooks, and other instructional aids? The issues here are the same as for reading instruction so we will not repeat our discussion.

Another major decision facing teachers, however, concerns the conceptual approach they take to mathematics. During the 1960s, a significant change occurred in elementary mathematics curriculum. Prior to that time, elementary mathematics consisted almost exclusively of rote instruction in arithmetic skills. Most of us who learned mathematics in that way remember it well, but unless we had an exceptional teacher, few of us remember it fondly. With the 1960s, however, came **new math.** This approach was based on Piaget's idea that *meaningful* mathematics learning consisted primarily of the develop-

ment and elaboration of the logical concepts that underlie mathematics. The drill-and-recite method, the new-math group suggested, served only to inhibit the child's understanding of what mathematical concepts really mean. Instead, it was felt that children would develop a better understanding of mathematics, would learn computational skills in a more meaningful and effective way, and would have a better attitude toward mathematics if elementary instruction focused on the logical meaning of mathematics. Prominent also in the thinking of the developers of this approach was the importance of providing instruction on these logical concepts in a sequence that paralleled Piaget's conception of normal intellectual development.

The new math approach fell into disfavor in the mid-1970s, however. Critics claimed

Examining set theory in a third-grade New Math text published in the mid-1960s

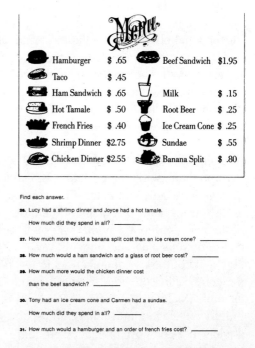

Page from a third-grade math text published in the mid-1970s using "real-life" examples to teach math

that it was too difficult conceptually for average and below-average children, that it produced as many "math phobias" as the old approach, and most significantly, that children who were taught using this approach were deficient in computational skills. While the new math may or may not be a good method to teach set and number theory, it does not *appear* to be a good way to teach addition and subtraction. It is always difficult to adequately evaluate an entire approach to instruction, but this was a telling criticism to the public and it brought the new math into some disfavor.

The emerging new approach to mathematics curriculum that seems most popular with teachers is, again, a compromise approach. Most new texts and workbooks combine some instruction in the logical foundations of mathematics with considerable practice on computation skills.

Many current curriculum materials for mathematics also contain a major innovation based on another of Piaget's notions that was largely ignored by the developers of the new math: Elementary-aged children learn best through *concrete* examples. Most new materials tie mathematics learning to concrete and inherently interesting real-life examples.

The use of examples is important in any area of instruction, but is particularly important in elementary mathematics. An experiment recently supported this. A wide range of fourth-grade students had significantly less difficulty in mastering the concept of the equilateral triangle when instruction covered the definition and concrete examples, when compared to just teaching the definition (Klausmeier & Felman, 1975).

Recent approach to math instruction: using familiar objects to teach math

Teaching Strategies for Mathematics

Regardless of the mathematics curriculum you adopt, however, your major task is to create the conditions that make learning happen. As in any type of instruction, this involves the implementation of the principles and methods discussed in Parts 1 through 3 of this book. A report from a consulting teacher in Vermont will give you a good idea of how this can be done (Coleman, Kaszuba, & Pierce, 1973). Two team teachers of an open design fourth-grade class requested assistance from the school system's consultant. Even though their class was for forty-nine normal children, nearly all the children were below grade level in mathematics achievement. The consultant suggested a reorganization of the curriculum to promote individualized instruction and mastery learning.

Their new curriculum stressed arithmetic computational skills and placed heavy emphasis on workbook exercises. Initially, students received instructions in groups on how to complete each daily unit while the teacher modeled examples on the board. Soon, however, students who scored 80 percent or above on each daily unit (their criterion for mastery) were allowed to work on as many units per day as they could, while others worked more slowly. Papers were corrected by the students and checked by the teachers.

As the program evolved, a routine was developed wherein the teachers first administered unit tests to those students who had completed one or more units since the preceding day. They next corrected and returned the unit tests along with the day's materials, and then gave brief small-group or individual instruction to those students who started a new unit. They spent the rest of the period working on a one-to-one basis with the students who scored below 80 percent. Figure 10–4 shows the change in the number of children who were above or below grade level as the school year went along. In September, thirty-five of the forty children were below the national average, whereas only two remained below grade level by April. Overall, the class gained an average of 2.5 years in computational skills and 1.9 years in mathematics concepts on the Stanford Diagnostic Arithmetic Test during the single school year. In addition, the teachers reported that student attitudes changed from aversion to enjoyment of mathematics. The use of individualization and mastery learning strategies is equally important for all types of basic skills learning.

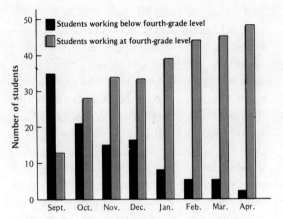

Figure 10–4. *Number of students working above or below grade level in an elementary mathematics class in which an individualized mastery learning strategy was introduced at the start of the school year. (From Coleman, Kaszuba, & Pierce, 1973)*

TEACHING "REAL-WORLD" SKILLS

There is a growing trend in the United States toward making education relevant to the specific day-to-day needs of students. We teach them to read and write, but we frequently do not do so in ways that facilitate the *transfer* of what they have learned to real-life situations. That is to say, we spend a great deal of time teaching students formal academic skills, but they may not be the skills students need when they leave school. Great strides have been made over the last decades in this regard, such as in teaching vocational skills, teaching students how to balance checkbooks, and so on, but good teachers still need to give thought to what their students need in order to succeed in life.

The research staff at Western Carolina Center, a treatment facility for exceptional youth, was concerned with the problems that their adolescent special-education students had in filling out job application forms. For the youths enrolled in Western Carolina Center, these forms were an important obstacle. Even when they had attained considerable skills in vocational and academic education, they could not successfully apply for many types of desirable positions because they could not fill out employment applications.

The researchers conducted a study (Clark, Boyd, & Macrae, 1975), therefore, using four male and two female delinquent individuals who were from fourteen to sixteen years of age, with scores on intelligence tests ranging from 65 to 85. We will describe the procedures in some detail to show you how a complex skill such as this can be taught. The students were first taught to copy the nine most frequently included items on an employment application. This included such items as names, telephone numbers, addresses and references, and so on. The students were reinforced for correct responses and given corrective feedback when the responses were incorrect. During this first phase, all written responses were made on pages of notebook paper. After each student had written each item correctly ten consecutive times, he or she would progress to the second stage.

AN ELEMENTARY-SCHOOL COURSE IN CONSUMER ECONOMICS

Elementary students are being taught a lot more than reading, writing, and arithmetic these days. The following excerpt describes a consumer economics unit that a teacher (Schurr, 1974) designed for her fourth-through sixth-grade classes. Two of her lesson plans are included.

"Elementary school children, as much as secondary students, should have an exposure to and an awareness of the basic economic concepts around which our country functions.

"The following set of activities show how consumer economics can be taught to a class of fourth-, fifth- or sixth-graders. The vehicle for getting across some very simple but basic economic concepts is toys. Topics covered answer such questions as: What makes a good buy? What is a quality product? How does one budget to get the most for one's money? What advertising strategies are aimed at the child? How can we protect ourselves against unfair consumer practices? How do businesses compete for customers? How does specialization help the consumer?

"Since children of elementary school age spend a considerable amount of time with toys of various kinds—games, sports equipment, crafts, hobby materials, books, building toys—they represent an effective device for introducing the children to economics.

"In this unit, sessions are short and can be covered in a two- to three-week unit. The activities suggested are varied and student-centered and include discussions, interviews, surveys, role playing, creative projects, simulation games and the use of community members—parents, local businessmen, local stores, etc. Critical-thinking skills stressed in the activities include observing, comparing,

summarizing, classifying, interpreting, criticizing, imagining, collecting and organizing of data, and finally applying facts and principles to new situations.

"All in all, using the child's natural love for and interest in toys to provide him with some basic understandings in consumer economic principles almost insures the teacher success in dealing with these materials. As Voltaire, the great French philosopher once said: 'Remember, play is the work of children!' . . .

SELECTING A TOY

Objective/Concept:
"One of the things a parent needs to learn is how to buy toys. Parents in the United States spend more than two billion dollars annually on toys. Unfortunately, too much of this money is wasted.

Procedure:
"Outline the criteria for a good toy. List on the board and have students take notes or copy list for future reference. Discuss each item as you go along using students' own toy experiences as much as possible. Here are the criteria I use:
1. A good toy is safe.
2. A good toy is durable.
3. Ninety percent of the play should be in the child and 10 percent in the toy. (Compare a push-button battery-operated toy with a set of wooden blocks.)
4. A good toy is fun.
5. A good toy must be suitable to the age and stage of development of the child as well as the special interests, hobbies, and skills of the child. (This list of criteria and the discussion idea that follows have been adapted from

material in *Toy Review,* Vol. 1, No. 3, Christmas, 1972, published by Toy Review, Newton, Mass.)

"Next, discuss the value of a cardboard box as a good toy for a child. Point out that a large cardboard box is big enough for a child to crawl into. It is abstract rather than specific so it can be many things—a fort, a boat, an igloo, a computer. It stimulates and enriches a child's powers of inventiveness. He can use it as it came originally. He can cut holes in it where he wishes. He can paint or crayon it any color he likes. There are few toys which you can buy in a toy store with the play value of a large cardboard box.

Assignment:

"Ask students to think of a toy that they now have which best fits the five criteria outlined above. In a good paragraph, they are to justify their choice. Follow up with a small or whole group discussion on the childrens' choices. Do the same toys come up again? Can the children agree with one another? Do they own many toys of this caliber? . . .

COMPETITION AND PROFIT

Objective/Concept:

"Competition is a contest among producers of goods and services to win the consumer's money. Producers compete with each other in many ways.

Materials:

"Several sheets of plain and colored construction paper. Glue, crayons, scissors.

Procedure:

"Divide the class into several small groups of 4 or 5. Teacher begins activity by stating that she is a businessman who owns a successful toy shop. She explains to the students that they, too, are owners of toy shops all competing with one another. 'Now as you know, businessmen watch very carefully what other businessmen who sell the same thing as they

sell are doing. Why do you think this is so?' Discussion.

"Teacher says, 'In playing this game, you are to watch very carefully what my business does and decide what you would do to stay in business.'

"Teacher starts game by placing a sign made of oaktag or cardboard on front of desk. Sign reads: TOYS FOR BOYS SHOP. Students respond by thinking of company names and making signs for their groups. Give students time to share their signs with other groups and award gumdrops (or some no-calorie toy) to the makers of the best and most creative sign. Students may use any of the materials to make their signs.

"Teacher puts out another sign that says: TOYS FROM AS LOW AS $1.00. Again students response may vary with prices that are lower, higher, or combination of values. Give students time to share once more and reward makers of signs where economy and value of items for sale are in the best balance.

"Proceed with similar signs, such as—TOYS MADE OF STURDY MATERIALS. TOYS GUARANTEED NOT TO BREAK. BUY ONE TOY AND GET ANOTHER ONE AT HALF PRICE. OUR SLOGAN: *BUY A TOY FOR YOUR FAVORITE BOY AND WATCH HIM JUMP FOR JOY!*

Follow Up: Discuss the following questions: Is competition good or bad? Why? How do businessmen compete with one another?

"Prepare a survey questionnaire sheet with which each student can interview a businessman—father, neighbor, friend, relative. Questions should include:

1. What made you go into your business?
2. Do you employ other people? How many?
3. Did you have any special aptitude, training or experience that have helped you succeed?
4. Would you like to expand your business? How?
5. How do you compete with other businessmen?" (pp. 48–51)

During the second phase, the students were taught to write each item correctly without continuous reference to a model that could be copied. Before the student could advance to the third phase, he or she had to write at least eight of ten items correctly. In the third phase, the students were taught to fill out one item at a time from a variety of different application forms; then they were given actual employment forms to fill out. After they completed this task, they were tested on a variety of unfamiliar employment forms. Although none of the students could successfully fill out an employment form before training, all six of the students were able to do so with near 100 percent accuracy after training, even on employment forms they had never seen before. The teaching of skills that increase the employability of students makes it more likely that they will have a chance to transfer their academic learning to their everyday working lives.

REVIEW 10–4

1. What should the relationship be between reading and spelling instruction?

2. Give an example of the method you might use to improve the amount of learning that takes place during spelling quizzes.

3. Give some examples of instructional objectives stated in behavioral terms for teaching composition.

4. What are the two major curriculum approaches to elementary mathematics instruction?

5. Why should "real-world" skills be taught?

SUMMARY

Age partly determines what a child will learn in school. In the preschool the focus is on ensuring that the child has the educational and social entering behaviors necessary for success in the first grade. The early elementary grades focus on the basic skills of reading, writing, and arithmetic, while later grades emphasize content courses such as government, biology, and so on. But today, considerable crossover of instruction takes place across age levels. Some content instruction goes on in some kindergartens, and increasing numbers of high schools offer reading instruction.

The specific objectives for each preschool program depend on the type of curriculum the child is being prepared to enter, but will often include teaching the child to attend to the teacher, to be an active participant, to interact with peers and teachers, and to communicate effectively using language. Once in the first grade, the "three Rs" become a major focus.

The field of reading instruction is characterized by many differences of opinion centering both around what skills should be taught and how they should be taught. In each case, compromise between the extreme points of view seems most productive. Some reading specialists advocate the teaching of generalizable skills for the pronunciation of all words (word-attack approaches), others recommend teaching words as individual units (whole-word approaches), while still others take an eclectic approach combining both methods. The second controversy surrounds the method of teaching reading. Some advocate basal reading programs in which the teacher presents suggestions on reading in group lectures, followed by practice in a text of reading passages. Others recommend programmed reading exercises, with most educators again choosing a combination of these methods.

The same controversies surround spelling instruction, but once a program has been chosen for reading instruction, it is probably best to follow the same type of program for spelling. The field of mathematics instruction also contains disagreements about basal-type textbooks versus programmed exercises, but its major controversy is over the teaching of "new math" versus computational skills. Many eclectic approaches in this area also combine instruction in the conceptual basis of mathematics with "old-fashioned arithmetic."

Throughout the chapter we emphasized that no matter which curriculum approach is chosen, the major function of teachers is to ensure that the principles of instruction are applied to teaching. Suggestions were provided for each type of subject matter, with composition being used as an example of a particularly complicated case. In all instances, effective learning requires excellent teaching.

ANSWERS TO REVIEW QUESTIONS

Review 10–1

1. The objectives of a preschool program depend on the nature of the elementary school program it leads into, but often include

(a) attending to the teacher of educational activity.

(b) volunteering to participate.

(c) interacting appropriately with peers and teachers.

(d) communicating effectively with language.

(e) having the intellectual and educational entering behaviors for first-grade work.

2. The zone defense approach seems superior to the man-to-man because the group does not have to wait on each child to finish each activity; rather, students can progress at their own rates.

Review 10–2

1. Reading is a valuable skill in providing recreation and information, but from the point of view of education, it is a necessary tool for the great majority of later learning and work.

2. Reading is not a single skill; rather, it combines many different skills, including, for example, saying sounds indicated by letters, oral reading, and reading comprehension.

3. The major approaches to reading instruction are the word-attack approaches, the whole-word approaches, and the eclectic approaches. The word-attack approaches seek to reach generalizable rules for pronouncing all letter combinations. The whole-word approaches advise that students memorize words as individual units. The eclectic approaches suggest combining these two strategies.

4. The phonics and linguistic approaches are both word-attack strategies that differ in that the phonics approach initially teaches the sounds of smaller groups of letters, while the linguistic approach teaches word-attack skills using intact words.

5. The advantage of the word-attack approaches is that they teach a relatively small number of rules for pronouncing all possible words, whereas the whole-word approaches teach all words as single units. On the other hand, the rules of pronunciation of the word-attack approaches are somewhat difficult to learn, and there are many exceptions to the rules. Pronunciation of words as single units, as in the whole-word approaches, is easier to learn, and because there are no rules of pronunciation, there are never any exceptions to confuse the beginning reader.

6. Research has failed to demonstrate the superiority of any of the major approaches to reading instruction, leading most experts to advocate eclectic methods.

Review 10–3

1. Three major curriculum approaches to reading instruction are basal readers, programmed instruction, and the experience approach.

2. Basal readers are primarily collections of graded passages in which the students practice reading silently or aloud. Programmed readers involve the students in solving problems and giving written answers to exercises that require silent reading. Teachers are most frequently required to lecture to the class in basal approaches, while in programmed approaches most of their time is spent in individual conferences with students who progress at different rates.

3. Boredom might be reduced through reinforcement or by supplementing with other programs.

4. In the experience approach, students read materials they have dictated to the teacher. Because it is not a systematic approach, but one that has high intrinsic interest, it might best be used as an occasional supplement to another type of basic reading program.

5. The more interested students are in the content of reading materials, the better their comprehension is. This is perhaps because the more interesting material is more meaningful to them. This is similar to the fact that meaningfulness improves memory.

Review 10–4

1. Because of the overlap between spelling and reading instruction, the same basic approach to the two types of instruction should be followed.

2. In the example in the text, spelling accuracy on daily tests was reinforced by allowing students who performed well to miss remedial tests. Other reinforcers could have been used, however.

3. Some examples of instructional objectives for teaching composition are increasing the number of different words or different parts of speech. It is clear that such objectives are only part of what is meant by learning an effective writing style.

4. The two major curriculum approaches to elementary mathematics instruction are the "new math," which emphasizes the conceptual basis of mathematics, and computational mathematics, which emphasizes the learning of skills of computation. A compromise approach between these two extremes seems most popular today.

5. As discussed in Chapter 4 in the section on transfer of learning, the more similar school learning is to the everyday situations in which we want education to help students, the more likely is positive transfer. In the example of teaching students to fill out actual employment forms, the learning has the extra advantage of helping them land a "real-life" job in the first place.

Chapter 11

Content Instruction

In the last chapter we discussed the teaching of basic educational skills. While these skills are important in their own right, basic skills such as reading and arithmetic are also important as tools for further learning. We *learn to read*, for example, so that we can *learn by reading*. The ideas, facts, and attitudes that we learn through reading (and lectures, etc.) are the *content* of education. Subjects such as history and science, for example, are mostly content, while reading and spelling are mostly skill. Other subjects such as English and art contain both skill and content aspects.

We will be concerned in this chapter with the teaching of various types of content. Our focus will be on helping students learn and remember the large amounts of content information that they must cope with in schools. Most content instruction occurs after the third grade, while the focus is on basic skills in kindergarten through the third grade. But much content instruction begins on the first day of school. When children learn to read, they must practice reading *something*. Increasingly, the subject matter of early reading materials and classroom discussions is meaningful educational content. A recent discussion with a five-year-old girl left no doubt about it:

Adult: "That's a pretty flower, isn't it?"
Child: "Yes, but the pistil and stamen are the same color on that one. I like it better when they are different colors."
Adult: "Oh."

In addition to being conducted at all grade levels, there is great variety among the various content subjects. To a greater extent than in the previous chapter, therefore, we will describe applications of the psychology of instruction to content teaching in somewhat general terms. But, even though there are important differences among content fields, such as literature and physics, the principles described in this chapter apply equally to all. It may take considerable thought on your part to see how you can tailor the principles to your specific teaching needs. To help you in this task, we will provide many examples in this chapter of how the principles have been applied to various aspects of content instruction.

WHAT SHOULD BE TAUGHT?

The first question that must be asked about all content instruction is *"which* subjects should we teach?" This question is so obvious that teachers often overlook it. It is a major concern of theoretical educators, especially to curriculum specialists and educational philosophers. Some of the dimensions of the problem are: "Should we teach liberal arts subjects such as literature and philosophy to broaden the students' minds?", or "Should we teach practical courses that will help the student land a job and be a better consumer?"

We are a long way from reaching unanimous agreement on such questions, as they touch our most deeply held beliefs and values. But, enough of a consensus exists among educators to suggest the following conclusions:

Learning is valuable in and of itself. There are probably no courses of study that are not

meaningful education will mean education that leads directly to employment and improved quality of daily life. The strong movement towards increased availability of vocational education is a step in that direction. So, too, is the increased offering of courses in consumer education, health, recreation, and so on.

But, regardless of what you teach, some ways of teaching it will be more effective than others. That is the main topic of this chapter.

PRESENTING CONTENT FOR LEARNING

The purpose of teaching is to help students learn. You should, therefore, create conditions that will make learning *easy*. This seems obvious when it is stated this way, but some teachers do not act as if they believe in facilitating learning. They present material in ways that make it seem more difficult than it is, perhaps to "impress" the students, or perhaps because they want to scare off the less capable students, or maybe because they think hard work is good for students. But, for whatever reason it is done, it has the effect of damaging learning and turning off students. Others make up tests that are extremely hard so that they will have a perfect normal distribution of grades. None of these practices is consistent with good content instruction.

If our goal is to make content learning efficient, then how do we do it? The following discussion outlines some of the most im-

beneficial in some way to the individual who studies them. But if schools are to improve the lives of students to the fullest extent, they must also teach those courses that will be *directly* meaningful to each student. For some, that will mean a heavy dose of science and mathematics, for others philosophy and the arts, but for most students

WHAT SHOULD THE CONTENT OF EDUCATION BE?

We have discussed already the difficulties involved in deciding what should be taught in schools. The following excerpt from a popular magazine summarizes one such controversy.

"In scores of communities from Vermont to Arizona, battles over school textbooks are raging. The textbook issue has become almost as heated a topic of dispute in these communities as teacher strikes, or integration, or busing. Parents in many areas are being warned that books and other materials now in use in the public schools are undermining the morals of their children and exposing them to alien, subversive doctrines. Underlying these charges are questions of deep personal concern to all parents of school-age children.

"What is your child learning in school? What should she or he be learning in addition to such basic skills as reading, writing, and arithmetic?

"Under particularly intense attack is a social-studies course for fifth and sixth graders called MACOS—short for "Man: A Course of Study." This course occupies one period of the school day for one year in the eight-year elementary-school curriculum of schools that use it; hence it does not impinge on the time needed for teaching the basic skills. Both critics and proponents of MACOS agree that it teaches children about salmon, herring gulls and baboons, and that it provides information on a band of Canadian Eskimos called the Netsilik, who as recently as 50 years ago were living under extremely hazardous and primitive conditions far north of the Arctic Circle. Beyond

that, there is very little agreement on anything about MACOS.

"'MACOS is designed to get young children to challenge every value taught them by their parents and to undermine their religious foundations,' one suburban parent alleges. 'The child . . . quickly learns that Mom's and Dad's view of the world is something to be ridiculed and supplanted. . . . It is time for every parent to warn his neighbor!'

"'These materials are making many of our children aliens in their own homes,' says Dr. Onalee McGraw, co-ordinator of the National Coalition for Children, an informal association of parents' organizations. 'We see our children being changed as by an unseen hand to reject everything we hold dear—every aspect of American society.'

"The dispute has reached even the halls of Congress. Representative John R. Conlan, of Arizona, national leader of the anti-MACOS forces, declares that MACOS is built up out of 'lurid examples of violence and sexual promiscuity and deviation,' and that it teaches ten- and eleven-year-olds to accept without moral condemnation such actions as 'wife-swapping and the abandoning of the aged to freeze to death.'

"Proponents of MACOS are equally outspoken. After seven years of teaching MACOS, Eileen Espovich, a sixth-grade teacher in the San Francisco Bay area, calls it 'one of the most exciting, comprehensive and enlightening curriculums I have ever encountered.' A fifth-grade California teacher says it is the 'most significant all-round educational program I've ever been involved with.' . . .

"Most fifth graders, for example, think of

food as something you buy in the supermarket. MACOS introduces children to a culture in which food is a seal that you must locate through the ice and spear with one swift thrust of your harpoon, using techniques as ingeniously adapted to seal hunting as computers are to supermarket operations. Food is also a caribou, which you cannot possibly capture by yourself—but which you may, with luck, be able to kill and share with your hunting partners if you and they co-operate in the hunt, pooling all your strength and cunning and the knowledge handed down to your generation by your fathers. Finally, food in the barren Arctic is so scarce that every last bit has to be eaten—even the eyeballs and the internal organs. . . .

"MACOS presents, again with little comment, the startlingly different Netsilik pattern of education. Educational failure in this Eskimo culture did not mean getting an F on a report card; it meant starving or freezing to death because you had not learned your lesson.

"Since the Eskimos lived through the winter on the very brink of starvation, they had to confront basic ethical issues on the harshest possible terms. The MACOS materials show, for example, a father, mother, three small children, and a grandmother down on their luck, limping their way across the Arctic ice from one winter camp to another. Their provisions are almost gone. The grandmother is much beloved—as the fifth graders have seen for themselves in an earlier scene, in which the entire family is eating and playing together in its igloo.

"But now the grandmother falls behind as the family hurries to find a better sealing site. What should be done? Should the seal hunter risk his own life, and thereby the survival of his wife and children, by returning for the grandmother and trying to carry her along? Does the grandmother, who loves her family as much as they love her, want him to return for her at the risk of five other lives?

"There are no easy answers, and MACOS offers none. But the problem of the Eskimo grandmother can lead to examination of the problems of the aged in our own society. How many of the aged are *we* leaving behind in nursing homes unfit for human habitation—without the Netsilik's reason of dire necessity? Fifth and sixth graders, teachers informed me, sometimes make this point in MACOS class discussions. One boy commented indignantly: 'I'm not going to leave *my* grandmother behind— or in a nursing home either!' " (Brecher, 1976, pp. 81–83)

Would you want MACOS in your classroom?

portant principles of presenting content for learning.

Meaningful Learning Is Effective Learning

We all know that we can learn and remember something better if we "understand it" than if it has no meaning for us. Instructions on how to take apart and clean a carburetor seem like so much gibberish if they are memorized in a rote, meaningless fashion. The instructions would be more meaningful and easier to understand if we also understand how the carburetor works and what each part does. The same is true for rules of grammar for a foreign language or the steps in balancing chemical equations. They are torture to learn unless we are lucky enough to see what they *mean*. Rote learning is difficult and soon forgotten; meaningful learning is easy and well retained.

Psychologists have conducted a variety of experiments to demonstrate the superiority of meaningful learning over rote. Although they approach the concept of meaningfulness in different ways, they all remind us to make sure our students understand the meaning behind what they learn. Levin and Rohwer (1968) at the Institute of Human Learning of the University of California in Berkeley asked fourth- and fifth-grade students to memorize a list of fourteen common nouns. As Figure 11−1 shows, some of the children were given the nouns in a simple list, while others memorized the nouns in a long sentence. Which group would be able to recall the greatest number of nouns?

Rote List	Meaningful Sentence
CAT	The grey **CAT**
LOG	jumped over the **LOG**
BOWL	to find the **BOWL**
MILK	of cold **MILK**
CHAIR	under the **CHAIR**
HOUSE	in the new **HOUSE**
LAKE	by the blue **LAKE**
BOY	where the young **BOY**
SHOE	lost his left **SHOE**
FISH	while eating the **FISH**
BOAT	on the wonder **BOAT**
STORM	during the **STORM**
YEAR	that came last **YEAR.**

Figure 11−1. *One group of children in the Levin and Rohwer (1968) experiment was asked to to memorize fourteen nouns as a simple rote list, while other children memorized the the nouns in a meaningful sentence, as shown above.*

The children who were given the sentence had to memorize a much greater total number of words than the children who memorized the simple list, but the material was presented to them in a more meaningful context. Which would be easier to memorize? Since this is a section on meaningfulness, you might expect the sentence group to have been superior. And they were. The group that memorized the nouns in the context of a meaningful sentence recalled more than 50 percent more of the nouns than did the children who memorized them in a rote fashion.

A group of Stanford University psychologists conducted another study that illustrates the value of meaningful learning in another context (Hilgard, Irvin, & Whipple, 1953). They taught two groups of students the steps to follow in performing a magician's card trick. One group learned the steps in a rote fashion, while the other learned the principle behind the card trick. Later, the group of students who had learned the trick in a meaningful way were better able to understand another trick than was the rote-learning group. They were better able to *transfer* their learning, or apply it to a new situation, because their learning was more meaningful.

These studies clearly suggest that content material is best taught to students in as meaningful a way as possible. Their learning and retention will be better when new information is placed in a meaningful context.

Taken one step further, however, this discussion suggests a basic strategy for education that relates to the previous section entitled, "What should be taught?" If we are better able to learn and remember meaningful concepts than simple facts, should we, then, focus more on the teaching of basic

concepts than on facts and details? We feel the answer is *yes*. Frutchey (1937), for example, found that high-school chemistry students recalled basic concepts fairly well a year later, but had little knowledge of specific facts. This and many similar studies show that we retain basic concepts much longer than specific facts and suggest that we should devote most of our teaching time to ensuring that the basic concepts will be learned. Some facts are important for students to learn and should be taught (in the most meaningful and effective ways possible), but since most names, dates, and insignificant facts will be forgotten anyway, spending valuable teaching time on them merely distracts students from more important kinds of learning. It is not difficult to teach facts and make up tests to evaluate factual learning, so we must be careful that we do not fall into an easy, but less meaningful style of teaching. Teach basic concepts first and foremost, and facts only to the extent that time permits. As you will read later in this section, teaching facts after concepts have been mastered will also make the learning and retention of facts more effective.

Organization of Content

Think of educational content as a message that must be communicated to students. That message will be understood by the greatest number of students if it is presented clearly, logically, and in a simple but precise vocabulary. We have mentioned this as a characteristic of good teaching before, but it is particularly important in content instruction.

Above all else, the content must be *understandable*. There are some simple techniques that you can use to improve the communication of content information to your students.

The teaching of content material can be easily facilitated by *adding* previews and reviews to lectures and reading assignments. These aid learning either by telling the students what they are going to learn or by reminding them of what they have just learned. That sounds too simple to be effective, but they can facilitate learning to a significant extent. Two types of previews and reviews have been studied extensively by educational psychologists: (1) general preview or review statements that give an overall picture of the content material, and (2) preview lists of important topics or review questions that highlight important items. Both improve the learning and retention of written content and can, in fact, be used together. The following sections will discuss each of these techniques.

Advance organizers and summaries.   An **advance organizer** is a brief statement that summarizes the content a reading passage or lecture in a general way. It does not include the specific facts or details that will be mentioned, but rather presents an overview of the content to be learned. The theory behind advance organizers (Ausubel, 1960) suggests that learning the most general concepts before the details gives the mind a "structure" to meaningfully "hang" the facts onto. Whether we concern ourselves with such theories or not, however, the use of

advance organizers does seem to be an effective method of improving classroom learning of content materials.

The classic study of advance organizers was conducted by Ausubel at the University of Illinois (Ausubel, 1960). He gave students a long passage to study on the metallurgy of carbon steel and later asked them factual questions about it. The students who had previously read a brief paragraph that described the basic concepts of carbon steel metallurgy did better on the test than students who had not read this advance organizer, even though the questions tested factual information rather than knowledge of the basic concepts. This facilitation of learning and memory by advance organizers has been replicated in experiments many times since. More recent evidence, however, suggests that the effects of advance organizers are just as good or better when they follow learning than when they precede it. This is why summaries appear at the end of each chapter.

Instructional objectives and review questions. Information that *highlights* ideas the instructor wants students to learn facilitates learning regardless of whether it comes before or after learning. These specific previews and reviews can be in the form of instructional objectives ("You will be expected to name two plants that grow well in moist, acid soil.") or questions ("What are two plants that grow well in moist acid soil?"). Research on the use of specific previews before learning suggests that they increase the amount of learning of the specific material relevant to the previews, but reduce the amount of learning for material that is not relevant to them (incidental learning).

For example, researchers at Florida State University (Duchastel & Brown, 1974) asked 58 students to read a 2,400-word passage entitled, "Conditions Under Which Mushrooms Grow and Thrive." The researchers identified twenty-four items of information in the passage and designed a test to evaluate the students' learning of them. Half the students were given a preview of the passage that referred to twelve of the items of information in the form of specific instructional objectives. The rest of the students were not given any preview material at all.

Figure 11–2 shows the results of the study. Overall, the two groups of students correctly answered about the same total number of questions. But, the group that read a specific preview answered *more* of the questions relevant to the previews than did the control group that had no previews and answered *fewer* of the incidental questions than did the control group.

Like general advance organizers and summaries, specific previews are useful, therefore, in focusing learning (Duchastel & Merrill, 1973). Students will not learn more information overall, but will learn more of the information you want them to learn. For this reason, you need to be sure that the previews you use are good ones. They will be effective only if they are clear and explicit and cover all the information you want the students to learn.

The influence of specific review questions on learning appears similar to previews or perhaps even stronger. In an experiment that involved 128 students reading biographical material (Frase, 1968), questions were found to increase the amount of relevant learning relative to incidental learning whether the questions preceded or followed learning, but the facilitation was greater when the questions followed the learning material. This is why review questions are used in this textbook after each section. Review questions are not just an important tool for textbook writers, however. On the contrary, review questions asked orally by teachers seem considerably more effective than written ones (Rothkopf & Bloom, 1970).

Some Guidelines for Teaching Concepts

Content instruction is more beneficial, then, when learning is made meaningful and when the communication is improved through the use of general and specific previews and reviews. In this section, we will discuss some specific suggestions for teaching new concepts to students. While we focused on ways to introduce and review the lecture or reading assignment in the previous section, now

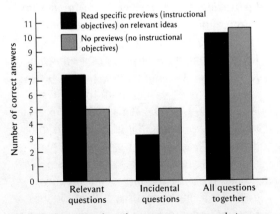

Figure 11–2. *Number of correct answers on a botany test for students who received specific previews (instructional objectives) on some of the test items, or who received no previews at all. (From Duchastel & Brown, 1974)*

we are concerned with the very heart of the content to be learned.

Perhaps the most challenging and certainly one of the most important goals of teaching is to explain new concepts to students. Just as reading and computation open up avenues of learning to students, ideas open up additional possibilities of thought and experience. Teaching new concepts can become an easier task for you if you follow a few simple guidelines of concept teaching. These guidelines are based primarily on the excellent analysis of concept learning provided by educational psychologist D. C. Clark (1971). They should usually be followed in the order given.

(1.) *Begin by giving a definition of the concept.* In teaching the concepts of prime numbers, for example, to eighth-graders, you might say, "Prime numbers are numbers that have no factors except the number one and themselves. The factors of a number are two numbers that equal that number when they are multiplied together." Definitions should be clear and accurate, but should not be more sophisticated than the students will understand. An experiment by Feldman and Klausmeier (1974), for example, compared the concept learning of fourth- and eighth-grade children under two conditions. Under one condition, both groups of children were given detailed technical definitions of a concept, and under the second condition they were given less detailed simpler definitions from a children's dictionary. The eighth-grade children learned the concept better when the

more detailed technical definition was given, but the fourth-graders learned more from the simpler definition. The younger students were unable to understand the technical definition, even though it was more detailed and informative than the simpler one.

(2.) *Give several different examples of the concept.* For example, you might say, "The numbers 1, 3, 7, 13, and 17 are all prime numbers because the only numbers that could be multiplied together to make these numbers are 1 and the number itself. Their only factors are 1 and themselves."

(3.) *Point out which features of the examples are actually critical features of the concept and which are not.* In the examples of prime numbers (1, 3, 7, and 13), point out that although all prime numbers are odd, not all odd numbers are prime (9 and 15, for example). Whether a number is odd, then, is not a critical feature of the concept.

(4.) *Give some examples that may appear to be members of the concept, but are not "negative instances."* Show the students, for example, that 9, 15, and 21 are not prime, even though they are odd.

(5.) *Test the students' knowledge of the concept by first giving them a mixture of positive and negative instances of the concept with explanation, and then test them on more positive and negative instances.* As always, give complete feedback when wrong and reinforcement when right, and then allow this information a moment to "sink in" before going on to the next practice item.

(6.) *Whenever possible, begin with easier instances of the concept and progress gradually to more difficult ones.* Also, try to keep all the positive and negative instances you have discussed in view at one time (on the blackboard, etc.).

(7.) *Finally, remember that some of the students will not have grasped the concept when most of them appear to understand it and will require some additional individual work.* It is not safe to move on just because most of the heads bob knowingly up and down when you ask them if they understand.

Discovery Learning Versus Expository Teaching

We have discussed at several points in the book the view that students learn best when they learn for themselves. Proponents of student-directed forms of "open education,"

such as Jean Piaget, argue that *teaching* new concepts to students (by following the guidelines presented above) does more harm than good. When teachers try to explain new ideas to students, they succeed only in inhibiting their students' natural interest in *discovering* new concepts for themselves. Student-guided "discovery" learning, these proponents argue, is more meaningful, enjoyable, and efficient. One thing is certain, the discovery of new concepts (letting students figure out for themselves that the sum of the interior angles of triangles is always equal to 180°) can be terrific fun for *some* students who are ready for new ideas and are tuned into education. But teacher-directed learning can be exciting as well. The key question is how efficient is discovery learning compared to expository teaching when concept learning is the primary goal?

Most recent research suggests that the discovery method is less effective than expository teaching, measured both in terms of rate of learning and amount retained. For example, a study comparing the two methods in teaching basic economics concepts to first-graders (Ryan & Carlson, 1973) found that the expository teaching group learned more during a seven-week economics unit than did the discovery group. Similarly, a study conducted in the public schools of Albuquerque, New Mexico, found that first- through sixth-graders learned novel concepts more easily, remembered them better, and applied them to new situations better (transferred them) when they were learned through expository teaching rather than a discovery method.

Most other research also supports the superiority of expository teaching over discovery learning, but that does not mean that there is no role for discovery exercises in the classroom. When used as change-of-pace learning experiences for children who can handle them, discovery exercises can be an excellent supplement to teacher-led learning.

Using Tests and Reviews as Learning Tools

One of the principles for good teaching mentioned in Chapter 1 says that students should take an active role in learning; they should overtly practice the new skills and ideas

GETTING ACTIVELY INVOLVED IN CONTENT LEARNING

Not all good learning happens while students are sitting passively at their desks. An important study conducted at the Frank Porter Graham Child Development Center in North Carolina gives an excellent illustration of that point.

Forty-eight second-grade children enrolled in a social studies unit on occupations and municipal services were given a unique alternative to the standard lecture course. They were allowed to construct a "city" out of inexpensive materials in which they acted out the functions of firemen, doctors, postmen, and so on. They participated in a fifteen- to twenty-five-minute dramatic play period each day, guided by teacher-led discussions on the jobs they were acting out. At the end of the unit, they were tested and compared to another class who covered the same material in a standard lecture-style method. The children who learned through participation correctly answered more than twice as many questions about the occupations they had "studied" than did the lecture group (Based on McKinney & Golden, 1973).

they are learning. One effective way of doing this for content instruction is to give practice tests or oral reviews between formal examinations. These can be learning experiences in and of themselves, and will provide

Feedback is important for making tests effective learning experiences.

both students and teachers an opportunity to find out just how much the students know at that point.   Here are some pointers for making tests learning experiences.

(1.) *Give feedback.* Students will learn little from practice tests and reviews unless they receive feedback on their answers (Wexley & Thornton, 1972). This feedback should be personalized and nonhostile, and it should clearly explain why the answer was wrong (Plowman & Stroud, 1942).

(2.) *Give feedback the next day.* Teachers vary greatly in the speed with which they give back corrected tests. This can annoy students at times, but more importantly, it

influences how much they will learn from the test. Students will learn and remember more if the feedback if given immediately after the test. Right? *Wrong!* A variety of studies show that *more is learned and retained when feedback is delayed rather than immediate.* Too much delay is not beneficial, however. The best time to give feedback on written test performance seems to be the next day. Delays of less than or greater than one day seem less effective (Kippel, 1974; Surber & Anderson, 1975). No firm explanation is available for this, but much evidence points to the superiority of a one-day delay. This beneficial effect of delayed feedback is limited, however, to tests and practice tests. At all other times, reinforcement and other forms of response consequences should be given immediately.

(3.) *Give frequent tests and reviews.* The effects of practice tests and reviews seem most helpful when they are given frequently. A group of researchers in Kansas (Rieth, Axelrod, Anderson, Hathaway, Wood, & Fitzgerald, 1974), for example, found that performance on weekly spelling tests for low-achievement middle-school students improved when they practiced on daily tests. Peterson, Ellis, Toohill, and Kloess (1935) similarly found that two reviews were better than one, which was better than none, in improving scores on a history examination.

(4.) *Contingent release from tests.* Tests and reviews can be powerful teaching tools, then. When carefully balanced with other learning experiences, they offer good times for learning. Beneficial though they may be, however, few students are crazy about taking them. Getting out of tests can, therefore, be used to stimulate as much learning as taking them. For example, as was mentioned in an earlier chapter, daily spelling test performance will improve if students are allowed to skip all remaining tests on the weekly spelling list if they make a perfect score on one of the daily tests (Lovitt, Guppy, & Blattner, 1969). Similar results have been found with older students enrolled in a psychology course (Bostow & O'Connor, 1973). When students who scored less than 90 percent correct on weekly quizzes were required to take remedial quizzes over the same material, they scored higher on the final examination than a group of students who

DO STUDENTS LEARN DIFFERENTLY FOR DIFFERENT KINDS OF TESTS?

It is folklore among teachers that students study differently for different styles of tests. For example, students learn lots of facts for teachers who give multiple-choice and true/false tests, but miss the basic concepts; while just the opposite is true when they study for essay tests. Studies on this topic suggest that part of this folklore is accurate, but that the most important part is not. Students do study differently for essay tests than they do for objective tests. McKenzie (1972) and King and Russell (1966) have found that students who study for essay-type questions learn the broader concepts better than students who study for factual questions, but that the essay students also do as well or better on the factual questions. Essay questions seem to produce better overall learning.

did not have to take remedial quizzes. Apparently, avoiding the remedial quiz proved a powerful reinforcer that stimulated improved learning and retention.

Mastery Learning Strategies for Content Instruction

As introduced in Chapter 1, the term *mastery learning* means that students should not progress from one topic to the next until they fully learn, or master, the first one. Students should not progress from plane geometry to trigonometry until they master plane geometry, and they should not start learning about balance of trade until they fully understand international currency exchange.

This is one of the primary reasons for individualized instruction. If students have not learned a basic topic, they will be unprepared for a more complicated topic based on the original one. In practice, it means that not all students will progress at the same rate; some will have to spend more time learning a given topic than others.

The mastery learning approach has been applied to content instruction with positive results. Bloom (1974) has found that the ratio between the amount learned by the top one-fifth and the bottom one-fifth in American schools is 3:1. That is, the best students regularly learn three times as much as the poorest students. When a mastery learning approach is used, however, (when each student is given enough time to master each topic before going on to the next) Bloom suggests that the ratio will drop to 1.5:1. Mastery strategies may cut the difference between the best and poorest students in half.

An interesting study conducted on high-school students enrolled in an automobile mechanics course provided a good test of the mastery approach (Wentling, 1973). Half of the 116 students progressed through the five-week course in the usual fashion. At the end of each of eight units, they took a test on the material covered in that unit, and then progressed on to the next one. The mastery learning group, in contrast, did not progress to the next unit until they had scored at least 80 percent correct on the test over the previous unit.

The results of the study showed that the mastery students did in fact score higher on the tests and on a later examination over the entire course. As in previous studies, although the difference was large enough to be important, it was not as large as Bloom predicted. In addition, Block and Tierney (1974) found that the effects of a mastery approach are considerably better when corrected unit tests are returned in small study groups rather than individually as in the Wentling (1973) study just described.

Using Positive Reinforcement to Improve Content Learning

You have heard many times by now that positive reinforcement can be used to improve classroom learning. This holds for all types of learning, including content learning. The ways in which it can be used are limited only by the imagination of the teacher. Some examples will illustrate the possibilities.

Brown, Huppler, Van Deventer, and Sontag (1973), in a study conducted at the University of Wisconsin Center on Mental Retardation, used positive reinforcement to increase comprehension of science filmstrips in mildly mentally retarded middle-school children. The children were repeatedly shown filmstrips on soil, air, water, and light. After each filmstrip, they were asked comprehension questions about its content. Figure 11–3 shows that comprehension was low on all three filmstrips during phase I when the children received no reinforcement. During phase II, the children saw two filmstrips and

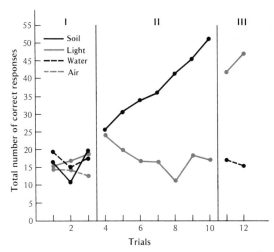

Figure 11–3. *Number of questions correctly answered by mildly retarded middle-school children after viewing science filmstrips. The students were reinforced for correct answers to questions about the soil filmstrip in Phase II and reinforced for questions on the light filmstrip in Phase III. (From Brown, Huppler, Van Deventer, & Sontag, 1973)*

school project conducted in a disadvantaged area of Knoxville, Tennessee. As above, students were given reinforcement (in the form of free time and points toward their final academic grades) for good behavior, but they were allowed to participate in the negotiation of a formal "behavior contract." The written contract specified that each student would earn points that could be exchanged for reinforcers for good performance on homework, classwork, and daily quizzes, and for good behavior (coming to class on time, bringing books and school supplies), and would lose points for misbehaviors such as hitting, throwing objects, and loud talking.

The students reacted well to this program. Figure 11–4 shows that the grades of the students in the experimental contracting classes improved over three grading periods, while the grades in a comparable control class, which did not use contracts, dropped slightly during the same period of time. Rein-

received monetary reinforcement after answers to questions on the soil filmstrip, but not after questions on light. The comprehension of soil questions went up markedly in this phase, but stayed low for light questions. In the third phase, correct answers to questions on light were reinforced, while answers on the water filmstrip were not. Performance on the reinforced questions again was much higher than for the nonreinforced answers. As the teacher of the students had predicted, the filmstrips were too difficult for the students to comprehend, but only when reinforcement was not given for correct answers.

A different strategy for using positive reinforcement was used by Williams and Anandam (1973) in an experimental junior high

Figure 11–4. *Grades of junior high school students who did and did not enter into contracts agreeing to follow classroom rules in exchange for positive reinforcement. (From Williams & Anandam, 1973)*

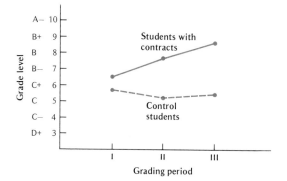

forcement, then, can clearly be used to stimulate content learning just as with the learning of basic skills.

Skillful content instruction, then, amounts to the clear presentation of concepts and facts in as meaningful a way as possible. This skill, as we portray it above, is neither mysterious nor difficult to acquire, but simply requires following some commonsense guidelines such as we have described. In addition, an individualized mastery learning approach using positive reinforcement to motivate learning is an essential part of content instruction.

REVIEW 11–1

1. What do you think should be taught as educational content?

2. Compare the effectiveness of rote and meaningful learning.

3. Discuss the effect of previews on learning.

4. List the seven guidelines for teaching concepts.

5. What have researchers found when comparing discovery learning and expository teaching?

TEACHING STUDY SKILLS TO STUDENTS

As we have been saying, content learning depends to a great extent on effective classroom instruction. But, much more than in the case of basic skills learning, it also depends on learning outside the classroom. It can only be successful if students are capable of learning by studying on their own. Many students are not competent independent learners and must be taught to be so. As such, you can greatly help your students

by teaching them effective study skills. Improved study skills will not only improve your students' learning in future academic courses, they will also give your students the capacity to be lifetime independent learners.

The following is a list of study rules that you may want to pass on to your students, or you may want to try yourself while you are still a student.

(1.) Choose an appropriate place to study. Studying will be most effective in a place that is comfortable and free from distractions. It is considerably more fun to study at "Arnold's Drive-In" or on a blanket at the beach, but it will be mostly wasted time.

(2.) Actually study.   Many students kid themselves into thinking they are studying when they are not. They stare at their books, talk to their friends, or listen to the radio when they think they are studying. Study time must be a time for studying and nothing else. If students find that they are not actually studying, they should give up the charade and go somewhere else until they are actually ready to study. In this way, the study area will become a place where only studying takes place.

(3.) Organize and reduce study material. Students need to learn that they must work *hard* in order to make learning *easy*. This work is mostly required before learning actually begins. For example, it is a lot of extra work to outline each chapter in the reading assignment and to rewrite lecture notes in

condensed form. It makes learning much easier, however, because the study material is much briefer and better organized.

Regardless of what ads in magazines imply, we cannot do much to make the human memory hold information more effectively. What we can do is to make the information we want to know easier to memorize. There are a few students who make excellent grades without any discernable effort, but the difference between most A students and C students is that the successful ones work harder at making learning easier.

(4.) Test yourself or use study partners. It is easy to study until you *think* you know the material, but that point usually falls short of actually knowing it. For this reason, you should give yourself tests on the material you are studying. For example, if you are studying German vocabulary, write the German words on one side of cards or a folded sheet of paper and the English translation on the other. Test yourself on translating the words both ways until you are *sure* that you know them (later in this section we will tell you what to do next). In this way, you will know what you know and do not know. Self-testing is an excellent way to learn, as well.

Sometimes it is even better to study with someone else so that you can test each other. This has the added advantage of someone else thinking of questions that you missed, finding gaps in your notes, and so on. Note that we did not say "study with a friend," however. The danger in studying with a friend is that socializing will distract from studying. Males should not study with females, for example, unless they have little interest in one another, or unless one partner has a savage, jealous fiancé.

(5.) Self-record and self-reinforce. Since studying is less fun than practically anything else, we need good "self-control." We need to make ourselves study when we would really rather be somewhere else. That magic quality of inner direction is not as elusive as it may seem and can rather easily be strengthened.

One simple way is to keep careful records of our study behavior. Research has shown that just recording our own behavior makes us behave more as we think we should. An eighth-grade girl named Lisa, for example, was having a great deal of trouble paying attention in history class (Broden, Hall, & Mitts, 1971). A psychologist working in her school suggested that she keep a record of the amount of time she was paying attention. Lisa was asked to put a "plus" on a sheet of paper when she attended and a "minus" when she did not, "whenever you think of it." Figure 11–5 shows that the amount of time that Lisa paid attention (as measured by independent observers) increased considerably when she recorded her own behavior. The same sort of thing may work for your students as well.

In addition to self-recording, students can even reinforce themselves for good study behavior. For example, if you want to go out for doughnuts later, you can make a deal with yourself not to go until you reach a prearranged criterion for studying..If you stick to it, such self-reinforcement contracts can be helpful.

(6.) Space out study time.   As was mentioned in Chapter 4, learning time is more effective if it is spaced out with breaks in between than if it is massed together. If a student studies ten hours for an examination, more will be learned and remembered if the study time is divided into five daily blocks of two hours each, instead of two blocks of five hours, or, worse yet, one ten-hour "cram" session. Learning is just not effective after a short period of time; thus, cramming at the last minute is an undesirable strategy. We are not suggesting here that students study more, only that they save themselves wear and tear and mediocre grades by spacing out their study time. Remember, however, that there are important differences in the way people learn. Some students may be able to learn effectively by cramming, but most would do even better using spaced study periods. Reynolds and Glaser (1964) found, in this light, that junior high school students remembered more from a programmed biology lesson if they read in small parts spread out through other lessons than if they read the lesson all at once. Similarly, a study conducted with a group of fifth-graders from Tecumseh, Kansas, showed that they learned more spelling words when they studied them five at a time on four days of the week, rather than twenty at a time on one day (Rieth, Axelrod, Anderson, Hathaway, Wood, & Fitzgerald, 1974). Figure 11–6 shows the pronounced magnitude of this difference.

Figure 11–5. *Percent of time spent by an eighth-grade girl when she was and was not recording the amount of her own study behavior. (From Broden, Hall, & Mitts, 1971)*

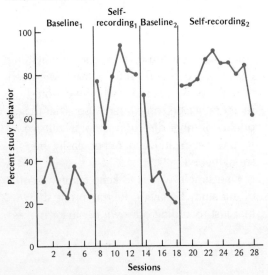

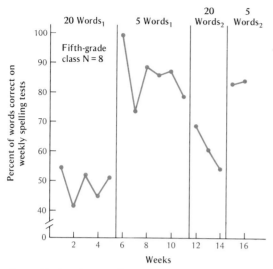

Figure 11–6. *Percent of words correct on weekly spelling tests in a class of fifth-graders when they studied five words at a time spaced out in four daily study periods, or when they studied twenty words at a time in one massed study period. (From Rieth, Axelrod, Anderson, Hathaway, Wood, & Fitzgerald, 1974)*

(7.) Use mnemonic devices. If you are going to be successful in this world, you have to be a little crafty. If you can come up with an honorable and honest strategy to help you with your trade, use it! The trade of students is learning and remembering, so their "bag of tricks" needs to include strategies for memorization. One effective strategy is to use **mnemonic devices.**

There are many types of mnemonic devices that can make content material easier to memorize. For example, one of the authors was having a hard time mastering the symptoms of psychological disorders in abnormal psychology until someone told him how to use acronyms for memorizing lists. For example, if the list of characteristics of a hypothetical type of neurosis contained the words

Gastrointestinal upset
Anxiety
Depression
Sleep disturbance
the first letters of the words could be formed into the word GADS. When the question calls for that list of symptoms, if GADS can be remembered, it will be easier to remember the whole list. Not all lists can be transformed into simple words, but they can all be transformed into a simplified form that can be more easily remembered, even if it is an awkward acronym like ARRANGLX.

Another mnemonic device that has been successful for some people is to form bizarre or silly associations between the words in the list. For example, in remembering the characteristics of a hypothetical neurosis, you could picture actor Don Knotts saying over and over, "I'm anxious, I'm anxious!", holding an aching stomach, alternately going to sleep and waking up, with a sign tied to his shoelace saying "depressed."

If they sound useful, try them. If not, invent your own. Mnemonics are limitless in form. Some medical students, for example, memorize a naughty poem to help them remember the location of the cranial nerves. But use whatever works for you.

(8.) Overlearn. This is the last of eight suggestions for making studying more efficient. This one promises that you will remember more if you *study more.* That is hardly earthshaking, but there is a twist to this recommendation that makes it much more important than it might first seem. As mentioned in Chapter 4, by far the most

important study time that you put in is *just after you have completely learned the material* you are studying. This is when most of us stop studying, of course, and run screaming gleefully out of the room. When we finally rattle off the principal exports of every country in Southeast Asia for the first time without an error, we applaud ourselves and stop studying. But how many times have you been unable to remember test material that you knew the night before? If students *overlearn,* that is, if they continue to study *after* they know the content perfectly the first time, that kind of forgetting will be reduced considerably. For example, Ausubel, Stager, and Gaite (1968) had two groups of high-school seniors read a 2,200-word passage on Zen Buddhism during a 35-minute study period. Even though the students in both groups "knew" the material after this amount of study, one group (the overlearning group) later studied the material for another thirty-five minutes. The overlearning group was able to answer 50 percent more questions on the passage on a later examination.

The ability to study and memorize well, when we look at it carefully, then, amounts to no more than some easily learned skills. Teaching them to your students, or to yourself, can be an important way to improve an individual's ability to function independently in society.

REVIEW 11–2

1. Does immediate feedback on test answers lead to better learning from the test than delayed feedback?

2. Do frequent quizzes and reviews lead to better learning?

3. Does being released from a test act as a reinforcer for learning?

4. Define mastery learning. Is it an effective approach?

5. List and explain eight rules for effective independent studying.

SUMMARY

Subjects such as reading, writing, and arithmetic are taught in schools partly because they are inherently valuable skills, but mostly so that they can be used as tools for further learning. This further learning—history, social studies, science, for example—is the *content* of education, which is mostly learned in the form of verbal concepts and facts. Content instruction begins with early schooling, but becomes the dominant focus after the third grade.

Once the subject matter of content instruction has been chosen, it must be presented in ways that facilitate learning and retention. Like all learning, it is most effective when it is meaningful and focuses on concepts rather than on trivial facts. But, the way that content material is presented also has a strong influence on how easily it is learned.

General summaries and instructional objectives presented before learning are effective, but summaries and review questions coming after learning are even more useful.

As is true with basic skills learning, a mastery learning approach produces better overall learning, as does positive reinforcement for good academic performance. Perhaps the most important asset that teachers can give to their students, however, is a knowledge of how to learn content on their own. Good study skills include choosing an appropriate place to study, actually studying, organizing and reducing study material, self-testing, self-recording and self-reinforcement, spacing out study time, using mnemonic devices, and overlearning.

ANSWERS TO REVIEW QUESTIONS

Review 11–1

1. The content that we choose for education reflects our views of what civilization should be like and how schools should prepare individuals for it. The authors feel that traditional academic content of an abstract and intellectual sort is valuable, but that education must be tailored to meet the needs of each individual, even if those needs are pragmatic and career oriented. There is no "correct" answer to this question, however, only opinions.

2. Learning is more efficient and retention and transfer are better when students understand what they are learning than when it is rote or meaningless.

3. Both previews that give a broad overview of the passage or lecture (advance organizers) and those that point out specific ideas or skills to be learned (instructional objectives) improve the amount of learning related to the preview. The effects of general summaries and specific objectives seem greater, however, when they follow learning in the form of general summaries and specific review questions.

Concepts are best presented in a sequential fashion that clearly defines their critical features and gives students a chance to practice the concept. Good expository teaching of concepts seems better than requiring students to discover concepts by themselves, but discovery learning can provide an exciting supplement to any curriculum. Practice tests and reviews are excellent facilitators of learning, especially if they are frequent. But, getting out of taking retests can effectively motivate students to learn well for the first test. Feedback on written test performance is important to effective learning, but the feedback should neither be given immediately nor after too long a delay.

4. The following guidelines for teaching concepts should be followed in order:

(a) Give a definition of the concept in a language that the students will understand.

(b) Present several different positive instances of the concept, pointing out the critical features.

(c) Explain which features are not critical features of the concept.

(d) Present several different negative instances of the concept, explaining why they lack the critical features of the concept.

(e) Present a mixture of positive and negative instances with explanation. Then test the students' knowledge with more positive and negative instances, giving feedback and allowing the feedback time to "sink in" before going to the next practice item.

(f) Begin with the easiest instances first, progressing to instances of the concept that are more difficult to understand.

(g) Give each student enough time to master the concept before allowing that student to move on to more difficult concepts.

5. Most studies suggest that good expository teaching leads to better learning than discovery methods.

Review 11–2

1. Research suggests that a delay of about one day leads to better learning than immediate feedback or than feedback delayed for longer periods of time.

2. More frequent tests and reviews apparently lead to better learning, but should not be overdone at the expense of other kinds of learning time.

3. Students who are allowed to miss remedial tests if they make a high grade on the first test will score higher on the first test and recall more of what they learned later.

4. In a mastery learning program, students are allowed to master each topic before going on to the next. It apparently leads to improved overall achievement.

5. The eight rules for effective independent studying are:

(a) Choose an appropriate place for studying that is comfortable and free from distractions.

(b) Actually study. Do not just go through the motions of studying.

(c) Organize and summarize the material to be learned to make learning easier.

(d) Test yourself or get a nondistracting study partner to test you.

(e) Record and reinforce your own good study behavior.

(f) Space out study time with breaks or other activities in between.

(g) Use mnemonic devices to make memorization easier.

(h) Overlearn material beyond the point of first mastery.

Chapter 12

Exceptional Children

Up to this point we have talked primarily about "normal, average" children, but we have also given some attention to the education of children with special problems. We have done this for two reasons: First, teachers have always played an important role in the identification of exceptional children. Referrals made by teachers to school psychologists and other specialists are our first and most important source of information about the problems of children. Regardless of what the expert finds, no assessment of children is complete without knowing fully how exceptional children function in the classroom.

There is a second and more important reason, however, for discussing exceptional children with teachers of average classes. Recent legal decisions and changes in educational policy mean that exceptional children will be segregated less completely from other children in the future and will spend a greater proportion of their time in regular classrooms. This suggests that all teachers, to some extent, will become teachers of exceptional children. They will be backed up in this role by a variety of specialists, but many exceptional children will henceforth spend most of their time in regular classrooms with their average peers.

For these reasons, then, it is important to discuss the nature of exceptionality and the reasons behind recent shifts in legal interpretation and educational policy. These changes in our attitudes and procedures for exceptional children, almost without exception, will bring important benefits to both exceptional and average children. They do, however, create special challenges for teachers. They are challenges, however, that the well-trained teacher can meet without great difficulty.

DEFINITION OF EXCEPTIONALITY

Our most important task, of course, is to understand what we mean when we say that a child is **exceptional.** Two factors must be present. First, the child's behavior must *deviate* markedly from the norm. This simply means that the child must be *very* different from other children. Second, the way in which the child is different must be seriously harmful, or **maladaptive,** to the child or to other members of society. This is not to say that all ways of being different are bad, of course. It is usually desirable to be an excellent athlete, artist, or mathematician. Many states administratively place their programs for "gifted" children in the exceptional child education department, but in this discussion, we will exclude these children from our definition of exceptionality.

Exceptional children are, therefore, children whose behavior deviates significantly from the norm in ways that are maladaptive to themselves or others in society. The category includes children who suffer because they are sad or angry much more frequently than others, children who are placed at a great disadvantage because they cannot learn to deal with complicated situations as well as others, children who hurt others through their physical aggression, and many, many, others.

There are great difficulties inherent in deciding whether a child is exceptional. First, how different from the norm does the child's behavior have to be before she or he is considered *deviant?* Psychologists try to quantify these decisions as much as possible using objective measures and well-developed norms, but in the end, it is largely a matter of judgment. If you will recall the concept of the "normal curve" from Chapter 6, this problem is easy to understand. The principle of the normal curve states that if you take a measurement of many people or phenomena, most of those measurements will cluster near the mean, with fewer measures being farther from the mean in either direction. Figure 12–1 shows a hypothetical distribution of measures of the number of times that eighth-grade students talk to one another during the course of the school day. These measures would most likely fall in the form of a normal curve, as shown in the figure. Most students talk close to fifty times per day (let us say), but fewer talk nine or ten times a day, or eighty or ninety times a day. But when are students *so* different from most others that we call them *deviant talkers?* Is it when they talk one hundred fifty times per day? Two hundred times? As you can see, it is a rather arbitrary decision.

Second, what is the norm for any given individual? We have long known that different cultures have different norms for behavior, but we have only recently begun to deal with this problem as it concerns the assessment of children. Ruth Benedict provides us with an invaluable lesson on this topic in her classic anthropology text, *Patterns of Culture* (1950). In it she describes the normal behavior of two Indian cultures that are now nearly extinct.

The Zuñi Indians, who flourished in the southwestern United States before the coming of European immigrants, had a highly communal culture. They held almost no individual possessions or property and rarely competed among themselves. Their normal pattern of behavior was extremely sober, showing little emotion or individuality of any sort. It was considered embarrassing among the Zuñi, in fact, to be noticed by the others for any act or deed. The only exception to this emphasis on blandness of personality was the desirability of having seizure-like "fits" that were taken as evidence of visitation by supernatural spirits.

Emphasis on soberness in interpersonal relationships also extended to patterns of courtship and marriage. The young Zuñi men and women had little opportunity to interact with members of the opposite sex until marriage. When a Zuñi male decided to marry a young female he saw from afar, he followed the tribe's conventional pattern of courtship. All young unmarried females were required to carry water from the river each evening to the family house in a stone jar. So, on his big night, the amorous male concealed himself in the bushes that lined the path of the river. When his young lady came unsuspectingly along, he emerged and asked her for a drink of water. If she wished

Figure 12–1. *Hypothetical distribution of the number of times that students talk to someone during the school day. How far from the mean do you have to be in order to be considered "abnormal"?*

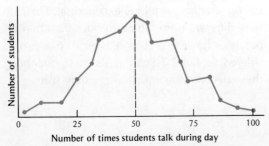

Number of times students talk during day

to become his bride, she gave him a drink and they were married the next morning. And that was that! I think you would agree that such behavior would be considered odd in our society, but it was normal for the Zuñi.

The normal pattern of behavior among the Dobu culture, however, is almost the exact opposite in every respect. This society lives on an island off the coast of New Guinea. The most obvious characteristic of the normal behavior of these people is their fierce competitiveness. The Dobu believe there is only a fixed amount of food and possessions available to all men. The only way for one man to prosper, therefore, is at the expense of his neighbor. They believe, for example, that there is no way for all the members of the tribe to increase their production of yams, but that one man can increase his production by interfering with his neighbor's ability to produce. Furthermore, it is completely normal and acceptable in Dobu culture to attempt to gain superiority over others by casting "spells." The favorite spell is a hex on one's neighbor's yams.

Courtship and marriage are similarly characterized by hostility. A degree of open heterosexuality is allowed and even encouraged among Dobu children and adolescents that would be surprising in the United States, and unheard of among the Zuñi. This almost total sexual freedom continues until about puberty when it is normal to select a mate. Sexual relationships between young Dobu males and females are restricted only in that they are expected to occur in the home of the female's parents. This may sound reasonable enough until you realize that they are one-room homes.

Nothing at all is said about these relationships until the male signals that he wants to take the female as his mate. He does this simply by remaining in the female's home until after sunrise. When this happens, his in-laws-to-be react with great mock surprise and rage, beating and stoning the young man with great ferocity. Because of the "embarrassment" he has inflicted upon the female's family, he is indentured as a slave to the family for a year, at which time his mother and father purchase his freedom with yams and blankets, and the couple is officially married.

The point of discussing these two cultures is this: Members of the Dobu tribe would be considered "abnormal" if they lived among the Zuñi, and vice versa. They would be considered perfectly normal living in their own cultures, but not as judged by the standards of another culture. This is important for us to keep in mind because America is a land of many cultures. The idea that America would be a "melting pot" in which its many immigrant cultures would dissolve into one American culture has been true to some extent; but far more than we realized, our Latin, African, Mediterranean, Northern European, Oriental, and other cultures have remained more or less distinct. We must, therefore, judge all students both by the norms of their *own subcultures* and by their ability to fit into a *multicultural* school system that is tolerant of differences among individuals.

In summary then, it is difficult to decide if a child should be considered "exceptional." Still, for all the difficulties in using the term, children who have special needs do exist. In order to provide them with special services, most school systems will need to

use the label "exceptional" in order to quali-
fy for outside financial assistance. The specialists who give these labels to children,
therefore, must be very careful to use them
wisely, and teachers should be careful to
interpret them cautiously. It cannot be pointed out too frequently that a label, in and of
itself, is meaningless. What really matters is
how children function in your classroom and
what you can do to help make their lives
better. You must be doubly sure that you do
not use a label of exceptionality as an excuse for not helping a child with his or her
problems. Even "exceptional" children can
be helped to live full and happy lives.

MODELS OF EXCEPTIONALITY

The way that we deal with exceptional children will be determined in large measure by
the way we conceptualize exceptionality.
There are three major models, or ways of
thinking, about exceptionality dominant in
psychology and education today. We will
discuss each of them to give you an idea of
the ways that different professionals view
exceptional children.

The Medical Model of Exceptionality

During the 1800s a revolutionary change
took place in the way that exceptional individuals were treated. Prior to the work of
Freud and other pioneers, abnormal behavior
was thought to be the result of evil spirits
inhabiting the body, or some other form of
retribution for a sinful life. In the new **medical model,** however, abnormal behavior was
seen as a *symptom* of a pathology of the
mind, or "mental illness." Freud replaced

evil spirits with sicknesses of the mind. This
was a great step forward, as it resulted in
treatment for exceptional individuals rather
than punishment for their supposed transgressions.

This new way of thinking was natural for
individuals trained in medicine. Just as a
sore throat and cough are viewed as symptoms of an underlying physical disease, so
deviant and maladaptive behaviors are taken
as symptoms of a presumed underlying mental sickness. This model places a great deal
of emphasis on the diagnosis of symptoms so
that the particular type of unseen mental
sickness can be determined and treatment
prescribed for it. This model has produced
terms such as "mental illness" that are so
much a part of our everyday culture that we
accept them without question. It is also the
reason for the existence of diagnostic categories that attempt to differentiate various
kinds of mental illness. Do not confuse the
medical model with the medical profession,
however. Many physicians do not believe in
the medical model, and many of those who
do believe in it are not physicians. The medical model is the oldest and still the most
dominant way of thinking about exceptionality (see, for example, Hartmann, 1967), but
there are other models as well.

The Humanistic Model of Exceptionality

A small but growing group of individuals has
developed a radically different view of exceptionality. The most important premise of
humanists is that each of us views reality in

our own personal way. No one can say what things *really* are like or should be, because each of us can only state our own subjective opinion. Humanists have little to say about exceptional children whose primary problems involve intellectual deficiencies, but they contribute much to our understanding of abnormal behavior. They see it as resulting from an individual's unique way of attempting to cope with reality as he or she sees it. We should not, therefore, always attempt to impose our standards of what is normal for us on other individuals.

There may be situations in which we should help individuals adjust better to their situations, but according to the humanistic viewpoint, we should first consider changing the situation to fit the individual. It might be decided, for example, to provide a special lunch for a child who does not wish to eat meat, rather than forcing that child to eat the standard school lunch. On the other hand, a child who has decided that he does not want to learn to read or write because he is going to become a cowboy might require intervention to change his behavior to fit reality as the teacher views it.

This model makes an important contribution to our understanding of all individuals, particularly in teaching us to have greater respect and understanding for individuals with differences that are not maladaptive. It does not provide us with a well-developed and unified frame of reference for dealing with all of exceptionality, however. It exists more as a reaction to what are viewed as the abuses of the medical model in labeling all individuals who violate society's norms as "sick" (see, for example, Lyons, 1973; Rogers, 1959).

The Behavioral Model of Exceptionality

The term *behaviorism* means many things. Used in its best sense, **behaviorism** is a point of view that says we should simply look at what people do and attempt to find ways of modifying their maladaptive behaviors (see, for example, O'Leary & Wilson, 1976). This is the essence of the behavioral model of exceptionality. Maladaptive behaviors are not viewed as symptoms of some underlying mental sickness; they are viewed as the problem itself. If a young man is unhappy because he does not interact well with young women, a behaviorist would try to teach him more appropriate patterns of social interaction. If we follow the medical model, we could attempt to determine what "mental disorder" (abnormal fears or hatred of females, lack of self-confidence, etc.) has caused this behavior disorder, but if we can teach better social skills to the individual and make him or her happy as a result, it is unnecessary to do so. More importantly, according to behaviorists, it is so difficult to deal with the unseen mental "causes" of deviant behavior that we will be more likely to help individuals by dealing directly with their behavior problems.

Think of it this way: Your tennis pro has adopted a behavioral model of poor tennis playing. If you go to him or her because most of your backhands are hitting the net, he or she will watch your backhand shots and suggest a change in that skill which will help you get the ball over the net more frequently. If your tennis pro used a medical model approach, however, he or she might put you on a couch and delve into your psyche to see if your poor backhands represent a symbolic way of taking out your hostility towards father figures, a desire to exorcise your feelings of inadequacy through self-punishment, and so on.

The point of view taken in this text might best be described as a "humanistic behaviorism." It is humanistic in its tolerance for differences among individuals and in its beliefs that no one group of people, regardless of the "excellence" of their educational background, knows what patterns of behavior are right for other people. On the other hand, the behavioral orientation of the book can be seen in the belief that when a pattern of behavior has been carefully and objectively determined to be maladaptive, direct steps should be taken to modify that behavior. (For further discussion of the concept of exceptionality, see Hewett & Forness, 1974.)

REVIEW 12–1

1. Define exceptionality.

2. What is the point made by Benedict's book, *Patterns of Culture?*

3. List the three models of exceptionality discussed in this book.

4. What is the major difference between the medical and behavioral models?

5. What is the main point made by proponents of the humanistic model?

MEANING OF DIAGNOSTIC CATEGORIES TO THE TEACHER

Because the medical model of exceptionality is still dominant among psychologists, psychiatrists, and educators today, it will be necessary to discuss further the diagnostic labels used in this model. As mentioned above, the first priority of the medical model is to "diagnose" the underlying cause of the individual's problems. Just as the physician attempts to determine whether a patient's sore throat is caused by a viral infection, a bacterial infection, or an allergic reaction, an attempt is made to determine which "type" of mental illness or deficiency is causing the individual's behavioral problems. The most frequently used diagnostic categories in school systems are *mental retardation, behavioral/emotional disturbance, learning disabilities,* and *physical handicaps.* These categories have been institutionalized in most of our school systems through state and federal funding formulas which usually dictate that children must be diagnosed as falling into one of these categories in order for the school system to receive reimbursement for providing special services.

This section will attempt to give you a working knowledge of what is meant by these categories. They are not discussed in order to encourage you to think in these terms, but rather to better equip you to understand what is, and is not, meant by such terms when others use them.

There are two striking features about the use of diagnostic categories. First, each category is extremely heterogeneous. An amazingly broad range of individuals is subsumed under each heading. This point will be amplified later in the chapter. Second, diagnostic categories are vague. There are many, many areas where it is difficult to determine whether an individual belongs in a given diagnostic category. Behavior is complicated and does not always fit easily into these Procrustean beds.* It is common, sadly, to look at a child's cumulative folder and see that three different diagnostic labels have been given by three different professionals.

Mental Retardation

According to the most recent guidelines of the American Association on Mental Deficiency, **mental retardation** is defined in terms of deficits of both intelligence and "adaptive behavior." This means that children are labeled mentally retarded when they score significantly lower on IQ tests than most other children and have been slow to acquire skills such as self-feeding, dressing, use of public transportation, and occupational skills. In spite of the recent emphasis on adaptive behavior, many professionals still use scores on a standardized intelligence test as the principal or the only criterion for diagnosing mental retardation.

The question is, then, how far below the mean must one score to be considered "mentally retarded"? Different organizations, states, and school systems have adopted different answers to this question. The most widely adopted schema in schools labels children with IQs below approximately 70 as "educable mentally retarded" and children with IQs below approximately 55 as "trainable mentally retarded." A score of 70 is

30 IQ points or 2 *standard deviations* below the mean of 100; 98 percent of the general population obtain a higher score. An IQ of 55 is exceeded by 99.9 percent of the general population. There are slight variations of these figures from one system to another and from one intelligence scale to another, but most school systems have adopted classification systems similar to this one.

Children who are classified as educable mentally retarded are most often considered capable of being "educated" in the normal sense. Programs are provided to teach them to read and write and to study other basic school subjects. There is, however, a strong emphasis placed on practical application of these educational skills, such as teaching the children to read directions at work and teaching them practical math skills such as balancing a checkbook. Individuals who are placed in a trainable mentally retarded category, on the other hand, are considered to be capable of only rudimentary levels of academic learning. They may be taught to read and do arithmetic at very basic levels, but most of their training will focus on teaching them *to take care of themselves*, to avoid dangerous situations, and to perform simple vocational skills in a sheltered workshop.

Keep in mind, however, the limitations on IQ scores discussed in Chapter 6. Many variables that have nothing to do with an individual's capacity for learning can produce low IQ scores. An individual who is from a culture alien to the one for which the test was developed, who felt bad on the day

*Procrustes was a mythical Greek robber who stretched or chopped his victims to make them conform to the length of his iron bed.

of the test, or who is shy or hostile may receive a score that is artifically low. Such children, especially minority-group children, do in fact receive the label of mental retardation far more frequently than they should. We must, therefore, be cautious in interpreting IQ scores, and be sure that individuals show deficits in many areas of their general behavior (their adaptive behavior) before we accept the term "mental retardation" as a label for them.

Heterogeneity among individuals labeled as mentally retarded. From the top to the bottom, the heterogeneity in the category of mental retardation is staggering. At the higher levels, retarded individuals' deficits are noticeably "different" only with close scrutiny. As children, individuals with an IQ of about 65 will learn to read and write, but will do so much more slowly than the average child. As adults, they will hold gainful employment, but will usually not rise above unskilled or semiskilled occupations. In general, they will behave like anyone else, but will occasionally appear "unintelligent" in their decision making.

At the lower end of the continuum, there are individuals who live their lives in comas, never speaking or moving in a purposeful way. They may require considerable training to even learn to swallow solid food. At the upper end of the continuum, retarded individuals usually look completely normal and rarely have detectable medical disorders accounting for their retardation. Toward the lower end of the continuum, brain damage and physical defects will be frequent.

Psychologist Edward Zigler (1967) has looked at the intelligence scores of children whose retardation apparently stems from organic causes and those for whom no organic cause can be found. As Figure 12–2 shows, the IQs of organically impaired retardates average 35, with very few individuals reaching an IQ above 65. Most retarded individuals without organic impairment, however, have IQs of about 70, with the number falling off rapidly at lower IQs. These data suggest that if a child has some type of organic impairment, the resulting retardation will usually, but not always, be serious. Most retarded individuals whose retardation does not result from organic causes, on the other hand, will be only mildly retarded.

While most retardates without organic impairment come from families in which at least one parent is also retarded, organic retardates come from all types of families and all walks of life. The most common types of

Figure 12–2. *Distribution of IQ scores of individuals whose mental retardation is related to organic causes and those where organic factors apparently play no part. (After Zigler, 1967, and Ross, 1974)*

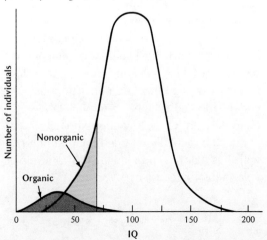

organic disorders are abnormalities of chromosomes that interfere with physical and intellectual development (as in Down's syndrome, or mongolism), or brain damage resulting from physical injury, lack of oxygen, infections, or chemical poisons. Most frequently, this damage occurs before or during birth.

The great majority of retarded individuals, however, are not organically impaired and fall at the highest end of the spectrum. Since the most frequent of all exceptionalities is mental retardation, by far the largest group of exceptional children fall in the educable mentally retarded category.

Perhaps describing some "typical" retarded children will help make this term more meaningful. First, a word of caution: Although the characteristics of these children will be commonly found among retarded children, there is such a wide range of differences in this group that there will be many other children of the same IQ levels who will be quite different in their characteristics. Consider the following case:

Mary is a twelve-year-old girl with an IQ of 40. In infancy, she was diagnosed as mentally retarded by a physician due to the slowness in her general behavioral development, some physical characteristics which are indicative of Down's syndrome, or mongolism, and findings of chromosomal damage. Although Mary is a happy, active child, she has a distinctly "dull" appearance. She is short and squat in appearance, heavyset with a thick neck, a dominant forehead, and an Oriental slant in the eyes. Her tongue is thickened and gives her a distinct speech impediment. Because of these physical factors, it takes many individuals a while to see that she is pretty in her own way.

She comes from an upper-middle class family and is well-dressed, well cared for, and obviously happy with her life. Mary was toilet trained, learned to feed and dress herself all by age nine, and at age twelve is now just learning to copy and identify letters. She speaks well except for problems in pronunciation and understands most statements made to her. Her attention span is short, however, and she sometimes disrupts the classroom in minor ways. She is unusually strong for her size, but rarely presents a serious problem to her teacher.

Mary represents a fairly typical case of Down's syndrome, but there are many differences among the individuals in this group, as in all types of exceptionality. Some are brighter, and some are less well behaved than Mary, while just the opposite is true in other cases.

The following case of a child whose retardation is unrelated to organic causes presents a different view of mental retardation:

Carl is a ten-year-old boy with an IQ of 65. He comes from a rural environment where he has recently learned to help his father with some of the farm chores. He rides to school each day on a regular school bus and seems to have many friends. He is particularly popular during baseball season, as he is one of the best pitchers in the class. No one ever suggested that Carl might be mentally retarded until he encountered considerable difficulty in the first and second grades. By the second grade, Carl had not learned to read beyond the primer level. When he was tested, he was diagnosed as educable mentally retarded by the school psychologist. At the school's request, Carl had been given a complete examination by a physician during the same year and was found to have no physical problems.

Now, at the age of ten, Carl reads at the second-grade level and has begun to master basic arithmetic skills. He learns much slower than other children in his class, but he shows notice-able progress nonetheless. Carl is a well-behaved young man, but many of the other students in his resource room for educable retarded children are disruptive.

VERY EARLY CHILDHOOD EDUCATION FOR EXCEPTIONAL CHILDREN IN SEATTLE

In Seattle, Washington, a group of educators (Hayden & Haring, 1975) and parents have started an educational program for educable and trainable retarded children that begins in early infancy. As early as it can be diag-nosed, children with a congenital form of retardation resulting from chromosome damage called Down's syndrome, or mon-golism, are enrolled in the special program. The program is situated in the Experimental Education Unit of the University of Wash-ington Child Development and Mental Re-tardation Center and is designed to stimulate and encourage educational and adaptive development using methods consistent with this textbook.

Before six months of age, the infants at-tend only one half-hour infant-mother in-struction session at the center, but the amount of involvement is gradually in-creased until the children are attending a full-time preschool program. By the time these children enter the first grade, they are significantly ahead of similar children who were not in the program. The results have prompted the spread of early intervention programs throughout the country in recent years.

There are many children like Carl in the schools. His hypothetical case paints a pic-ture of an individual who seems normal, has no physical handicaps, and is learning to perform useful tasks both inside and outside the classroom. Many other educable retarded children are less intelligent, however, and less well behaved.

Teaching mentally retarded children.
Teachers of regular classes rarely come into contact with children below the educable mentally retarded level. This is partly be-cause the impairments and deficits of train-able-level children are almost always obvious to parents and professionals before school age, and because they generally require help in special classrooms or sometimes in resi-dential institutions. Nearly all educable men-tally retarded children, on the other hand, start the first grade in regular classrooms, with many such children not being separated from regular classes until later grades. More-over, as will be discussed below, children who have been identified as educable men-tally retarded frequently spend some or most of their school day in regular classrooms.

For this reason, it is important that regular classroom teachers be aware of the charac-teristics and methods of teaching of educa-ble mentally retarded children. This is a criti-cal issue, but if you expect to be taught something profound and complicated at this point, you will be quite disappointed. On the contrary, what we hope to accomplish in

this chapter is to "debunk" diagnostic labels so that regular classroom teachers will not be misled by them. As common sense dictates, teachers should ask for the opinions of other professionals *whenever* a child behaves quite differently from other children in the classroom, but the more you learn about educable retarded children, the more you will see that they are more like other children than they are *different* from them. Educable mentally retarded children learn exactly like other children, except that it is *particularly* important to teach your slowest learners in the best ways possible. If the conditions for learning are good, even slow-learning children will learn a great deal. If the conditions for learning are poor, on the other hand, your good learners will continue to learn at a slow pace, but your slowest children may not learn anything at all. And, as we will discuss in the next chapter, your discipline skills may need to be a bit more sophisticated with these students.

Behaviorally/Emotionally Disturbed Children

For all the problems inherent in using the term *mental retardation*, the diagnostic category **behavioral** or **emotional disturbance** is even less precise. In theory, this category

includes children whose intelligence is normal, but whose behavior and learning in the classroom is deviant due to underlying emotional problems. In attempting to determine whether to diagnose an individual as mentally retarded, the professional has an inadequate guideline in the intelligence test, but at least it provides some degree of objectivity. No widely accepted objective measure of behavioral/emotional disturbance exists at all; it is strictly a matter of professional judgment. As a result, the kinds of problem behaviors exhibited by children who are identified as emotionally disturbed

differ widely from one school system to another. Again, the range in this diagnostic category is enormous. At the higher levels the children simply do not pay attention, do not complete their work, or make a lot of noise. At the lower end of the continuum, there are children whose behavior is so grossly deviant that they must be hospitalized. But, as in mental retardation, the greatest majority of children who are placed in this category have the least severe problems.

Originally, the term most frequently used for this diagnostic category was *emotional disturbance*. More recently, however, professionals who did not want to drop this term altogether, but who had become concerned with the difficulties inherent in deciding whether a child has problems with his or her "emotions," have adopted the term *behavioral disturbance* for this diagnostic category. Both terms, therefore, are widely used.

Again, we will describe some hypothetical cases to give more meaning to the diagnostic labels:

Carolyn was placed in a self-contained classroom for "behaviorally disturbed" children when she was thirteen years old. She was held back when she was in the third grade and has a general history of poor academic achievement. Her tested IQ is 102, and her teachers have never noticed any problems with learning except a lack of "interest and attention." Her school records are filled with comments about her poor conduct and misbehavior, but she was first brought to the attention of the school psychologist when she began having temper tantrums in the classroom. When she was twelve years old, she got into several fights on the school grounds with other girls, and by the time she was thirteen, this had become a regular occurrence. She frequently refused to follow the teacher's instructions and on several occasions tore up her work and refused to do anything for the entire day. She has only a few friends who are generally regarded as troublemakers by the school administration. She appears to come from a solid middle-class family, but the school officials have been able to learn little about her home life because her parents have never kept their appointments for parent-teacher conferences. She completes the majority of her schoolwork and is making progress, but much more slowly than the teachers feel she could do if she tried.

Calvin is an extremely quiet boy. He is fifteen years old and has been in a class for the "emotionally disturbed" for a year. His grades have always been mediocre, in spite of a tested IQ of 115. He has no history of causing problems in the classroom, but in recent years has seemed to become increasingly sad and to have less contact with other students. He is painfully thin and unattractive, and seems to participate in no student activities at all. When the school psychologist asked him how things were going for him, he stated that everything was fine, but showed little emotion in his statements. He has little family life, as his father left the family when he was young and his mother works at night.

These hypothetical cases give you some flavor of what behaviorally/emotionally disturbed children are like, but, again, the variability among children assigned to this and all categories of exceptionality is tremendous. The primary role of the teacher is to encourage appropriate rule following and social behavior in these children. Specific procedures for doing this will be discussed in the next chapter, but they amount only to applications of the principles of learning and motivation described in Chapters 5 and 9. In addition, many children classified as behaviorally/emotionally disturbed also have serious learning problems. This means that excellent teaching will also be required. The methods of teaching and discipline required for these children, however, do not differ fundamentally from those required for normal children. But it is more important that exceptional children receive *excellent* instruction. If they receive appropriate teaching and discipline, the behavior of the majority of exceptional children with less serious problems will not differ significantly from normal children, and those with serious problems will be far more normal.

Learning Disabilities

Since the early 1960s, a new diagnostic category has come into wide use in school systems. **Learning disabled** children have serious problems in one or more areas of academic learning, but have basically normal overall intelligence. They do not have behavioral/emotional problems which can be viewed as the cause of their academic problems, have no serious physical handicaps which might interfere with learning, and do not come from seriously deprived backgrounds. They are, therefore, "normal" children who have serious problems with academic learning. Much has been written about these types of problems recently, and there are almost as many theories as there are books and articles about them. Most specialists in this area, however, suggest that the learning problems are due to some *specific* rather than global problem of intellectual functioning, such as disorders of visual or auditory perception, attention span, or activity level.

Joy is the eight-year-old daughter of a prominent family. She is a pretty, friendly, and well-liked child whose overall IQ score is 110. She scored poorly on some of the subtests, however, particularly those that involved visual perception and fine motor coordination. She writes almost all her letters in right-to-left sequence and backwards. When she tries to read, she frequently confuses letters like b, p, d, and q, and sometimes seems to read words backwards. She does well in school subjects that do not require reading, but has not progressed beyond the first-grade level in that subject. Lately, her attitude towards school has become poor and she has begun making negative remarks about her ability.

Many different recommendations for dealing with such problems have been proposed, but it seems that the most productive strategy for teachers to follow is the same as mentioned above. Seek advice whenever children seem to be learning much less well than their peers, and deal with slow learners by improving the conditions of learning.

Rex is a ten-year-old boy who has been scheduled to see the learning disability resource teacher once a day. His IQ is 95 and he has no serious physical or behavior problems. He is a bit more active than most other children, and is reported to have been extremely active when in the first and second grade. His reading, writing, and science achievement are a little below grade level, but his academic progress would not be a serious source of concern were it not for his first-grade skill level in mathematics. He seems to have no interest at all in this subject and forgets almost everything he has been taught within a few minutes. Rex can be taught math in much the same way as other children, in spite of his past failures. He may require extra attention and patience, his learning experiences may need to be more carefully programmed, and his positive reinforcers may need to be more powerful, but he is capable of learning math in a fairly normal way.

Physical Handicaps

We have spoken thus far about psychological and educational handicaps. There are also, of course, many children who have serious problems in school learning because of their physical limitations. This group includes children with problems of motor control, such as children who are partially paralyzed or spastic, and children who have sensory deficits, particularly in hearing and vision. Decisions as to how to educate these children should be made in close liaison

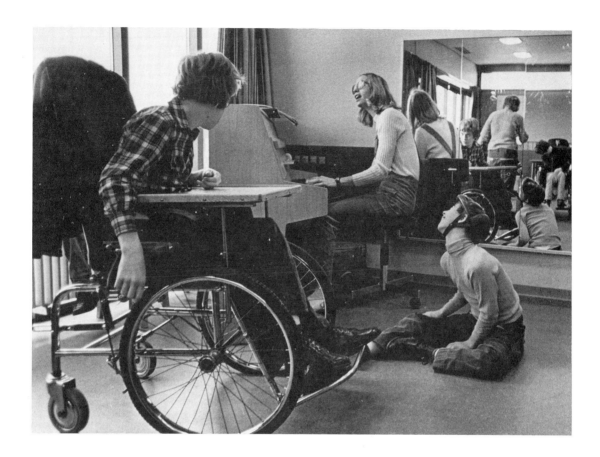

with the resource persons responsible for their education. Each pattern of physical handicap has its own special educational needs. Teachers and children can contribute greatly to the adjustment of these children, however, by offering them an atmosphere of acceptance of their strengths, rather than rejection of their weaknesses.

The Meaning of Related Diagnostic Terms

Although the four categories listed above are the major diagnostic categories used in schools, there are many other diagnostic labels that you will encounter and will need to know something about. Some of the most frequently encountered terms are discussed in the remainder of this section.

Hyperactivity/hyperkinesis.   These terms are used to refer to children who have very high activity levels and short attention spans.

A SIMPLE METHOD FOR DEALING WITH "PERCEPTUAL-MOTOR" DISORDERS

A substantial number of children diagnosed as learning disabled and mentally retarded have severe problems in handwriting and other fine visual-motor skills. Figure 12–3 shows handwriting samples of an eleven-year-old learning disabled boy with pronounced problems in handwriting who was treated by one of the authors and his associates (Lahey, Busemeyer, O'Hara, & Beggs, 1977). The samples in the extreme left-hand panel of the figure show his attempts to copy simple words. This performance was typical of his handwriting in the classroom in spite of the fact that he was in the fifth grade. The handwriting samples in the next panel were taken when he was being reinforced with pennies and praise for completely correct words, during which time over 80 percent of his words were legibly printed. The samples in the next two panels were obtained in phases when reinforcement was discontinued and then reinstituted. Similarly striking results were found for three other children in this study, and

two others in another study (Lahey & Dotts, 1976). In these cases, what appeared to be an extremely complex and difficult problem was easily treated using a simple motivational technique. If you want to encourage the occurrence of any behavior, reinforce it.

Figure 12–3. *Handwriting and positive reinforcement. (From Lahey, Busemeyer, O'Hara, & Beggs, 1977)*

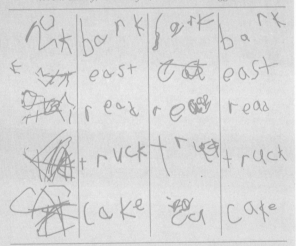

In this sense, activity means jumping from one activity to another, having a very brief attention span, constantly moving and fidgeting, never wanting to rest or take a nap, and so on. This is a diagnostic term that has been much abused. The obvious problem with it is in determining how much activity is abnormal. Children do not come in two kinds, those that have normal activity and those that are hyperactive; rather, activity levels

vary along a continuum. It is extremely difficult, therefore, to know when a child's activity level is excessive.

There have been several scandals in recent years in which 50 percent or more of the children in some school systems have been found to be on medication for "hyperactivity." This is obviously inappropriate. It is unnecessary, however, to decide whether a child should be labeled hyperactive in order to decide to do something about his or her activity level. Whenever a child's level of activity interferes to any significant degree with the goals of the classroom, the teacher could try reducing the activity by reinforcing behavior that is incompatible with those distracting activities. An excellent experimental example of this procedure will be discussed in the next chapter.

Minimal brain dysfunction.   Children who have learning or behavior problems and who show some signs of neurological dysfunction are often labeled as having a **minimal brain dysfunction.** This means that the diagnoser believes the child has some minor functional disorder of the nervous system, even though there is insufficient evidence to warrant a diagnosis of brain damage. Children who are diagnosed as learning disabled or who are considered hyperactive are particularly likely to be placed in this category. This is a controversial term, as many professionals feel that the equivocal signs of neurological dysfunction used in this diagnosis are too unreliable to warrant such a speculation. Individuals who feel that minor dysfunctioning of the brain is a major cause of learning and behavior problems, however, defend the necessity of the term. The teacher need not become involved in this controversy, however, but should, as in the case of *any* child, determine the specific learning characteristics of each individual child and develop appropriate learning conditions.

Dyslexia.   The root words of the term *dyslexia* literally mean "poor reading." This is an alternative diagnosis used for children

who meet the criteria for learning disabilities and whose primary academic deficit is in reading. As with any child, the solution to this problem is simply (we are aware that is not always a *simple* matter) to teach them to read in a more effective way.

Autism.   Autism or childhood psychosis is a term that refers to extremely deviant children. The label is most frequently given to children who have many of the following characteristics: lack of language, a seemingly lack of interest in being with other individuals, a lack of responsiveness to praise from other individuals, and a tendency to spend a great deal of time in activities that seem to serve no purpose except self-stimulation (rocking back and forth, twirling objects, etc.). Autistic children also may engage in frequent temper tantrums and self-injurious behavior such as scratching or biting themselves. These problems are also common among lower-level retarded individuals, however.

NONCATEGORICAL EDUCATION
FOR EXCEPTIONAL CHILDREN

We have discussed above the principal diagnostic categories used in the medical model for the diagnosis of school-age individuals. It is worth pointing out again that because these categories were discussed does not mean that they actually "exist." When we sort fruit into different categories, we can be pretty sure that types of fruit such as apples and oranges exist, but when we are given the job of classifying children, we should not hastily conclude that there is such a "thing" as an emotionally disturbed or mentally retarded child. There is no question that their *problems* exist, but do we need to *classify* children in order to deal with them? A sizeable segment of psychologists and educators answer *no*. They do so for three reasons.

First, diagnostic labels often have a negative effect on the life of the child. As we strongly pointed out above, each diagnostic category contains a very broad range of individuals. Although each individual is unique in his or her behavioral characteristics, diagnostic labels create stereotyped expectations as to how an individual will behave. These can frequently have negative consequences. For example, an individual who functions at a high level of competence, but whose IQ barely places him or her in the category of mental retardation, might not be employed if a potential employer learns of this diagnosis. That employer might already employ many individuals who are less capable, but the employer's interpretation of the meaning of the term retardation could color his or her perceptions of this individual. In the same way, children who are diagnosed as emotionally disturbed because they are

unusually loud and obstreperous might lead teachers into "humoring" them and letting them get away with inappropriate behavior. The term suggests that the child is "insane" whereas he or she may simply be hard to manage.

Guidelines for these categories are frequently vague, making it difficult in many cases to decide which label to assign to an individual. In a case, for example, where a child shows characteristics of both learning disabilities and behavioral/emotional disturbance, the expectations created by applying one of these labels would differ sharply from those created by giving the child the other. In summary, then, the use of diagnostic labels often detracts from our understanding of each individual as a unique person.

A second objection to the use of diagnostic labels is a pragmatic one. Children are typically grouped for part or all of the school day according to their diagnostic classification. Most schools, for example, have separate resource rooms or classes for mentally retarded, behavioral/emotional disturbance, and learning disabilities. This is based on an assumption of the medical model approach that because each group of children is believed to share common "disorders," they will benefit from the same types of special programs. In practice, however, this does not seem to be the case. Not only do the children within one diagnostic category differ greatly from one another, but the categories overlap. For example, children whose primary problem seems to be inattentiveness will be found in all three diagnostic categories. The same is true of problems in reading, visual discrimination, interpersonal behavior, and so on.

MAINSTREAMING: THE MADISON SCHOOL PLAN

Frank M. Hewett, professor of special education and psychiatry at the University of California at Los Angeles, has worked for several years on the development of a model special education program in a public school. The program, known as the Madison School Plan (Hewett & Forness, 1974), utilizes a structured approach to instruction similar to the one described in this text, and emphasizes three basic premises of the mainstreaming approach to special education.

1. Almost all exceptional children can benefit from placement in the regular school program during some part of the school day.

2. Exceptional children should be segregated and grouped together *only* for instructional purposes. That is, children with problems in arithmetic should be briefly grouped together for special instruction in that subject, but only for as much time as necessary.

3. When exceptional children are grouped for special instruction, it should be only on the basis of what academic subject they need help in rather than on the diagnostic label ("mental retardation," "learning disabled," etc.) they have been assigned.

This highly successful model program has been a major factor in the elimination of total segregation of exceptional children and in the growing disinterest in diagnostic labeling.

For this reason, it has been proposed (Hewett & Forness, 1974) that when children are grouped, they should be *grouped according to the kind of special teaching they need.* Children who need extra help in developing fine motor skills for handwriting could be grouped for this type of instruction during some part of the day, but it should make no difference which diagnostic label each child had been given. Part of this recommendation involves an empirical question: Do children from different diagnostic labels who have the same problem react in the same way to remedial procedures? Research indicates that they do. This approach to exceptional child education has been called the "noncategorical" approach. It recommends that children not be categorized into medical model classifications, but should only be grouped for short periods of time for instructional purposes. This is a relatively new approach, but one that has received considerable and growing support from educators and psychologists.

As mentioned before, the third possible disadvantage of diagnostic labels is that they can lead teachers to believe that nothing can be done to help their exceptional students. Exceptional children can learn, too.

MAINSTREAM EDUCATION FOR EXCEPTIONAL CHILDREN

There is another controversial development in the education of exceptional children closely related to the noncategorical approach, which has been termed *mainstreaming.* Individuals who voice opinions under this banner object to the segregation of exceptional children into self-contained class-rooms. They believe that when school systems provide special help to exceptional children by providing them with special classrooms and teachers, they inadvertently do more harm than good. By taking these children away from contact with average children, the exceptional children are deprived of social contact and intellectual stimulation, and society is harmed by depriving normal children of the opportunity to learn to live with people with handicaps.

For this reason, mainstreamers propose that exceptional children should be kept out of self-contained classrooms and be given special assistance in other ways. The primary alternative is the use of *resource rooms*. Resource rooms are staffed by exceptional-child teachers who are trained in providing help for special problems. Exceptional children would spend most of their school day in regular classrooms with their average peers, but would be scheduled in the resource room on a regular basis to receive special help. This concept has been widely adopted in recent years and promises to be the dominant strategy of the 1970s and 1980s.

The resource room concept has many advantages, but it is also subject to a special kind of abuse. School systems are required by law in many states to provide special educational services for all children who are in need of them. They rarely receive enough funds to do this in an adequate way, however. As a result, school systems sometimes meet the letter of the law by scheduling children to meet with the resource teacher two or three hours per week, when they need to receive special assistance two or three hours per day. The number of school systems that

do this out of an intentional desire to short-change exceptional children is small, but it is a situation that exists nonetheless. The mainstreaming concept also has special implications for regular classroom teachers. The most obvious one is the necessity for you to learn to provide adequate educational experiences to a broader range of people. This is both a problem and an opportunity for you. It is a problem in that, almost by definition, children with learning problems are more difficult to teach. It offers you the opportunity, however, to teach yourself and your students how to accept the differences among individuals.

AN OVERVIEW OF THE TEACHER'S ROLE

Children are placed in special educational programs because their learning or behavior is deficient compared to other children. This means that they have not benefited from the teaching and discipline of their teachers as much as other children. This state of affairs should not lead you to believe that exceptional children need something *other* than effective teaching and discipline. In nearly all cases, a pill from a physician or counseling from a psychologist will not "cure" their problems. While medical and psychological consultation may be useful in some cases, the greatest educational need of exceptional children is *excellent teaching and discipline*. At the risk of being repetitious, we will make the important point once more that the approach to instruction described in this book represents an effective way of improving classroom instruction.

FULL-SCALE EDUCATIONAL PROGRAMS FOR BEHAVIORALLY DISTURBED AND LEARNING DISABLED CHILDREN

This text has described a number of principles and procedures that you can use to improve the learning of both normal and exceptional children. Several large-scale experiments have been conducted to evaluate the effectiveness of classrooms organized around these principles. Herbert Quay and his associates, for example, conducted a major study of the education of behaviorally disordered children in Philadelphia which suggests that even children with serious behavioral handicaps can learn effectively (Quay, Glavin, Annesley, & Werry, 1972).

Quay and his associates helped the teachers of three special education classrooms design optimal teaching and discipline programs. Two of the three experimental classrooms contained predominantly white children, while the third contained predominantly black children, but all the sixty-nine children were classified as behaviorally/emotionally disturbed. The children were ten years old on the average, came from a variety of economical levels, and most often exhibited problems of aggression and overactivity. A group of forty-eight children with similar behavior problems served as controls. They were placed in three similar special education classrooms that did not receive consultation from the experimenters.

The nine-month instructional program for the experimental classrooms embodied nearly all of the principles described in this text, but its core features were individualization of instructional objectives and positive reinforcement for correct academic work. These features were less evident in the control classrooms. It is important to note that even though the researchers helped the teachers design the program, they played no part in its day-to-day activities. The instructional programs were conducted by the teachers themselves under typical conditions for classrooms of this type.

The results of the study measured at the end of the nine months strongly favored the experimental classrooms. The mean gain in achievement on the California Achievement Test was .99 years (1.0 is the national average), whereas the gain for the control group was .59. This means that the behaviorally disturbed children in the experimental classrooms learned at a "normal" rate for the first time in their lives, while the control children continued in their pattern of learning about half of what they are supposed to learn each year and consequently falling farther behind their normal peers.

Similar results have been found for experimental programs for learning disabled children by Norris Haring and his colleagues at the University of Washington (Haring & Hauck, 1969; Nolen, Kunzelmann, & Haring, 1967). They found achievement gains of over one year in a group of learning disabled children whose previous achievement had been less than one-half year per school year.

The principles of instruction discussed in this book, therefore, are important to the teaching of both normal and exceptional children. It is even more important to understand the way people learn to teach exceptional learners, as productive learning can only occur in these individuals when the conditions of learning have been maximized.

REVIEW 12–2

1. What two factors are used in the diagnosis of mental retardation?

2. How would a school psychologist determine whether to label a child mentally retarded or learning disabled?

3. Why is it said that diagnostic categories are "heterogeneous"?

4. What are three objections to the use of diagnostic labels?

5. What does noncategorical special education mean?

6. What are the implications of the mainstreaming concept for the teacher, the child, and society?

7. In what ways should the teaching and discipline of exceptional and normal children differ?

SUMMARY

Teachers in average classrooms play an essential role in both the identification and teaching of exceptional children. We have defined exceptional children as those who are markedly deviant (different) from others in ways that are maladaptive for the individual or society, and have discussed three ways of viewing exceptionality. The medical model sees abnormal behavior as resulting from underlying mental disturbances, while the behavioral model suggests we deal directly with the deviant behavior. The humanistic model sees exceptionality as resulting from problems in individuals' unique attempts to cope with the world as they see it. It cautions us to at least consider changing the world to accept "different" individuals in addition to changing individuals to fit the world. The behavioral model seeks to find ways of directly changing the deviant behavior that led to the label of exceptionality.

Because the medical model is dominant today, the major diagnostic labels were discussed. The term *mental retardation* refers to individuals whose IQ is markedly below average and who show deficits in adaptive behavior. Behavioral/emotional disturbance refers to individuals with deviant behavior, but who generally show satisfactory intelligence. Learning disabled children have normal overall scores on IQ tests, no physical handicaps, no serious emotional/behavioral problems, and yet have serious problems with one or more areas of school learning. Physically handicapped children have physical conditions such as paralysis or blindness that interfere with learning.

Alternatives to self-contained classrooms based on the medical model are found in both the noncategorical and mainstreaming concepts. Recently it has been suggested that exceptional children should not be diagnosed at all, should be kept with average children as much as possible, and should only be grouped separately for instructional purposes. The opposition to diagnosis comes from the tendency of individuals to misunderstand the meaning of the terms and to have stereotyped expectations for children with certain labels, and because grouping by instructional needs may be more useful.

ANSWERS TO REVIEW QUESTIONS

Review 12–1

1. Exceptionality is defined as characteristics of an individual that deviate markedly from the norm and are maladaptive for that individual or for members of society.

2. Benedict makes the point that exceptionality is relative. What is normal in one culture may be considered abnormal in another.

3. The three models of exceptionality discussed in this book are the medical, the behavioral, and the humanistic models.

4. The medical model views maladaptive behavior as a symptom of an underlying illness of the mind that must be treated indirectly; whereas the behavioral model views maladaptive behavior as the problem itself and seeks to find ways to change it directly.

5. The main thrust of the humanistic model is to recommend that we respect the differences in people and be less ready to label individuals as "mentally ill" simply because they are different.

Review 12–2

1. Mental retardation is defined in terms of deficits in both measured intelligence and general adaptive behavior.

2. Children diagnosed as learning disabled differ from those diagnosed as mentally retarded primarily because learning disabled children score in the normal or high range on IQ tests.

3. All diagnostic categories are heterogeneous in the sense that each one contains children who have a variety of different problems. They often share some common characteristics, but are not alike.

4. Three objections to the use of diagnostic labels with children are:

(a) They often create negative expectations about the child.

(b) They lead to grouping the children into classrooms according to labels rather than to their actual educational needs.

(c) They sometimes lead teachers to believe they cannot help these children.

5. Noncategorical special education is an approach that advocates not giving children diagnostic labels, but rather giving them special educational help according to their individual needs.

6. The mainstreaming approach recommends the placement of exceptional children in regular classrooms, except when they need to be temporarily regrouped into special classes on the basis of their special needs. It is hoped that this approach will result in better learning and increased tolerance and appreciation for individual differences.

7. Teaching and discipline procedures for exceptional children should generally be the same as for normal children. In some cases, however, more powerful discipline procedures may be necessary, learning experiences may need to be programmed in smaller steps, and special methods for dealing with specific problems may have to be devised based on the principles of instruction.

Chapter 13

Discipline and the Encouragement of Learning

Discipline and Positive Reinforcement
Some Guidelines for Discipline Using Reinforcement

Self-Control and Related Methods
Self-Instruction
Self-Recording
Daily Report Cards

Methods of Discipline for Serious Misbehaviors
Quiet Corners, Loss of Reinforcement, and Punishment
Using Free Time as Reinforcement
Token Economies

Special Methods for Special Problems
Truancy
School Phobias

Peer Tutoring as an Aid to Teaching and Discipline

Summary

One of the major concerns of beginning teachers is discipline. Although many of your experiences with children have been positive (or you probably would not have chosen teaching as your profession), you no doubt have also known some big and little "monsters." Are there thoughts lurking in your head that you might not be able to handle the ones in your first classroom? Disciplining disruptive students can be a serious problem, but it need not be a stumbling block. If you apply a few of the principles that you have learned very thoroughly by this point to your discipline practices, you can reduce considerably the amount of problem behavior that you cannot successfully deal with.

The origins of discipline problems are varied and complex. Parents sometimes model aggressive and other forms of inappropriate behavior, reinforce their children's coercive demands by giving in to them, or in many other ways "teach" their children inappropriate behavior. In addition, peer groups often encourage rule breaking, and the general tenor of our society, especially as reflected in television, motion pictures, and "comic" book content, may contribute to a mood of aggression and defiance.

Fortunately, it is not necessary to be able to deal with the origins of misbehavior in order to redirect it in constructive ways. If you use appropriate and effective discipline procedures, these methods will usually produce appropriate behavior in the classroom, even if some students will continue to misbehave outside of it. In some cases, however, your ability to help a child will be greatly enhanced if you are able to work with school psychologists, counselors, and social workers in a team approach that involves both the school and the family. In any case,

the most important element in encouraging effective behavior in the classroom is the classroom discipline program of the teacher.

DISCIPLINE AND POSITIVE REINFORCEMENT

"What rules should I set for my classroom and how will I enforce them?" Recall the goals of teaching mentioned in Chapter 1 before attempting to answer this question: *Teachers should strive to make learning meaningful, efficient, and joyful.* Rules that regiment children without adding to learning, therefore, should be carefully scrutinized and publicly discussed before you implement them. For example, if children are learning well, does it matter that some quiet talking is going on and that some children are working on the floor? Adopt the rules that you and your community feel comfortable with, but do not automatically adopt the rules you followed as a child. A *minimum* number of flexible rules will probably work best. On the other hand, consistent and firm (but not harsh) enforcement of some rules that prohibit violence or state that assignments must be completed at a given level of accuracy prior to enrichment activities seems essential. But effective classroom discipline involves more than just the enforcement of rules; maintaining student interest, building positive relationships with students, and arranging classroom environment to promote orderly behavior are all aspects of good discipline methods (Gnagy, 1975). Still, the enforcement of an appropriate set of rules is the heart of any discipline program.

How then should you enforce your rules? Two general principles provide important guidelines:

(1.) Just as it is a good idea to have a small number of simple, sensible rules, you should use the least powerful method of discipline. There are some classes that can be managed quite well with a lot of praise and an occasional gentle reprimand. It would be unwise to use a complicated system of token reinforcement or physical punishment with such classes.

(2.) Manage behavior as much as possible by telling your students what you expect of them, by encouraging them to behave appropriately, by modeling appropriate and effective behavior, and by using positive reinforcement for appropriate behavior (children cannot be ''bad'' while they are being ''good''). Use punishment and loss of reinforcement procedures for inappropriate behavior only as a last resort. It is far more effective (and far more enjoyable from the point of view of both the student and the teacher) to take a positive approach to discipline—and that means using the resources at your disposal to *increase* appropriate behavior.

There are a number of old as well as recently developed ways to do this, but they all carry an important caution. The irony of this and all other books about instruction is that you cannot simply read about effective teaching and discipline and then automatically become an excellent teacher. With some pluck and effort, you *can* and *will* develop expertise, but it takes more than just reading about it. A good analogy is driving a car. Driving is a relatively easy task, but would you let a person who has never seen a car, drive yours after just reading a book about driving? Similarly, your development of effective teaching skills will require observation of good teaching, consultation with others, and, most importantly, trial and error. The reason for our making this point is this: If you try the methods described in this or any other book and they fail, seek additional guidance before you decide that the methods themselves do not work. There are many discipline methods that will work for teachers and students, but it may take time for you to perfect them.

Some Guidelines for Discipline Using Reinforcement

The following guidelines describe some effective, positive ways of encouraging appropriate general behavior in your students.

Tell students in clear terms what you expect of them.   Be *explicit and clear* in communicating your rules and expectations to your students. As in the case of instructional objectives, be sure you phrase these in terms of positively stated *specific actions* on the part of the students. Say, ''Please talk quietly,'' rather than vague statements such as, ''Please do not interfere with the learning atmosphere,'' or ''Do not show a lack of respect for others.'' As mentioned before, it also helps to involve the children in a democratic selection of the rules.

Use positive reinforcement for appropriate behavior.   Show your approval of good conduct and good academic performance by giving strong descriptive praise (''That's terrific!'', or ''You really are good at math!''),

ELEMENTS OF EFFECTIVE CLASSROOM DISCIPLINE

Charles Madsen, Wesley Becker, and Don Thomas were among the first researchers to systematically study methods of classroom discipline. Their studies have had a strong influence on this text, particularly on our advocacy of clearly specified rules for behavior, positive reinforcement of appropriate behavior, and nonreinforcement (ignoring) of inappropriate behavior. One of their most interesting experiments (Madsen, Becker, & Thomas, 1968) demonstrates the effectiveness of these elements, but shows clearly that they will only work in *combination*.

Following a baseline period of observing the normal behavior of a class of second-grade children, the teacher gave the class a list of specific rules of behavior. These consisted of a few simple rules of conduct stated in positive terms ("Sit quietly when working," instead of, "Don't talk to your neighbors."); the teacher went over these rules several times to make sure that the students understood them. After a few days, the teacher began ignoring misbehaviors such as talking out or being out of seat, in-

stead of criticizing them. Then, after two weeks of ignoring, the teacher combined rules and ignoring with praise for good behavior. As Figure 13–1 shows, rules and ignoring alone had no effect on misbehavior, but the combination of rules, ignoring, and praise resulted in pronounced improvements.

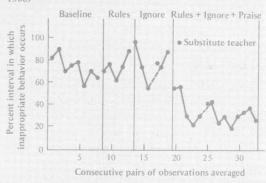

Figure 13–1. *The inappropriate behavior of a problem child in a class in which rules and ignoring were used separately and in combination with praise for appropriate behavior. (From Madsen, Becker, & Thomas, 1968)*

but remember to give it only when your students are doing what they should. Do not give lavish praise to a student who has just goofed off to "encourage" her. It may have just the opposite effect.

Use shaping. Remember that you must adjust your expectations when you deal with different students. In deciding what to praise and encourage, ask yourself what you expect of *this* particular student. Some students' good behavior may be worse than the bad behavior of others. As your praise leads to improvement, you can raise your criteria for reinforcement.

√*Keep individual teacher-student contacts frequent, but brief.*   One major advantage of the instructional strategies suggested in this text is that they allow the teacher to spend less time lecturing and more time in individual contact with students. Unless you have an aid to take over your regular duties, however, you should keep these contacts brief. Researchers found that when teachers kept their contacts with individual students for at least fifty seconds the rest of the class engaged in much more off-task behavior than when they kept contacts below twenty seconds in duration (Scott & Bushell, 1974).

√*Make academic learning meaningful and exciting.*   The time-worn notion that good teaching reduces the need for discipline is true. If the students are *involved* in their academic work because it is inherently interesting, because it is presented in an exciting way, because it requires active participation (solving problems or working problems rather than just reading, memorizing, and listening), and because they are reinforced for doing it, they will have much less time for mischief. Similarly, if the students are making progress and are visibly successful, they will not experience the frustrations that can produce negative reactions.

A number of studies on the importance of "attention" for school learning provides an excellent case in point. Studies conducted on first- through sixth-graders find that academic achievement is highest for those children who most often *attend* (look at, orient to) to their work (Hops & Cobb, 1974; Lahaderne, 1968). Our informal experience suggests that the importance of attention continues through secondary levels as well. Clearly, then, a prime consideration for teachers is to get their students to pay attention.

The obvious strategy, then, is to make your assignments, lectures, and discussion interesting enough to grab the students' attention. But when you have made your best efforts, what about the large number of students who are still not paying as much attention as they should?

First, you could teach them to pay attention. You probably could, by now, design a fairly effective and usable method for reinforcing attending, but the old adage, "You can lead a horse to water, but you can't make him drink," has special meaning here. You can easily teach children to *look* at their work, but can you get them to *see* it? Will they learn anything? Research on teaching children to attend better suggests that improved attention often does *not* result in better learning (Ferritor, Buckholdt, Hamblin, & Smith, 1972).

But if all you really want the horse to do is drink, why bother to lead him to the water at all? If you teach the horse to drink, he will lead himself to the water. By the same token, why teach students to attend in order to learn, when we can directly teach them to learn? A study conducted in the Atlanta Public Schools (Ayllon & Roberts, 1974) illustrates this principle. The teacher of a group of fifth-grade children who rarely paid the slightest bit of attention to classroom tasks sought help from a consultant. Instead of suggesting that the teacher reinforce the children for sitting down, being quiet, and working on their assignments, the consultant recommended that the teacher reinforce the students only when they *accurately completed assignments*. This program resulted not only in improved academic performance, but also in a decrease in disruption. These results are shown in Figure 13–2. Children do

not necessarily learn better when they attend and behave better, but they do behave better when they learn better. Stated differently, the better you teach, the fewer discipline problems you will have.

SELF-CONTROL AND RELATED METHODS

Recently, a number of discipline procedures have been tried out that reduce the role played by teachers in the management of behavior and place that responsibility, instead, on the students themselves. While it is too early to tell how useful these procedures will be across a wide variety of classroom situations, they appear effective in the few situations in which they have been used. More importantly, the emphasis on self-control inherent in these approaches may well teach attitudes and skills to students that will be valuable in later life.

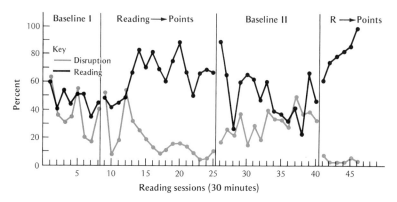

Figure 13–2. *The amount of disruption and of accuracy in reading workbooks when accurate reading answers were reinforced by token points. No reinforcement was given in the baseline phases, but was given during the points phases. (From Allyon & Roberts, 1974)*

WHAT SHALL I REINFORCE?

If you have effective positive reinforcers, you have the ability to increase the frequency of nearly any behavior that occurs in the classroom. When correctly applied, the principle of positive reinforcement is an obviously powerful tool for teachers. But which behaviors should you reinforce? Most children who create problems for themselves or others in school settings engage in a lot of disruptive behavior and spend little time studying. Our first tendency, therefore, is to reinforce students for attending to their assignments and not engaging in misbehaviors. A study conducted at the Central Midwestern Regional Educational Laboratory in Missouri, however, suggests that this is an ineffective strategy (Ferritor, Buckholdt, Hamblin, & Smith, 1972).

These researchers reinforced disadvantaged third-graders with tokens for attending to their arithmetic lessons instead of engaging in disruptive behavior and found increases in attending, decreases in disruption, but *no increases* in accuracy of arithmetic performance. The token reinforcement program made the children *look like* better students, but did not help them become better learners. Fortunately, Ayllon's studies discussed elsewhere in this chapter indicate that giving reinforcement for correct *academic behavior* results in both better learning and better behavior. That is where you should focus your efforts, with occasional discipline programs designed to deal with particularly difficult problem behaviors on a supplementary basis.

⟩ Self-Instruction

Bornstein and Quevillon (1976) of the University of Montana have suggested that children often behave inappropriately in the classroom because they do not "tell" themselves what to do. Well-behaved children, they theorize, have a set of rules that they repeat silently to guide their behavior. Working on this assumption, these psychologists set up an experimental program to help three preschool children who were described as "overactive," "disciplinary problems," and "out of control in the classroom."

Using typical classroom tasks, an adult trainer modeled appropriate behavior while saying aloud appropriate self-instructions such as, "What does the teacher want me to do here? Oh, that's right, I'm supposed to copy that picture. O.K., first I draw a line here . . ." Meanwhile, the students imitated the trainer. The students were first encouraged to give themselves overt self-instructions, but gradually the trainer and students spoke their self-instructions more softly until they were not being said at all.

Each child received instruction for two fifty-minute sessions. Sessions were given at different times to different students to allow an evaluation of their effects on behavior. Later, the three children were observed again in their regular classroom settings. As Figure 13–3 shows, pronounced improvements in on-task behavior resulted and were maintained over two months' time.

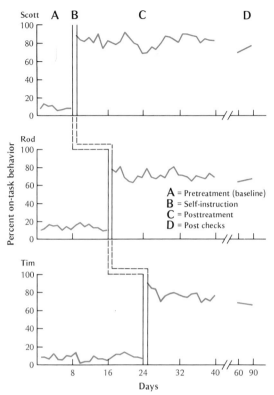

Figure 13–3. *Percent of time that three children were on-task before and after receiving "self-instruction" counseling. (From Bornstein & Quevillon, 1976)*

Self-Recording

Researchers in New Zealand have tested similar procedures for teaching children to manage their own behavior (Thomas, 1976). During mathematics exercises, the teacher of thirty-one second-graders asked her students to monitor their own attentiveness. When she gave a signal every two or three minutes, the children noted on a card whether they were on- or off-task. Independent observers found that (1) the children were accurate in their self-recording, and (2) their rate of on-task behavior increased dramatically when they recorded their own behavior. Such a procedure may not work with all children, but since it requires little effort from the teacher, it may be worth a try.

Daily Report Cards

Another recently developed discipline procedure that involves little direct interaction with students is the use of daily report cards. Although this method requires you to provide feedback on the student's behavior, considerable responsibility is placed on the student for self-management. This method has an added advantage in that it involves the parents in discipline matters. Daily report cards were recently tested by Lahey, Gendrich, Gendrich, Schnelle, Gant, and Mc-Nees (1976). After a baseline period, brief daily report cards were given to two kindergarten classes. In order to study the effects of the reports, they were introduced into one classroom several days before the other. Figure 13–4 shows that the amount of distracting behaviors dropped considerably when the reports were given at the end of each day. Marked improvements in appropriate behavior also resulted.

It may have occurred to you that we have no way of knowing if the children actually repeated their rules silently to themselves. This is so, but it does not really matter. We may not be able to know what, if anything, students are telling themselves, but the results of this experiment suggest that telling students to guide their own behavior in this manner was effective, for whatever the reasons.

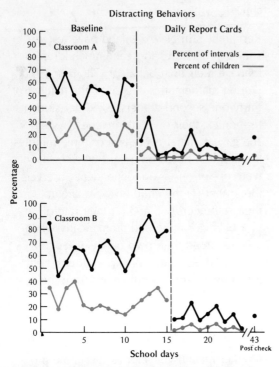

Figure 13–4. *Amount of distracting behavior in two classes of kindergarten children before and during the use of daily report cards. Data are presented for the percent of intervals in which at least one child was distracting, and for the percent of children who were engaged in distracting behavior. (From Lahey, Gendrich, Gendrich, Schnelle, Gant, & McNees, 1976)*

This method was as easy to use as it was effective. The daily report cards (shown in Figure 13–5) were easy to fill out and the teachers felt the extra work was well worth the effort. Several other teachers in the school, in fact, voluntarily adopted the procedure after hearing about it. Even though the parents received no special instructions on how to handle the reports at home, their reactions on a questionnaire also were very positive, and the great majority of parents

asked that the program be continued after the experiment ended. You would probably want to have some contact with parents to discuss the report cards, particularly to caution them not to use punishment for poor reports. The evidence is still tentative for this and the other self-control methods, so you will have to carefully monitor it to be certain that it is working in your classroom.

METHODS OF DISCIPLINE FOR SERIOUS MISBEHAVIORS

Most teachers of average children will be able to manage their classrooms and encourage effective learning by using only the procedures described above. But if you are teaching exceptional children or normal children who are poorly behaved or are significantly below grade level in academic achievement, you will need stronger methods. These are slightly more complicated and time consuming in the beginning, but once you successfully implement them, they will save you time, trouble, and headaches, and will benefit your students.

Quiet Corners, Loss of Reinforcement, and Punishment

Occasionally you will have to deal with a behavior problem that is either very persistent or very inappropriate. Your first efforts should be directed at eliminating this behavior by increasing the frequency of appropriate behavior; but if that fails, you will need to *also* use some method to directly reduce the frequency of the problem behavior (regardless of what procedure you use to eliminate an undesirable behavior, it is

BRADLEY BRAGS

Name _____ Date _____ Yes

1. Your child followed instructions well today. ....

2. Your child was a good rester today. ....

3. Your child fell asleep during rest period. ....

4. Your child completed all of his work today. ....

5. Your child got along with his classmates. ....

6. Something Happened Today!

7. We worked on this skill today!

Signed _____

Figure 13–5. *Sample daily report card used with kindergarten students. (From Lahey, Gendrich, Gendrich, Schnelle, Gant, & McNees, 1976)*

essential that you also continue to reinforce desirable behaviors to take its place).

You must be careful not to conclude that we recommend the use of *verbal* punishment, however. As we have said, some children will respond well to verbal reprimands, especially gentle ones (O'Leary, Kaufman, Kass, & Drabman, 1970), but most will not. In fact, as we cautioned in Chapter 5, reprimands are frequently reinforcing to students. Becker, Engelmann, and Thomas (1975) suggest that teachers who use verbal punishment frequently find themselves in a **criticism trap.** They begin the year by reprimanding and criticizing their students for a few inappropriate behaviors. Instead of eliminating these problem behaviors, however, the criticism serves to increase their frequency.

This leads the teacher to criticize the students more, which leads to even more inappropriate behavior, and so on. Verbal punishment encourages the very behavior it intends to eliminate.

One of the simplest and most effective procedures is to punish the behavior using the "quiet corner" or "timeout" procedure. This involves putting the student into a corner or a closed-off area every time the undesirable behavior occurs. For example, an aggressive student might be put in the corner for ten minutes after each and every episode of aggression. This will nearly always be effective if the teacher follows a few rules:

(1.) Be *consistent. Always* put the student in the corner after every episode of undesirable behavior.

(2.) Be *persistent.* The student may change slowly, or may even get worse before getting better. Students often seem to test your willingness to be firm. If you give in to them,

you will acknowledge that they lead and you follow. Your problems will just be beginning then.

(3.) Ignore the student while you are marching him or her to the timeout area. Do not scold, apologize for the punishment, plead for a cessation of hostilities, or say anything except "Go into the corner for ten minutes for doing— — —." Do not even make eye contact with the student. Avoid these actions so that you will not inadvertently reinforce the student's inappropriate behavior.

(4.) If the student misbehaves while in the timeout area, start the required time over. For instance, if the student yells out an obscenity after only three minutes in the corner, say that he or she will have to stay in for an additional period of time.

(5.) Tailor the punishment somewhat to fit the crime, but mostly to fit the student. Some students will be amply impressed by one minute in timeout, while ten minutes will be required to impress others. Keep in mind, also, that some students will be physically too *strong* to put into a timeout area and you will have to adopt other methods. Never start a program that you cannot carry through.

Another way of eliminating a behavior is to use the principle of loss of reinforcement. If the children are receiving token reinforcement (discussed below) or are earning free time, you can achieve good results if you deduct free time or tokens when rule infractions occur. The guidelines listed above for using the quiet corner/timeout technique apply here also.

Using Free Time as Reinforcement

Another way to have a strong impact on classroom behavior and achievement is to use reinforcers that are stronger than praise and approval. One effective reinforcer for most children is being allowed to engage in activities of their own choosing (within loose guidelines). For example, contingent upon good performance, students could be allowed to socialize quietly, to read supplementary materials, to play math games, or to listen to recorded music through earphones.

It is useful to have a separate "free-time area" in the classroom so that you can admit only children who have earned the privilege and limit their time in the area, but it is not necessary. An inexperienced, but innovative seventh-grade teacher used the following procedure with thirty-two inner-city disadvantaged youths (Long & Williams, 1973). The students were told that they would have eighteen minutes of free time as a group at the end of every math and geography period if they followed the classroom rules. Each rule infraction cost the entire class one minute, which the teacher recorded by flipping

over one card in a rotary file after each misbehavior. As a result, the general classroom behavior greatly improved. If academic learning is a problem in a class, the teacher could modify this system after general behavior improves so that the students could first *earn* the free time through completing assignments and scoring at criterion levels on quizzes. It is generally found that when free time is used as a reinforcer, the children accomplish much more in the time that is devoted to academics than if they work the entire period at a slower, less interested rate (Long & Williams, 1973).

REVIEW 13–1

1. How should a teacher set up classroom rules for behavior? How should they be enforced?

2. What are the five specific guidelines for discipline using positive reinforcement discussed in this chapter?

3. What are two alternatives to punishment that can be effectively used in the classroom? When should punishment be used? What must always be used with these procedures?

4. What is the relationship between attention and learning?

5. What is the "criticism trap"?

Token Economies

The strongest, and most complicated, system of reinforcement is token reinforcement. This involves giving the children poker chips, coupons, points, or other tokens that they can later trade for reinforcers. It will almost never be necessary to use a full token system with normal children who are achieving at close to grade level. Almost every educational goal can be accomplished using praise and positive reinforcement. But there are some exceptions, and these special problems will require special methods. The majority

of extreme discipline problems will arise with exceptional children, but they may be found in all classrooms to some extent. If your school system uses the mainstreaming concept, you will have at least partial responsibility for the education of exceptional children. What we have not told you, however, is that many students that your school psychologist feels should not be placed in a program for exceptional children may be

A SIMPLIFIED TOKEN REINFORCEMENT SYSTEM FOR REGULAR ELEMENTARY-SCHOOL CLASSROOMS

We have taken the position that teachers should use positive reinforcement in the most natural manner that will be effective with their children. For average children, this usually means the systematic use of social reinforcement (praise, interested comments, etc.), but some teachers will prefer a more structured system. A teacher of twenty-eight second-graders in Tampa, Florida, for example, adopted a simplified token economy for average children that avoids the artificiality often associated with such methods.

She assigned four categories of written work to be done daily between 9:00 and 11:30A.M. As soon as a student was finished with an assignment, the teacher checked the work at the student's desk. If 80 percent of the work was correct, the student was allowed to go to the teacher's desk and place one check mark next to his or her name. If the work was less than 80 percent correct, the teacher gave assistance as needed and required the student to rework the assignment until it reached criterion. At 11:30 A.M., students who had received all four check marks were allowed to engage in thirty minutes of free-time activities that included painting pictures, playing with clay, listening to records through earphones, and playing games such as "Lotto" (Rapport & Bostow, 1976). The effectiveness of this simple program is shown in Figure 13–6.

Figure 13–6. *Academic performance of one student in each of the four assignment areas each day. Tokens were in use in the second and fourth phases, but not during the first and third phases. (From Rapport & Bostow, 1976)*

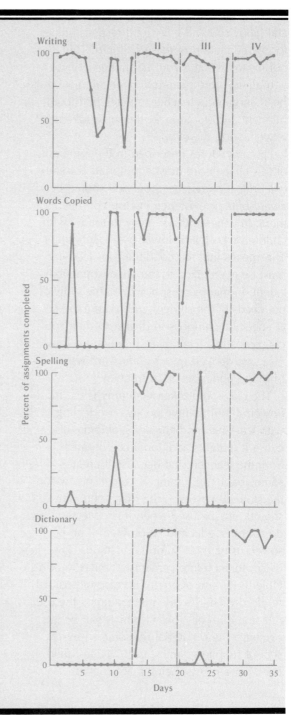

even worse than the ones that receive special help. You will have total responsibility for the education of these children. This is not meant to scare you, but rather to give you an accurate picture of your job. Like a heart surgeon, a teacher requires both commitment and stamina. By the same token, it is well worth the effort.

The procedures described in the remainder of this chapter are most appropriate for special education teachers, but you should be aware of their existence in case you need them. In general, the strategy to follow with children who learn slowly is to teach better. This means that the conditions for learning must be maximized to the greatest possible extent. In many cases, however, the individual needs of the student will require the use of special techniques to deal with their special problems. Even these procedures, however, are derived in straightforward ways from the principles of instruction.

The classroom **token economy** is the most powerful tool that we possess for dealing with learning and behavior problems. Because it requires additional commitment from the teacher, and because it creates somewhat of an "artificial" environment for the student, however, the token economy should only be used when it is necessary to do so. Most educational problems can be solved using more informal methods. The use of token reinforcement is similar in principle to the use of any other type of positive reinforcement. Its essential feature is the use of some form of "token" which can be later exchanged for material reinforcers (toys, school supplies, games) or privileges (field trips, extra recess, being team captain).

Psychologists Brian Iwata and Jon Bailey (1974) of Florida State University conducted a study with a teacher of a self-contained class for exceptional children. The fifteen students in the classroom had a mean age of ten years and a mean IQ of 70. The major problem of the children in this class was their extreme disruptive behavior and time spent off-task. Iwata and Bailey conducted the study during the daily forty-minute math class in which the students were assigned individualized work in math workbooks. For the first twenty-six days, the researchers observed the behavior and academic performance of the children. On the twenty-seventh day, the teacher reminded the children of the classroom rules and explained the token economy to the children. The rules included staying seated, raising hands to get assistance, not talking or disturbing other students, and going to the bathroom only when no one else was using it.

The teacher placed a cup on each student's desk and told the group that they could earn tokens if they obeyed the classroom rules and worked hard. They were told that they had to have at least six tokens in their cups by the end of the math period in order to earn a snack. The teacher also told the students that on "surprise days" the three or four students who had the most tokens since the last surprise day would earn a special bonus. This feature of the procedure emphasized the importance of earning as many tokens as possible on each day.

Every three to five minutes, as signaled by the timer, the teacher went around and gave a token to each child that she felt had behaved well. The children thus had an opportunity to earn a total of ten tokens during the forty-minute period. After five days, the

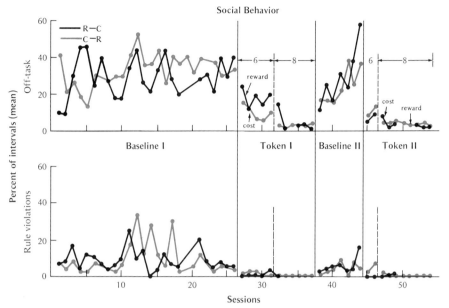

Figure 13–7.   *Rule violations and off-task behavior of children who were placed on a reward token system and then on a reward-cost (loss of reinforcement) token system (R-C), and a group of children who were placed on the same programs in reverse order (C-R). The shift from a criterion of six tokens to eight tokens needed to earn a reward is indicated by the vertical broken line in Token I and Token II. No reward program was in effect during the baseline phases. (From Iwata & Bailey, 1974)*

teacher raised the requirement for earning a snack to a total of eight tokens during the period. As Figures 13 – 7 and 13 – 8 show, the amount of time spent off-task and in rule violations dropped markedly with the introduction of the token system. The amount of off-task behavior dropped even further when the teacher raised the criterion for earning a snack to eight tokens. At the same time, the number of math problems completed in the workbooks rose considerably, while the percent correct remained between 80 and 90 percent.

When the token system was discontinued during Baseline II in order to be sure that it was the cause of the positive behavior changes, the time spent off-task and the number of rule violations increased again, while the amount of work completed dropped. During a second phase, the gains in appropriate behavior and academic output were again in evidence. As a sidelight, researchers found that the use of the token system slightly increased the frequency of positive remarks made by the teacher to the students. It would probably be unnecessary to rate the children's performance this frequently in most situations; rather, teachers could

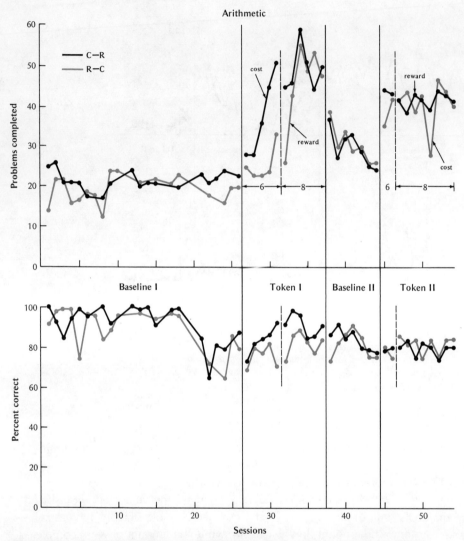

Figure 13–8. *Academic performance of children who were placed on a reward token system and then on a reward-cost (loss of reinforcement) token system (R-C), and a group of children who were placed on the same programs in reverse order (C-R). The shift from a criterion of six tokens to eight tokens is indicated by the vertical broken line in Token I and Token II. No reward program was in effect during the baseline phases. (From Iwata & Bailey, 1974)*

conduct a mini-experiment to determine the frequency of ratings required in their classrooms.

A study conducted by Teodoro Ayllon and his associates at Georgia State University (Ayllon, Layman, & Kandel, 1975) illustrates another important use of the token economy technique. These researchers were particularly interested in the behavior and academic performance of three children enrolled in an elementary learning disabilities classroom. They had been diagnosed as learning disabled and hyperactive and were currently receiving medication. Even though the medication (Ritalin) controlled their activity level to a great extent, they still exhibited serious learning problems. After several days of baseline in which their activity

levels and amount of academic performance were monitored during math and reading periods, their physicians stopped the medication. At this point, activity levels rose sharply. The teacher in the math class, however, began reinforcing the students for accurate performance in their math workbooks. This resulted in marked increases in correct academic performance and also resulted in a drop in activity to the level previously obtained through medication. Later, token reinforcement was given for accurate performance in reading with the same result. The results are shown in Figure 13–9. The effects of token reinforcement for academic performance on activity level is understandable if we consider that children must be reasonably still and attentive if they are to produce

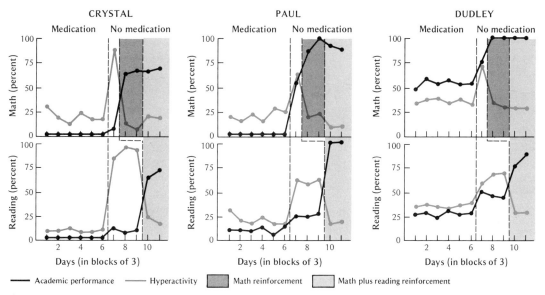

Figure 13–9. *Behavior and academic performance of three hyperactive learning disabled children. During the initial phase, all of the children received medication to control their hyperactivity, which was withdrawn in the second phase. The students were then reinforced for good work in a math workbook, and then reinforced for good work in a reading workbook. (From Allyon, Layman, & Kandel, 1975)*

accurate academic work. Similar results were found with children who were extremely disruptive, but who had less serious learning problems (Ayllon & Roberts, 1974).

SPECIAL METHODS FOR SPECIAL PROBLEMS

Even if you successfully adopt procedures that encourage learning and keep general behavior under control, you will most likely have to develop special methods to deal with special problems, particularly if you teach exceptional children. These methods are based on the principles of instruction which we have covered throughout this text, but it will take considerable expertise (and downright luck) to develop methods that will handle all the problems you will encounter. Short of gaining practical experience yourself, perhaps the best way to learn is to review some of the many ways which other educators and psychologists have used the principles of instruction in dealing with special problems. The following examples cover two of the more difficult problems that educators face.

Truancy

It is a sure bet that your students will not learn much if they do not come to class. And it is just those students who need every bit of help they can get who seem to skip school most frequently. This has long been a problem for public school systems that require attendance. It has even prompted local governments to pay the salaries of "truant officers" in an attempt to deal with the situation. And yet, in spite of these measures,

it remains an unsolved problem for most schools. An extremely creative and effective solution was developed by a counselor and some psychologists in the state of Hawaii that may provide a useful alternative to traditional practices, however (MacDonald, Gallimore, & MacDonald, 1970).

Six ninth-grade chronic truants who were enrolled in a "special motivation class" were chosen for this experimental program. The program was organized by a counselor who involved parents, teachers, and other individuals to assist with the program. During the six-week baseline phase, the counselor collected attendance data on the six students. They attended school on the average of one day out of three. Next, the counselor and other individuals negotiated "contracts" with the truant adolescents. Each day that the student attended school for an entire day, he or she would be given a card signed by the counselor that would be taken to one of the "mediators." These individuals were persons who knew the students well and had volunteered to work with them on the deal. Included were two mothers, one father, one grandmother, the mother of a student's girlfriend, and a kindly poolhall owner. The mediators and the students themselves negotiated for the terms of the contract. One contract stated that a boy could spend time in the afternoon with his girlfriend only if he presented her mother with the daily attendance card. Another involved receiving money for attendance, while the friendly poolhall owner gave free time at the pool table to another student for each signed card. During the six weeks that the contracts were in effect,

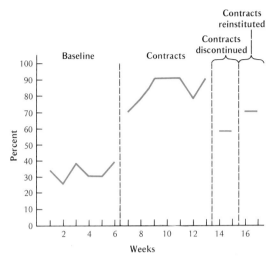

Figure 13–10. *Percent of truant middle-school students who attended school in four phases of the experiment. From left to right, the figure shows data taken before contracts for attendance were initiated, during contracts, when contracts were dropped, and when contracts were reinstituted. (From MacDonald, Gallimore, & MacDonald, 1970)*

daily attendance rose to approximately 85 percent, a gain of over 150 percent. In order to be sure that the contracts were responsible for the changes in attendance, they were discontinued for two weeks, during which time attendance fell to approximately 60 percent; attendance rose again when they were reinstated. Figure 13–10 shows these results.

School Phobias

Closely related to the problem of truancy is the dilemma of the "school phobic" child. Students labeled as school phobic are usually young children who not only dislike going to school, but become extremely upset when asked to do so. This does not mean

THE WITHDRAWN CHILD

The problem behaviors that cause the greatest concern for teachers are usually the "active" ones. You will most likely aim your discipline methods at curbing the frequency of misbehaviors such as hitting, yelling, and not following instructions. Many students, however, have "problem" behaviors that often go unnoticed. These are withdrawn children who rarely break classroom rules, but who often have trouble with school and peer relationships because of their inappropriate behavior. In coordination with other professionals such as counselors and school psychologists, you also have an obligation to help these children with their "silent" behavior problems.

One teacher found that she was able to significantly help a severely withdrawn seven-year-old girl by spending a few minutes a day with her having a special conversation (Butler, Doster, & Lahey, 1976). The teacher encouraged the student to talk more audibly and to make eye contact more often by smiling and praising her for appropriate conversation and by promoting her with phrases such as, "and what did you do then?" Within a few days, the child's behavior had improved markedly.

One of the procedures developed by psychologists accomplishes the same end in a much more pleasant and efficient manner. The parents use a *shaping* procedure to encourage the child to go to school without fear. At first they ask the child to perform acts that he or she associates with going to school, such as getting dressed and walking towards the school, but do not make the child follow through. They praise and reward the child for these actions, even though the child does not actually go to school on those days. As the child becomes more comfortable with these actions, they are extended to walking to the school grounds and staying outside the school building for thirty minutes or so. Again, the parents respond with praise. Finally, the child is rewarded for entering the school room and staying without a parent for a short period of time, which is gradually lengthened until the child is staying the entire day. Not only is this procedure effective, but it can accomplish its purpose without the shedding of a single tear. If the child shows emotionality at any point along the way, the parents can drop back a few steps and start over again. This technique enables parents to solve the problem in an efficient, yet relatively painless way (G. Patterson, 1965).

that they have a disease called "school phobia," but only that some children are much more extreme than others in their crying, begging, and pleading not to be made to go to school. How can we solve this problem?

We could require these children to come to school anyway and, making sure that no one reinforces their emotional behavior, simply let them cry until they get over it. They would, eventually, stop crying and learn to enjoy themselves if the school had a positive environment, but this would be unnecessarily stern.

PEER TUTORING AS AN AID TO TEACHING AND DISCIPLINE

The discussion above should give you a general idea of how to handle most discipline problems. Critical to the success of both teaching and discipline, however, is having enough time and energy to carry out your programs. The use of peers as tutors has

recently received a great deal of attention as a method of freeing teachers from an overload of responsibilities, while actually improving learning.

If you are committed to meeting the needs of each student as an individual, you will often need to be in two places at once to give individual assistance. Peer tutors (or any other type of volunteer) can be extremely useful in just this type of situation. Several studies have shown that peer tutors can teach very effectively on a one-to-one basis and that the tutors often learn something from it themselves (Harris & Sherman, 1973;

Lippett & Lohman, 1965; Johnson & Bailey, 1974). The secret seems to be to use responsible tutors who are a little older than the student (they can easily be recruited from study halls or free-time periods) and to give them clear instructions on how to perform simple teaching tasks. Do not require them to make many decisions on their own, however; you do the creative teaching and let them help you with the repetitive part.

Peer tutoring takes a little extra effort to set up, but those teachers who have made this initial effort are usually enthusiastic about the direct advantages it has for their students and about the work and time it saves, time that can be put to much better use. A few tutors working a few hours a day can improve your discipline and educational plan through their savings in time and effort. It works by keeping the children learning instead of getting into trouble, and it is so popular with students that it can even be used as a reinforcer. Robertson, Dereus, and Drabman (1976) found that second-graders were much better behaved when they had to earn the right to work with a peer or adult tutor through good behavior.

REVIEW 13–2

1. To what use should we restrict token economies? Why?

2. Describe a hypothetical token economy designed to reinforce participation in group discussions and that uses the principle of loss of reinforcement to control extreme misbehavior.

3. What are the values of tutoring by peers or volunteers?

SUMMARY

Discipline is a major concern of teachers, but most discipline problems can be handled through the use of a few simple methods. The use of positive reinforcement to encourage learning and appropriate behavior is the first principle of all discipline methods. Some guidelines for use of this approach include positively stating clear expectations for behavior, using positive reinforcement and shaping, making frequent brief contacts with students, and making academic learning meaningful and exciting. These methods will handle most misbehavior, but on some occasions quiet corners, loss of reinforcement, and even punishment may also be necessary in conjunction with positive reinforcement. Recently, some promising new methods that place more emphasis on self-management of behavior by students through self-recording or daily report cards have been studied with good preliminary results, but additional research is needed to validate the use of these procedures.

In more extreme cases, it may be necessary to use token reinforcement to control behavior. These methods require more effort than other methods and are somewhat artificial, but you may need their extra power in some circumstances. Regardless of which methods of discipline you choose, however, the first strategy should be to reinforce academic learning to indirectly decrease misbehavior, and to firmly and consistently enforce a minimal number of necessary classroom rules. At the end of the chapter, two examples illustrated how the principles of instruction may need to be adapted to solve special problems.

ANSWERS TO REVIEW QUESTIONS

Review 13–1

1. Teachers should set up the *minimum* number of *necessary* classroom rules for behavior, but should enforce those rules firmly (but not harshly) and consistently.

2. The five guidelines for discipline using positive reinforcement given in this chapter are

(a) Tell students what you expect of them.

(b) Use positive reinforcement for appropriate behavior.

(c) Use shaping.

(d) Keep individual student contacts frequent, but brief.

(e) Make academic learning meaningful and exciting.

3. Quiet corners and loss of reinforcement can be used with some students. Punishment should be used only when reinforcement for appropriate behavior, quiet corners, and loss of reinforcement has failed. All three of these must be used with reinforcement for good behavior.

4. Children cannot learn without attending to their work, but they will not necessarily learn just because they look as if they are paying attention. We should not focus our reinforcement procedures on attending, therefore, but rather on effective learning.

5. The term *criticism trap* refers to the tendency of teachers to make inappropriate behavior worse when they are trying to make it better. Criticism often reinforces the behavior it means to punish, thus leading to more inappropriate behavior, which leads to more criticism, and so on. We can break out of the criticism trap by using effective discipline procedures instead of criticism.

Review 13–2

1. Token economies are the most powerful methods of discipline and motivation for learning available to teachers. They should only be used when other methods are not sufficient, because they are somewhat artificial and because they require extra effort from the teacher. When token economies are called for, however, they are worth the effort.

2. It may be necessary under some circumstances to encourage participation in group discussions through the use of token reinforcement, such as with some mentally retarded students or juvenile delinquents. In such a case, a token could be given to the students after each contribution to the discussion, or a tally could be kept by the teacher. Students could later exchange the tokens for free time, privileges, food, money, and so on. Methods for reducing inappropriate behavior will only be effective when used with positive reinforcement for appropriate behavior.

3. In addition to its value as a teaching aid, peer tutoring saves time and energy for the teacher, involves students more in learning and thus indirectly reduces misbehavior, and is popular enough with students to even be used as a reinforcer.

GLOSSARY

accelerated readiness. A theoretical term that proposes readiness is learned and can be intentionally accelerated.

acceleration. The term used to refer to the intentional speeding up of intellectual and academic development.

accommodation. According to Piaget's theory of learning, *accommodation* is the learning process in which the existing intellectual structure is changed to accept new information.

accountability. The concept that the community should hold teachers and schools responsible for what children learn in the same way that industries should be held responsible for the quality of the products and services they produce.

achievement motivation. A theoretical term that refers to the fact that success and the things that go along with it are more rewarding to some individuals than others.

advance organizer. A statement summarizing material that is to be learned. Most research suggests that *advance organizers* (as well as summaries presented after learning) facilitate learning and retention.

affective domain. Bloom's term for the emotional and attitudinal goals of education. See also *cognitive domain* and *psychomotor domain.*

age-level scale. A type of intelligence or achievement test in which items are grouped according to age levels, with items becoming more difficult at each successive age level.

applied behavior analysis. An approach to psychology and education that is concerned with the application of laboratory principles of learning to human problems.

articulation. The control of vocal sounds in speaking.

assimilation. According to Piaget's theory of learning, assimilation is the learning process in which new information is changed to fit the existing intellectual structure.

attitude. A set of feelings towards other people, situations, or things that is associated with actions towards them.

authoritarian leaders. Leaders who strongly direct the activities of a group with little input from group members.

autism. A term used to refer to the behavior of some extremely deviant or psychotic children.

aversive stimulus. A negative or unpleasant event which serves to punish behavior that precedes it.

basal readers. Series of graduated books of prose reading material, usually prepared as a set for grades one through six.

behavioral disturbance. Serious behavior problems that interfere with learning and conduct in classroom and other situations. The term "behavior disorders" is frequently used as a synonym. These terms are often used in place of the term "emotional disturbance."

behaviorists. Psychologists and educators who emphasize the measurement and modification of overt behavior.

choice items. Test items, such as multiple-choice or true/false items, that require the student to select a response from among the given alternatives.

chronological age. The actual age of an individual in years and months.

clustering. The arrangement of the words of a list into related groups to facilitate memorization.

cognitive domain. Bloom's term for the intellectual goal of education. See also *affective domain* and *psychomotor domain.*

cognitive strategies. According to Gagné, cognitive strategies are skills such as asking questions, focusing attention, and evaluating which are used to organize thought processes.

cohesiveness. A characteristic that describes tightly knit social groups that are attractive to their members and satisfy their needs.

concept. Concepts are the common characteristics shared by many otherwise different ideas or things.

conservation. The concept that objects maintain their essential identity even though surface features, such as shape and length, have been changed.

content validity. A psychological or educational test has content validity if experts agree that it is an adequate measure of the characteristic of behavior that it was designed to measure.

conventional moral reasoning. According to Kohlberg, conventional moral reasoning involves an understanding of the necessity for rules of behavior.

cooperative play. Playing interactively with other children.

creativity. Unusual and useful solutions to problems or the production of something new and enjoyable.

criterion-referenced tests. Tests in which students are compared against some absolute criterion of proficiency, rather than against the performance of other students. See also *norm-referenced tests.*

critical periods. Periods of development during which the growing individual is particularly susceptible to specific learning experiences or imprinting.

criticism trap. The term used by Becker, Engelmann, and Thomas (1975) to refer to a self-defeating cycle teachers can get into. They may criticize (instead of actually disciplining) the misbehavior of some children which makes their misbehavior worse rather than better, which leads to more criticism, which leads to even more misbehavior, and so on.

cross-sectional method.   The method of studying developmental changes in which children of different ages are studied at approximately the same time. See also *longitudinal method*.

decentered thought.   According to Piaget, thought is decentered when the child is able to focus on more than one aspect of a situation at one time. Decentered thought is necessary for the acquisition of *conservation*.

deferred imitation.   The ability to imitate at a later time what has been previously observed.

democratic leaders.   Leaders who allow the members of a group to participate in decision making within limits.

developmental norms.   The typical age (mean or median) at which key developmental changes occur, such as walking or talking. Developmental norms are often used as guidelines for judging development, but usually do not explain the wide degree of variability that is a normal part of development.

developmental psychology.   The field of psychology that studies the ways in which behavior changes with age.

developmental stages.   A theoretical term that refers to periods of development that are marked by qualitative changes (changes in kind) at the beginning and end, but only minor quantitative changes (changes in degree) during the stage. For example, children change suddenly when they learn to crawl, and change suddenly again when they give up crawling for walking, but change very little during the "crawling stage."

deviation IQs.   Scores of intelligence tests that are based on *standard scores* rather than actual quotients of *mental age* divided by *chronological age*.

discovery learning.   Presenting students with the ideas and materials necessary to allow them to learn by solving problems on their own.

distributed practice.   Spreading study time out into short periods with breaks in between. Generally, distributed practice is more effective than *massed practice*.

dyslexia.   A term that means the same thing as *learning disabilities* when there are problems only in reading.

egocentric.   Piaget's term that refers to the tendency of young children to see the world from their point of view only.

emotional disturbance.   Serious behavior problems that interfere with learning and conduct in classroom situations. The term theoretically implies that the behavior problems are caused by emotional problems. See also *behavioral disturbance*.

enactive representation.   According to Bruner's theory, enactive representation is the representation of past experience through motor acts. This type of *representation* predominates in infancy and very early childhood.

entering behaviors.   The knowledge, skills, attitudes, and motives that students bring to new learning situations and upon which new learning is based. If entering behaviors are insufficient, the new learning will likely be inadequate.

errors of measurement.   All test scores are considered to be inaccurate to some extent because of the uncontrolled influence of such factors as lighting, noise, mood of the student, and so forth on test scores. These inaccuracies are referred to as *errors of measurement*.

exceptional children.   Children whose behavior deviates from the norm in ways that are maladaptive to the child or society. See also *maladaptive behavior*.

extinction.   If the source of a change in behavior is removed, such as positive reinforcement or a model, the behavior will tend to return to its original state. This process is called *extinction*.

extrinsic motives.   Rewards that are given to encourage learning but that are not inherent in the process of learning.

fine motor coordination.   Control of small movements, especially of the hands, as in handwriting and painting. See also *gross motor coordination*.

formal discipline.   The nineteenth-century theory that training in subjects such as Latin and logic strengthens the "mental faculties."

frequency distribution.   A list of scores, ranked from the highest to the lowest, that indicates how many individuals received each score.

grade equivalents.   A type of score used by some standardized achievement tests. If a raw score of 17, for example, is the average raw score of students in the third month of the sixth grade, then an individual who obtains a raw score of 17 will be assigned a grade equivalent of sixth grade, third month.

gross motor coordination.   Control of the large movements of the body, as in running and throwing. See also *fine motor coordination*.

hierarchy of motives. According to Maslow, motives exist in a hierarchy from the most basic to the least basic. In this conception, basic motives must be satisfied before higher-order motives can be active.

humanism. An approach to psychology which suggests that each person views the world in his or her own way and has his or her own "reality."

hyperactivity. Serious problems of high activity levels and short attention spans that interfere with school learning.

hyperkinesis. A synonym for *hyperactivity*.

iconic representation. According to Bruner's theory, iconic representation is the representation of past experiences through visual images. This type of representation predominates during preschool and early elementary-school years.

insight. The sudden understanding and solution of a problem.

instructional objectives. Detailed statements that describe the goals of instruction.

intellectual skills. According to Gagné, intellectual skills allow students to cope with new situations in their environment. For example, knowing phonic rules allows a student to approximate the pronunciation of most words.

internalized thought. Piaget's term that refers to problem solving using mental images rather than overt trial and error.

intrinsic motives. A theoretical term that suggests learning is inherently rewarding. See also *extrinsic motives*.

laissez-faire leaders. Leaders who exert no control over the activity of a group, but let each member go his or her own way.

lateral transfer. When learning in one situation facilitates later learning in another situation of different concepts or skills that are at the same level of complexity.

learning. Any relatively permanent change in behavior that is due to experience.

learning disabilities. Serious deficits in school learning in children who have normal intelligence, do not show serious behavior problems, do not have serious physical handicaps, and are not from disadvantaged environments.

learning hierarchy. A chart that shows the relationship between the prerequisites and the final skill to be learned.

linguistic approach. An approach to basic reading instruction in which children are taught general skills for pronouncing words using only intact words. See also *phonic approach* and *whole-word approach*.

longitudinal method. The method of studying developmental changes in which the same child or group of children are studied at different ages. See also *cross-sectional method*.

loss of reinforcement. When behavior is regularly followed by the loss or elimination of a reinforcer, it will be weakened.

mainstreaming. The practice of keeping exceptional children in regular classrooms as much as possible, often with special instruction being given to them part of the day.

maladaptive behavior. Behavior that is harmful to the individual or society.

massed practice. Using study time in one block without breaks. Usually massed practice, or "cramming," is less effective than *distributed practice*.

mastery learning. An approach to education advocated by Bloom which says that students should not progress from one learning task to another until each student has been given enough time to master (fully learn) the task.

maturation. A theoretical term that attributes changes in behavior which occur with increasing age to genetically determined biological changes which occur independent of experience.

mean. The average of all scores in a distribution, obtained by dividing the sum of all of the scores by the number of scores in the distribution.

meaningful learning. In theory, learning is considered meaningful if the learner understands what he or she is learning and relates it to previous knowledge.

medical model. The approach to abnormal behavior advocated by Freud that views abnormal behavior as a symptom of some underlying sickness of the mind or "mental illness" in much the same way that a physician views a cough and a sore throat as symptoms of an underlying physical illness.

mental age. The age level for which the raw score on an intelligence test is the average score. For example, if an individual obtains a score of 28 raw score points on an intelligence test, and 28 points is the average score for children 9 years, 2 months of age, the individual's mental age is 9 years, 2 months regardless of what the individual's *chronological age* is.

mental retardation. Serious deficits in intelligence and general adaptive skills.

minimal brain dysfunction. A controversial theoretical label given to some children with learning or behavior problems. The label implies that minor neurological disorders have caused the behavior and learning problems in cases where no clear evidence for neurological disorders exists.

mnemonic devices. Aids to improve memorization, such as creating acronyms out of the first letters of words in a list or clustering words in a list into related subgroups.

modeling. The procedure of intentionally presenting desirable behavior to others in hopes that they will imitate it.

moral realism. According to Piaget, children from four through ten years of age typically think of moral rules in rigid terms, and often judge acts according to their consequences rather than the motive behind the act.

moral relativists. In Piaget's terminology, children become moral relativists when they can see that a given behavior can be right in one situation, but wrong in another.

motor skills. Activities that require a precise sequence of bodily movements.

natural readiness. A theoretical term that proposes that readiness develops naturally and cannot be taught.

negative reinforcement. When behavior regularly terminates an *aversive stimulus* or prevents it from occurring that behavior will increase in strength. This process is called *negative reinforcement.*

negative transfer. When what is learned in one situation interferes with later learning in another situation.

new math. An approach to mathematics instruction introduced during the 1960s which stresses teaching basic mathematical concepts more than computational mathematics.

noncategorical special education. Grouping exceptional children according to similar educational needs rather than on the basis of diagnostic categories such as mental retardation and behavioral disturbance.

nonsense syllables. Meaningless syllables developed by Ebbinghaus for the experimental study of memory.

normal curve. A mathematical concept that describes a bell-shaped distribution in which most scores cluster around the mean with fewer scores at the extreme ends of the distribution.

norm-referenced tests. Tests in which students are compared against the performance of a group of other students (the *norm*), rather than against an absolute criterion of performance. See also *criterion-referenced tests.*

norms. The scores of a large number of individuals (the *standardization group*) against whom scores on a standardized test are compared for interpretation.

operant conditioning. Refers to the four principles of learning (positive reinforcement, punishment, negative reinforcement, and loss of reinforcement) in which behavior is strengthened or weakened by its consequences.

object permanence. Piaget's term that refers to the developmental change in which children act as if they know that objects exist even when they are out of sight.

objectivity. A necessary characteristic of psychological and educational tests meaning that the biases and prejudices of the examiner can have little influence on the score given on the test.

overlearning. Learning material beyond the point of initial mastery.

parallel play. Playing beside other children but not playing interactively with them.

percentile rank. A *standardized score* that expresses the percent of individuals who obtained raw scores lower than that of an individual.

phonic approach. An approach to basic reading instruction in which children are taught general skills for pronouncing words beginning with isolated letters and syllables and building to complete words. See also *linguistic approach* and *whole-word approach.*

positive reinforcement. When any behavior is followed by a *reinforcer*, that behavior will be strengthened. This process is called *positive reinforcement.*

positive transfer. When what is learned in one situation facilitates later learning in another situation.

principled moral reasoning. According to Kohlberg, *principled moral reasoning* involves the ability to go beyond the conventional standards of one's own society and see a need for broad universal values.

preconcepts. The term used by Piaget to refer to young children's immature early concepts, such as referring to all four-legged animals as "dogs."

preconventional moral reasoning. Kohlberg's first stage of moral development (typically ages six through eight) in which children adhere to moral standards to avoid punishment or to gain rewards.

predictive validity. A psychological or educational test has *predictive validity* if scores on the test adequately predict performance on some criterion behavior. For example, scores on a reading test that predict with some accuracy which children would be reading in texts that were above or below their grade level would have *predictive validity.*

proactive interference. Interference with the recall of later learning by material that was learned earlier.

psychomotor domain.   Bloom's term for the motor-skill goals of education. See also *cognitive domain* and *affective domain*.

punishment.   When behavior is regularly followed by an *aversive stimulus*, it will be weakened. This process is called *punishment*.

range.   A measure of the *variability* among the scores of a distribution calculated by subtracting the lowest score from the highest score.

readiness.   Children are considered to exhibit *readiness* for new learning when they have the *entering behaviors* necessary to base new learning upon.

recall.   The measure of memory that requires the learner to reproduce what was learned earlier. See also *recognition* and *relearning*.

recognition.   The measure of memory that requires the learner to identify what was learned earlier from among other alternatives. See also *relearning* and *recall*.

reinforcer.   An approximate synonym for reward; any event that serves to strengthen a behavior when it regularly follows the behavior.

relearning.   The measure of memory in which the learner relearns to some mastery criterion what had been learned earlier. The measure of memory is the extent to which the relearning is more efficient than the original learning.

reliability.   A necessary characteristic of psychological and educational tests meaning that a test must yield similar test scores when given to the same individual on different occasions.

representation.   The term in Bruner's theory of development that refers to the cognitive behaviors that occur when people process and remember information.

resource rooms.   When the *mainstreaming* approach to exceptional child education is followed, the children are brought to the *resource room* part of the time for work with a special teacher. The *resource room* contains special materials, games, and so forth, for the children's use.

retention.   A synonym for the memory of learned skills or knowledge.

retroactive interference.   Interference of later learning with the recall of material that was learned earlier.

rote learning.   Learning that is mechanically memorized without understanding.

rules.   Verbal statements that tell students how to perform, such as "the area of a rectangle equals the width times the height."

scaled scores.   The *standard scores* used on the subtests of the Wechsler Intelligence Test for Children-Revised which have a *mean* of 10 and a *standard deviation* of 3.

serial position effect.   The tendency for items at the beginning and end of a list to be remembered better than those in the middle.

sex-typing.   The process of learning the patterns of behavior associated with male or female roles in a given culture.

socialization.   The process of learning the values, standards, attitudes, and patterns of behavior of a culture.

sociometry.   Procedures for describing and measuring group structure.

solitary play.   Playing alone and at a distance from other children.

standard deviation.   A statistical measure of the variability of scores in a distribution.

standard error of measurement.   A statistic reported with some standardized test scores that estimates the extent to which uncontrolled inaccuracies may affect scores on that test. See also *errors of measurement*.

standard scores.   Standard scores express the individual's distance from the mean in terms of the *standard deviation* of the *norm*.

standardization group.   The group of individuals to whom a test is initially administered to develop the *norms* for interpreting scores on a standardized test.

stanine.   A type of standard score in which the raw scores of the individuals taking a test are divided into nine groups ranging from the highest (nine) to the lowest (one). The stanine indicates in which group the individual's raw score falls.

stimulus.   An object or event in the environment.

stimulus control.   A *stimulus* is said to control behavior if the probability of the occurrence of a behavior is different in its presence than in its absence.

stimulus repetition.   When a stimulus is presented repeatedly or for a prolonged period of time it will lose some or all of its stimulus function.

subculture.   The smaller cultures that make up a larger, more varied culture, such as the Chicano, black, and Southern white subcultures in the United States.

supply items.   Test items, such as essay and fill-in-the-blank items, that require the student to construct the response. See also *choice items*.

symbolic representation.   According to Bruner's theory, symbolic representation is the use of abstract rather than concrete mental images in memory and thought. This type of representation predominates after the elementary-school years.

systematic instruction.   The approach to education in

which testing is an integrated part of the teaching process and in which the teacher intentionally and systematically guides learning.

teacher expectancy effect.   According to Rosenthal, the expectations that teachers have for the way a child will perform may actually influence the child's performance in that direction. For example, if a teacher thinks a child will learn poorly, that expectation might be subtly communicated to the child and impair learning.

telegraphic speech.   The speech of young children that is so named because it often resembles a telegram message, such as "give milk" or "mommy go store."

terminal behaviors.   The knowledge or skill that the instructor wants the student to learn.

token economy.   A system using tokens such as poker chips or points (that can later be exchanged for reinforcers such as privileges, objects, or free time) to encourage learning and control misbehavior.

transductive reasoning.   Piaget's term that refers to the young child's erroneous reasoning that unrelated events are causally related. For example, young children may feel that wearing bathing suits makes the weather warm even though these two events are not causally related in this way.

transfer.   Transfer has occurred when what has been learned in one situation affects behavior in another situation, such as when skills learned in a driver's education simulator improve driving a car. See also *vertical transfer* and *horizontal transfer*.

transposing.   The task of completely reversing a stimulus array used in Bruner's experiments designed to study the process of representation.

validity.   Psychological and educational tests are valid if they measure the aspect of behavior they are designed to measure. See also *content validity* and *predictive validity*.

variability.   The degree to which the scores in a distribution differ from one another.

verbal information.   According to Gagné's analysis of learning, verbal information consists of labels and facts.

vertical transfer.   When learning in one situation facilitates later learning of more advanced or complex concepts or skills in another situation.

whole-word approach.   An approach to basic reading instruction in which children are taught to memorize the pronunciation of words as intact units. See also *word-attack approaches*.

word-attack approaches.   Approaches to reading instruction in which general rules of pronunciation are taught. See also *phonic approach, linguistic approach*, and *whole-word approach*.

REFERENCES

Adams, R. L., & Phillips, B. N. Motivational and achievement differences among children of various ordinal birth positions. *Child Development*, 1972, **43**, 155–164.

Ainsworth, M. D. S. *Infancy in Uganda*. Baltimore: Johns Hopkins Press, 1967.

Ainsworth, S. The education of children with speech handicaps. In W. M. Cruickshank and G. O. Johnson (Eds.), *Education of exceptional children and youth*. Englewood Cliffs, N. J.: Prentice-Hall, 1967.

Allen, K. E., Hart, B. M., Buell, J. S., Harris, F. R., & Wolf, M. M. Effects of social reinforcement on isolate behavior of a nursery school child. *Child Development*, 1964, **35**, 511–518.

Allinsmith, B. B. Expressive styles. II. Directness with which anger is expressed. In D. R. Miller & G. E. Swanson (Eds.), *Inner conflict and defense*. New York: Holt, 1960.

Allyon, T., Layman, D., & Kandel, H. J. A behavioral-educational alternative to drug control of hyperactive children. *Journal of Applied Behavior Analysis*, 1975, **8**, 137–146.

Allyon, T., & Roberts, M. Eliminating discipline problems by strengthening academic performance. *Journal of Applied Behavior Analysis*, 1974, **7**, 71–76.

Anastasi, A. *Psychological testing*. New York: Macmillan, 1976.

Anderson, G. J. Effects of classroom social climate on individual learning. *American Educational Research Journal*, 1970, **2**, 135–152.

Asch, S. E. Studies in independence and conformity. *Psychological Monographs*, 1956, **70**, No. 416.

Ausubel, D. P. The use of advance organizers in the learning and retention of meaningful verbal material. *Journal of Educational Psychology*, 1960, **51**, 267–272.

Ausubel, D. P., Stager, M., & Gaite, A. J. H. Retroactive facilitation in meaningful verbal learning. *Journal of Educational Psychology*, 1968, **59**, 250–255.

Baer, D. M. The control of developmental process: Why wait? In J. R. Nesselroade & H. W. Reese (Eds.), *Life-span developmental psychology*. New York: Academic Press, 1973.

Baer, D. M., & Wright, J. C. Developmental psychology. In M. R. Rozenzweig & L. W. Porter (Eds.), *Annual review of psychology*. Palo Alto, Calif.: Annual Reviews Inc., 1974.

Bandura, A. *Social learning theory*. Englewood Cliffs, N. J.: Prentice-Hall, 1977.

Bany, M. A., & Johnson, L. V. *Educational social psychology*. New York: Macmillan, 1975.

Barnes, K. E. Preschool play norms: A replication.

Developmental Psychology, 1971, **5**, 99–103.

Bartlett, F. C. *Remembering*. London: Cambridge University Press, 1932.

Bayley, N. Research in child development: A longitudinal perspective. *Merrill-Palmer Quarterly of Behavior and Development*, 1965, **11**, 8–35.

Becker, W., Englemann, S., & Thomas, D. *Teaching: A course in applied psychology*. Chicago: Science Research Associates, 1975.

Belcher, T. L. Modeling original divergent responses: An initial investigation. *Journal of Educational Psychology*, 1975, **67**, 351–358.

Belmont, L., & Marolla, A. F. Birth order, family size, and intelligence. *Science*, 1973, **182**, 1096–1101.

Benedict, R. *Patterns of culture*. Boston: Houghton Mifflin, 1950.

Berdiansky, B., Cronnel, B., & Koehler, K. Spelling-sound relations and primary form-class descriptions for speed-comprehension vocabularies of 6–9 year olds. Southwest Regional Laboratory for Educational Research and Development. Technical Report, No. 15, 1969. See also **Smith, F.** *Understanding reading*. New York: Holt, Rinehart and Winston, 1971, which discusses the report.

Bereiter, C., & Engelmann, S. *Teaching disadvantaged children in the preschool*. Englewood Cliffs, N.J.: Prentice-Hall, 1966.

Berlyne, D. E. Novelty and curiosity as determinants of exploratory behavior. *British Journal of Psychology*, 1950, **41**, 68–80.

Bernstein, B. A sociolinguistic approach to socialization: With some reference to educability. In F. Williams (Ed.), *Language and poverty*. Chicago: Markham, 1970.

Bijou, S. W. Ages, stages, and the naturalization of human development. *American Psychologist*, 1968, **23**, 419–427.

Bijou, S. W. *Child development: The basic stage of early childhood*. Englewood Cliffs, N.J.: Prentice-Hall, 1976.

Bijou, S. W., & Baer, D. M. *Child development: A systematic and empirical theory*. New York: Appleton-Century-Crofts, 1961.

Bijou, S. W., & Baer, D. M. *Child development: Universal stage of infancy*. New York: Appleton-Century-Crofts, 1965.

Block, J. H., & Tierney, M. L. An exploration of two correction procedures used in mastery learning approaches to instruction. *Journal of Educational Psychology*, 1974, **66**, 962–967.

Bloom, B. S. *Stability and change in human characteristics*. New York: John Wiley & Sons, 1964.

Bloom, B. S. Time and learning. *American Psychologist*, 1974, **29**, 681–688.

Bloom, B. S., Engelhart, M. D., Furst, E. J., Hill, H. W.,

& Krathwohl, D. R. *Taxonomy of educational objectives: Handbook I, Cognitive domain.* New York: Longmans, Green, and Co., 1956.

Bloom, B. S., Hastings, J. T., & Madaus, G. F. *Handbook on formative and summative evaluation of student learning.* New York: McGraw-Hill, 1971.

Bonney, M. E. The relative stability of social, intellectual, and academic status in grades II to IV, and the interrelationships between these various forms of growth. *Journal of Educational Psychology,* 1943, **34,** 88–102.

Bornstein, P., & Quevillon, R. P. The effects of a self-instructional package on hyperactive preschool boys. *Journal of Applied Behavior Analysis,* 1976, **9,** 179–188.

Bostow, D. E., & O'Connor, R. J. A comparison of two college classroom testing procedures: Required remediation versus no remediation. *Journal of Applied Behavior Analysis,* 1973, **6,** 599–607.

Bower, G. H., Clark, M. C., Lesgold, A. M., & Winzenz, D. Hierarchical retrieval schemes in recall of categorized word lists. *Journal of Verbal Learning and Verbal Behavior,* 1969, **8,** 323–343.

Brecher, E. M. Do you know what your children are learning in school? *Redbook,* April 1976, 81–83.

Broden, M., Hall, R. V., & Mitts, B. The effect of self-recording on the classroom behavior of two eighth-grade students. *Journal of Applied Behavior Analysis,* 1971, **4,** 191–199.

Brown, L., Huppler, B., VanDeventer, P., York, R., & Sontag, E. Use of reinforcement principles to increase comprehension of instructional filmstrips. *Education and Training of the Mentally Retarded,* 1973, **8,** 50–56.

Brown, P., & Elliott, R. Control of aggression in a nursery school class. *Journal of Experimental Child Psychology,* 1965, **2,** 103–107.

Bruner, J. S. The course of cognitive growth. *American Psychologist,* 1964, **19,** 1–15.

Bruner, J. S. *The process of education.* Cambridge, Mass.: Harvard University Press, 1960.

Bruner, J. S. *The relevance of education.* New York: Norton & Co., 1971.

Bruner, J. S., & Kenney, H. J. On multiple ordering. In J. S. Bruner, et al., *Studies in cognitive growth.* New York: Wiley & Sons, 1966.

Burt, C. The genetic determination of difference in intelligence: A study of monozygotic twins reared together and apart. *British Journal of Psychology,* 1966, **57,** 137–153.

Busemeyer, M. K., O'Hara, C., & Beggs, V. E. Treatment of severe perceptual-motor disorders in children diagnosed as learning disabled. *Behavior Modification,* 1977, **1,** 123–140.

Bushell, D. The Behavior Analysis Follow Through project: An engineering approach to the elementary school classroom. In T. A. Brigham & A. C. Catania (Eds.), *Analysis and modification of social and educational behaviors.* New York: Wiley, in press.

Butler, C., Doster, J. T., & Lahey, B. B. Parent and teacher mediated social skills in a very withdrawn disadvantaged girl. *Corrective and Social Psychiatry,* in press.

Carew, J. V., Chan, I., & Halfar, C. *Observing intelligence in young children: Eight case studies.* Englewood Cliffs, N. J.: Prentice-Hall, 1976.

Carmichael, L., Hogan, H. P., & Walter, A. A. An experimental study of the effect of language on the reproduction of visually perceived form. *Journal of Experimental Psychology,* 1932, **15,** 73–86.

Clarizio, H. Natural versus accelerated readiness. In H. F. Clarizio, R. C. Craig, and W. A. Mehrens (Eds.), *Contemporary issues in educational psychology.* Boston: Allyn & Bacon, 1974.

Clark, D. C. Teaching concepts in the classroom: A set of teaching prescriptions derived from experimental research. *Journal of Educational Psychology,* 1974, **66,** 481–485.

Clark, H. B., Boyd, S. B., & Macrae, J. W. A classroom program teaching disadvantaged youths to write biographic information. *Journal of Applied Behavior Analysis,* 1975, **8,** 67–75.

Coleman, J. C. *Abnormal psychology and modern life.* Glenview, Ill.: Scott, Foresman and Company, 1976.

Coleman, J. S. *Equality of educational opportunity.* Washington, D. C.: U.S. Government Printing Office, 1966.

Coleman, P., Kaszuba, K., & Pierce, M. The effects of a sequential computational skills program on an underachieving fourth-grade class. *Journal of Behavioral Education,* 1973, **67,** 174–178.

Costanzo, P. R., & Shaw, M. E. Conformity as a function of age level. *Child Development,* 1966, **37,** 967–975.

Covington, M. V., Crutchfield, R. S., Davies, L., & Olton, R. M. *The Productive Thinking Program.* Columbus, Ohio: Merrill, 1972.

Crossman, E. R. F. A theory of acquisition of speed-skill. *Ergonomics,* 1959, **2,** 153–166.

Crowl, T. K., & MacGinnitie, W. H. The influence of students' speech characteristics on teachers' evaluations of oral answers. *Journal of Educational Psychology,* 1974, **66,** 304–308.

Crutchfield, R. S. Creative thinking in children: Its teaching and testing. In O. G. Brim, Jr., R. S. Crutchfield, & Wayne H. Holtzman (Eds.), *Intelligence: Perspectives 1965.* New York: Harcourt Brace Jovanovich, Inc., 1966.

Daniels, N. The smart white man's burden. *Harpers*, 1973, **247** (1481), 24–40.

Dennis, W. Infant development under conditions of restricted practice and of minimum social stimulation. *Genetic Psychology Monographs*, 1941, **23**, 143–189.

Dennis, W., & Dennis, M. The effect of cradling practices upon the onset of walking in Hopi children. *Journal of Genetic Psychology*, 1940, **56**, 77–86.

Dewey, J. *How we think*. Boston: Heath, 1910.

Dick, W., & Carey, L. *The systematic design of instruction*. Glenview, Ill.: Scott, Foresman, 1978.

DiVesta, F. J., & Gray, G. S. Listening and note taking. *Journal of Educational Psychology*, 1972, **63**, 8–14.

Dorsel, T. N. Preference-success assumption in education. *Journal of Educational Psychology*, 1975, **67**, 514–520.

Drabman, R. S., & Lahey, B. B. Feedback in classroom behavior modification: Effects on the target child and her classmates. *Journal of Applied Behavior Analysis*, 1974, **7**, 591–598.

Duchastel, P. C., & Brown, B. R. Incidental and relevant learning with instructional objectives. *Journal of Educational Psychology*, 1974, **66**, 481–485.

Duchastel, P. C., & Merrill, P. F. The effect of behavioral objectives on learning: A review of empirical studies. *Review of Educational Research*, 1973, **43**, 53–69.

Dunphy, D. C. The social structure of urban adolescent peer groups. *Sociometry*, 1963, **26**, 230–246.

Durkin, D. A six-year study of children who learned to read in school at the age of four. *Reading Research Quarterly*, 1975, **10**, 9–61.

Durkin, D. *Teaching them to read*. Boston: Allyn & Bacon, 1970.

Dyer, H. S. Toward objective criteria of professional accountability in schools. In A. C. Ornstein (Ed.), *Accountability for teachers and school administrators*. Belmont, Calif.: Fearon, 1973.

Ebbinghaus, H. *Memory*. H. A. Ruger & C. E. Bussenius (Trans.). New York: Dover, 1964.

Ebel, R. L. *Essentials of educational measurement*. Englewood Cliffs, N.J.: Prentice-Hall, 1972.

Elkind, D. Piagetian and psychometric conceptions of intelligence. *Harvard Educational Review*, 1969, **39**, 319–337.

Engelmann, S. The effectiveness of direct verbal instruction on IQ performance and achievement in reading and arithmetic. In J. Hullmuth (Ed.), *Disadvantaged child, Volume 3, Compensatory education: A national debate*. New York: Brunner/Mazel, 1970.

Erikson, E. H. *Childhood and society*. New York: Norton, 1950.

Erlenmeyer-Kimling, L., & Jarvik, L. F. Genetics and intelligence: A review. *Science*, 1963, **142**, 1477–1479.

Feldman, K. V., & Klausmeier, H. J. Effects of two kinds of definition on the concept attainment of fourth and eighth graders. *Journal of Educational Research*, 1974, **67**, 219–223.

Felixbrod, J. J., & O'Leary, K. D. Self-determination of academic standards by children: Toward freedom from external control. *Journal of Educational Psychology*, 1974, **66**, 845–850.

Ferguson, L. R., & Maccoby, E. E. Interpersonal correlates of differential abilities. *Child Development*, 1966, **37**, 549–571.

Ferinden, W. E., Jacobson, S., & Linden, N. J. Early identification of learning disabilities. *Journal of Learning Disabilities*, 1970, **3**, 589–593.

Ferritor, D. E., Buckholdt, D., Hamblin, R. L., & Smith, L. The noneffects of contingent reinforcement for attending behavior on work accomplished. *Journal of Applied Behavior Analysis*, 1972, **5**, 7–17.

Feshbach, S., & Adelman, H. Remediation of learning problems among the disadvantaged. *Journal of Educational Psychology*, 1974, **66**, 16–28.

Festinger, L., Schacter, S., & Back, K. W. *Social pressures in informal groups: A study of human factors in housing*. New York: Harper & Brothers, 1950.

Fillmer, H. T. Sexist teaching—What can you do? *Teacher*, January 1974, 30–32.

Firestone, G., & Brody, N. Longitudinal investigation of teacher-student interactions and their relationship to academic performance. *Journal of Educational Psychology*, 1975, **67**, 544–550.

Fisher, J. L., & Harris, M. B. Effect of note taking and review on recall. *Journal of Educational Psychology*, 1973, **65**, 321–325.

Francis, E. W. Grade level and task difficulty in learning by discovery and verbal reception methods. *Journal of Educational Psychology*, 1975, **67**, 146–150.

Franzini, L. R., Litrownik, A. J., & Choisser, L. *Modification of serial recall ability in children via modeling*. Paper presented at the meeting of the Rocky Mountain Psychological Association, Las Vegas, May 1973.

Frase, L. T. Effect of question location, pacing, and mode upon retention of prose material. *Journal of Educational Psychology*, 1968, **59**, 244–249.

Frutchey, F. P. Retention in high school chemistry. *Educational Research Bulletin*, 1937, **16**, 34–37.

Furth, H. G., & Wachs, H. *Thinking goes to school*. New York: Oxford University Press, 1974.

Gagné, R. M. *The conditions of learning.* New York: Holt, Rinehart, and Winston, 1970.

Gagné, R. M., & Briggs, L. J. *Principles of instructional design.* New York: Holt, Rinehart and Winston, 1974.

Gelman, R. Conservation acquisition: A problem of learning to attend to relevant attributes. *Journal of Experimental Child Psychology,* 1969, **7,** 167–187.

Gesell, A. The ontogenesis of infant behavior. In L. Carmichael (Ed.), *Manual of child psychology.* New York: John Wiley & Sons, 1954.

Gesell, A., & Ilg, F. L. *The child from five to ten.* New York: Harper & Brothers, 1946.

Gesell, A., & Ilg, F. L. *Infant and child in the culture of today.* New York: Harper & Brothers, 1943.

Gesell, A., Ilg, F. L., & Ames, L. B. *The years from ten to sixteen.* New York: Harper & Brothers, 1956.

Gesell, A., & Thompson, H. Learning and growth in identical twins: An experimental study by the method of co-twin control. *Genetic Psychology Monographs,* 1929, **6,** 1–124.

Glaser, R. Psychology and instructional technology. In R. Glaser (Ed.), *Training research and education.* New York: John Wiley & Sons, 1962.

Glavin, J. P., Quay, H. C., Annesley, F. R., & Werry, J. S. An experimental resource room for behavior problem children. *Exceptional Child,* 1971, **38,** 131–137.

Gnagy, W. J. *The psychology of discipline in the classroom.* New York: Macmillan, 1975.

Goebel, L. G. An analysis of teacher-pupil interaction when programmed instruction materials are used. Unpublished doctoral dissertation, University of Maryland, 1966.

Goldberg, M. L., Passow, A. H., & Justman, J. *The effects of ability grouping.* New York: Teachers College Press, 1966.

Goldfarb, W. Psychological privation in infancy and subsequent adjustment. *American Journal of Orthopsychiatry,* 1945, **15,** 247–255.

Goldfarb, W. Variations in adolescent adjustment of institutionally reared children. *American Journal of Orthopsychiatry,* 1947, **17,** 449–457.

Goodlad, J. I. Classroom organization. In C. W. Harris (Ed.), *Encyclopedia of educational research.* New York: Macmillan, 1960.

Gottesman, I. I., & Shields, J. *Schizophrenia and genetics.* New York: Academic Press, 1972.

Gronlund, N. E. *Measurement and evaluation in teaching.* New York: Macmillan, 1976.

Guilford, J. P. *The nature of human intelligence.* New York: McGraw-Hill, 1967.

Hall, R. V., Fox, R., Willard, D., Goldsmith, L., Emerson, M., Owen, M., Davis, F., & Porcia, E. The teacher as observer and experimenter in the modification of disputing and talking-out behaviors. *Journal of Applied Behavior Analysis,* 1971, **4,** 141–149.

Haring, N. G., & Hauck, M. A. Improved learning conditions in the establishment of reading skills with disabled readers. *Journal of Exceptional Children,* 1969, **35,** 341–352.

Harlow, H. F., Blazek, N. C., & McClearn, G. E. Manipulatory motivation in the infant rhesus monkey. *Journal of Comparative and Physiological Psychology,* 1956, **49,** 444–448.

Harris, V. W., & Sherman, J. A. Effects of peer tutoring and consequences on the math performance of elementary classroom students. *Journal of Applied Behavior Analysis,* 1973, **6,** 587–597.

Harrison, M. L. *Reading readiness.* New York: Houghton Mifflin, 1939.

Hart, B. M., Reynolds, N. J., Baer, D. M., Brawley, R., & Harris, F. R. Effect of contingent and noncontingent social reinforcement on the cooperative play of a preschool child. *Journal of Applied Behavior Analysis,* 1968, **1,** 73–76.

Hartmann, H. Psychoanalysis as a scientific theory. In T. Millon (Ed.), *Theories of psychopathology.* Philadelphia: W. B. Saunders, 1967.

Haskett, G. J., & Lenfestey, W. Reading-related behavior in an open classroom: Effects of novelty and modeling on preschoolers. *Journal of Applied Behavior Analysis,* 1974, **1,** 233–241.

Havighurst, R. J., & Breese, F. H. Relation between ability and social status in a midwestern community. III. Primary mental abilities. *Journal of Educational Psychology,* 1947, **38,** 241–247.

Hayden, A. H., & Haring, N. G. Programs for Down's syndrome children at the University of Washington. In T. Tjossen (Ed.) *Intervention strategy for high risk infants and young children.* Baltimore: University Publications Press, 1975.

Heber, R., Garber, H., Harrington, S., Hoffman, C., & Falenger, C. Rehabilitation of families at risk for mental retardation. Progress Report, University of Wisconsin, 1972.

Helmreich, R. Birth order effects. *Naval Research Reviews.* 1968, **21.**

Herrnstein, R. IQ. *The Atlantic Monthly,* 1971, **228**(3), 43–64.

Hewett, F., & Forness, S. R. *Education of exceptional learners.* Boston: Allyn & Bacon, 1974.

Hildreth, G. Individual differences. In W. S. Monroe (Ed.), *Encyclopedia of educational research.* New York: Macmillan, 1950.

Hilgard, E. R., Irvin, R. P., & Whipple, J. E. Rote memorization, understanding, and transfer: An extension of Katona's card trick experiments. *Journal of Experimental Psychology*, 1953, **46,** 288–292.

Hollander, E. P. Conformity, status, and idiosyncrasy credit. *Psychological Review*, 1958, **65,** 117–127.

Holt, G. L. Effect of reinforcement contingencies in increasing programmed reading and mathematics behaviors in first grade children. *Journal of Experimental Child Psychology*, 1971, **12,** 362–369.

Hops, H., & Cobb, J. A. Initial investigations into academic survival-skill training, direct instruction, and first-grade achievement. *Journal of Educational Psychology*, 1974, **66,** 548–553.

Houston, S. H. A reexamination of some assumptions about the language of the disadvantaged child. *Child Development*, 1970, **41,** 947–963.

Hunt, J. McV. *Intelligence and experience.* New York: Ronald Press, 1961.

Husén, T. *International study of achievement in mathematics.* Vol. 2. Uppsala, Sweden: Almquist and Wiksells, 1967.

Inhelder, B. & Piaget, J. *The growth of logical thinking from childhood to adolescence.* New York: Basic Books, 1958.

Iwata, B. A., & Bailey, J. S. Reward versus cost token systems: An analysis of the effects on students and teachers. *Journal of Applied Behavior Analysis, 1974,* **7,** 567–576.

Jencks, C. *Inequality: A reassessment of the effects of family and schooling in America.* New York: Basic Books, 1972.

Jensen, A. R. How much can we boost IQ and scholastic achievement? *Harvard Educational Review,* 1969, **39,** 1–123.

Jensen, A. R. Spelling errors and the serial-position effect. *Journal of Educational Psychology*, 1962, **53,** 105–109.

Jersild, A. T., & Holmes, F. B. *Children's fears.* New York: Bureau of Publications, Teachers College, Columbia University, 1935.

Johnson, D. W. *The social psychology of education.* New York: Holt, Rinehart and Winston, 1970.

Johnson, M. J., & Bailey, J. S. Cross-age tutoring: Fifth graders as arithmetic tutors for kindergarten children. *Journal of Applied Behavior Analysis*, 1974, **7,** 223–232.

Kagan, J. Reflection-impulsivity: The generality and dynamics of conceptual tempo. *Journal of Abnormal Psychology*, 1966, **71,** 17–24.

Kagan, J., & Madsen, M. C. Cooperation and competition of Mexican, Mexican-American, and Anglo-American children of two ages under four instructional sets. *Developmental Psychology*, 1971, **5,** 32–39.

Kagan, J., & Moss, H. A. *Birth to maturity: a study in psychological development.* New York: John Wiley, 1962.

Kamii, C. K., and DeVries, R. Piaget for early education. In R. K. Parker (Ed.), *The preschool in action.* Boston: Allyn & Bacon, 1975.

Kaufman, K. F., & O'Leary, K. D. Reward, cost, and self-evaluation procedures for disruptive adolescents in a psychiatric hospital school. *Journal of Applied Behavior Analysis*, 1972, **5,** 293–309.

Kennedy, W. A. *Intelligence and economics: A confounded relationship.* Morristown, N. J.: General Learning Corporation, 1973.

Kennedy, W. A. *Child psychology.* Englewood Cliffs, N.J.: Prentice-Hall, 1975.

King, D. J., & Russell, G. N. A comparison of rote and meaningful learning of connected meaningful material. *Journal of Verbal Learning and Verbal Behavior*, 1966, **5,** 478–483.

Kippel, G. M. Information feedback schedules, interpolated activities, and retention. *Journal of Psychology*, 1974, **87,** 245–251.

Kirby, F. D., & Shields, F. Modification of arithmetic response rate and attending behavior in a seventh-grade student. *Journal of Applied Behavior Analysis*, 1972, **5,** 79–84.

Klausmeier, H. J., & Felman, K. V. Effects of definition and a varying number of examples and nonexamples of concept attainment. *Journal of Educational Psychology*, 1975, **67,** 174–178.

Kohlberg, L. The development of children's orientations toward a moral order: I. Sequence of the development of moral thought. *Vita Humana*, 1963, **6,** 11–33.

Kohlberg, L. Early education: A cognitive developmental view. *Child Development*, 1968, **39,** 1013–1062.

Kohlberg, L. Stage and sequence: The cognitive developmental approach to socialization. In D. A. Goslin (Ed.), *Handbook of socialization theory and research.* Chicago: Rand McNally, 1969, 347–480.

Komaki, J. Child-managed sharing: Learning to take turns with a minimum of adult monitoring. Unpublished manuscript, Emory University, 1976.

Krathwohl, D. R., Bloom, B. S., & Masia, B. B. *Taxonomy of educational objectives: Handbook II, Affective domain.* New York: David McKay Co., 1964.

Krueger, W. C. F. The effect of overlearning on retention. *Journal of Experimental Psychology*, 1929, **12,** 71–78.

Labov, W. The logic of nonstandard English. In F. Williams (Ed.), *Language and poverty*. Chicago: Markham, 1970.

Lahaderne, H. M. Attitudinal and intellectual correlates of attention: A study of four sixth-grade classrooms. *Journal of Educational Psychology*, 1968, **59,** 320–324.

Lahey, B. B. Modification of the frequency of descriptive adjectives in the speech of Head Start children through modeling without reinforcement. *Journal of Applied Behavior Analysis*, 1971, **4,** 19–22.

Lahey, B. B. Treatment of severe perceptual-motor disabilities in children diagnosed as learning disabled. *Behavior Modification*, 1977, **1,** 123–140.

Lahey, B. B., & Dotts, J. T. Rapid treatment of perceptual-motor disorders in disadvantaged preschool children. *Journal of Instructional Psychology*, 1976, **3,** 38–40.

Lahey, B. B., Gendrich, J. G., Gendrich, S. I., Schnelle, J. F., Gant, D. S., & McNees, M. P. An evaluation of daily report cards with minimal teacher and parent contacts as an efficient method of classroom intervention. *Journal of Behavior Modification*, 1977, **1,** 381–394.

Lahey, B. B., McNees, M. P., & McNees, M. C. Control of an obscene "verbal tic" through timeout in an elementary school classroom. *Journal of Applied Behavior Analysis*, 1973, **6,** 101–104.

Lee, D. M., & Allen, R. V. *Learning to read through experience.* New York: Appleton-Century-Crofts, 1963.

LeLaurin, K., & Risley, T. R. The organization of day care environments: The "Zone defense" versus the "man-to-man defense." *Journal of Applied Behavior Analysis*, 1972, **5,** 225–232.

Lessinger, L. M. Accountability and humanism: A productive educational complementarity. In C. D. Sabine (Ed.), *Accountability: Systems planning in education.* Homewood, Ill.: ETC Publications, 1973.

Lessinger, L. M. The powerful notion of accountability in education. In H. F. Clarizio, R. C. Craig, & W. A. Mehrens (Eds.), *Contemporary issues in educational psychology.* Boston: Allyn & Bacon, 1974.

Levin, J. R., & Rohwer, W. D. Verbal organization and the facilitation of serial learning. *Journal of Educational Psychology*, 1968, **59,** 186–190.

Lewin, K., Lippitt, R., & White, R. K. Patterns of aggressive behavior in experimentally created social climates. *Journal of Social Psychology*, 1939, **10,** 271–299.

Lippett, P., & Lohman, J. E. Cross-age relationships: An educational resource. *Children*, 1965, **12,** 113–117.

Lippitt, R., & White, R. K. The "social climate" of children's groups. In R. G. Barker, J. S. Kounin, & H. F. Wright (Eds.), *Child behavior and development.* New York: McGraw-Hill, 1943.

Long, J. D., & Williams, R. L. The effects of group and individually contingent free time with inner city junior high school students. *Journal of Applied Behavior Analysis*, 1973, **6,** 465–474.

Lorenz, K. The companion in the bird's world. *Auk*, 1937, **54,** 245–273.

Lovitt, T. C., & Curtiss, K. A. Academic response rate as a function of teacher and self-imposed contingencies. *Journal of Applied Behavior Analysis*, 1968, **2,** 85–92.

Lovitt, T. C., Guppy, T. E., & Blattner, J. E. The use of a free-time contingency with fourth graders to improve spelling accuracy. *Behavior Research and Therapy*, 1969, **1,** 151–156.

Lyons, J. *Experience: Introduction to a personal psychology.* New York: Harper & Row, 1973.

Maccoby, E. E., & Jacklin, C. N. *The psychology of sex differences.* Stanford, Ca.: Stanford University Press, 1974.

MacDonald, W. S., Gallimore, R., & MacDonald, G. Contingency counseling by school personnel: An economical model of intervention. *Journal of Applied Behavior Analysis*, 1970, **3,** 175–182.

Madden, P. Skinner and the open classroom. *School Review*, 1972, **81,** 100–107.

Madsen, C. H., Becker, W. C., & Thomas, D. R. Rules, praise, and ignoring: Elements of elementary classroom control. *Journal of Applied Behavior Analysis*, 1968, **1,** 139–150.

Madsen, C. H., & Madsen, C. K. *Teaching/discipline: A positive approach for educational development.* Boston: Allyn & Bacon, 1974.

Mager, R. *Preparing instructional objectives.* Palo Alto, Calif.: Fearon, 1962.

Maloney, K. S., & Hopkins, B. L. The modification of sentence structure and its relationship to subjective judgments of creativity in writing. *Journal of Applied Behavior Analysis*, 1973, **6,** 425–434.

Marwit, S. J., & Neumann, G. Black and white children's comprehension of standard and nonstandard English passages. *Journal of Educational Psychology*, 1974, **66,** 329–332.

Maslow, A. H. *Motivation and personality.* New York: Harper, 1954.

Matheny, K. B., & Edwards, C. R. Academic improvement through an experimental classroom management system. *Journal of School Psychology*, 1974, **12,** 222–232.

McClelland, D. C. *The achieving society.* Princeton: Van

Nostrand, 1961.

McGraw, M. B. Neural maturation as exemplified in achievement of bladder control. *Journal of Pediatrics,* 1940, **16,** 580–590.

McKenzie, G. R. Some effects of frequent quizzes on inferential thinking. *American Educational Research Journal,* 1972, **9,** 231–240.

McKinney, J. D., & Golden, L. Social studies dramatic play with elementary school children. *Journal of Educational Research,* 1973, **67,** 172–176.

McLaughlin, T. F., & Malaby, J. Intrinsic reinforcers in a classroom token economy. *Journal of Applied Behavior Analysis,* 1972, **5,** 263–270.

McNeil, D. *The acquisition of language.* New York: Harper & Row, 1970.

Meichenbaum, D., & Goodman, J. Reflection-impulsivity and verbal control of motor behavior. *Child Development,* 1969, **40,** 785–789.

Mellon, J. C. *National assessment and the teaching of English.* Urbana, Ill.: National Council of Teachers of English, 1975.

Mercer, J. R. Sociocultural factors in labeling mental retardates. *Peabody Journal of Education,* 1971, **48,** 188–203.

Money, J., & Ehrhardt, A. A. *Man and woman, boy and girl: Differentiation and dimorphism of gender identity.* Baltimore: Johns Hopkins University Press, 1972.

Moore, O. K. Autotelic responsive environments and exceptional children. In O. J. Harvey (Ed.), *Experience, structure, and adaptability.* New York: Springer Publishing Company, 1966.

Mosher, F. A., & Hornsby, J. R. On asking questions. In J. S. Bruner et al., *Studies in cognitive growth.* New York: Wiley & Sons, 1966.

Neill, A. S. *Summerhill: A radical approach to child rearing.* New York: Hart, 1960.

Nelson, G. K., & Klausmeier, H. J. Classificatory behaviors of low socioeconomic status children. *Journal of Educational Psychology,* 1974, **66,** 432–438.

Newman, H. H., Freeman, F. N., & Holzinger, K. J. *Twins: A study of heredity and environment.* Chicago: University of Chicago Press, 1937.

Nolen, P. A., Kunzelman, H. P., & Haring, N. E. Behavioral modification in a junior high learning disabilities classroom. *Exceptional Children,* 1967, **34,** 163–168.

Nunnally, J. C. *Educational measurement and evaluation.* Englewood Cliffs, N.J.: Prentice-Hall, 1972.

O'Connell, E. J., Dusek, J. B., & Wheeler, R. J. A follow-up study of teacher expectancy effects. *Journal of Educational Psychology,* 1974, **66,** 325–328.

O'Connor, R. D. Modification of social withdrawal through symbolic modeling. *Journal of Applied Behavior Analysis,* 1969, **2,** 15–22.

O'Leary, K. D., Kaufman, K. F., Kass, R. E., & Drabman, R. S. The effects of loud and soft reprimands on the behavior of disruptive students. *Exceptional Children,* 1970, **37,** 145–155.

O'Leary, K. D., & Wilson, T. *Behavior therapy: Application and outcome.* New York: Prentice-Hall, 1976.

Olver, R. R., & Hornsby, J. R. On equivalence. In J. S. Bruner, et al., *Studies in cognitive growth.* New York: Wiley & Sons, 1966, 68–85.

Palermo, D. S., & Molfese, D. L. Language acquisition from age five onward. *Psychological Bulletin,* 1972, **78,** 409-428.

Patterson, G. R. A learning theory approach to the treatment of the school phobic child. In L. P. Ullman & L. Krasner (Eds.), *Case studies in behavior modification.* New York: Holt, Rinehart & Winston, 1965.

Peterson, H. A., Ellis, M., Toohill, N., & Kloess, P. Some measurements of the effects of reviews. *Journal of Educational Psychology,* 1935, **26,** 65–72.

Piaget, J. *The language and thought of the child.* New York: Harcourt, Brace, & World, 1929.

Piaget, J. *The moral judgment of the child.* M. Gibain (Trans.). Boston: Routledge and Kegan Paul, 1932.

Piaget, J. *The origin of intelligence in children.* New York: International Universities Press, 1952.

Piaget, J. *The construction of reality in the child.* New York: Basic Books, 1954.

Piaget, J. *Science of education and the psychology of the child.* New York: Grossman, 1970.

Piaget, J. Intellectual evolution from adolescence to adulthood. *Human Development,* 1972, **15,** 1–12.

Plowman, L., & Stroud, J. B. Effects of informing pupils of the consequences of their responses to objective test questions. *Journal of Educational Research,* 1942, **36,** 16–20.

Quay, H. C., Glavin, J. T., Annesley, F. R., & Werry, J. S. The modification of problem behavior and academic achievement in a resource room. *Journal of School Psychology,* 1972, **10,** 187–197.

Quilitch, H. R., & Risley, T. R. The effects of play materials on social play. *Journal of Applied Behavior Analysis,* 1973, **6,** 573–578.

Rappaport, M. M., & Rappaport, H. The other half of the expectancy equation: Pygmalion. *Journal of Educational Psychology,* 1975, **67,** 531–536.

Rapport, M. D., & Bostow, D. E. The effects of access

to special activities on the performance in four categories of academic tasks with third-grade students. *Journal of Applied Behavior Analysis*, 1976, **9**, 372.

Raugh, M. R., & Atkinson, R. C. A mnemonic method for learning a second-language vocabulary. *Journal of Educational Psychology*, 1975, **67**, 1–16.

Reynolds, J. H., & Glaser, R. Effects of repetition and spaced review upon retention of a complex learning task. *Journal of Educational Psychology*, 1964, **55**, 297–308.

Rieth, H., Axelrod, S., Anderson, R., Hathaway, F., Wood, K., & Fitzgerald, C. Influence of distributed practice and daily testing on weekly spelling tests. *Journal of Educational Research*, 1974, **68**, 73–77.

Risley, T. R. Learning and lollipops. In P. Cramer (Ed.), *Readings in developmental psychology today.* Del Mar, Calif.: CRM Books, 1967.

Roberts, M. D., & Allyon T. Training third grade educated women to teach cognitive skills to disadvantaged children. *Journal of Applied Behavior Analysis*, 1974, **7**, 71–76.

Robertson, S., Dereus, D., & Drabman, R. S. Peer and college student tutoring as reinforcement in a token economy. *Journal of Applied Behavior Analysis*, 1976, **9**, 169–177.

Rogers, C. A theory of personality. In S. Koch (Ed.), *Psychology: A study of a science.* New York: McGraw-Hill, 1959.

Rohwer, W. D., Jr. Prime time for education: Early childhood or adolescence? *Harvard Educational Review*, 1971, **41**, 316–341.

Rollins, H. A., McCandless, B. R., Thompson, M., & Brassell, W. R. Project Success Environment: An extended application of contingency management in inner-city schools. *Journal of Educational Psychology*, 1974, **66**, 167–178.

Rosenshine, B., & Furst, N. The use of direct observation to study teaching. In R. Travers (Ed.), *Second handbook of research on teaching.* Chicago: Rand McNally, 1973.

Rosenthal, R., & Jacobson, L. *Pygmalion in the classroom: Teacher expectation and pupils' intellectual development.* New York: Holt, Rinehart & Winston, 1968.

Ross, A. O. *Psychological disorders of children: A behavioral approach to theory, research, and therapy.* New York: McGraw-Hill, 1974.

Rothkopf, E. Z., & Bloom, R. D. Effects of interpersonal interaction on the instructional value of adjunct questions in learning from written material. *Journal of Educational Psychology*, 1970, **61**, 417–422.

Russell Sage Foundation. *Guidelines for the collection, maintenance, and dissemination of pupil records.*

Report of a Conference on the Ethical and Legal Aspects of School Record Keeping, May 1969.

Ryan, F. L., & Carson, M. A. The relative effectiveness of discovery and expository strategies in teaching toward economic concepts with first grade students. *Journal of Educational Research*, 1973, **66**, 446–450.

Saegert, S., Mackintosh, E., & West, S. Two studies of crowding in urban public spaces. *Environment and Behavior*, 1975, **7**, 159–184.

Sattler, J. M. *Assessment of children's intelligence.* Philadelphia: W. B. Saunders, 1974.

Schacter, S. *The psychology of affiliation.* Stanford, Ca.: Stanford University Press, 1959.

Schmidt, T. H. Remaking the reading program. *Teacher*, January 1974, 40 ff.

Schmuck, R. Some aspects of classroom social climate. *Psychology in the Schools*, 1966, **3**, 59–65.

Schurr, S. Consumerism. *Teacher*, February 1974, 48–51.

Schwartz, M., & Schwartz, J. Evidence of a genetical component to performance on IQ tests. *Nature*, March 1974, **248**, 84–85.

Scott, J. W., & Bushell, D. The length of teacher contacts and students' off-task behavior. *Journal of Applied Behavior Analysis*, 1974, **7**, 39–44.

Shaw, M. E. *Group dynamics: The psychology of small group behavior* (2nd ed.). New York: Harper & Row, 1976.

Shaw, M. E., & Shaw, L. M. Some effects of sociometric grouping upon learning in a second-grade classroom. *Journal of Social Psychology*, 1962, **57**, 453–458.

Sheppard, W. C., & Willoughby, R. H. *Child behavior.* Chicago: Rand McNally, 1975.

Sherif, M., & Sherif, C. W. *Groups in harmony and tension.* New York: Harper & Row, 1953.

Skeels, H. M. Adult status of children with contrasting early life experiences. *Monograph of the Society for Research in Child Development*, 1966, **31**, 1–65.

Skeels, H. M., & Dye, H. B. A study of the effects of differential stimulation on mentally retarded children. *Program of the American Association of Mental Deficiency*, 1939, **44**, 114–136.

Smedlund, J. The acquisition of conservation of substance and weight in children: Extinction of conservation of weight acquired "normally" and by means of empirical controls on a balance scale. *Scandinavian Journal of Psychology*, 1971, **2**, 71–84.

Sonquist, H., Kamii, C., & Derman, L. A Piaget-derived preschool curriculum. In I. J. Athey, & D. O. Rubadeau, (Eds.), *Educational implications of Piaget's theory.* Waltham, Mass.: Ginn-Blaisdell, 1970.

Spearman, C. *The abilities of man.* New York:

Macmillan, 1927.

Stanley, J. C., & Hopkins, K. D. *Educational and psychological measurement and evaluation.* Englewood Cliffs, N. J.: Prentice-Hall, 1972.

Starch, D. Periods of work in learning. *Journal of Educational Psychology*, 1912, **3**, 209–213.

Stevenson, H. W., Parker, T., Wilkinson, A., Hegion, A., & Fish, E. Longitudinal study of individual differences in cognitive development and scholastic achievement. *Journal of Educational Psychology*, 1976, **68**, 377–400. (a)

Stevenson, H. W., Parker, T., Wilkinson, A., Hegion, A., & Fish, E. Predictive value of teachers' ratings of young children. *Journal of Educational Psychology*, 1976, **68**, 507–517. (b)

Stuart, R. B. Teaching facts about drugs: Pushing or preventing? *Journal of Educational Psychology*, 1974, **66**, 189–201.

Suchman, J. R. Inquiry training: Building skills for autonomous discovery. *Merrill-Palmer Quarterly*, 1961, **7**, 147–171.

Suppes, P. The use of computers in education. *Scientific American*, 1966, **203**, 207–220.

Surber, J. R., & Anderson, R. C. Delay-retention effect in natural classroom settings. *Journal of Educational Psychology*, 1975, **67**, 170–173.

Tanner, J. M., Whitehouse, R. H., & Takaishi, M. Standards from birth to maturity for height, weight, height velocity, and weight velocity: British children, 1965. *Archives of Diseases in Childhood*, 1966, **41**, 455–471.

Terman, L. M., & Merrill, M. A. *Stanford-Binet Intelligence Scale: Manual for the third revision form L-M.* Boston: Houghton Mifflin, 1973.

Thomas, J. D. Accuracy of self-assessment of on-task behavior by elementary school children. *Journal of Applied Behavior Analysis*, 1976, **9**, 209–210.

Thorndike, E. L. Mental discipline in high school studies. *Journal of Educational Psychology*, 1924, **15**, 83–98.

Thurstone, L. L. *Primary mental abilities.* (Psychometric Monograph No. 1), Chicago: University of Chicago Press, 1938.

Torrance, E. P. *Rewarding creative behavior in classroom creativity.* Englewood Cliffs, N. J.: Prentice-Hall, 1965.

Torrance, E. P. "Structure" can improve the group behavior of five-year-old children. *The Elementary School Journal*, 1971, **72**, 102–108.

Tuckman, B. W. *Measuring educational outcomes: Fundamentals of testing.* New York: Harcourt Brace Jovanovich, 1975.

Tulkin, S. R., & Kagan, J. Mother-child interaction in the first year of life. *Child Development*, 1972, **43**, 31–41.

Tyler, L. E. *Individual differences.* New York: Appleton-Century-Crofts, 1974.

Underwood, B. J. *Experimental psychology: An introduction.* New York: Appleton-Century-Crofts, 1949.

Vandenberg, S. G. Hereditary factors in normal personality traits (as measured by inventories). In J. Wortis (Ed.), *Recent advances in biological psychiatry* (Vol. 9). New York: Plenum Press, 1967, 65–104.

Vargas, J. S. *Writing worthwhile behavioral objectives.* New York: Harper & Row, 1972.

Watson, J. B. *Behaviorism.* Chicago: University of Chicago Press, 1925.

Watson, J. B. *Psychological care of the infant and child.* New York: Norton & Co., 1928.

Watson, J. B., & Raynor, R. A. Conditioned emotional reactions. *Journal of Experimental Psychology*, 1920, **3**, 1–4.

Wechsler, D. *Manual for the Wechsler Intelligence Scale for Children—Revised.* New York: The Psychological Corporation, 1974.

Wentling, T. Mastery versus nonmastery instruction with varying test item feedback treatments. *Journal of Educational Psychology*, 1973, **65**, 50–58.

Wexley, K. N., & Thornton, C. L. Effect of verbal feedback of test results upon learning. *Journal of Educational Research*, 1972, **66**, 119–120.

White, S. H. Evidence for a hierarchical arrangement of learning processes. In L. P., Lipsitt, & C. C. Spiker, (Eds.), *Advances in child development and behavior* (Vol. 2). New York: Academic Press, 1965.

Willerman, L. Activity level and hyperactivity in twins. *Child Development*, 1973, **44**, 288–293.

Williams, R. L., & Anandam, K. The effect of behavior contracting on grades. *Journal of Educational Research*, 1973, **66**, 231–236.

Williams, R. L., Cormier, W. H., Sapp, G. L., & Andrews, H. B. The utility of behavior management techniques in changing interracial behaviors. *Journal of Psychology*, 1971, **77**, 127–138.

Winnet, R. A., & Winkler, R. C. Current behavior modification in the classroom: Be still, be quiet, be docile. *Journal of Applied Behavior Analysis*, 1972, **5**, 499–504.

Womar, F. B. *What is National Assessment?* Denver: National Assessment of Educational Progress, 1970.

Zigler, E. Familial mental retardation: A continuing dilemma. *Science*, 1967, **155**, 292–298.

ACKNOWLEDGMENTS

PHOTOGRAPHS

Cover   Scott, Foresman Staff

7   Elizabeth Hamlin/Stock, Boston

15   Jean-Claude Lejeune

20   Scott, Foresman Staff

22   Joanne Leonard

26   Jean-Claude Lejeune

28   Joanne Leonard

29   Joanne Leonard

34   Nils Johan

35   Nils Johan

47   Richard Stromberg

52   Michael Mauney

58   Suzanne Szasz/Photo Researchers

72   Richard Stromberg

73   Elizabeth Crews/Jeroboam

86   Scott, Foresman Staff

88   Karen Preuss/Jeroboam

91   Christopher Morrow/Stock, Boston

96   Alex Webb/Magnum

101   Miriam Reinhart/Photo Researchers

121   Alex Webb/Magnum

128   Bob Adelman/Magnum

138   Elizabeth Hamlin/Stock, Boston

139   Elizabeth Hamlin/Stock, Boston

155   Marion Bernstein

161   Abigail Heyman/Magnum

169   Van Bucher/Photo Researchers

187   Richard Stromberg

197   Elizabeth Crews/Jeroboam

212   Scott, Foresman Staff

219   Charles Harbutt/Magnum

225   F. Siteman/Stock, Boston

227   Abigail Heyman/Magnum

231   Thomas S. England

234   Elizabeth Hamlin/Stock, Boston

236   Karen R. Preuss/Jeroboam

238   Charles Gatewood/Magnum

243   Marilyn Silverstone/Magnum

254   Scott, Foresman Staff

258   Charles Harbutt/Magnum

279   Bill Grimes/Black Star

281   Bohdan Hrynewych/Stock, Boston

288   Owen Franken/Stock, Boston

293   St. Louis Post Dispatch/Black Star

300   Jean-Claude Lejeune

305   Charles Harbutt/Magnum

312   Joanne Leonard

323   Martha Leonard

324   Hiroji Kubota/Magnum

327   F. Siteman/Stock, Boston

329   Hella Hammid /Photo Researchers

336   Hiroji Kubota/Magnum

340   Thomas S. England

346   Elizabeth Crews/Jeroboam

348   Marion Bernstein

356   Michael Mauney

All photographs appearing on the following pages were photographed by Michael Mauney for Scott, Foresman:
i, ii, vi, vii, viii, ix, x, xi, xii, 5, 10, 12, 64, 68, 81, 99, 116, 133, 143, 146, 180, 184, 193, 209, 214, 248, 252, 256, 263, 271, 275, 285, 290, 298, 309, 357, 360, 363, 371, 383, 389

FIGURES AND TABLES

3   Fig. 1–1   From Haskett, G. J., & Lenfestey, W. Reading-related behavior in an open classroom: Effects of novelty and modeling on preschoolers. *Journal of Applied Behavior Analysis*, 1974, *1*, 233–241. Reprinted by permission.

30   Fig. 2–1   From McGraw, M. B. Neutral maturation as exemplified in achievement of bladder control. *Journal of Pediatrics*, 1940, *16*, 580–590. Reprinted by permission.

41   Fig. 2–3   From Bruner, J. S., & Kenney, H. J. On multiple ordering. In J. S. Bruner et al., *Studies in cognitive growth*. New York: Wiley & Sons, 1966. Reprinted by permission of the publisher.

56   Fig. 3–1   From Jersild, A. T., & Holmes, F. B. *Children's fears*. New York: Teachers College Press © 1935 by Teachers College, Columbia University. Reprinted by permission of the publisher.

65   Fig. 3–2   From Mosher, F. A., & Hornsby, J. R. On asking questions. In J. S. Bruner et al., *Studies in cognitive growth*. New York: Wiley & Sons, 1966. Reprinted by permission of the publisher.

66   Fig. 3–3   From Olver, R. R., & Hornsby, J. R. On equivalence. In J. S. Bruner et al., *Studies in cognitive growth*. New York: Wiley & Sons, 1966, 68–85. Reprinted by permission of the publisher.

70   Fig. 3–4   From Tanner, J. M., Whitehouse, R. H., & Takaishi, M. Standards from birth to maturity for height, weight, height velocity, and weight velocity: British children, 1965. *Archives of Diseases in Childhood*, 1966, *41*, 455–471. Reprinted by permission.

71   Fig. 3–5   From Costanzo, P. R., & Shaw, M. E. Conformity as a function of age level. *Child Development*, 1966, *37*, 967–975. Reprinted by permission of the Society for Research in Child Development, Inc. © 1966.

76, 77   Fig. 3–6, 3–7   From Bayley, N. Research in child development: A longitudinal perspective. *Merrill-Palmer Quarterly of Behavior and Development*, 1965, *11*, 8–35. Reprinted by permission.

82   Fig. 3–10   From *Teaching 2: Cognitive Learning and Instruction* by Wesley C. Becker, Siegfried Engleman. © 1975, Science Research Associates, Inc. Reprinted by permission of the publisher.

94   Fig. 4–2   From *Principles of Instructional Design* by Robert M. Gagné and Leslie J. Briggs. Copyright © 1974 by Holt, Rinehart and Winston, Inc. Reprinted by permission of Holt, Rinehart and Winston, Inc.

97   Fig. 4–3   From Crossman, E. R. F. A theory of acquisition of speed-skill. *Ergonomics*, 1959, *2*, 153–166. Reprinted by permission of the publisher, Taylor & Francis, Ltd.

103   Fig. 4–4   From Ebbinghaus, H. *Memory*. H. A. Ruger & C. E. Bussenius (Trans.) New York: Dover, 1964.

105   Table 4–1   From Raugh, M. R., & Atkinson, E. C. A mnemonic method for learning a second-language vocabulary. *Journal of Educational Psychology*, 1975, *67*, 1–16. Copyright 1975 by the American Psychological Association. Reprinted by permission.

106   Fig. 4–5   From Bower, G. H., Clark, M. C., Lesgold, A. M., & Winzenz, D. Hierarchial retrieval schemes in recall of categorized word lists. *Journal of Verbal Learning and Verbal Behavior*, 1969, *8*, 323–343. Reprinted by permission.

107   Fig. 4–6   From Starch, D. Periods of work in learning. *Journal of Educational Psychology*, 1912, *3*, 209–213.

109   Fig. 4–7   From Jensen, A. R. Spelling errors and the serial-position effect. *Journal of Educational Psychology*, 1962, *53*, 105–109. Copyright 1968 by the American Psychological Association. Reprinted by permission.

109   Fig. 4–8   From Carmichael, L., Hogan, H. P., & Walter, A. A. An experimental study of the effect of language on the reproduction of visually perceived form. *Journal of Experimental Psychology*, 1932, *15*, 73–86. Copyright 1932 by the American Psychological Association. Reprinted by permission.

118   Fig. 5–1   From Allen, K. E., Hart, B. M., Buell, J. S., Harris, F. R., & Wolf, M. M. Effects of social reinforcement on isolate behavior of a nursery school child. *Child Development*, 1964, *35*, 511–518. Copyright 1964 by The Society for Research in Child Development, Inc. Reprinted by permission.

119   Fig. 5–2   From Kirby, F. D., & Shields, F. Modification of arithmetic response rate and attending behavior in a seventh-grade student. *Journal of Applied Behavior Analysis*, 1972, *5*, 79–84. Reprinted by permission.

120   Fig. 5–3   From Kaufman, K. F., & O'Leary, K. D. Reward, cost, and self-evaluation procedures for disruptive adolescents in a psychiatric hospital school. *Journal of Applied Behavior Analysis*, 1972, *5*, 293–309. Reprinted by permission.

123   Fig. 5–4   From Lahey, B. B., McNees, M. P., & McNees, M. C. Control of an obscene "verbal tic" through timeout in an elementary school classroom. *Journal of Applied Behavior Analysis*, 1973, *6*, 101–104. Reprinted by permission.

125   Fig. 5–5   From O'Connor, R. D. Modification of social withdrawal through symbolic modeling. *Journal of Applied Behavior Analysis*, 1969, *2*, 15–22. Reprinted by permission.

126   Fig. 5–6   From Lahey, B. B. Modification of the frequency of descriptive adjectives in the speech of Head Start children through modeling without reinforcement. *Journal of Applied Behavior Analysis*, 1971, *4*, 19–22. Reprinted by permission.

131   Fig. 5–7   From Hall, R. V., Fox, R., Willard, D., Goldsmith, L., Emerson, M., Owen, M., Davis, F., & Porcia, E. The teacher as observer and experimenter in the modification of disputing and talking-out behaviors. *Journal of Applied Behavior Analysis*, 1971, *4*, 141–149. Reprinted by permission.

141   Table 5–1   Data for diagram based on Hierarchy of Needs (pp. 35–51) in a theory of Human Motivation from *Motivation and Personality*, 2nd ed. by Abraham H. Maslow © 1970 by Abraham H. Maslow. Reprinted by permission.

153   Fig. 6–2   Data for figure based on: Burt, C. The genetic determination of difference in intelligence: A study of monozygotic twins reared together and apart. *British Journal of Psychology*, 1966, *57*, 137–153. Reprinted by permission of Cambridge University Press.

158   Fig. 6–3   From Belmont, L., & Marolla, A. F. Birth order, family size, and intelligence. *Science*, 1973, *182*, 1096–1101. Copyright 1973 by the American Association for the Advancement of Science. Reprinted by permission.

170   Table 6–2   From "Samples of Test Items at Various Age Levels on the Stanford-Binet Intelligence Scale" Table 6.2 in the *Stanford-Binet Intelligence Test*. Reprinted by permission of Houghton Mifflin Company.

173   Table 6–3   Reproduced by permission from the *Wechsler Intelligence Scale for Children-Revised*. Copyright © 1974 by The Psychological Corporation, New York, N. Y. All rights reserved. Reprinted by permission.

182   Table 7–1   Reprinted with permission of Macmillan Publishing Co., Inc. from *Psychological Testing* by Anne Anastasi. Copyright © 1976 Anne Anastasi.

189   Table 7–3   From *Taxonomy of Educational Objectives Handbook 1 Cognitive Domain* by Benjamin Bloom, Max O. Engelhart, Edward J. Furst, Walter H. Hill, and David R. Krathwohl. Copyright © 1956 by Longmans, Green and Co. Reprinted by permission.

199   Fig. 7–1   From Glaser, R. Psychology and instructional technology. In R. Glaser (Ed.), *Training research and education*. New York: Wiley & Sons, 1962. Reprinted by permission of the author.

216   Fig. 8–1   From Torrance, E. P. "Structure" can improve the group behavior of five-year-old children. *The Elementary School Journal*, 1971, *72*, 102–108. Reprinted by permission of the University of Chicago Press. © 1971.

223   Fig. 8–2   From Drabman, R. S., & Lahey, B. B.

Feedback in classroom behavior modification: Effects on the target child and her classmates. *Journal of Applied Behavior Analysis,* 1974, *7,* 591–598. Reprinted by permission.

250   Fig. 9–2   From Bushell, D. The Behavior Analysis Follow Through project: An engineering approach to the elementary school classroom. In T. A. Brigham & A. C. Catania (Eds.), *Analysis and modification of social and educational behaviors.* New York: Irvington Press, In Press. Reprinted by permission of the author.

261   Fig. 10–1   From Komaki, J. Child-managed sharing: Learning to take turns with a minimum of adult monitoring. Unpublished manuscript, Emory University, 1976. Reprinted by permission of the author.

271   From *Programmed Reading* © 1973 by Behavioral Research Laboratories. Reprinted by permission of Behavioral Research Laboratories.

272   Fig. 10–2   From Holt, G. L. Effect of reinforcement contingencies in increasing programmed reading and mathematics behaviors in first grade children. *Journal of Experimental Child Psychology,* 1971, *12,* 362–369. Reprinted by permission.

276   Fig. 10–3   From Lovitt, T. C., Guppy, T. E., & Blattner, J. E. The use of a free-time contingency with fourth graders to improve spelling accuracy. *Behavior Research and Therapy,* 1969, *1,* 151–156. Reprinted by permission.

280   Fig. 10–4   From Coleman, P., Kaszuba, K., & Pierce, M. The effects of a sequential computational skills program on an underachieving fourth-grade class. *Journal of Behavioral Education,* 1973, *67,* 174–178.

293   Fig. 11–1   From Levin, J. R., & Rohwer, W. D. Verbal organization and the facilitation of serial learning. *Journal of Educational Psychology,* 1968, *59,* 186–190. Copyright 1968 by the American Psychological Association. Reprinted by permission.

296   Fig. 11–2   From Duchastel, P. C., & Brown, B. R. Incidental and relevant learning with instructional objectives. *Journal of Educational Psychology,* 1974, *66,* 481–485. Copyright 1974 by the American Psychological Association. Reprinted by permission.

303   Fig. 11–3   From Brown, L., Huppler, B., Van Deventer, P., York, R., & Sontag, E. Use of reinforcement principles to increase comprehension of instructional filmstrips. *Education and Training of the Mentally Retarded,* 1973, *8,* 50–56.

303   Fig. 11–4   From Williams, R. L., & Anandam, K. The effect of behavior contracting on grades. *Journal of Educational Research,* 1973, *66,* 231–236. Reprinted by permission.

306   Fig. 11–5   From Broden, M., Hall, R. V., & Mitts, B. The effect of self-recording on the classroom behavior of two eighth-grade students. *Journal of Applied Behavior Analysis,* 1971, *4,* 191–199. Reprinted by permission.

307   Fig. 11–6   From Rieth, H., Axelrod, S., Anderson, R., Hathaway, F., Wood, K., & Fitzgerald, C. Influence of distributed practice and daily testing on weekly spelling tests. *Journal of Educational Research,* 1974, *68,* 73–77. Reprinted by permission.

320   Fig. 12–2   From Zigler, E. Familial mental retardation: A continuing dilemma. *Science,* 1967, *155,* 292–298. © 1967 by the American Society for the Advancement of Science.

339   Fig. 13–1   From Madsen, C. H., Becker, W. C., & Thomas, D. R. Rules, praise, and ignoring: Elements of elementary classroom control. *Journal of Applied Behavior Analysis,* 1968, *1,* 139–150. Reprinted by permission.

341   Fig. 13–2   From Allyon, T., & Roberts, M. Eliminating discipline problems by strengthening academic performance. *Journal of Applied Behavior Analysis,* 1974, *7,* 71–76. Reprinted by permission.

343   Fig. 13–3   From Bornstein, P., & Quevillon, R. P. The effects of a self-instructional package on hyperactive preschool boys. *Journal of Applied Behavior Analysis,* 1976, *9,* 179–188. Reprinted by permission.

344, 345   Fig. 13–4, 13–5   From Lahey, B. B., Gendrich, J. G., Gendrich, S. I., Schnelle, J. F., Gant, D. S., & McNees, M. P. An evaluation of daily report cards with minimal teacher and parent contacts as an efficient method of classroom intervention. *Journal of Behavior Modification,* 1977, *1,* 381–394. Reprinted by permission.

349   Fig. 13–6   From Rapport, M. D., & Bostow, D. E. The effects of access to special activities on the performance in four categories of academic tasks with third-grade students. *Journal of Applied Behavior Analysis,* 1976, *9,* 372. Reprinted by permission.

351, 352   Fig. 13–7, 13–8   From Iwata, B. A., & Bailey, J. S. Reward versus cost token systems: An analysis of the effects on students and teachers. *Journal of Applied Behavior Analysis,* 1974, *7,* 567–576. Reprinted by permission.

353   Fig. 13–9   From Allyon, T., Layman, D., & Kandel, H. J. A behavioral-educational alternative to drug control of hyperactive children. *Journal of Applied Behavior Analysis,* 1975, *8,* 137–146. Reprinted by permission.

355   Fig. 13–10   From MacDonald, W. S., Gallimore, R., & MacDonald, G. Contingency counseling by school personnel: An economical model of intervention. *Journal of Applied Behavior Analysis,* 1970, *3,* 175–182. Reprinted by permission.

QUOTED MATERIAL

4   From Bloom, B. S., "Time and Learning," *American Psychologist,* September 1974, 682–688, *29,* 9. Reprinted by permission.

9   From "How Much Must a Student Master?" in *Time,* February 28, 1977. Reprinted by permission from *Time,* The Weekly Newsmagazine; Copyright Time Inc. 1977.

14   From "And Now, Teaching Emotions" by L. E. Bourne and B. R. Estrand, *Time,* February 22, 1971. Reprinted by permission from *Time,* The Weekly Newsmagazine; Copyright Time Inc. 1971.

31   From *Behaviorism* by John B. Watson. Copyright 1924,

1925 by The People's Institute Publishing Company, Inc. Copyright 1930 by W. W. Norton & Company, Inc. Copyright Renewed 1952, 1953, 1958 by John B. Watson. Reprinted by permission of W. W. Norton & Company, Inc.

31   From *Psychological Care of Infant and Child* by John B. Watson, Ph. D. Copyright 1928 by W. W. Norton & Company, Inc. Reprinted by permission.

38   Carew, Chan and Halfar, *Observing Intelligence in Young Children: Eight Case Studies*, © 1976, pp. 59–61. Reprinted by permission of Prentice-Hall, Inc., Englewood Cliffs, New Jersey.

45   From *Intelligence and Experience* by J. McV. Hunt. Copyright © 1961 The Ronald Press Company, New York. Reprinted by permission.

47   Reprinted by permission of Hawthorn Books, Inc. from *Child Development*, Volume One, A Systematic and Empirical Theory, by Sidney W. Bijou and Donald M. Baer. Copyright © 1961 by Appleton-Century-Crofts, Inc. All rights reserved.

68   Kohlberg, "Stage and Sequence: The Cognitive-Developmental Approach to Socialization," Goslin, David A. (Ed.), *Handbook of Socialization Theory and Research*, © 1969 by Rand McNally College Publishing Company, Chicago, Table 6.5, pp. 379–380.

124   R. C. Jurgensen, A. J. Donnelly, and M. P. Dolciani, *Modern Geometry*. Boston: Houghton Mifflin Company, 1965. Reprinted by permission.

134–135   From "Skinner and the Open Classroom" by Peter Madden, *School Review*, Vol. 81, 1972–73. © 1972 and 1973 by The University of Chicago. Reprinted by permission.

135   From *Principles of Instructional Design* by Robert M. Gagné and Leslie J. Briggs. Copyright © 1974 by Holt, Rinehart and Winston, Inc. Reprinted by permission.

140   Winett, R. A., & Winkler, R. C. Current Behavior Modification in the Classroom: Be still, be quiet, be docile. *Journal of Applied Behavior Analysis*, 1972, 5, 499–504 (p. 502). Reprinted by permission.

157, 158   From "Birth Order, Family Size and Intelligence" by Lillian Belmont and Francis Marolla, *Science*, Vol. 182,

December 14, 1973, pp. 1096–1101. Copyright 1973 by the American Association for the Advancement of Science. Reprinted by permission.

164–166   From *I. Q. in the Meritocracy* by Richard J. Herrnstein, by permission of Little, Brown and Co. in association with the Atlantic Monthly Press and Penguin Books Ltd. Originally appeared in *The Atlantic Monthly* (September 1971), pp. 51–53. Copyright © 1971 by Richard J. Herrnstein.

183   From *Measuring Educational Outcomes: Fundamentals of Testing* by Bruce W. Tuckman © 1975 by Harcourt Brace Jovanovich, Inc. and reprinted with their permission.

187   From the book, *Preparing Instructional Objectives*, 2nd Ed. by Robert F. Mager, Copyright © 1975 by Fearon Publishers, Inc. Reprinted by permission of Fearon Publishers, Inc.

206   From "The Powerful Notion of Accountability in Education" by Leon M. Lessinger, *Journal of Secondary Education*, Dec. 1970, Vol. 45, No. 8, pp. 339–347. Reprinted by permission of the author.

207–208   From "Accountability and Humanism" by Leon Lessinger from *Accountability: Systems Planning in Education* by Leon Lessinger & Associates. Copyright © 1973 by ETC Publications. Reprinted by permission of ETC Publications, 700 E. Vereda del Sur/Palm Springs, California 92262.

242   Arthur R. Jensen, "How much can we boost IQ and scholastic achievement?" *Harvard Educational Review*, 39, Winter 1969, pp. 2–3. Copyright © 1969 by President and Fellows of Harvard College.

259   From "Learning and Lollipops" by Todd Risley, *Psychology Today*, Vol. 1, No. 8, January 1968, pp. 28–31, 62–65. Reprinted by permission of *Psychology Today* Magazine. Copyright © 1967 Ziff-Davis Publishing Company.

268   Reprinted from the January 1974 issue of *Teacher* magazine with permission of the publisher. This article is copyrighted. © 1974 by Macmillan Professional Magazines, Inc. All rights reserved.

282–283   Excerpted from the February 1974 issue of *Teacher* magazine with permission of the publisher. This article is copyrighted. © 1974 by Macmillan Professional Magazines, Inc. All rights reserved.

INDEX